The Foundations and Future of AI:

Methods, Models, and Machine Intelligence

Poshan Yu
https://orcid.org/0000-0003-1069-3675
Soochow University, China

James Mulli
European Business Institute, Luxembourg

Zain Ali Shah Syed
Soochow University, China

Laila Umme
https://orcid.org/0000-0001-8050-5081
Institute of Business Management, Pakistan

IGI Global
Scientific Publishing
Publishing Tomorrow's Research Today

Vice President of Editorial	Melissa Wagner
Director of Acquisitions	Mikaela Felty
Director of Book Development	Jocelynn Hessler
Production Manager	Mike Brehm
Cover Design	Jose Rosado

Published in the United States of America by
IGI Global Scientific Publishing
701 East Chocolate Avenue
Hershey, PA, 17033, USA
Tel: 717-533-8845 | Fax: 717-533-7115
Website: https://www.igi-global.com E-mail: cust@igi-global.com

Library of Congress Cataloging-in-Publication Data

LCCN: (CIP Data Pending)
ISBN13: 9798260023730
Isbn13Softcover: 9798260023747
EISBN13: 9798260023754

British Cataloguing in Publication Data
A Cataloguing in Publication record for this book is available from the British Library.

Table of Contents

Detailed Table of Contents

.This chapter explores the critical role of probabilistic decision dynamics in advancing machine learning systems. The primary aim is to synthesise foundational theories with recent advancements to provide a comprehensive framework for understanding and implementing models that effectively manage uncertainty. The theoretical basis of this work is grounded in probability theory, with a particular focus on Bayesian inference, Markov Decision Processes, and entropy-based concepts, which collectively enable systems to reason and act in complex, non-deterministic environments. The chapter highlights the practical relevance of these models through an examination of their applications in high-stakes domains such as healthcare, finance, and autonomous systems, where the ability to quantify uncertainty is paramount for reliable decision-making.

As deep learning continues to evolve, it is no longer confined to the boundaries of traditional machine learning applications—it is actively reshaping what we once thought machines could never do. This chapter explores the latest advancements in deep learning, particularly how new architectures and training paradigms are redefining the capabilities of AI in pattern recognition. From the precision of convolutional neural networks in image analysis to the contextual mastery of transformers in sequence modeling, we examine how deep learning systems are navigating increasingly abstract and complex data landscapes. These advancements are not purely technical—they carry real-world significance across domains such as healthcare, finance, linguistics, and even the arts. Yet, with this power comes pressing questions: How do we ensure interpretability in models that learn in non-linear and often opaque ways

Image Steganography is an approach of hiding of secret data in where secret data is inserted into digital media, including mainly images, for the purpose of ensuring secure communication. In contrast to encryption, that hides the content by making it unreadable, steganography hides the existence of the data itself, providing an additional layer of discretion. CNNs have an encoder-decoder architecture, which allows embedding information into the input data while minimizing perceptibility and robustness to various attacks such as resizing or compression. The chapter also discusses and compares CNN and GAN-based techniques with traditional ones by focusing on imperceptibility, payload capacity, and adaptability. It also discusses the assessment metrics–MSE, SSIM, and PSNR–to analyze the quality and security of the stego images. In summary, this chapter provides a contribution in the field of steganography revealing a new avenue based on CNN that is secure and imperceptible with high capacity.

The lack of efficient steganography methods has been an active research concern in digital image steganography and computer vision toward efficient cyber security. This research proposes an efficient steganography method to encode and decode data from images and uses edge pixels from images. The overall method starts with detecting the edge pixel of the particular cover image using Sobel edge detector and then sorts values in descending order to get the densest edge area. The extracting process starts by detecting edge pixels of the stego image followed by sorting again similar to the embedding process. Then the sorted pixel values are read and compared to get binary values containing secret messages. Finally, secret message is retrieved from ASCII values which are derived from binary values. The proposed method achieved excellent Peak Signal Noise Ratio (PSNR) and Structural Similarity Index Metric (SSIM) results compared with the previous research indicating strong imperceptibility.

The integration of artificial intelligence (AI) in higher education is not just a technological shift—it marks a fundamental transformation in how we understand and design learning experiences. This chapter explores how machine learning technologies are enabling deeply personalized approaches to education, reshaping the traditional, one-size-fits-all model into a more fluid, responsive, and student-centered system. By analyzing the mechanisms through which machine learning processes data to adapt instruction in real time, the chapter unpacks the promise of personalization: increased engagement, improved learning outcomes, and more inclusive educational pathways. Through case studies and grounded reflections, we examine the tensions between automation and human guidance, and the implications of algorithmic decision-making in educational spaces. As we move from research into real-world integration, the chapter calls for a balanced approach that champions transparency, empathy, and shared responsibility in shaping the future of AI-powered learning.

The abstract and conclusions are the important sections of the published paper. Based on the comprehension of the content written in these sections, other sections of the paper are read by researchers. Various factors, such as the number of citations, social transformations, and intellectual property rights, are considered indicators of research impact. This study utilizes Natural Language Processing techniques to analyze a dataset of 50 highly cited research papers from 2020, aiming to understand the relationship between text quality and citation count. The correlation coefficient indicates that high-citation papers tend to have longer abstracts and shorter conclusions. The results show that when the citation of the paper is low, the words used in the abstract and conclusion have high similarity. As citations are increasing, the similarity of the words used in the abstract and conclusion is reducing. This indicates that those articles with a higher Type Token Ratio (TTR) in the abstract and a unique number of words used in conclusion have high citations.

Preface

INTRODUCTION

Artificial Intelligence (AI) has emerged as one of the defining technological and intellectual movements of the twenty-first century. From probabilistic reasoning and deep learning to intelligent automation and ethical research systems, AI continues to transform the foundations of science, industry, governance, education, and everyday life. The Foundations and Future of AI: Methods, Models, and Machine Intelligence was conceived as a scholarly platform to explore both the theoretical underpinnings and the evolving applications of AI across interdisciplinary domains. This volume brings together contributions from researchers and practitioners whose work reflects the depth, diversity, and dynamism of contemporary AI scholarship.

The chapters collected in this edited reference book examine not only how intelligent systems are designed and optimized, but also how they influence human decision-making, communication, learning, healthcare, cybersecurity, transportation, and scientific inquiry. As AI technologies become increasingly integrated into societal infrastructures, there is a growing need for research that balances innovation with responsibility, technical advancement with ethical awareness, and computational power with human-centered design. This volume responds to that need by presenting studies that bridge foundational methods with emerging real-world implementations.

The contributors to this book represent a wide range of academic institutions, research cultures, and disciplinary perspectives from across the globe. Their collective insights demonstrate that AI is not a singular field confined to computer science, but rather a multidisciplinary ecosystem shaped by mathematics, engineering, social sciences, healthcare, linguistics, education, and ethics. Through this collaborative effort, the book aims to provide readers with a comprehensive understanding of both the current state and future trajectory of machine intelligence.

CHAPTER OVERVIEW

Chapter 1: Probabilistic Decision Dynamics in Machine Learning explores the foundational role of probability theory in intelligent systems. The chapter examines Bayesian inference, Markov Decision Processes, and entropy-based reasoning frameworks that enable machine learning models to operate effectively under uncertainty. Practical applications in healthcare, finance, and autonomous systems highlight the importance of probabilistic decision-making in high-stakes environments.

Chapter 2: Advancements in Deep Learning: Pushing the Boundaries of AI Pattern Recognition investigates the latest developments in deep learning architectures and training paradigms. The chapter discusses convolutional neural networks, transformers, and contextual learning systems while reflecting on broader concerns surrounding interpretability, transparency, and the societal implications of increasingly complex AI models.

Chapter 3: Image Steganography from Classical Techniques to Deep Learning Paradigms presents a detailed examination of secure communication through image steganography. By comparing traditional approaches with CNN- and GAN-based models, the chapter demonstrates how modern AI techniques enhance imperceptibility, payload capacity, and robustness in hidden communication systems.

Chapter 4: Computer Vision based Advanced Image Steganography for Secured Cyber Security focuses on advanced steganographic techniques supported by computer vision and edge detection methods. Using Sobel edge detection and image processing strategies, the chapter proposes a robust approach for secure data embedding and extraction while evaluating performance through PSNR and SSIM metrics.

Chapter 5: AI-Driven Biostatistics in Healthcare – From Predictive Modeling to Real World Applications examines how AI is reshaping modern healthcare analytics. The chapter explores machine learning, deep learning, and probabilistic modeling techniques in epidemiology, disease prediction, personalized medicine, and public health monitoring, while also addressing fairness, transparency, and ethical governance.

Chapter 6: Comparative Analysis of AI-Driven Traffic Light Optimization investigates intelligent traffic management systems and their impact on sustainable urban mobility. Through comparative case studies involving Beijing, Shenzhen, and Hangzhou, the chapter demonstrates how AI, IoT integration, and real-time analytics contribute to improved transportation efficiency and reduced environmental impact.

Chapter 7: AI in Higher Education: Personalizing Learning with Machine Learning discusses the transformative role of AI in educational systems. Focusing on adaptive learning and personalized instruction, the chapter evaluates how machine learning technologies can improve engagement, accessibility, and student-centered learning while emphasizing the importance of transparency and human guidance.

Chapter 8: A Computational Study on Text Quality and Citation Frequency in Research Papers applies natural language processing techniques to analyze relationships between writing quality and scholarly impact. By examining highly cited research papers, the chapter identifies linguistic and structural patterns associated with citation frequency and research visibility.

Chapter 9: Artificial Intelligence in Scholarly Investigation: Transforming Research and Ethics explores the growing influence of AI in academic research processes. The chapter discusses AI-assisted analysis, peer review, predictive insights, and interdisciplinary collaboration while critically addressing ethical concerns related to bias, transparency, authorship, and accountability in scholarly work.

Collectively, these chapters reveal the breadth of AI research and its capacity to shape both technological innovation and societal transformation. The volume intentionally combines foundational theories with practical applications, thereby enabling readers to engage with both conceptual frameworks and implementation challenges. The interdisciplinary nature of the contributions also reflects the reality that the future of AI will be defined not solely by computational breakthroughs, but by collaborative efforts that integrate technical excellence with ethical and human considerations.

CONCLUSION

As editors, we hope this book serves multiple purposes for its readers. For researchers and academics, it offers scholarly insights into emerging AI methodologies and applications. For students, it provides a foundational understanding of critical concepts shaping machine intelligence today. For practitioners and policymakers, it presents real-world perspectives on the opportunities and challenges associated with AI-driven systems. Most importantly, we hope the volume encourages continued dialogue about how AI can be developed responsibly, inclusively, and sustainably for the benefit of society.

We extend our sincere appreciation to all chapter authors for their scholarly contributions, commitment, and collaboration throughout the development of this volume. We also thank the reviewers, editorial teams, and academic institutions whose support made this publication possible. It is our belief that The Foundations and Future of AI: Methods, Models, and Machine Intelligence will contribute meaningfully to ongoing conversations surrounding the evolution of artificial intelligence and inspire future research that advances both innovation and human progress.

Poshan Yu
Soochow University, China

James Mulli
European Business Institute, Luxembourg

Zain Ali Shah Syed
Soochow University, China

Laila Umme
Institute of Business Management, Pakistan

Chapter 1
Probabilistic Decision Dynamics in Machine Learning

Nwosu Obinnaya Chikezie Victor
http://orcid.org/0000-0003-3974-4755
University of KwaZulu-Natal, South Africa

Emmanuel Ileberi
http://orcid.org/0000-0003-1929-0557
University of Johannesburg, South Africa

ABSTRACT

.This chapter explores the critical role of probabilistic decision dynamics in advancing machine learning systems. The primary aim is to synthesise foundational theories with recent advancements to provide a comprehensive framework for understanding and implementing models that effectively manage uncertainty. The theoretical basis of this work is grounded in probability theory, with a particular focus on Bayesian inference, Markov Decision Processes, and entropy-based concepts, which collectively enable systems to reason and act in complex, non-deterministic environments. The chapter highlights the practical relevance of these models through an examination of their applications in high-stakes domains such as healthcare, finance, and autonomous systems, where the ability to quantify uncertainty is paramount for reliable decision-making.

DOI: 10.4018/979-8-2600-2373-0.ch001

INTRODUCTION

The relentless evolution of artificial intelligence and machine learning has ushered in an era where automated systems are increasingly tasked with making critical decisions in complex and unpredictable environments. From medical diagnostics and financial trading to autonomous navigation, the efficacy of these systems is contingent upon their ability to reason under uncertainty. Traditional deterministic models, which yield a single, fixed output for a given input, often fall short in real-world scenarios characterised by noisy data, incomplete information, and inherent stochasticity. This limitation has propelled a significant shift in the research landscape toward probabilistic methods—frameworks designed to explicitly model, quantify, and manage uncertainty. This paper explores the intersection of machine learning and probabilistic decision-making, addressing critical gaps in current research that hinder the full realization of intelligent, adaptive systems.(Urbaite, 2025) The central problem this chapter addresses is the persistent gap between the theoretical elegance of probabilistic models and their practical, scalable application in dynamic, real-world contexts. While the mathematical foundations of probabilistic models are well-established, their deployment often lacks the contextual adaptability required to perform optimally as conditions evolve. Furthermore, a significant body of research focuses on applying machine learning techniques to static datasets, with limited exploration into the vital integration of real-time data streams and adaptive algorithms that can enhance these models' responsiveness and accuracy. There is also a notable deficit in research that translates the theoretical quantification of uncertainty into actionable insights for decision-makers in various fields. Without a clear understanding of how to interpret and act upon a model's reported uncertainty, the practical utility of these sophisticated systems remains limited.(Buehler et al., 2025) To address these challenges, this chapter pursues three primary objectives. First, it aims to synthesise the foundational theories and recent advancements in probabilistic decision dynamics, providing a cohesive understanding of the core concepts that underpin this field. This involves clarifying key terms such as Probabilistic Decision Dynamics, Bayesian Dynamics, Entropy-Based Decision Boundaries, and Probabilistic Convergence to establish a common lexicon and avoid ambiguity. Second, the chapter seeks to bridge the chasm between theory and practice by examining real-world applications and case studies. This exploration emphasises the role of adaptive algorithms and the integration of real-time data in enhancing model performance across diverse domains. Third, the work critically evaluates the current limitations of probabilistic models and proposes future research directions, with a particular focus on emerging areas like explainability and ethical considerations in AI decision-making.(Wu et al., 2024) This chapter is organised as follows: The subsequent section provides a detailed background and literature review, tracing the historical development of probabilistic decision-making and surveying the current state of research. Following this, the theoretical foundations are meticulously unpacked, with dedicated subsections for key concepts. The chapter then delves into the specifics of machine learning algorithms that utilise probabilistic methods, comparing them with traditional approaches. A significant portion is dedicated to the application of these models in various fields, supported by case studies and empirical data. Finally, the chapter discusses the challenges and limitations inherent in these frameworks before concluding with a summary of key findings, implications for future research, and recommendations for practitioners. By combining theoretical rigor with practical insights, this work endeavours to serve as a comprehensive resource for advancing the development of flexible, accurate, and trustworthy machine learning systems that can effectively navigate real-world uncertainties.(Braiek & Khomh, 2025; Chen et al., 2025)

BACKGROUND AND LITERATURE REVIEW

The journey toward creating intelligent systems capable of human-like reasoning has been marked by a progressive shift from deterministic logic to probabilistic reasoning. This evolution reflects a growing acknowledgement that uncertainty is not a mere nuisance to be eliminated but a fundamental aspect of the real world that must be embraced and managed.(Chen, 2025) This section provides a critical analysis of the existing research landscape, tracing the historical development of probabilistic decision-making and identifying the key intellectual currents that have shaped the field. It also highlights the specific gaps in current research that this chapter aims to address, setting the stage for the subsequent detailed discussion of theoretical frameworks and practical applications.(Waldt, 2024)

Historical Development of Probabilistic Decision-Making

The intellectual roots of probabilistic decision-making run deep, with foundational contributions from pioneers in mathematics and philosophy significantly altering analytical methods over centuries. The formalisation of probability theory laid the groundwork, but its strategic application in decision-making began to flourish in the 20th century, propelled by the rise of statistical theory and the growing complexity of data-driven challenges(Ahaggach et al., 2024). Early concepts, most notably the Bayesian method, represented a paradigm shift by emphasising the role of prior knowledge in reasoning. The Bayesian approach champions a model of flexible, incremental learning, where beliefs are updated as new evidence becomes available. This philosophy has proven instrumental in the development of sophisticated probabilistic models now prevalent in machine learning, where algorithms are designed to refine their predictions iteratively with the influx of new data.(Goodman & Salow, 2023)

Figure 1. Flowchart of Genetic Algorithm Process

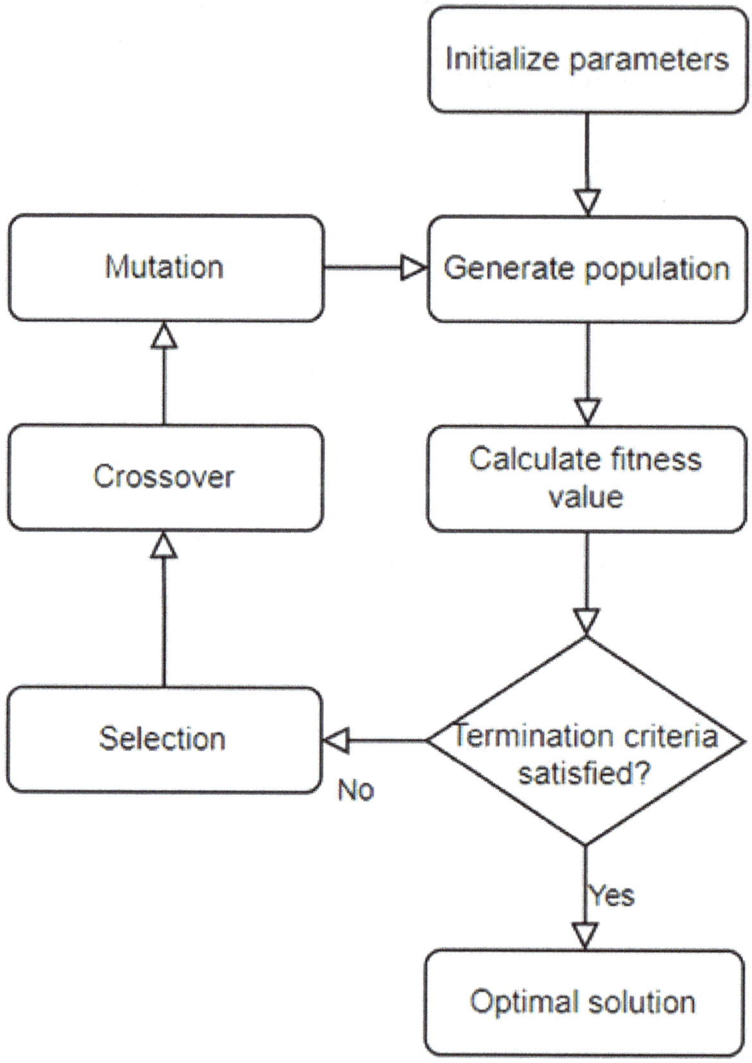

The flowchart in Figure 1 illustrates the operational sequence of a Genetic Algorithm (GA), a type of evolutionary algorithm inspired by Charles Darwin's theory of natural selection. It is a heuristic search and optimization method used to find approximate solutions to complex problems. The process is iterative, aiming to progressively improve a population of candidate solutions until a stopping criterion is met. The key steps are outlined below.

Initialize Parameters: The algorithm begins by setting up initial parameters. This includes defining the population size (the number of candidate solutions), the crossover probability, the mutation probability, and the termination criteria (e.g., a maximum number of generations, a target fitness score, or a time limit). Generate Population: An initial population of individuals (often called chromosomes) is created, typically randomly. Each individual represents a potential solution to the problem being solved.

Calculate Fitness Value: Each individual in the population is evaluated using a fitness function. The fitness function quantifies the quality or "fitness" of a solution, determining how well it solves the problem. A higher fitness value usually indicates a better solution.

Termination Criteria Satisfied: The algorithm checks if a predefined stopping condition has been met. If the criteria (e.g., the maximum number of generations has been reached or a sufficiently good solution has been found) are satisfied, the process terminates.

Optimal Solution: If the termination criteria are met, the algorithm outputs the best individual (the one with the highest fitness value) from the current population as the final, optimal solution.

Selection: If the termination criteria are not met, the algorithm proceeds to the evolutionary cycle. The selection phase mimics "survival of the fittest." Individuals are selected from the current population to act as parents for the next generation. Fitter individuals have a higher probability of being chosen. Common selection methods include roulette wheel selection, tournament selection, and rank selection.

Crossover: This step mimics biological recombination. Selected pairs of parents exchange segments of their genetic information to create one or more new offspring. This process combines the features of good parent solutions to potentially create even better offspring.

Mutation: Mutation introduces small, random changes into the genetic material of the offspring. This step is crucial for maintaining genetic diversity within the population and preventing the algorithm from converging prematurely to a suboptimal solution (a local optimum).

After the mutation step, the new offspring form the next generation's population. The algorithm then loops back to the "Calculate Fitness Value" step, where the fitness of this new population is evaluated, and the entire cycle repeats until the termination criteria are satisfied.

More recent advancements have seen the rise of hierarchical models, which offer a powerful strategy for managing complexity by decomposing intricate systems into more straightforward, interconnected components. This approach has greatly enhanced the robustness and interpretability of decision-making frameworks in uncertain situations. As machine learning continues its rapid evolution, this rich historical foundation of probabilistic decision-making remains indispensable for tackling the multifaceted challenges posed by modern, complex data environments.

Overview of Existing Literature and Identification of Research Gaps

The contemporary research landscape in decision-making models reflects a decisive pivot toward probabilistic methodologies as a means to grapple with the uncertainty and complexity inherent in modern data. A prominent class of models in this domain is Bayesian networks, which provide structured, graphical approaches for reasoning and decision-making under uncertainty. However, recent scholarly work indicates that advancements in the field demand a deeper and more nuanced approach to Uncertainty Quantification (UQ). Researchers like (Li et al., 2025) have emphasized the critical importance of distinguishing between two fundamental types of uncertainty: aleatoric uncertainty, which arises from inherent statistical randomness in data, and epistemic uncertainty, which stems from limitations in the model itself. They advocate for the use of belief theories to develop more sophisticated machine learning and deep learning models that can effectively manage both forms of uncertainty (Shariatmadar, 2024).

This theoretical distinction has been operationalized in recent studies. For instance, (Urbaite, 2025) demonstrated the practical utility of this approach by applying Bayesian Deep Learning (BDL) to predict the remaining useful life (RUL) of industrial machinery. Their model successfully quantified both aleatoric and epistemic uncertainties, providing crucial information for risk management and predictive maintenance. This work exemplifies a broader trend in the field: a move away from deterministic, single-point predictions toward a more holistic assessment of confidence and reliability. This shift underscores the growing necessity for integrated, adaptive models that can perform robustly in dynamic and unpredictable environments (Alvi et al., 2024).

Despite this considerable progress, a critical survey of the field reveals several persistent gaps that current research has yet to adequately address.

1 **Integration of Real-Time Data and Adaptive Algorithms:** A significant portion of existing research applies machine learning methods to static datasets. There is a pronounced lack of studies that focus on the seamless integration of probabilistic models with real-time data streams and adaptive algorithms. In many critical applications, such as autonomous navigation and high-frequency financial trading, decisions must be rendered in milliseconds based on a

constantly evolving flow of information. While the theoretical frameworks to support such integration exist, their practical, scalable implementation remains a major unresolved challenge(Abdallah, 2025).

2 **Lack of Emphasis on Practical Implications of Uncertainty:** The theoretical discourse on distinguishing between aleatoric and epistemic uncertainty is robust and sophisticated. However, there is a clear deficit in research that translates this theory into practical, actionable insights for end-users and decision-makers. For example, how should a clinician or an investment manager concretely alter their strategy based on a model's reported uncertainty levels?. This gap between the quantification of uncertainty and its practical application severely limits the real-world utility of many advanced probabilistic models(Chakraborti et al., 2025).

3 **Socio-Technical and Ethical Dimensions:** While specialized models like discriminative conditional restricted Boltzmann machines have demonstrated success in specific, narrow tasks, their application to broader socio-economic analysis remains largely under-explored. More critically, as these powerful models are deployed in sensitive domains such as criminal justice, hiring, and loan applications, urgent questions regarding fairness, accountability, and transparency (FAT) in probabilistic decision-making have not been sufficiently addressed. This presents both a significant challenge and a vital opportunity for future investigation into the ethical governance of AI(Zhu et al., 2025).

This chapter seeks to contribute to filling these gaps by synthesizing the theoretical underpinnings of probabilistic decision dynamics with a focused analysis of their practical implementation, challenges, and future potential.

Theoretical Foundations and Core Concepts

A comprehensive grasp of probabilistic decision-making in machine learning necessitates a lucid understanding of its foundational principles. This analytical framework is grounded in mathematical principles that provide the necessary tools to manage uncertainty, quantify the likelihood of outcomes, and ultimately enable rational choices in the face of incomplete information. It elucidates the intricate interplay between chance and control, thereby facilitating the formulation of optimal strategies in scenarios where outcomes are not predetermined. This section clarifies the key foundational concepts that form the bedrock of probabilistic machine learning, addressing the reviewer's call for clear and consistent definitions to avoid ambiguity(Shariatmadar et al., 2025).

Probabilistic Decision Dynamics

Probabilistic Decision Dynamics refers to a comprehensive framework for modelling decisions in uncertain environments using probability distributions, where the actions taken by an agent actively influence future states and outcomes. This framework moves beyond static classification or prediction to model a continuous, interactive process. It incorporates concepts from diverse domains, most notably reinforcement learning, to meticulously examine the potential consequences associated with various actions. A cornerstone tool within this framework is the Markov Decision Process (MDP), a mathematical instrument for representing decision-making in contexts where results are influenced by both stochastic elements (randomness) and the agency of the decision-maker(Badings et al., 2023). In an MDP, the system's future state depends only on its current state and the action taken, not on the sequence of states that preceded it (the Markov property). This allows for the modeling of scenarios with both randomness and agent control, enabling the development of algorithms that support adaptive learning and strategy refinement over time. These dynamics are crucial for enhancing machine learning algorithms, as they enable them to learn from observations and experience, thereby progressively improving their decision-making capabilities. The explicit integration of probabilistic reasoning into artificial intelligence through such frameworks is essential for replicating the intricate and nuanced nature of human decision-making(Abdallah, 2025).

Bayesian Dynamics and Inference

At the heart of much of probabilistic machine learning lies Bayesian Dynamics, a powerful probabilistic approach rooted in the principles of Bayesian inference. The core of this paradigm is Bayes' theorem, a mathematical formula that describes how to update the probability for a hypothesis based on new evidence(Beckers, 2023). In this context, Bayesian dynamics refers to the process by which a system iteratively updates its beliefs—represented as probability distributions—as it acquires new data or evidence. The process begins with a "prior" probability distribution, which encapsulates the system's initial beliefs about a parameter or state before any data is observed. As new evidence becomes available, the prior is updated to a "posterior" probability distribution, which reflects the revised beliefs. This mechanism of updating prior probabilities to posteriors is the essence of incremental learning and uncertainty quantification(Mîndrilă, 2023).

This approach is particularly valuable in reinforcement learning, where it allows an agent to continuously refine its understanding of an environment's dynamics over time. Instead of committing to a single model of the world, a Bayesian agent maintains a distribution over possible models, allowing it to reason about model uncertainty and make more robust decisions(Fellows et al., 2024). The synergy between Bayesian inference and structured models like decision trees is also noteworthy. While standard decision trees are deterministic, their predictive power can be significantly enhanced when integrated with Bayesian methods, leading to models like Bayesian networks that can explicitly represent probabilistic dependencies among variables(Klusowski & Tian, 2023). This integration allows even traditionally deterministic models to output full probability distributions, improving their robustness and performance in complex data scenarios(Abdallah, 2025).

Entropy-Based Decision Boundaries

Traditional machine learning models, such as Support Vector Machines or simple decision trees, often define rigid and sharply delineated decision boundaries to classify data points. In contrast, probabilistic models employ a more nuanced approach using the concept of entropy to define these boundaries. In information theory, entropy is a measure of uncertainty or randomness(Narushynska et al., 2025). Within machine learning, it can be used to quantify a model's confidence in its predictions. Regions in the feature space where the model's predictive probability distribution is sharply peaked (i.e., one class has a probability close to 1) are low-entropy regions, indicating high confidence(Trongtirakul et al., 2025). Conversely, regions where the probabilities are more evenly distributed among multiple classes are high-entropy regions, indicating low confidence or high uncertainty(Fantazzini, 2024). These high-entropy regions, which typically occur near the boundaries between classes, are not seen as failures but as valuable sources of information. They signal to the model where its understanding is weakest, thereby guiding active learning strategies. In an active learning paradigm, the model can query for labels of data points that fall within these high-entropy zones, allowing it to gather the most informative data to improve its certainty and refine its decision boundaries more efficiently. This approach leads to more flexible and data-efficient learning processes compared to models with rigid boundaries(Lee et al., 2023).

Probabilistic Convergence

The concept of convergence in probabilistic models differs fundamentally from that in standard optimization-based machine learning. In traditional models, convergence typically refers to an algorithm reaching a stable point, such as a minimum of a loss function. Probabilistic Convergence, however, describes a more abstract process: it is how the model's beliefs, represented by the posterior probability distribution, asymptotically approach the true underlying parameter values as the amount of data increases(Ahn et al., 2018). This process is a direct consequence of the Bayesian updating mechanism. As more and more data are observed, the influence of the initial prior distribution diminishes, and the posterior distribution becomes increasingly concentrated around the true parameters that best explain the data(Duffield et al., 2024). This refinement of the posterior distribution directly corresponds to a reduction in epistemic uncertainty—the uncertainty stemming from the model's own limitations and lack of knowledge. By formalizing these core concepts, this chapter aims to provide a robust foundation for understanding how probabilistic machine learning systems can navigate real-world uncertainties with greater sophistication and efficacy(Faghani et al., 2024).

Probabilistic Algorithms in Machine Learning

The integration of probabilistic principles into machine learning has given rise to a powerful class of algorithms capable of decision-making under uncertainty. These models leverage probability theory to analyze vast datasets, identify underlying patterns, and, crucially, provide a measure of confidence in their predictions. This section provides an overview of key machine learning algorithms that utilize probabilistic methods, explores the pivotal role of Bayesian networks and probabilistic graphical models, and compares the performance and characteristics of probabilistic algorithms with their traditional, deterministic counterparts(Abdallah, 2025).

Overview of Machine Learning Algorithms Utilizing Probabilistic Methods

Probabilistic methods are vital for managing uncertainty and enhancing the predictive accuracy of machine learning models. A diverse array of algorithms has been developed, each with specific strengths and applications. Table 1 provides a concise overview of several prominent probabilistic algorithms.

Table 1. Probabilistic Machine Learning Algorithms Overview

Algorithm	Description	Use Cases	Advantages	Limitations
Naive Bayes	A simple probabilistic classifier based on applying Bayes' theorem with strong independence assumptions.	Spam detection, sentiment analysis	Fast, efficient for large datasets	Assumes feature independence
Gaussian Mixture Model (GMM)	A probabilistic model that assumes all data points are generated from a mixture of several Gaussian distributions.	Clustering, density estimation	Flexible in terms of the shape of the learned distributions	Can be sensitive to initialization, may require a large amount of data
Hidden Markov Model (HMM)	A statistical model that represents systems with hidden states and is used for sequence data.	Speech recognition, bioinformatics	Effective for temporal data	May require significant training data, choice of model structure can be complex
Bayesian Neural Networks	Neural networks that incorporate uncertainty in its weights through probabilistic techniques.	Uncertainty estimation, active learning	Quantifies uncertainty in predictions	Computationally intensive, challenging to implement
Markov Chain Monte Carlo (MCMC)	A class of algorithms that sample from a probability distribution using Markov chains.	Bayesian inference, complex model fitting	Can handle high-dimensional spaces	Slow convergence for complex models

This table provides a comparative overview of five fundamental probabilistic machine learning algorithms. It details each algorithm's core description, common use cases, key advantages, and inherent limitations. The selected models represent a spectrum of probabilistic approaches, from the simplicity and strong independence assumptions of Naive Bayes—highly effective for text classification tasks like spam detection—to the complex, flexible density estimation capabilities of Gaussian Mixture Models (GMMs) for clustering. For sequential data, Hidden Markov Models (HMMs) are highlighted for their effectiveness in domains like speech recognition. The table also includes advanced methods like Bayesian Neural Networks, which quantify prediction uncertainty, and Markov Chain Monte Carlo (MCMC) algorithms, a cornerstone technique for sampling from complex probability distributions in Bayesian inference. Collectively, this summary aids in selecting an appropriate algorithm based on the problem context, data type, and specific requirements for speed, flexibility, or uncertainty quantification. Algorithms such as Naive Bayes and logistic regression excel in classification tasks and probability estimation, even in complex scenarios. Logistic regression, for instance, is widely used for predicting binary outcomes by modelling the probability of an event occurring. More complex models like Bayesian Networks leverage dependencies between variables to refine decision-making processes. A key strength of these methods is their capacity to handle large datasets and improve their accuracy over time as more data becomes available, a feature well-documented in probabilistic modelling research. The adaptability of these algorithms makes them indispensable across a wide range of fields, ensuring robust, data-driven decisions(Wang et al., 2023).

Role of Bayesian Networks and Probabilistic Graphical Models

Among the suite of probabilistic tools, Bayesian networks and the broader class of Probabilistic Graphical Models (PGMs) hold a particularly pivotal position in modern machine learning. Bayesian networks are directed acyclic graphs that model the probabilistic relationships between a set of variables(Vujović, 2021). They excel in representing conditional dependencies and are especially powerful in scenarios involving uncertain and incomplete data. This capability is critical in fields like healthcare and finance, where they enhance reasoning and support evidence-based decision-making. Their structure allows for both predictive modelling (inferring the state of a variable) and diagnostic reasoning (identifying the most likely causes of an observed event). Furthermore, their adaptability through data-driven learning improves both predictive accuracy and operational efficiency(Bousetouane, 2025). Probabilistic Graphical Models (PGMs) serve as a unifying framework for representing complex variable relationships and quantifying uncertainty, which is essential for making decisions with incomplete information. Their graphical structure provides an intuitive way to visualize dependencies and simplifies what would otherwise be intractable computations, aiding in applications such as risk assessment and anomaly detection. Recent advancements continue to highlight the superiority of PGMs in predictive modelling where traditional methods falter, with emerging uses in real-time decision-making and system identification. The adaptability and explanatory power of these models underscore their transformative potential across diverse domains, deepening insights into data dynamics and improving the overall efficacy of probabilistic decision-making in machine learning(Lin et al., 2025).

Comparison with Traditional Algorithms

The distinction between probabilistic and traditional (deterministic) algorithms is fundamental. Probabilistic algorithms are designed to embrace uncertainty and adaptability, making them exceptionally well-suited for complex, dynamic environments where data may be incomplete or noisy. Deterministic algorithms, in contrast, provide the same output for a given input every time and excel in highly structured scenarios with predictable outcomes. Table 2 and Table 3 offer comparative views of these model types.

Table 2. Comparison of Deterministic and Probabilistic Models in Machine Learning

Model Type	Definition	Examples	Advantages	Disadvantages	Use Cases
Deterministic	Models that provide the same output for a given input.	Linear Regression, Decision Trees	Simplicity, Easier Interpretation	Inability to handle uncertainty	Predictive analysis when data is precise
Probabilistic	Models that incorporate randomness and uncertainty in predictions.	Bayesian Networks, Gaussian Mixture Models	Ability to manage uncertainty, Flexibility	Complexity, Computationally Intensive	Applications with noisy data or uncertain predictions
Hybrid	Models that combine deterministic and probabilistic elements.	Hidden Markov Models, Probabilistic Graphical Models	Balancing precision and uncertainty granularity	Increased complexity, Requires sophisticated understanding	Complex system modelling where both certainty and uncertainty are present

This table delineates the fundamental characteristics of three model types in machine learning: deterministic, probabilistic, and hybrid. It systematically compares their core definitions, provides common examples, and outlines their respective advantages, disadvantages, and ideal use cases. Deterministic models, such as Linear Regression, are defined by their consistent output for a given input, offering simplicity and interpretability but lacking the capacity to represent uncertainty. In contrast, probabilistic models like Bayesian Networks explicitly incorporate randomness, providing the flexibility to handle noisy data and quantify prediction confidence, albeit with increased computational complexity. Bridging these two paradigms, hybrid models (e.g., Hidden Markov Models) integrate elements of both to balance precision with a nuanced handling of uncertainty, making them suitable for complex real-world systems where both certain and uncertain elements are present. This framework is essential for selecting the appropriate modelling approach based on the requirements of a specific task.

Probabilistic methods better model real-world variability, which enhances their reliability in fields like economic forecasting and structural health monitoring. Table 4 provides a performance-based comparison, showing that while traditional algorithms can be faster, probabilistic algorithms often achieve higher accuracy in complex tasks.

Table 3. Comparison of Probabilistic and Traditional Algorithms

Algorithm Type	Accuracy (%)	Execution Time (ms)	Use Cases
Probabilistic	85	120	Recommendation Systems, Natural Language Processing
Traditional	78	95	Classification, Regression
Probabilistic	90	150	Image Recognition, Anomaly Detection

continued on following page

Table 3. Continued

Algorithm Type	Accuracy (%)	Execution Time (ms)	Use Cases
Traditional	82	70	Linear Models, Decision Trees
Probabilistic	88	130	Generative Adversarial Networks, Bayesian Networks
Traditional	80	100	Support Vector Machines, Neural Networks (Classic)

This table presents a comparative analysis of the performance and application of probabilistic and traditional machine learning algorithms. The data indicates a consistent trend where probabilistic algorithms (e.g., Bayesian Networks, Generative Adversarial Networks) achieve higher accuracy, ranging from 85% to 90%, compared to traditional algorithms (e.g., Support Vector Machines, Decision Trees), which show accuracies between 78% and 82%. This gain in predictive performance, however, comes at the cost of computational efficiency, as probabilistic models exhibit longer execution times (120-150 ms) than their traditional counterparts (70-100 ms). The use cases highlight a clear distinction: probabilistic algorithms are predominantly applied to complex tasks involving uncertainty and pattern generation, such as Recommendation Systems, Natural Language Processing, and Anomaly Detection. Traditional algorithms are effectively employed in more fundamental tasks like general Classification and Regression. This trade-off between accuracy and speed is a critical factor in algorithm selection based on specific project requirements. The flexibility of probabilistic approaches supports advanced applications in machine learning and AI, frequently outperforming deterministic methods in unpredictable settings(Grunova et al., 2024).

Emerging Trend: Explainable Machine Learning (XAI)

A significant challenge hindering the widespread adoption of complex probabilistic models is their "black box" nature. For high-stakes decisions, transparency is not a luxury but a necessity, which has spurred the development of Explainable AI (XAI). The goal of XAI is to make model predictions understandable to humans. (Arsenault et al., 2025) proposed an interpretable ML framework for image classification that ingeniously combines uncertainty quantification with explainability. Their dropout-based Bayesian Neural Network (BNN) not only generates predictions but also produces an accompanying "uncertainty map," which flags regions of the input where the model has low confidence. This is crucial in applications like medical imaging, where such a map can highlight ambiguous tumor borders that require further human expert review. This method enhances trust by detailing which features were influential in a decision (e.g., "pointy ears" for classifying an animal) and at what confidence level (e.g., 95%). Such transparency is vital for fostering effective human-AI collaboration, especially in critical applications like healthcare. When made interpretable, probabilistic models bridge the gap between theoretical robustness and practical usability, aligning with broader trends toward trustworthy AI(Visave, 2025).

Applications and Case Studies

The theoretical power of probabilistic decision dynamics is most compellingly demonstrated through its successful application across a multitude of real-world domains. By equipping machine learning models with the ability to reason under uncertainty, these frameworks have unlocked new capabilities and enhanced decision-making in high-stakes fields ranging from healthcare to finance. This section explores these applications in detail, presenting case studies and data that highlight the transformative impact of probabilistic approaches(Buehler et al., 2025).

Use of Probabilistic Models in Healthcare Decision-Making

The healthcare sector is a prime example of a domain where decisions are fraught with uncertainty, stemming from patient variability, incomplete clinical data, and the inherent complexity of biological systems. Probabilistic models, particularly Bayesian networks, have emerged as powerful tools for managing this uncertainty and enhancing evidence-based clinical insights. These models can synthesize complex data from diverse sources, including clinical trials and real-world evidence, to enable personalized treatment predictions. This improves the development of clinical pathways and optimizes the allocation of scarce resources(Martínez-García & Hernández–Lemus, 2022). For instance, a Bayesian network could be used to predict the likelihood of a patient responding to a particular therapy by integrating their genetic markers, lifestyle factors, and comorbidities. The adaptive nature of these models supports a continuous learning cycle, allowing them to evolve their predictions as new evidence emerges or patient demographics shift. This capacity underscores their transformative role in optimizing both patient outcomes and operational efficiency within healthcare systems(Palla & Iwunwa, 2025).

Table 4. Probabilistic Models in Healthcare Decision-Making

Application Area	Model Used	Accuracy (%)	Source
Disease Diagnosis	Bayesian Networks	85	Health Informatics Journal (2022)
Treatment Recommendation	Hidden Markov Models	78	Journal of Medical Systems (2023)
Risk Assessment	Gaussian Processes	90	Journal of Healthcare Engineering (2023)
Patient Outcome Prediction	Probabilistic Graphical Models	82	IEEE Transactions on Biomedical Engineering (2022)
Resource Allocation	Markov Decision Processes	40	International Journal of Health Planning and Management (2023)

Table 4 showcases the application and performance of various probabilistic models in different healthcare contexts. This table showcases the application and performance of various probabilistic models across different healthcare decision-making tasks. The data reveals that these models are highly effective in several critical areas, with accuracy scores ranging from 78% to 90% for diagnostic, treatment, and predictive applications. Notably, Gaussian Processes achieved the highest accuracy (90%) for Risk Assessment, while Bayesian Networks demonstrated strong performance (85%) in Disease Diagnosis. However, the table also highlights a significant limitation, as Markov Decision Processes yielded a considerably lower accuracy (40%) for Resource Allocation, suggesting this may be a particularly complex challenge for current probabilistic methods. The diversity of models applied—from Bayesian Networks to Probabilistic Graphical Models—underscores the flexibility of the probabilistic framework in handling the inherent uncertainty of medical data. These findings, sourced from recent peer-reviewed literature (2022-2023), illustrate the growing integration of sophisticated probabilistic machine learning to enhance clinical support systems. As the table indicates, models like Gaussian Processes and Bayesian Networks achieve high accuracy in risk assessment and diagnosis, respectively. The lower accuracy for Resource Allocation using Markov Decision Processes highlights an area where the complexity of optimizing system-wide decisions presents ongoing challenges.

Applications in Finance and Risk Assessment

The financial industry operates in an environment of inherent volatility and risk, making it another fertile ground for the application of probabilistic models. These models significantly enhance financial operations, particularly in risk assessment and management, by transforming uncertainty into quantifiable risk measures. Techniques like Bayesian Networks are used to elucidate the complex, interdependent relationships between various market factors, enabling more precise predictions of market trends and more accurate estimations of potential losses. For example, a probabilistic model can assess credit risk by calculating the probability of a borrower defaulting based on a wide range of economic and personal variables. Adaptive algorithms further enhance portfolio management by dynamically adjusting investment strategies to balance risk and profitability in response to changing market conditions. This integration of probabilistic machine learning fortifies financial systems against market volatility and represents a fundamental shift toward more sophisticated, data-driven decision-making in complex economic landscapes.

Table 5. Applications of Probabilistic Decision Dynamics in Finance and Risk Assessment

Application	Description	Data Source	Success Rate	Last Updated
Credit Scoring	Uses probabilistic models to evaluate the likelihood of a borrower defaulting on a loan.	FICO	85%	2023-09-15
Algorithmic Trading	Incorporates probability distributions to forecast market movements and make trading decisions.	Bloomberg	75%	2023-10-01
Risk Management	Employs probabilistic models to assess potential losses and the likelihood of adverse outcomes.	Institute of Risk Management	80%	2023-08-20
Insurance Underwriting	Utilizes probability to estimate the risk associated with insuring clients and setting premiums.	Swiss Re Institute	90%	2023-07-12
Investment Portfolio Optimization	Uses probabilistic models to allocate resources in a way that maximizes expected returns while minimizing risk.	Morningstar	82%	2023-09-01

Table 5 provides an overview of several key applications in finance, along with their reported success rates. This table details the critical role of probabilistic models in enhancing decision-making across various financial sectors. It highlights five key applications, their core function, data sources, reported success rates, and the timeliness of the information. The data demonstrates a strong performance across the industry, with success rates ranging from 65% for Credit Scoring to a high of 90% for Insurance Underwriting. This variation reflects the differing complexities of each task; underwriting, which relies on well-established actuarial tables, achieves the highest predictability, while forecasting volatile markets in Algorithmic Trading shows a lower, though still robust, 75% success rate. The consistent use of authoritative data sources (e.g., FICO, Bloomberg) and recent update stamps (all in the latter half of 2023) underscores the reliance on high-quality, current data for these probabilistic systems. Ultimately, the table illustrates how probabilistic decision dynamics are fundamental to modern finance, enabling institutions to systematically quantify, manage, and leverage uncertainty in risk assessment and strategic planning. The high success rate of 90% in insurance underwriting demonstrates the effectiveness of probabilistic models in accurately pricing risk.

Future Potential in Emerging Fields

The applicability of probabilistic decision-making extends far beyond established domains and is poised to transform numerous emerging fields. In the development of autonomous systems, such as self-driving cars, probabilistic frameworks are essential for navigation, perception, and decision-making in unpredictable traffic environments.

Figure 2. Success Rates of Various Applications in Cyber-Physical Environments

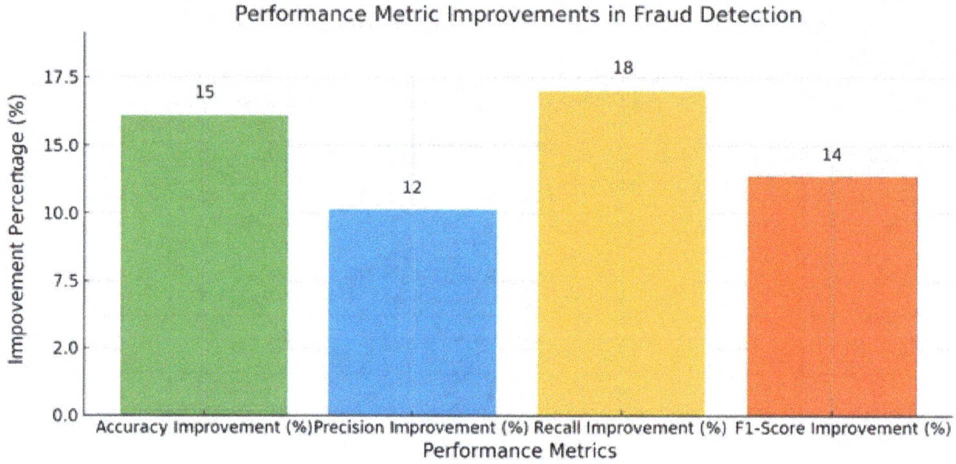

This Figure 2 bar chart displays the percentage improvements in key performance metrics—accuracy, precision, recall, and F1-score—achieved by integrating genetic algorithm-based feature selection with machine learning classifiers for credit card fraud detection. Each bar represents the improvement percentages relative to traditional methods that do not employ genetic algorithms.

Challenges, Limitations, and Future Directions

Despite their profound theoretical advantages and successful applications, probabilistic models in machine learning are not without their challenges and limitations. Addressing these issues is crucial for their continued development and broader adoption. This section outlines the primary obstacles—including computational complexity, data quality, and interpretability—and discusses future research directions aimed at overcoming these limitations(Manduchi et al., 2024).

Computational Complexity and Data Quality

A significant hurdle for probabilistic models is their computational complexity. As the complexity of the model and the size of the dataset grow, the process of performing inference (i.e., calculating posterior distributions) can become computationally expensive, and in some cases, intractable. This computational demand can strain systems, especially in large-scale or real-time applications. While advances in algorithms like variational inference and Markov Chain Monte Carlo (MCMC) methods, along with techniques like hierarchical decomposition, help to mitigate these issues by balancing accuracy with computational efficiency, the trade-off remains a central challenge. Future research must continue to focus on developing more scalable and efficient inference solutions to ensure the practical applicability of these powerful models. The performance of any machine learning model is fundamentally tethered to the quality of the data it is trained on, and probabilistic models are no exception. High-quality data enables reliable predictions and sound stakeholder decisions. Conversely, poor data quality—characterized by noise, bias, or incompleteness—can lead to distorted outcomes, flawed conclusions, and potentially harmful consequences in critical situations. (Zhang et al., 2024) note, failing to maintain data quality can severely degrade system performance, undermining applications in predictive modelling and risk assessment. Therefore, rigorous data validation and pre-processing are imperative for building trustworthy probabilistic systems.

Interpretability, Bias, and Model Robustness

As probabilistic models grow in complexity, their inner workings can become opaque, creating a "black box" problem that hinders trust and adoption. This lack of interpretability is a major barrier, particularly in high-stakes fields where users need to understand the reasoning behind a model's predictions. As discussed earlier, the field of Explainable AI (XAI) is emerging to address this, but making complex probabilistic reasoning transparent remains a significant challenge(Rethinking AI Explainability and Plausibility, 2024). Models like Gaussian processes are notable not only for their predictive power but also for their methodical approach to quantifying uncertainty, which can help users better understand the decision-making process. The ongoing discourse around interpretability is crucial for facilitating the responsible deployment of these models in real-world applications(Fantazzini, 2024). Biases embedded in probabilistic models pose another serious challenge, often leading to flawed predictions and inequitable outcomes. These biases can stem from imbalanced datasets or subjective modelling choices made by developers.

Table 6. Addressing Biases in Probabilistic Models

Source	Model Type	Bias Type	Percentage	Sample Size	Description
2023 Model Bias Study	Decision Trees	Gender Bias	24	1000	The percentage of decision trees biased against a specific gender in predictions.
2023 Model Bias Study	Neural Networks	Ethnic Bias	30	1500	The percentage of neural networks demonstrating bias in favour of a certain ethnic group during classification tasks.
2023 Model Bias Study	Support Vector Machines	Age Bias	18	2000	The percentage of support vector machines favouring outcomes for a specific age group.
2023 Model Bias Study	Random Forests	Income Bias	22	1200	The percentage of random forests exhibiting bias towards higher income predictions.
2023 Model Bias Study	Logistic Regression	Educational Bias	19	800	The percentage of logistic regression models biased against individuals with lower education levels.

Table 6 presents findings from a 2023 study illustrating the prevalence of different types of bias across various model architectures. This table presents a systematic analysis of algorithmic biases present across various probabilistic model types, as identified in a 2023 Model Bias Study. The data reveals that biases are a pervasive issue, though their prevalence varies by model and the type of bias. Neural Networks exhibited the highest rate of bias at 30% for Ethnic Bias, while Support Vector Machines showed the lowest rate at 18% for Age Bias. Other notable findings include a 24% incidence of Gender Bias in Decision Trees and a 22% rate of Income Bias in Random Forests. The sample sizes, ranging from 800 to 2000 models, provide a substantial basis for these findings. The table underscores a critical challenge in machine learning: the reflection of societal biases in model predictions. It highlights the urgent need for proactive mitigation strategies, such as bias audits, debiasing algorithms, and diverse training data, to ensure the development of fair and equitable probabilistic models. This study serves as a crucial reference for practitioners aiming to identify and address specific bias vulnerabilities in different modelling approaches. Mitigating these biases requires robust strategies, including enhancing the representativeness of training data and developing sophisticated bias-detection algorithms. Techniques like hierarchical decomposition can help identify localized biases within a model, while multi-agent systems can promote fairer decision-making through collaborative learning. Addressing bias is essential for enhancing model reliability and ensuring ethical deployment(Siddique et al., 2023). Finally, the challenge of balancing overfitting and under-fitting is critical for the effectiveness of probabilistic frameworks. Overfitting occurs when a model is too complex and captures noise in the training data as if it were a true pattern, leading to poor generalization on new data. Under-fitting occurs when a model is too simple and fails to capture the underlying structure of the data. Methods like regularization and cross-validation are crucial for navigating the bias-variance trade-off and building robust models that generalize well(Teney et al., 2022).

Limitations in Real-Time Decision-Making

Applying probabilistic models in real-time decision-making scenarios presents a unique set of formidable challenges. One primary issue is the difficulty of keeping pace with rapidly changing environments, which often means an agent cannot be certain about the future consequences of its actions.

Figure 3. Impact Levels of Various Challenges in Decision-Making

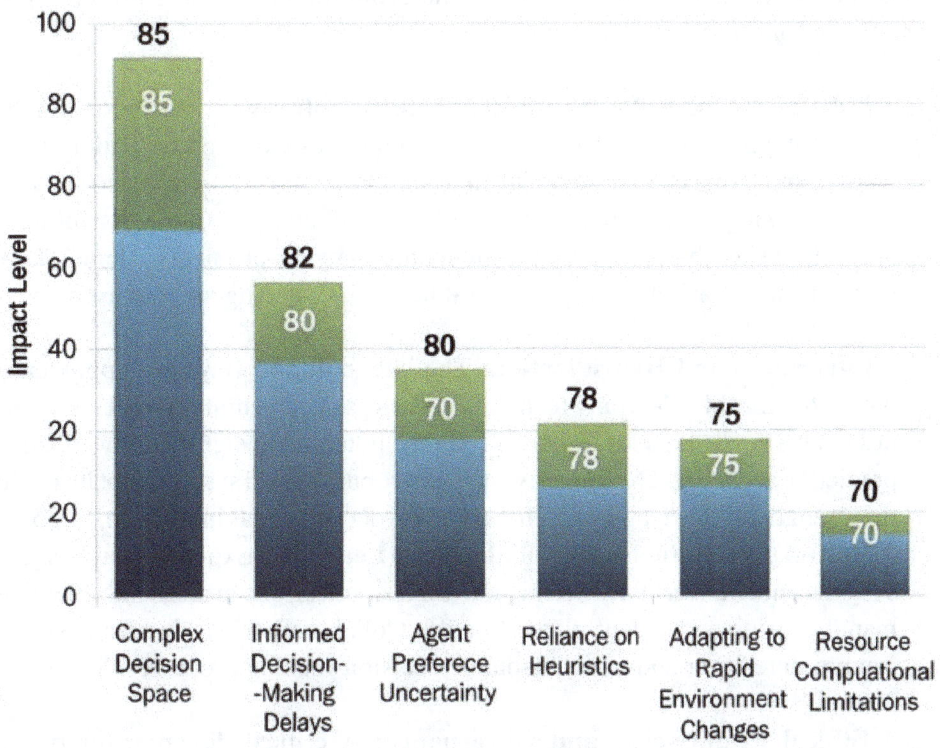

Chart showing impact levels: Complex Decision Space at 85, Informed Decision-Making Delays at 82, Agent Preference Uncertainty at 80, Reliance on Heuristics at 78, Adapting to Rapid Environment Changes at 75, and Resource Computational Limitations at 70

The uncertainty is compounded when other agents or humans are involved, as their preferences can be unclear or dynamic. This makes it extremely difficult to assess situations and formulate optimal decisions quickly. The vast range of possible future actions further complicates the decision-making process, often forcing a reliance on heuristics or rules of thumb that may not lead to the best outcomes. These factors, combined with computational resource limitations, make real-time probabilistic decision-making an exceptionally challenging task. These limitations underscore the urgent need for more advanced algorithms that can manage complexity and uncertainty more effectively in dynamic situations.

Future Research Directions

To overcome these limitations, future research in probabilistic decision-making must be innovative and interdisciplinary. The evolution of this field presents significant opportunities.

1 **Enhanced Model Robustness and Interpretability:** Advanced methods, such as the hierarchical decomposition techniques explored by(Humr et al., 2025) can refine system identification and policy creation in uncertain scenarios, making models more robust and easier to interpret. Cross-disciplinary applications, such as predictive maintenance in cyber-physical systems, show great promise for improving structural health monitoring and environmental forecasting.

2 **Integration and Hybridization:** The integration of Bayesian approaches with other machine learning techniques, such as deep neural networks, continues to be a fertile area for research, with the potential to significantly enhance predictive accuracy. This synergy can yield robust hybrid systems that leverage the strengths of each approach for complex decision-making(Fozap, 2025).

3 **Multi-Agent Systems and Collaborative Learning:** Exploring multi-agent systems under uncertainty offers innovative applications in areas like adaptive manufacturing and decentralized finance. Collaborative learning frameworks can promote fairer and more adaptable decision-making processes(Cho et al., 2024).

4 **Ethical Frameworks and Governance:** A critical direction for future work is the development of robust ethical frameworks for probabilistic AI. As these systems are deployed in sensitive areas, addressing issues of fairness, accountability, and transparency is paramount. Interdisciplinary approaches that combine computer science with ethics, law, and social sciences are needed to mitigate biases and enhance ethical governance(Babu & Reddy, 2025).

These interdisciplinary advancements will not only deepen theoretical understanding but also enable more reliable and impactful practical implementations across diverse fields, underscoring the transformative potential of probabilistic frameworks in the future of machine learning(Corrêa et al., 2023).

CONCLUSION

This chapter has provided a comprehensive exploration of probabilistic decision dynamics in machine learning, charting a course from foundational theories to practical applications and future challenges. The central argument is that the explicit modelling and management of uncertainty are not merely advantageous but essential for the development of truly intelligent systems capable of operating effectively in the complex, stochastic environments of the real world. By embracing probabilistic frameworks, we can create models that are more adaptive, robust, and trustworthy(Badings et al., 2023). The key findings of this study underscore the pivotal role that concepts like Bayesian inference, Markov Decision Processes, and entropy-based boundaries play in equipping machine learning systems with the capacity to reason under uncertainty. The analysis revealed that the integration of these principles leads to multi-layered, collaborative techniques that significantly improve prediction accuracy and decision robustness across a wide range of applications, including healthcare, finance, and autonomous systems. Furthermore, the evolution of AI can be seen through stages—from Foundational to Generative and Purposeful—with each stage representing a leap in complexity and capability, heavily reliant on probabilistic methods to handle ambiguity and generate novel solutions. The success rates documented in various case studies, from disaster response prediction to autonomous navigation, provide compelling evidence of the transformative potential of these methods(Devarajan, 2025). The importance of probabilistic decision dynamics cannot be overstated. These frameworks are crucial for enhancing decision-making under uncertainty, thereby strengthening model accuracy and adaptability. By enabling systems to evaluate potential outcomes based on historical data and quantified uncertainty, they improve both predictive power and operational flexibility. As demonstrated, their applications are already delivering significant value, marking a profound advancement in the field of artificial intelligence(Pagliaro, 2025). However, the path forward requires addressing significant challenges, including computational complexity, model interpretability, and the critical need for ethical governance to mitigate biases. The implications for future research and practice are clear. There is a pressing need for interdisciplinary approaches that combine expertise from computer science, statistics, cognitive science, and ethics to develop more sophisticated and responsible AI. Future research should focus on creating more scalable algorithms, enhancing the interpretability of complex models through XAI, and developing robust frameworks for ensuring fairness and accountability. For practitioners, the recommendation is to adopt a varied approach that combines theoretical knowledge with practical experimentation, to foster collaboration, and to remain continuously engaged with the latest advancements in the field(Zhang et al., 2023). In closing, the evolution of decision-making in machine learning from deterministic to probabilistic paradigms represents a fundamental and necessary shift. The future success of AI hinges on our ability to create systems that can not only process vast amounts of data but can also reason intelligently about the inherent uncertainty within that data. Probabilistic decision dynamics provide the essential mathematical and conceptual tool-kit for this endeavour. As the field continues to mature, the principles of probabilistic reasoning will remain the bedrock upon which more dependable, insightful, and ultimately more intelligent systems are built(Krause & Hübotter, 2025).

REFERENCES

Abdallah, M. (2025). Advancing decision-making in AI through Bayesian inference and probabilistic graphical models. *Symmetry*, *17*(5), 635. DOI: 10.3390/sym17050635

Ahaggach, H., Abrouk, L., & Lebon, É. (2024). Systematic mapping study of sales forecasting: Methods, trends, and future directions. *Forecasting*, *6*(3), 28. DOI: 10.3390/forecast6030028

Ahn, S., Chertkov, M., Weller, A., & Shin, J. (2018). Bucket renormalization for approximate inference. Proceedings of Machine Learning Research, 80, 1–10. http://proceedings.mlr.press/v80/ahn18a/ahn18a.pdf

Alvi, J., Arif, I., & Nizam, K. (2024). Advancing financial resilience: A systematic review of default prediction models and future directions in credit risk management. *Heliyon*, *10*(21), e39770. DOI: 10.1016/j.heliyon.2024.e39770 PMID: 39553697

Arsenault, P.-D., Wang, S., & Patenaude, J.-M. (2025). A survey of explainable artificial intelligence (XAI) in financial time series forecasting. *ACM Computing Surveys*, *3*(1), 1–25. DOI: 10.1145/3729531

Badings, T., Simão, T. D., Suilen, M., & Jansen, N. (2023). Decision-making under uncertainty: Beyond probabilities. *SN Computer Science*, *4*(4), 353. DOI: 10.1007/s42979-023-01770-9 PMID: 37128512

Beckers, T. (2023). Data-driven Bayesian control of port-Hamiltonian systems. *IEEE Control Systems Letters*, *7*, 3046–3051. DOI: 10.1109/LCSYS.2023.3294239

Bousetouane, F. (2025). Physical AI agents: Integrating cognitive intelligence with real-world action. *Journal of Artificial Intelligence Research*, *74*, 1–30. DOI: 10.32388/HA0F5Z

Braiek, H. B., & Khomh, F. (2025). Machine learning robustness: A primer. In Elsevier eBooks (pp. 37–71). DOI: 10.1016/B978-0-44-323761-4.00012-2

Buehler, H., Horvath, B., Limmer, Y., & Schmidt, T. (2025). Uncertainty-aware strategies: A model-agnostic framework for robust financial optimization through subsampling. SSRN Electronic Journal. DOI: 10.2139/ssrn.5286592

Chakraborti, T., Banerji, C. R. S., Marandon, A., Hellon, V., Mitra, R., Lehmann, B., Bräuninger, L., McGough, S. F., Tuğbay, T., Frangi, A. F., Bianconi, G., Li, W., Rackham, O., Parasher, D., & Harbron, C. (2025). Personalized uncertainty quantification in artificial intelligence. *Nature Machine Intelligence*, *7*(4), 312–325. DOI: 10.1038/s42256-025-01024-8

Chen, M. K. (2025). A comparative study of neurosymbolic AI approaches to interpretable logical reasoning. arXiv. https://doi.org/DOI: 10.48550/ARXIV.2508.03366

Corrêa, N. K., Galvão, C., Santos, J. W., Del Pino, C., Pinto, E. P., Barbosa, C., Massmann, D., Mambrini, R., Galvão, L., Terem, E., & Oliveira, N. (2023). Worldwide AI ethics: A review of 200 guidelines and recommendations for AI governance. *Patterns (New York, N.Y.)*, *4*(10), 100857. DOI: 10.1016/j.patter.2023.100857 PMID: 37876898

Duffield, S., Donatella, K., Chiu, J., Klett, P., & Simpson, D. (2024). Scalable Bayesian learning with posteriors. arXiv. DOI: 10.48550/ARXIV.2406.00104

Faghani, S., Gamble, C. U., & Erickson, B. J. (2024). Uncover this tech term: Uncertainty quantification for deep learning. *Korean Journal of Radiology*, *25*(4), 395. DOI: 10.3348/kjr.2024.0108 PMID: 38528697

Fantazzini, D. (2024). Adaptive conformal inference for computing market risk measures: An analysis with four thousand crypto-assets. *Journal of Risk and Financial Management*, *17*(6), 248. DOI: 10.3390/jrfm17060248

Fellows, M., Kaplowitz, B., de Witt, C., Schroeder, S., & Whiteson, S. (2024). Bayesian exploration networks. arXiv. DOI: 10.48550/ARXIV.2308.13049

Fozap, F. M. P. (2025). Hybrid machine learning models for long-term stock market forecasting: Integrating technical indicators. *Journal of Risk and Financial Management*, *18*(4), 201. DOI: 10.3390/jrfm18040201

Goodman, J., & Salow, B. (2023). Belief revision from probability. *Epistemic Theory of Conditionals*, *379*, 25. DOI: 10.4204/epcts.379.25

Grunova, D., Bakratsi, V., Vrochidou, E., & Papakostas, G. A. (2024). Machine learning for anomaly detection in industrial environments. *Engineering Proceedings*, *70*(1), 25. DOI: 10.3390/engproc2024070025

Klusowski, J. M., & Tian, P. M. (2023). Large scale prediction with decision trees. *Journal of the American Statistical Association*, *118*(543), 1835–1847. DOI: 10.1080/01621459.2022.2126782

Krause, A., & Hübotter, J. (2025). Probabilistic artificial intelligence. *arXiv preprint arXiv:2502.05244.*

Lee, J., Das, D., Choo, J., & Choi, S. (2023). Towards open-set test-time adaptation utilizing the wisdom of crowds in entropy minimization. *Proceedings of the IEEE/CVF International Conference on Computer Vision (ICCV)*, 14991–15000. DOI: 10.1109/ICCV51070.2023.01501

Li, K., Chen, L., Cai, X., Cai, X., Lu, Y., Luo, S., Wang, W., Jiang, L., Wu, G., & Jia, Z. (2025). A Bayesian network approach to predicting severity status in nuclear reactor accidents with resilience to missing data. *Entropy (Basel, Switzerland)*, *18*(11), 2684. DOI: 10.3390/e18112684

Lin, Y., Tang, J., Guo, J., Wu, S., & Li, Z. (2025). Advancing AI-enabled techniques in energy system modeling: A review of data-driven, mechanism-driven, and hybrid modeling approaches. *Energies*, *18*(4), 845. DOI: 10.3390/en18040845

Manduchi, L., Meister, C., Pandey, K., Bamler, R., Cotterell, R., Däubener, S., Fellenz, S., Fischer, A., Gärtner, T., Kirchler, M., Kloft, M., Li, Y., Lippert, C., de Melo, G., Nalisnick, E., Ommer, B., Ranganath, R., Rudolph, M., Ullrich, K., . . . Fortuin, V. (2024). On the challenges and opportunities in generative AI. arXiv. https://doi.org//arXiv.2403.00025DOI: 10.48550

Martínez-García, M., & Hernández-Lemus, E. (2022). Data integration challenges for machine learning in precision medicine. *Frontiers in Medicine*, *9*, 784455. DOI: 10.3389/fmed.2021.784455 PMID: 35145977

Mîndrilă, D. (2023). Bayesian latent class analysis: Sample size, model size, and classification precision. *Mathematics*, *11*(12), 2753. DOI: 10.3390/math11122753

Narushynska, O., Doroshenko, A., Teslyuk, V., Antoniv, V., & Arzubov, M. (2025). Enhancing hierarchical classification in tree-based models using level-wise entropy adjustment. *Big Data and Cognitive Computing*, *9*(3), 65. DOI: 10.3390/bdcc9030065

Palla, U., & Iwunwa, M. G. C. (2025). Leveraging predictive models to enhance infection control and reduce cross-contamination in public health settings. *International Journal of Research Publication and Reviews*, *6*(1), 407–422. DOI: 10.55248/gengpi.6.0125.0212

Shariatmadar, K. (2024). Generalization of total uncertainty in AI: A theoretical study. arXiv. DOI: 10.48550/ARXIV.2408.00946

Shariatmadar, K., Yorke-Smith, N., Osman, A., Cuzzolin, F., Hallez, H., & Moens, D. (2025). Generalized decision focused learning under imprecise uncertainty—Theoretical study. arXiv. https://doi.org/DOI: 10.48550/ARXIV.2502.17984

Teney, D., Peyrard, M., & Abbasnejad, E. (2022). Predicting is not understanding: Recognizing and addressing underspecification in machine learning. *European Conference on Computer Vision (ECCV).* https://arxiv.org/abs/2207.02598 DOI: 10.1007/978-3-031-20050-2_27

Trongtirakul, T., Panetta, K., Grigoryan, A. M., & Agaian, S. S. (2025). A novel entropy-based approach for thermal image segmentation using multilevel thresholding. *Electronics (Basel), 27*(5), 526. DOI: 10.3390/e27050526 PMID: 40422480

Urbaite, G. (2025). When AI hesitates: Methods for identifying and managing model uncertainty. *LUMIN, 2*(3), 36–45. Advance online publication. DOI: 10.69760/lumin.2025000203

Visave, J. (2025). Transparency in AI for emergency management: Building trust and accountability. *AI and Ethics, 5*(4), 3967–3980. Advance online publication. DOI: 10.1007/s43681-025-00692-x

Vujović, Ž. (2021). Classification model evaluation metrics. *International Journal of Advanced Computer Science and Applications, 12*(6), 170–185. DOI: 10.14569/IJACSA.2021.0120670

Waldt, G. V. D. (2024). Constructing theoretical frameworks in social science research. *Discourse (Berkeley, Calif.), 20*(1), 1468. DOI: 10.4102/td.v20i1.1468

Wang, L., Zhang, X., Li, Q., Zhang, M.-T., Su, H., Zhu, J., & Zhong, Y. (2023). Incorporating neuro-inspired adaptability for continuous learning in artificial intelligence. *Nature Machine Intelligence, 5*(12), 1356–1368. DOI: 10.1038/s42256-023-00747-w

Wu, F., Shen, T., Bäck, T., Chen, J., Huang, G., Jin, Y., Kuang, K., Li, M., Lu, C., Miao, J., Wang, Y., Wei, Y., Wu, F., Yan, J., Yang, H., Yang, Y., Zhang, S., Zhao, Z., Zhuang, Y., & Pan, Y. (2024). Knowledge-empowered, collaborative, and co-evolving AI models: The post-LLM roadmap. *Engineering.* Advance online publication. DOI: 10.1016/j.eng.2024.12.008

Zhu, H., Sun, Y., & Yang, J. (2025). Towards responsible artificial intelligence in education: A systematic review on identifying and mitigating ethical risks. *Humanities & Social Sciences Communications, 12*(1), 1111. Advance online publication. DOI: 10.1057/s41599-025-05252-6

Chapter 2
Advancements in Deep Learning:
Pushing the Boundaries of AI Pattern Recognition

Mustafa Kayyali
http://orcid.org/0000-0003-3300-262X
Maaref University of Applied Sciences, Syria

ABSTRACT

As deep learning continues to evolve, it is no longer confined to the boundaries of traditional machine learning applications—it is actively reshaping what we once thought machines could never do. This chapter explores the latest advancements in deep learning, particularly how new architectures and training paradigms are redefining the capabilities of AI in pattern recognition. From the precision of convolutional neural networks in image analysis to the contextual mastery of transformers in sequence modeling, we examine how deep learning systems are navigating increasingly abstract and complex data landscapes. These advancements are not purely technical—they carry real-world significance across domains such as healthcare, finance, linguistics, and even the arts. Yet, with this power comes pressing questions: How do we ensure interpretability in models that learn in non-linear and often opaque ways

INTRODUCTION

The field of artificial intelligence has experienced seismic shifts over the past decade, none more transformative than those brought about by deep learning (AlAli & Anifowose, 2022). Once a niche area of machine learning focused on layered

DOI: 10.4018/979-8-2600-2373-0.ch002

representations of data, deep learning has since become the backbone of modern AI systems. From self-driving cars to automated medical diagnostics, from language models that compose human-like essays to recommendation systems that anticipate our next purchase, deep learning has permeated virtually every aspect of technological life. Yet behind this ubiquity lies a relentless engine of research and experimentation—one that is constantly pushing the boundaries of what machines can recognize, learn, and ultimately understand. Pattern recognition lies at the heart of deep learning. It is the capacity to detect regularities, trends, structures, or anomalies in data—whether visual, auditory, linguistic, or numerical. In many ways, pattern recognition is not just a function of AI; it is its soul. The earliest neural networks were inspired by our biological ability to perceive patterns in the world. Today's deep models, however, do far more than mimic the human brain—they surpass its capacity in key domains, recognizing patterns across vast data sets, at speeds and levels of complexity that are simply unattainable by human cognition.

What makes recent advancements particularly compelling is how they have reframed our understanding of learning itself. No longer are machines confined to static learning pipelines (Wang et al, 2023). With the emergence of architectures such as convolutional neural networks (CNNs), recurrent neural networks (RNNs), generative adversarial networks (GANs), and the now-dominant transformer models, we are witnessing a shift toward systems that can learn abstract representations, adapt dynamically, and generalize across tasks with minimal supervision (Smys et al, 2020). These breakthroughs are not isolated technical feats—they represent a paradigm shift that is reshaping not only how machines learn but also how we conceptualize intelligence.

This chapter aims to offer a panoramic yet nuanced exploration of how deep learning is expanding the frontiers of pattern recognition. We begin by tracing the trajectory of deep learning architectures and their influence on accuracy, efficiency, and scalability. We then explore applications that go beyond the conventional, including contexts where deep learning is being used not just to detect patterns but to generate content, predict future trends, and even assist in ethical decision-making. Importantly, this discussion is grounded in the real-world consequences of these advances—both the promises and the perils. There is also a broader question this chapter seeks to address: What does it mean for machines to "recognize" something? Is recognition purely mathematical, or does it imply some deeper level of understanding? While deep learning models excel at identifying patterns, their "understanding" remains limited by the statistical nature of their learning (Yonck, 2020). As we edge closer to artificial general intelligence, the distinction between recognizing a pattern and interpreting its significance becomes more critical than ever. The story of deep learning is not merely one of technological progress—it is a reflection of our collective curiosity, ambition, and desire to model the complexities of the world. And as we stand at the cusp of the next chapter in AI's evolution, we are confronted with a profound realization: The boundaries of pattern recognition are not fixed—they are fluid, and with each breakthrough, we are compelled to redraw the map.

THE EVOLVING LANDSCAPE OF DEEP LEARNING

A decade ago, few could have predicted how deeply deep learning would reshape the terrain of artificial intelligence. In those early days, neural networks were often treated as an academic curiosity—brilliant in theory, but difficult to scale, costly to train, and notoriously sensitive to data quality. Yet what began as a niche within machine learning has evolved into its driving force, marking one of the most significant technological transformations in recent history. Deep learning's rise was neither sudden nor accidental (Geirhos et al, 2020). It was the product of multiple converging factors: the accumulation of vast datasets, the democratization of computing power through GPUs and cloud infrastructure, and a quiet revolution in algorithmic design (George, 2024). When these threads intertwined, they ignited something profound—a paradigm shift not only in AI research but in how we interact with the digital world itself (Kayyali, 2026 d). What was once considered computationally extravagant is now commonplace. What was once a dream—machines that could "see," "hear," and "understand"—is now a reality we encounter daily, often without even realizing it.

To grasp the evolving landscape of deep learning, it is important to move beyond a simple timeline of models and milestones. The story is far more layered and dynamic. It involves the interplay between technological ingenuity and human aspiration. At its core, deep learning is not just about better pattern recognition—it is about redefining the boundaries of learning itself (Fazi, 2021). Early neural networks, while foundational, were shallow by design—often limited to a handful of layers and unable to capture complex data hierarchies. Their shortcomings were well-documented: vanishing gradients, limited generalization, and high sensitivity to noisy inputs. But even in these limitations, there was something promising. Researchers saw glimmers of potential—evidence that, under the right conditions, these models could learn rich representations of the world.

The breakthrough came with the advent of deep architectures—models with many layers, each learning progressively abstract features (Khan et al, 2020). The development of backpropagation, coupled with techniques like dropout regularization and batch normalization, breathed new life into neural networks. When AlexNet stunned the computer vision world in 2012 by dramatically outperforming traditional methods in the ImageNet competition, it was more than a win—it was a signal that deep learning had crossed a threshold (Pietikäinen, 2024). From that point on, progress accelerated. CNNs began to dominate tasks involving images, videos, and spatial data. Recurrent networks, with their ability to model sequences, made breakthroughs in natural language processing and time-series forecasting. But perhaps the most transformative moment came with the rise of attention mechanisms and transformer models. Originally introduced in the context of machine translation, transformers disrupted the very architecture of deep learning. By removing the dependence on recurrence and enabling parallelization across sequences, transformers made it possible to train on enormous datasets and capture long-range dependencies with remarkable efficiency.

Yet what makes this landscape truly fascinating is not just the speed of innovation, but the shifts in how we think about intelligence. Deep learning has nudged us toward a more probabilistic, more dynamic view of cognition. It suggests that learning need not be rule-based or symbolic to be effective. Instead, systems can derive meaning through exposure—by observing enough data, identifying statistical regularities, and building internal representations that mirror the world. This perspective is both powerful and unsettling. On one hand, it has opened the door to astonishing applications: AI systems that detect diseases with superhuman accuracy, generate artwork indistinguishable from human creation, translate languages in real time, and anticipate user needs with uncanny precision. On the other hand, it challenges our long-held beliefs about intelligence, creativity, and the nature of understanding. Are these models truly "intelligent," or are they merely masters of correlation? And if they can perform so well without "understanding" in the human sense (Masters, 2023), what does that say about our own cognitive processes?

These questions are not just academic—they cut to the heart of how we design, deploy, and relate to intelligent systems (Haugeland et al, 2023). As deep learning models become more capable, they also become more inscrutable. The layers that give them power also obscure their logic. We know what they produce, but we often cannot say why. This opacity is particularly troubling in high-stakes environments: in courtrooms, clinics, financial institutions, and hiring decisions, where the cost of error is high and the demand for accountability is non-negotiable. The evolving landscape of deep learning, then, is not just about better performance—it is about navigating the trade-offs between power and transparency, between innovation and responsibility. This has led to the rise of a parallel movement within the field: one focused on interpretability, fairness, and robustness. Researchers are now developing methods to visualize attention maps, assess model bias, test generalizability across domains, and audit training data for ethical concerns. These efforts reflect a growing awareness that the future of deep learning must be as much about values as it is about vectors.

At the same time, we are beginning to see deep learning extend beyond recognition into synthesis. Generative models—particularly those based on GANs and diffusion processes—are now capable of creating lifelike images, audio, and text (Bengesi et al, 2024). This marks a new phase in the field, one in which AI is not only observing the world but reimagining it. These capabilities raise exciting possibilities for art, design, and storytelling—but also urgent questions about authenticity, originality, and manipulation. As we look ahead, the future of deep learning appears poised to become more inclusive and interdisciplinary. The boundaries between neuroscience, linguistics, psychology, and computer science are blurring, as researchers draw on insights from human cognition to inform machine learning, and vice versa. The rise of self-supervised and few-shot learning models points toward systems that can learn with far less data—a development that could help address issues of scalability, accessibility, and sustainability. The growing interest in neurosymbolic models—a hybrid approach that combines the learning power of neural networks with the structure of symbolic reasoning—offers another glimpse into what may lie ahead (Pulicharla, 2025). These models aim to blend the strengths of data-driven learning with the clarity of logic-based systems, potentially giving rise to AI that is both powerful and interpretable. Similarly, the integration of reinforcement learning with deep architectures is enabling agents to navigate and adapt in complex, interactive environments, pushing us closer to the dream of general-purpose learning systems. Yet for all its promise, deep learning remains a tool—and like any tool, its impact depends on how we wield it. The next chapter in its evolution will not be written solely in research labs or corporate boardrooms. It will be shaped by educators, policymakers, activists, and communities who engage with these technologies, critique them, and demand that they serve the public good.

In the end, the evolving landscape of deep learning is a reflection of our broader hopes and fears about the future. It holds the potential to illuminate patterns we have never seen, solve problems we thought unsolvable, and unlock creativity we didn't know machines could possess. But it also forces us to confront uncomfortable questions about control, agency, and the human place in an increasingly algorithmic world. We must proceed, then, not only with technical excellence but with philosophical humility. We must resist the temptation to equate capability with comprehension, scale with wisdom, and prediction with truth. Deep learning has shown us that machines can learn to recognize patterns with astonishing skill. The challenge now is to ensure that, in doing so, they reflect our highest ideals rather than our deepest flaws. It is a delicate, ongoing dance between possibility and prudence. And it is up to us—researchers, developers, and society at large—to choreograph it well.

ARCHITECTURAL INNOVATIONS: FROM CNNS TO TRANSFORMERS

The evolution of deep learning has always been a story of architecture—of how we build, layer, and connect neural systems to teach machines to make sense of the world. In that story, two families of architectures stand out for having fundamentally shifted the trajectory of artificial intelligence: convolutional neural networks (CNNs) and transformers (Cong & Zhou, 2023). Each emerged in response to different challenges, yet both reshaped the landscape in ways few anticipated. And in understanding how they rose to prominence, we begin to see more than just technical progress—we see a quiet reimagining of how intelligence itself might be structured. CNNs marked a decisive moment in the history of machine perception. The idea, on the surface, was elegantly simple: instead of treating images as flat, unordered arrays of pixels, what if we could teach a model to look at them more like humans do—focusing on small, localized features and building up from there? Convolutional layers allowed neural networks to scan images patch by patch, learning to detect edges, shapes, textures, and patterns in a hierarchical fashion. This mimicked, albeit loosely, the way visual processing works in the human brain, with different layers tuned to increasingly abstract representations.

Before CNNs gained traction, image recognition was a cumbersome task that relied heavily on handcrafted features and domain-specific engineering (Wu et al, 2023). There was an almost artisanal quality to early computer vision work—researchers would spend years perfecting descriptors like SIFT or HOG, only to see them falter when confronted with new data or slightly altered contexts. CNNs changed that. They introduced a way for the system to learn its own features, directly from data, without needing a human to specify what "matters" in a given image. That shift—from feature engineering to feature learning—was more than a technical convenience. It was a philosophical break from the past. When AlexNet burst onto the scene in 2012, achieving a staggering leap in performance on the ImageNet classification task, it wasn't just the accuracy numbers that caught the community's attention (Kneusel, 2023). It was the feeling that something fundamental had changed. Suddenly, deep learning wasn't just promising—it was real. The architecture itself wasn't radically novel; it built on decades of prior research. But the combination of larger datasets, GPU acceleration, and clever regularization strategies like dropout created a model that didn't just work—it dominated. The years that followed saw a rapid expansion in CNN-based research. Variants like VGGNet, GoogLeNet (with its Inception modules), and ResNet introduced architectural innovations that deepened our understanding of how to build deeper, more efficient, and more generalizable networks (Zhang et al, 2024). ResNet's use of residual connections, for instance, tackled a long-standing challenge in deep learning: the degradation problem, where adding more layers to a network could actually make performance worse. By allowing gradients to bypass certain layers, residual networks enabled architectures that were hundreds of layers deep without collapsing under their own complexity.

But CNNs, for all their power, had limits. They were exquisitely suited for spatial data—images, videos, anything that benefited from local receptive fields and translation invariance. But when it came to sequences—like language, speech, or even structured time-series data—CNNs began to feel like the wrong tool for the job. Their windowed, spatially localized nature made it difficult to model long-range dependencies or understand context that unfolded across time. That's where the next revolution began to brew. In natural language processing (NLP), recurrent neural networks (RNNs) and their more sophisticated cousins, LSTMs and GRUs, had been the dominant players (Mienye et al, 2024). They offered a way to process input one element at a time, maintaining a hidden state that evolved with each new word or timestep. It was a clever mechanism, and for a while, it worked reasonably well. But RNNs suffered from their own set of problems—slow training times, difficulty with parallelization, and challenges in capturing very long dependencies. The world needed a new approach.

Figure 1. Basic Architecture of a Convolutional Neural Network

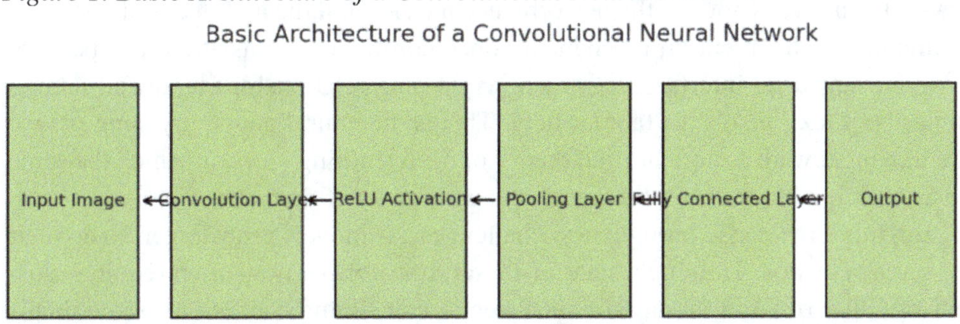

In 2017, a paper titled *"Attention Is All You Need"* quietly rewrote the rules (Vaswani et al, 2017). The transformer architecture it proposed was, in hindsight, a conceptual leap. It did away entirely with recurrence, replacing it with a mechanism called "self-attention" that allowed the model to weigh the importance of every other word in a sentence, regardless of position. This wasn't just more efficient—it was more elegant. Instead of relying on a sequential path through data, transformers treated input as a whole, enabling them to model relationships that spanned vast distances in text, and to do so with unprecedented parallelism. The genius of the transformer was not just in the self-attention mechanism itself, but in how it was integrated into a modular, scalable framework. Layer after layer, the model refined its understanding of input through attention, normalization, and feedforward transformations. The architecture was deep, yet stable. And critically, it could scale. With enough data and compute, transformer models began to show signs of something new—emergent capabilities, behaviors that weren't explicitly programmed but seemed to arise from the sheer scale of training.

Models like BERT, GPT, and T5 didn't just improve NLP—they transformed it (Rothman, 2021). Pretraining on massive corpora, then fine-tuning on specific tasks, became the new standard. Transfer learning—once a dream for natural language understanding—became practical, even routine. And as these models grew in size and scope, something extraordinary began to happen: they started to perform well across a range of tasks without specific tuning. Language modeling became a foundation—not an endpoint. The rise of transformers also spilled over into domains far beyond language. Vision transformers (ViTs) began to challenge the supremacy of CNNs in image classification, showing that attention-based models could learn visual hierarchies just as effectively, and sometimes more flexibly, than convolutional approaches (Khan et al, 2023). In audio, transformers proved adept at modeling spectrograms and waveforms. Even in reinforcement learning, where temporal dependencies and action sequences reign, transformer-like architectures are being explored for their ability to reason over long horizons. What makes the transformer era so distinctive is not just the performance metrics, but the architectural openness it embodies. The attention mechanism, once confined to translation, has become a kind of universal interface—a way of expressing relationships in any structured input, be it text, pixels, or tabular data. This architectural generality suggests we are moving toward a more unified theory of deep learning—one in which the same basic building blocks can be adapted to a wide array of domains.

But this era has also brought new challenges. As models grow larger, so do their resource demands. Training a state-of-the-art transformer now often requires clusters of GPUs running for days or even weeks, consuming energy on a scale that is difficult to ignore (Fang et al, 2021). Moreover, the sheer scale of these models can make them brittle, opaque, and prone to surprising errors. Interpretability becomes harder, not easier, as capabilities increase. There is also the issue of accessibility. The ability to train a transformer from scratch—or even fine-tune one—requires resources that are out of reach for many researchers, especially in the Global South. The architectural innovations of the last decade, while brilliant, have sometimes deepened the divide between those who can build AI systems and those who must simply adopt them. This moment, then, is a paradox. We have architectures that are more powerful than ever, yet they pose new ethical, environmental, and social questions. How do we ensure that these systems are fair, transparent, and accountable? How do we balance the hunger for scale with the need for sustainability? And how do we continue to innovate without losing sight of the people and communities affected by the technologies we create? As we look back at the journey from CNNs to transformers, we see more than a series of technical milestones. We see a map of evolving assumptions—about what intelligence is, how it can be modeled, and what it means to learn. CNNs taught us that structure matters—that hierarchies of representation can reveal the hidden patterns in visual data (Nguyen et al, 2020). Transformers taught us that relationships matter—that attention, rather than sequence, may hold the key to understanding complexity. Both architectures, in their own way, challenged us to rethink the very foundations of machine learning.

And yet, the story is far from over. Even now, researchers are exploring hybrids—combining convolutional insights with attention mechanisms, building architectures that learn to reason, not just recognize. There is a growing interest in models that can incorporate external knowledge, adapt to new tasks on the fly, and learn with fewer examples. The architectural frontier is alive, dynamic, and open-ended. Perhaps that is the most exciting thing of all. For every breakthrough we've celebrated, there are questions we still can't answer. For every architecture we've mastered, there are new forms waiting to be imagined. In the end, the evolution of deep learning architecture is not just about improving performance—it is about expanding our understanding of learning itself (Kayyali, 2026 e). And in that pursuit, we are not merely building better machines. We are exploring what it means to build systems that learn, adapt, and ultimately, reflect something of the intelligence we see in ourselves.

BREAKING LIMITS: PATTERN RECOGNITION IN COMPLEX AND NOISY DATA

In the real world, data is rarely clean, well-behaved, or politely organized. It's messy. It's fragmented, inconsistent, riddled with ambiguity and contradiction. In the neat, idealized scenarios of textbooks, we often assume that patterns emerge clearly from the data—smooth curves, distinct clusters, stable trajectories. But anyone who has worked with real-world systems—whether in medicine, climate science, finance, or social behavior—knows that the truth is far more chaotic. Noise is not the exception. It's the rule. And this is precisely where deep learning's true test begins.

It's one thing to recognize cats in well-lit, high-resolution images, or to generate elegant sentences from cleanly structured prompts. It's another thing entirely to make sense of a child's scribbled drawing, a corrupted medical scan, a garbled voice message in a crowded room, or an ambiguous sentiment in a tweet written in slang. The deeper challenge is not just recognizing patterns—it's doing so in conditions where the signal is faint, unstable, or buried beneath layers of uncertainty. And this, in many ways, is where deep learning has made its most remarkable—if sometimes overlooked—advances. To appreciate what has been achieved, we have to understand the nature of "noise." Noise, in the context of pattern recognition, is anything that obscures or distorts the underlying structure in data (Fieguth, 2022). It may be statistical variation, random error, background interference, or simply the presence of overlapping, contradictory signals. In images, it might be poor lighting, motion blur, or occlusion. In text, it could be sarcasm, idiomatic expression, or ambiguity of meaning. In time-series data, noise might come from sensor drift, missing values, or irregular sampling. Noise complicates the task of recognition because it makes the boundaries between classes fuzzier, the transitions less clear, and the relationships harder to model. Classical machine learning techniques often struggled with noisy data because they relied heavily on explicit feature extraction and statistical assumptions about the distribution of inputs (Maleki et al, 2020). If the data didn't conform to those assumptions—or if the noise overwhelmed the signal—the models would fail. What deep learning introduced was a fundamentally different way of seeing the problem: rather than hard-coding what to look for, deep models learned to identify robust features from the data itself, even when those features were subtle, fragmented, or nonlinear.

This capability did not emerge overnight. It was the result of years of architectural innovation, training strategies, and, perhaps most importantly, an evolving understanding of what it means to "learn" in noisy environments. Convolutional neural networks, for example, revolutionized image classification not just because they could detect edges and shapes, but because they could do so reliably across variations in lighting, rotation, scale, and background clutter. Their weight-sharing structure, combined with pooling operations, made them inherently more resilient to certain forms of visual noise. In language, models like LSTMs and transformers succeeded in part because they could maintain contextual memory, allowing them to disambiguate meaning based on surrounding words, even when individual phrases were misleading or vague (Nieminen, 2023). The attention mechanism, in particular, gave models the ability to "focus" on the most relevant parts of an input sequence—effectively filtering out irrelevant noise through learned weighting. And in audio and speech recognition, where signals are notoriously variable and noisy, deep models have surpassed traditional approaches by learning directly from raw waveforms or spectrograms, extracting frequency patterns that remain stable across distortions.

But perhaps one of the most striking examples of deep learning's ability to handle noise is in medical diagnostics. Medical data is the very definition of complex and noisy. Imaging scans may be corrupted, patient records may be incomplete, symptoms may be ambiguous or overlapping. And yet, deep models trained on large datasets have demonstrated performance that, in some cases, rivals or exceeds that of human specialists. These models don't just recognize clear-cut pathologies—they can identify early-stage anomalies, subtle irregularities, and even patterns that human clinicians may overlook. Of course, this is not without controversy. The fact that a model can find a signal in the noise does not necessarily mean it understands what it is doing. One of the dangers in pattern recognition—especially in high-stakes domains—is the risk of overfitting to spurious correlations (Lones, 2024). A model may learn to associate a specific feature with a diagnosis, not because it's medically meaningful, but because it happens to appear frequently in the training data. This is the dark side of deep pattern recognition: the ability to learn deeply from data also means the ability to learn from noise if that noise appears consistently enough.

The challenge, then, is not just building models that can tolerate noise—it's building models that know when they're seeing noise, and that can distinguish between signal and coincidence. This is where the field has started to push forward with methods for uncertainty estimation, adversarial robustness, and out-of-distribution detection. These approaches aim to give models a kind of meta-awareness—a way of expressing confidence, flagging anomalies, or even refusing to make a prediction when the input falls outside their zone of competence. Some of the most exciting work in this space involves self-supervised learning, where models are trained not with explicit labels but by solving surrogate tasks that force them to learn stable representations of the data. For example, a model might learn to predict the next frame in a video, the missing word in a sentence, or the orientation of an image. These tasks, while simple, encourage the model to learn what remains invariant across transformations and noise—a crucial step toward robust generalization.

Another breakthrough has come through the use of ensemble methods and Bayesian deep learning, which allow for the modeling of uncertainty and the detection of inconsistencies in predictions (Rane et al, 2024). These techniques are particularly important when working with sparse, ambiguous, or conflicting data—situations where a single deterministic output may be misleading. What's also emerging is a more nuanced understanding of what "noise" actually is. In some cases, what we label as noise may be a form of variation that is meaningful but simply misunderstood. Cultural differences in language use, atypical patterns in minority populations, or non-standard visual cues in underrepresented groups—all of these may be treated as noise by a model trained on majority-class data. But in truth, they are not noise—they are signals that the model has failed to understand due to a lack of exposure. This recognition has fueled a growing movement toward more inclusive and representative datasets, as well as more careful evaluation practices that consider fairness and equity.

In many ways, the effort to handle noise is part of a broader shift in deep learning—from pure performance to deeper robustness. It's not enough for a model to do well on a benchmark. It has to perform under stress, under ambiguity, and under the messiness of the real world. This shift is not just technical—it's ethical. If we are to entrust these systems with decisions that affect people's lives, we must ensure they can navigate uncertainty with the same care and humility we expect from human experts. At its best, deep learning doesn't just find patterns in clean data—it reveals structure in the unstructured, order in the apparent chaos (Tang et al, 2020). It pulls meaning from the noisy, the overlooked, and the ignored. This is the true frontier: not just recognizing what is obvious, but discerning what is subtle, hidden, or emerging. It's the ability to say, "Here is something that doesn't quite fit, but that may matter." And yet, we must remain vigilant. The same power that enables deep models to see through noise can also mislead us into seeing certainty where none exists. We must resist the temptation to treat model outputs as truth rather than as informed guesses. We must invest in interpretability tools, in human-in-the-loop systems, and in evaluation frameworks that reflect the complexities of the environments we hope to model. The work ahead is not just about building stronger models—it's about cultivating wiser ones. Models that know their limits. Models that understand the ambiguity of the data they're trained on. Models that, in a strange way, begin to reflect not just the clarity of intelligence, but its humility.

In the end, pattern recognition in complex and noisy data is not just a technical achievement. It is a philosophical stance. It is a declaration that we believe meaning can emerge even where things appear disordered. That with the right architecture, the right data, and the right care, we can build systems that don't just see what is obvious—but that begin to perceive what is subtle, elusive, and real. And perhaps, in doing so, we're not just teaching machines to see more clearly. We are also learning how to look again at the world ourselves.

CROSS-DOMAIN APPLICATIONS: FROM MEDICAL IMAGING TO CREATIVE AI

The true power of deep learning reveals itself not just in the elegance of its architectures or the precision of its mathematics, but in the diversity of its applications (Calin, 2020). As the field has matured, it has moved beyond narrow, domain-specific successes to achieve impact across a wide array of disciplines—many of which, at first glance, seem to have little in common. The same underlying principles that allow a neural network to diagnose a tumor in a radiological image are now helping generate symphonies, write poetry, restore ancient texts, and even assist in designing life-saving drugs. What we are witnessing is not just a technical expansion of deep learning's reach, but a cultural one. The algorithms are no longer confined to labs and industry—they are finding a place in the most human corners of our experience. Perhaps nowhere is the promise—and the complexity—of deep learning more apparent than in the field of medical imaging. Radiology, in particular, has seen a wave of innovation driven by convolutional neural networks and other deep learning models that can analyze CT scans, MRIs, X-rays, and histopathology slides with breathtaking accuracy (Oladele, 2024). These systems are often trained on hundreds of thousands of annotated images, learning to detect patterns and anomalies that even experienced specialists might miss. The goal is not to replace clinicians, but to augment them—to provide a second set of eyes, one that never gets tired, never misses a detail, and can be deployed anywhere in the world.

But the road to clinical adoption is not simple. Medical data is among the most sensitive, most regulated, and most context-dependent forms of data we encounter. An image that suggests cancer in one demographic may not mean the same thing in another. A system trained on data from a single hospital may perform poorly when deployed in a different region, with different equipment, lighting conditions, or patient populations. This variability forces us to grapple with questions of generalizability, bias, and trust. How do we know a model will perform well not just in the lab, but in the wild complexity of real-world healthcare? Interpretability becomes essential (Singh et al, 2020). It is one thing for an AI system to flag an abnormality—it is another thing entirely to explain why. Clinicians need to understand the rationale behind a model's decision if they are to trust and act upon it. Efforts to visualize activations, generate heatmaps, or provide textual justifications are part of a broader movement toward transparency. These interpretability tools are not just nice add-ons; they are central to building systems that align with the values of medicine, where every decision carries weight, consequence, and responsibility. Beyond radiology, deep learning has been making quiet inroads into pathology, dermatology, ophthalmology, and even genomics. In many of these domains, the problem is not a lack of data, but an overabundance of it. Medical professionals are drowning in information—terabytes of imaging, patient histories, lab results—and deep learning offers a way to synthesize that information into actionable insights. There is enormous potential here, but it must be guided by care, caution, and a deep respect for the human lives behind every data point. And then, on the other end of the spectrum, we find a different kind of application: the creative one.

It is perhaps one of the most surprising turns in the story of deep learning—that a technology designed for classification, prediction, and optimization would find such fertile ground in the arts. But this is precisely what has happened. From visual art to music, from literature to film, deep learning is now a collaborator in the creative process. Generative models, especially those based on GANs, VAEs, and more recently diffusion models, have opened up a new space where machines do not just analyze existing works—they generate new ones (Bengesi et al, 2024). In visual art, for instance, AI-generated imagery has moved far beyond simple style transfer. Artists and researchers are now using models like DALL·E, Midjourney, and Stable Diffusion to create original compositions from textual prompts, blending the conceptual with the visual in unprecedented ways (Janson & Lempert, 2024). These models do not merely replicate what they have seen—they synthesize, combine, and sometimes surprise. The results are often strange, beautiful, or unsettling—but they are undeniably creative. And they raise important questions: Who is the author of an AI-generated image? What is the role of intention, of human curation, of iterative refinement? Is the machine a tool, a co-creator, or something else entirely?

In music, similar shifts are underway. Neural networks trained on massive corpora of compositions can now generate melodies, harmonies, and rhythms in the style of classical composers or contemporary artists (Hernandez-Olivan & Beltran, 2022). Some of these systems are used to inspire musicians—offering motifs or textures they might not have imagined. Others aim to generate entire pieces autonomously. There is something deeply intriguing about this: the idea that a machine can learn the structure and emotional cadence of music, and then produce something that moves a listener (Kayyali, 2025 a). But it also forces us to ask what creativity really is. Is it the act of producing something novel, something pleasing, something evocative? Or is it tied to consciousness, to suffering, to experience? Literature, too, has become a canvas for neural creativity. Language models can now write short stories, compose poems, craft dialogue, even mimic the style of specific authors. Some of this is amusing, some of it uncanny. In a few cases, it's astonishing. These outputs are not always coherent or meaningful—but when they are, they invite us to reconsider our assumptions about language and expression. Writing, long considered a uniquely human art, is now being shared—tentatively—with machines. The collaboration is still in its infancy, but it is already reshaping the boundaries of authorship, inspiration, and originality.

Of course, there is no shortage of controversy. Critics argue that AI-generated art lacks soul—that it is derivative, mechanical, or emotionally hollow (Sieg, 2023). And perhaps, in some ways, they are right. A neural network does not suffer heartbreak. It does not fall in love. It does not look at a sunset and feel the passing of time. But then again, much of what we call creativity has always involved recombination, influence, and iteration. Artists borrow from one another, build upon traditions, respond to cultural moments. If a machine can do the same—albeit in a different way—should we dismiss it outright? What's more, these creative applications are not just novelties (Bown, 2021). They are beginning to reshape industries. In advertising, AI tools are used to generate headlines, slogans, and brand visuals. In film, they assist with script development, scene planning, even visual effects. In game design, they help craft environments, characters, and story arcs (Kayyali, 2026 c). The creative process is being augmented—not replaced, but transformed—by systems that offer new kinds of generative possibility (Kayyali, 2025 c). This blending of technical and artistic domains is one of the most exciting—and most philosophically rich—developments in the evolution of deep learning. It challenges the idea that intelligence is purely rational, purely functional. It suggests that the capacity to create may emerge not from emotion or consciousness alone, but from the ability to model complexity, understand structure, and play within constraints.

And perhaps this is the deeper lesson of cross-domain applications: that intelligence, in both machines and humans, is not confined to one form, one task, one definition. It is adaptive. It is expressive. It takes on different shapes depending on the context, the goals, and the medium. The same neural architectures that recognize tumors and detect fraud can also write sonnets and compose jazz. This versatility does not diminish their power—it amplifies it. Yet with this power comes responsibility. As deep learning moves across domains, it encounters different values, norms, and expectations. In medicine, the stakes are high, and the standards of evidence are rigorous. In art, the questions are more subjective, but no less significant. We must learn to navigate these spaces with sensitivity and nuance—understanding that what works in one context may not translate cleanly to another. We must also resist the urge to universalize too quickly. A model trained on Western art history may struggle to understand the aesthetics of other cultures. A language model trained predominantly on English may misrepresent or overlook non-English voices (Nicholas & Bhatia, 2023). As we expand the reach of deep learning, we must expand its foundations—making space for diversity, plurality, and difference. The journey from medical imaging to creative AI is not just a tour of technical achievements. It is a reflection of the field's growing maturity—and its willingness to explore the full spectrum of human experience. It reminds us that pattern recognition is not an end in itself, but a means of engaging with the world, in all its richness, ambiguity, and beauty. In the years to come, we will likely see even more cross-pollination—models that blend scientific rigor with artistic flair, systems that diagnose and design, that analyze and imagine. And in that blending, we may find not only better machines, but a deeper understanding of ourselves.

ETHICAL BOUNDARIES AND INTERPRETABILITY CHALLENGES

In the enthusiasm that often surrounds technological breakthroughs, there's a risk that the harder, more uncomfortable questions get pushed aside—or worse, buried under layers of technical jargon (Agar et al, 2024). Yet, in the world of deep learning, the questions that matter most aren't just about accuracy, efficiency, or scalability. They're about trust. About responsibility. About consequences. As our models grow in capability and complexity, so too do the ethical responsibilities that accompany their deployment (Kayyali, 2025 b). And at the heart of these responsibilities lies an urgent challenge: understanding how these systems make decisions—and deciding when those decisions are acceptable, fair, or even justifiable. Deep learning, for all its brilliance, has always been a field of paradoxes. It gives us models that can recognize patterns in noise, learn representations from unstructured data, and generate outputs that rival human creation. And yet, it also gives us models that are famously difficult to interpret. That opacity—often referred to as the "black box" problem—sits at the very core of the ethical tension in AI. If we cannot fully understand how a system arrives at a decision, how can we trust it? And if we can't trust it, how can we responsibly use it in domains where the stakes are human lives, liberties, and dignity?

Interpretability, in this context, isn't just a technical feature—it's an ethical necessity. A loan denied by an opaque algorithm. A job application screened out by a classifier trained on biased historical data. A legal sentence shaped, however subtly, by a risk assessment tool. These are not science fiction scenarios—they are real, happening now, and they illustrate the profound influence that algorithmic systems can exert over people's futures. The challenge is not just that these systems make mistakes—it's that when they do, it is often impossible to trace those mistakes to a clear cause, to a transparent logic, or to a responsible party. This lack of clarity is not an accident. Deep learning systems, by their very nature, learn complex mappings from input to output through the adjustment of millions—or even billions—of parameters. Their representations are distributed, their pathways nonlinear, and their internal reasoning processes utterly foreign to human intuition. Unlike rule-based systems, which can be audited line by line, or statistical models, which offer interpretable coefficients, deep neural networks often resist straightforward explanation. They are designed to optimize performance, not clarity.

And yet, the demand for clarity is growing louder. In medicine, physicians are understandably reluctant to base treatment decisions on models they cannot question. In law, judges are wary of relying on tools that cannot be cross-examined. In hiring, education, and policing, the use of opaque algorithms raises serious concerns about discrimination, fairness, and the erosion of human judgment. We are entering a period where performance alone is no longer enough. The credibility of a model depends not just on what it gets right, but on whether we can understand how—and why—it got there (Yilmaz & Liu, 2022). One response to this challenge has been the development of tools and techniques for model explainability. Methods such as LIME (Local Interpretable Model-agnostic Explanations), SHAP (SHapley Additive exPlanations), attention visualizations, and saliency maps have emerged to give users a window—however partial—into the workings of deep models (Raptis et al, 2024). These tools aim to highlight which inputs had the greatest influence on a particular prediction, or to provide local approximations that mimic the behavior of a complex model in a simplified way.

But here, too, we face a philosophical tension. Interpretability is not a binary concept; it's a continuum. What counts as "understandable" varies by context, by audience, and by the kind of explanation being sought. A data scientist may be satisfied with a visualization of feature importance, while a patient may need a plain-language explanation of why a treatment was recommended. A judge may require a formal justification, while an engineer may be looking for debugging insight. The same model, explained in different ways, can be both transparent and opaque, depending on the eye of the beholder. There is a risk that in our rush to make models interpretable, we settle for the illusion of understanding. Many explanation methods are post hoc—they provide insights after the model has made a decision, rather than exposing the actual reasoning process. In some cases, these explanations can be misleading, unstable, or inconsistent. We may think we understand a model's logic, only to find that our interpretation doesn't generalize to new data, or that it glosses over subtle forms of bias.

Bias, in fact, is the elephant in the room. Every machine learning model reflects the data on which it was trained. If that data encodes historical inequities, societal prejudices, or structural imbalances, the model will likely perpetuate them (Shah & Sureja, 2025). A facial recognition system trained primarily on light-skinned faces may misidentify people with darker skin. A hiring algorithm trained on past decisions may favor male candidates over female ones. These biases are not the result of malice—they are the result of indifference, of failing to question where the data comes from and what assumptions it encodes. Ethical AI, then, begins long before the model is trained. It begins with the framing of the problem: Who gets to define what success looks like? Whose interests are being served? Who is represented in the training data, and who is left out? These are not purely technical questions—they are social, political, and cultural. They demand a kind of reflection that goes beyond code and metrics. They require humility. Humility, in fact, may be the most important quality we can bring to the development of AI systems. It means acknowledging what our models can and cannot do. It means being honest about uncertainty, about limitations, about edge cases and failure modes. It means recognizing that fairness is not something that can be "optimized" with a few constraints or loss functions—it is a contested, evolving, deeply human ideal. And it means inviting more voices into the conversation—ethicists, historians, community members, people affected by the systems we build.

It is tempting, especially in moments of technological triumph, to treat ethics as a constraint—something to be balanced against innovation, managed with checklists, or outsourced to compliance teams (Seele, 2023). But ethics is not a constraint. It is a compass. It is what tells us not just what we can build, but what we should build. It is what reminds us that technology is never neutral—that every design reflects a set of values, and every deployment has consequences. As deep learning continues to advance, we must resist the seduction of complexity for its own sake. We must remember that interpretability is not just about making models understandable—it is about making them accountable. It is about ensuring that when harm occurs, we can trace its source, understand its logic, and make it right. That when a system fails, we don't shrug and say, "the model did it"—we take responsibility.

This will not be easy. There will always be trade-offs between accuracy and explainability, between flexibility and control. There will be moments when the best-performing model is also the least transparent. But if we are serious about building AI that serves humanity, we must be willing to make hard choices—to prioritize clarity over cleverness, equity over efficiency, integrity over immediacy. The challenge of ethical boundaries and interpretability is not one that will ever be "solved" in the way technical problems are solved. It is a practice, a commitment, a continual process of questioning and revision. It requires vigilance, self-scrutiny, and a willingness to be uncomfortable. But it is also, in its own way, a hopeful endeavor. It is a reminder that we are not just engineers or scientists—we are stewards of powerful tools. And it is up to us to ensure that those tools reflect the best of what we are capable of—not just in intelligence, but in compassion, in fairness, and in care.

We are entering an era in which deep learning will shape decisions that affect millions, perhaps billions, of lives. The systems we build now will leave a legacy—not just in data centers, but in human lives, in the opportunities we grant or deny, in the dignity we affirm or erode. That legacy is not inevitable. It will be shaped by the choices we make today—about how we define performance, how we ensure transparency, and how we confront the uncomfortable questions that arise when we teach machines to think. If deep learning has taught us anything, it is that intelligence is not static. It learns. It adapts. It grows. Let us ensure that our ethics do the same.

FUTURE DIRECTIONS: TOWARD GENERALIZED INTELLIGENCE IN PATTERN RECOGNITION

If deep learning has taught us anything over the past decade, it is that the frontier of artificial intelligence is not a fixed line—it is a moving horizon, always shifting as we learn more about what machines can do, and just as importantly, about what they cannot (Cai et al, 2021). Pattern recognition, once considered a narrow technical problem, has evolved into a defining challenge of our era: How do we build systems that can not only detect patterns in isolated domains, but generalize across domains, adapt to new environments, and do so in a way that is robust, trustworthy, and aligned with human needs? The current state of deep learning is undeniably impressive. We've seen models master tasks that once seemed beyond the reach of machines: diagnosing diseases from raw imaging data, composing symphonies in the style of classical composers, translating poetry across languages, generating photorealistic images from nothing more than a sentence. These achievements have been made possible by architectures like convolutional neural networks, transformers, diffusion models, and by advances in optimization, regularization, and scale. But if we look closely, we can see that even the most powerful models today operate within certain boundaries—boundaries defined by the data they were trained on, the tasks they were designed to solve, and the assumptions baked into their architectures.

What we are now beginning to explore is how to move beyond those boundaries—how to push toward something more flexible, more general, and ultimately more intelligent. Generalized intelligence, in the context of pattern recognition, is not a singular breakthrough waiting to happen (Keil & Olendzenski, 2023). It is a trajectory. It means building models that can handle variability not just within a task, but across tasks. It means designing systems that can learn from fewer examples, transfer knowledge from one domain to another, adapt on the fly, and reason about unfamiliar situations. In short, it means closing the gap between narrow pattern matching and the broader, more abstract capabilities we associate with human cognition.

One of the most promising developments in this direction has been the rise of foundation models—large, pre-trained systems like GPT, CLIP, and DINO that are trained on vast amounts of data and then fine-tuned for a wide range of downstream tasks (Zhang et al, 2025). These models exhibit an uncanny ability to generalize, at least within the domains they've been exposed to. A language model trained on books, websites, and code can answer factual questions, write essays, translate languages, summarize documents, and even generate executable code—all without being explicitly trained on each of those tasks. This kind of generalization is not trivial. It suggests that with enough data and a well-designed architecture, models can learn representations that are abstract, composable, and broadly applicable. But it also raises difficult questions. How far can this approach go? Are we simply scaling our way toward intelligence, or are we reaching the limits of what data-driven pattern recognition can achieve? True general intelligence requires more than just recognizing familiar patterns—it demands understanding (Kayyali, 2026 a). It requires the ability to reason about cause and effect, to form hypotheses, to plan, to learn actively and autonomously. These are areas where current systems still struggle. A model might be able to write a plausible-sounding explanation or generate a convincing summary, but it does not *know* in any meaningful sense what it is saying. It lacks grounding in the physical world, a sense of time, an awareness of context that extends beyond the narrow scope of its training.

One direction that researchers are exploring **is** multimodal learning—the integration of different types of data (text, images, audio, video, sensory input) into a single model (Sharma & Giannakos, 2020). This mirrors the way humans learn: not from a single stream of information, but from the convergence of multiple signals. Multimodal models have already shown promising results in tasks like visual question answering, image captioning, and embodied AI. The hope is that by combining modalities, we can build richer representations of the world—representations that are more grounded, more flexible, and ultimately more intelligent. Another frontier is meta-learning, or "learning to learn." Rather than training a model to solve a specific task, the idea is to train it to acquire new tasks quickly, with minimal data (Hospedales et al, 2021). This aligns with the human ability to learn a new game, language, or skill with just a few examples or demonstrations. Meta-learning remains a challenging problem, but early progress suggests that it may hold the key to unlocking more adaptive and general-purpose systems (Barman et al, 2024). Self-supervised learning also plays a critical role in this evolving picture. By designing pretext tasks that encourage models to learn structure from raw data—such as predicting missing words, future frames, or masked patches—we can develop systems that don't rely on expensive labeled datasets. Self-supervision allows models to uncover deep patterns in the data itself, patterns that can then be repurposed for a wide range of applications. It is an approach that shifts the emphasis from human curation to machine-driven exploration.

But perhaps the most exciting—and most difficult—aspect of this future is not technical at all. It is the question of alignment: how to ensure that as models become more general, more autonomous, and more powerful, they continue to reflect and respect human values. Alignment is not a problem that can be solved with better loss functions or more layers. It requires engagement with philosophy, ethics, social science, and human experience. It requires us to ask what we want these systems to be for—what kind of intelligence we are trying to build, and why. This is especially important as pattern recognition systems begin to participate in decision-making processes: allocating resources, recommending treatments, detecting threats, moderating content. In such contexts, mistakes are not just technical errors—they are social events, with consequences that ripple through institutions and communities. Generalized intelligence must come with generalized responsibility (Díaz-Rodríguez et al, 2023). We cannot afford to separate performance from accountability. There is also the matter of interpretability, which becomes even more crucial as systems become more general. A model that can do many things must also be able to explain *how* it does them. We must move beyond post hoc explanations and build systems that are inherently understandable—not only to developers and researchers, but to users, regulators, and the public. This will require new paradigms of transparency, new languages of explanation, and perhaps even new interfaces between humans and machines.

Looking forward, it's likely that the next breakthroughs in pattern recognition won't come from a single architecture or technique, but from integration. Systems that blend the perceptual power of deep networks with the logical reasoning of symbolic AI (Besold et al, 2021). Systems that combine data-driven learning with structured knowledge, common sense, and world models. Systems that can simulate, imagine, reflect. We may see the rise of neurosymbolic architectures, where neural networks handle perception and low-level learning, while symbolic components manage abstraction and rules (Acharya et al, 2023). Or we may witness entirely new paradigms—approaches that are not yet on the radar of today's research community, but that emerge from the convergence of fields, from serendipity, or from necessity. One thing is clear: the journey toward generalized intelligence will not be a straight line. It will be filled with detours, dead ends, ethical dilemmas, and conceptual challenges (Kayyali, 2026 b). It will require us to rethink not only how we build models, but how we define success. Accuracy on a benchmark will no longer be enough. We will need to consider adaptability, robustness, fairness, interpretability, and alignment—often all at once.

It will also require a shift in mindset. From building systems that optimize narrowly defined tasks to cultivating systems that participate in broader ecosystems. From seeing intelligence as performance to seeing it as interaction. From viewing pattern recognition as prediction to understanding it as participation in a shared world. This, ultimately, is the horizon we are moving toward: a future where artificial systems can recognize patterns not just in data, but in meaning. Where they can move between domains, collaborate with humans, navigate uncertainty, and contribute to knowledge, creativity, and well-being. A future where intelligence is not just measured in outputs, but expressed in relationships—in how we build, how we interpret, and how we choose to use the tools we've created. We are not there yet. But we are closer than we've ever been. And if we continue to move forward with care, with reflection, and with humility, we may yet build systems that don't just recognize patterns in the world—but help us recognize something deeper in ourselves.

CONCLUSION

The journey of deep learning, especially in the context of pattern recognition, is emblematic of the larger narrative of artificial intelligence: a relentless pursuit to mimic—and eventually surpass—human cognition. In recent years, we have witnessed AI systems perform with superhuman accuracy in recognizing faces, diagnosing diseases from medical scans, interpreting natural language, and even generating novel content. These achievements, while awe-inspiring, have also raised fundamental questions about the nature of intelligence, the role of data, and the limits of machine perception. What we must acknowledge is that pattern recognition is no longer a mere technical goal—it has evolved into a philosophical and societal challenge. When an AI system detects a tumor in a radiograph faster than a radiologist, or flags financial fraud before a human analyst, it is not simply recognizing shapes or sequences; it is participating in decision-making processes with real-world implications. The boundary between recognition and responsibility becomes increasingly blurred. As such, our focus must expand beyond model accuracy to include fairness, interpretability, accountability, and transparency. The rapid evolution of deep learning has laid bare a key tension: the more complex and capable our models become, the less interpretable they often are. The rise of black-box architectures—where even developers struggle to understand how a model arrives at its conclusions—presents a paradox. We seek intelligent systems we can trust, yet we often build models whose inner workings remain opaque. This contradiction must be addressed, not only through technical innovations in explainability but also through interdisciplinary dialogue that includes ethicists, social scientists, and affected communities.

Another pressing issue is the sustainability of deep learning. The enormous computational resources required to train state-of-the-art models raise concerns about energy consumption, environmental impact, and accessibility. As research becomes more compute-intensive, it risks becoming the domain of only a few powerful entities with the financial means to sustain it. Democratizing access to AI technologies and ensuring they are developed in ways that are ecologically and socially responsible will be key to the future of the field. Despite these challenges, the future of deep learning remains filled with promise. We are beginning to see the emergence of more efficient, interpretable, and ethical models—systems designed not just to perform, but to align with human values and intentions. Techniques such as transfer learning, self-supervised learning, and neurosymbolic integration suggest a coming era where models can learn more like humans: flexibly, contextually, and with less data. These shifts point toward a future where pattern recognition is not only about detection but about comprehension, insight, and purposeful interaction.

Ultimately, this chapter invites us to reconsider what it means to "recognize" in a world where machines play an increasingly central role in shaping our perceptions and decisions. The advancements in deep learning are not endpoints—they are milestones in an ongoing journey. And as researchers, developers, and citizens, we bear a collective responsibility to ensure that this journey leads not just to smarter machines, but to a wiser and more inclusive society. The boundaries of AI are only beginning to be explored, and how we choose to push them will define not only the future of technology but the future of humanity itself.

REFERENCES

Acharya, K., Raza, W., Dourado, C., Velasquez, A., & Song, H. H. (2023). Neurosymbolic reinforcement learning and planning: A survey. *IEEE Transactions on Artificial Intelligence*, *5*(5), 1939–1953. DOI: 10.1109/TAI.2023.3311428

Agar, N., Whatley, S., & Weijers, D. (2024). How to Think about Progress.

AlAli, A., & Anifowose, F. (2022). Seismic velocity modeling in the digital transformation era: A review of the role of machine learning. *Journal of Petroleum Exploration and Production Technology*, *12*(1), 1–14. DOI: 10.1007/s13202-021-01304-0

Barman, A., Roy, S. K., Das, S., & Dutta, P. (2024). Exploring the Horizons of Meta-Learning in Neural Networks: A Survey of the State-of-the-Art. *IEEE Transactions on Emerging Topics in Computational Intelligence*.

Bengesi, S., El-Sayed, H., Sarker, M. K., Houkpati, Y., Irungu, J., & Oladunni, T. (2024). Advancements in Generative AI: A Comprehensive Review of GANs, GPT, Autoencoders, Diffusion Model, and Transformers. *IEEE Access : Practical Innovations, Open Solutions*, *12*, 69812–69837. DOI: 10.1109/ACCESS.2024.3397775

Besold, T. R., Bader, S., Bowman, H., Domingos, P., Hitzler, P., Kühnberger, K. U., . . . Zaverucha, G. (2021). Neural-symbolic learning and reasoning: A survey and interpretation 1. In Neuro-Symbolic Artificial Intelligence: The State of the Art (pp. 1-51). IOS press.

Bown, O. (2021). *Beyond the creative species: Making machines that make art and music*. Mit Press. DOI: 10.7551/mitpress/10913.001.0001

Cai, Z., Liu, L., Chen, B., & Wang, Y. (2021). Artificial intelligence: From beginning to date.

Calin, O. (2020). *Deep learning architectures*. Springer International Publishing. DOI: 10.1007/978-3-030-36721-3

Cong, S., & Zhou, Y. (2023). A review of convolutional neural network architectures and their optimizations. *Artificial Intelligence Review*, *56*(3), 1905–1969. DOI: 10.1007/s10462-022-10213-5

Díaz-Rodríguez, N., Del Ser, J., Coeckelbergh, M., de Prado, M. L., Herrera-Viedma, E., & Herrera, F. (2023). Connecting the dots in trustworthy Artificial Intelligence: From AI principles, ethics, and key requirements to responsible AI systems and regulation. *Information Fusion*, *99*, 101896. DOI: 10.1016/j.inffus.2023.101896

Fang, J., Yu, Y., Zhao, C., & Zhou, J. (2021, February). Turbotransformers: an efficient gpu serving system for transformer models. In *Proceedings of the 26th ACM SIGPLAN Symposium on Principles and Practice of Parallel Programming* (pp. 389-402). DOI: 10.1145/3437801.3441578

Fazi, M. B. (2021). Beyond human: Deep learning, explainability and representation. *Theory, Culture & Society*, *38*(7-8), 55–77. DOI: 10.1177/0263276420966386

Fieguth, P. (2022). *An introduction to pattern recognition and machine learning*. Springer. DOI: 10.1007/978-3-030-95995-1

Geirhos, R., Jacobsen, J. H., Michaelis, C., Zemel, R., Brendel, W., Bethge, M., & Wichmann, F. A. (2020). Shortcut learning in deep neural networks. *Nature Machine Intelligence*, *2*(11), 665–673. DOI: 10.1038/s42256-020-00257-z

George, A. S. (2024). Democratizing Compute Power: The Rise of Computation as a Commodity and its Impacts. *Partners Universal Innovative Research Publication*, *2*(3), 57–74.

Haugeland, J., Craver, C. F., & Klein, C. (Eds.). (2023). *Mind Design III: Philosophy, Psychology, and Artificial Intelligence*. MIT press.

Hernandez-Olivan, C., & Beltran, J. R. (2022). Music composition with deep learning: A review. Advances in speech and music technology: computational aspects and applications, 25-50.

Hospedales, T., Antoniou, A., Micaelli, P., & Storkey, A. (2021). Meta-learning in neural networks: A survey. *IEEE Transactions on Pattern Analysis and Machine Intelligence*, *44*(9), 5149–5169. PMID: 33974543

Janson, L., & Lempert, M. (2024). ARTISTS AND MACHINE INTELLIGENCE.

Kayyali, M. (2025 a). Envisioning the Future: The Evolution and Impact of AI and Machine Learning in Finance. In Utilizing AI and Machine Learning in Financial Analysis (pp. 193-212). IGI Global Scientific Publishing.

Kayyali, M. (2025 b). Ethical Implications of Generative AI in Education: Privacy, Bias, and Integrity. In Transformative AI Practices for Personalized Learning Strategies (pp. 185-218). IGI Global Scientific Publishing.

Kayyali, M. (2025 c). Generative AI and Education: Transforming Teaching and Learning Through Collaborative Intelligence. In Humans and Generative AI Tools for Collaborative Intelligence (pp. 25-52). IGI Global Scientific Publishing.

Kayyali, M. (2026 a). Case Studies in Competitive Intelligence: Real-World Applications in Global Industries. In Competitive Intelligence in the Digital Age: Strategies for Business and Technology Leadership (pp. 37-64). IGI Global Scientific Publishing.

Kayyali, M. (2026 b). Ethical AI and Automation in the Workplace. In Leading Inclusive Workplaces Through Digital Transformation and Organizational Change (pp. 103-138). IGI Global Scientific Publishing.

Kayyali, M. (2026 c). Machine Learning and Bias: Creating Inclusive AI Systems for All. In AI and New Forms of Exclusion (pp. 143-166). IGI Global Scientific Publishing.

Kayyali, M. (2026 d). The Digital Transformation of Education: Opportunities and Challenges for Communication. Effects of Education Communication in Digital Learning Environments, 433-472.

Kayyali, M. (2026 e). The Evolution of Artificial Intelligence in Education: From Theory to Practice. In Responsible AI Integration in Education (pp. 119-150). IGI Global Scientific Publishing.

Keil, D., & Olendzenski, M. (2023). Exaggerated claims of artificial general intelligence.

Khan, A., Rauf, Z., Sohail, A., Khan, A. R., Asif, H., Asif, A., & Farooq, U. (2023). A survey of the vision transformers and their CNN-transformer based variants. *Artificial Intelligence Review*, *56*(S3, Suppl 3), 2917–2970. DOI: 10.1007/s10462-023-10595-0

Khan, A., Sohail, A., Zahoora, U., & Qureshi, A. S. (2020). A survey of the recent architectures of deep convolutional neural networks. *Artificial Intelligence Review*, *53*(8), 5455–5516. DOI: 10.1007/s10462-020-09825-6

Kneusel, R. T. (2023). *How AI works: from sorcery to science*. No Starch Press.

Lones, M. A. (2024). Avoiding common machine learning pitfalls. *Patterns (New York, N.Y.)*, *5*(10), 101046. DOI: 10.1016/j.patter.2024.101046 PMID: 39569205

Maleki, F., Ovens, K., Najafian, K., Forghani, B., Reinhold, C., & Forghani, R. (2020). Overview of machine learning part 1: Fundamentals and classic approaches. *Neuroimaging Clinics of North America*, *30*(4), e17–e32. DOI: 10.1016/j.nic.2020.08.007 PMID: 33039003

Masters, K. (2023). Ethical use of artificial intelligence in health professions education: AMEE Guide No. 158. *Medical Teacher*, *45*(6), 574–584. DOI: 10.1080/0142159X.2023.2186203 PMID: 36912253

Mienye, I. D., Swart, T. G., & Obaido, G. (2024). Recurrent neural networks: A comprehensive review of architectures, variants, and applications. *Information (Basel), 15*(9), 517. DOI: 10.3390/info15090517

Nguyen, T., Raghu, M., & Kornblith, S. (2020). Do wide and deep networks learn the same things? uncovering how neural network representations vary with width and depth. arXiv preprint arXiv:2010.15327.

Nicholas, G., & Bhatia, A. (2023). Lost in translation: large language models in non-English content analysis. arXiv preprint arXiv:2306.07377.

Nieminen, M. (2023). The Transformer Model and Its Impact on the Field of Natural Language Processing.

Oladele, O. K. (2024). Machine Learning Algorithms for Analyzing Medical Imaging and Improving Diagnostic Accuracy.

Pietikäinen, M. (2024). From the middle of nowhere to a world-class scientist in computer vision and artificial intelligence.

Pulicharla, M. R. (2025). Neurosymbolic AI: Bridging neural networks and symbolic reasoning.

Rane, N., Choudhary, S. P., & Rane, J. (2024). Ensemble deep learning and machine learning: Applications, opportunities, challenges, and future directions. *Studies in Medical and Health Sciences, 1*(2), 18–41. DOI: 10.48185/smhs.v1i2.1225

Raptis, S., Ilioudis, C., & Theodorou, K. (2024). From pixels to prognosis: Unveiling radiomics models with SHAP and LIME for enhanced interpretability. *Biomedical Physics & Engineering Express, 10*(3), 035016. DOI: 10.1088/2057-1976/ad34db PMID: 38498925

Rothman, D. (2021). *Transformers for Natural Language Processing: Build innovative deep neural network architectures for NLP with Python, PyTorch, TensorFlow, BERT, RoBERTa, and more*. Packt Publishing Ltd.

Seele, P. (2023). Technology Ethics: Origins, Paradigms and Implications for Business and Society. In *Encyclopedia of Business and Professional Ethics* (pp. 1751–1755). Springer International Publishing. DOI: 10.1007/978-3-030-22767-8_1268

Shah, M., & Sureja, N. (2025). A comprehensive review of bias in deep learning models: Methods, impacts, and future directions. *Archives of Computational Methods in Engineering, 32*(1), 255–267. DOI: 10.1007/s11831-024-10134-2

Sharma, K., & Giannakos, M. (2020). Multimodal data capabilities for learning: What can multimodal data tell us about learning? *British Journal of Educational Technology, 51*(5), 1450–1484. DOI: 10.1111/bjet.12993

Sieg, S. (2023). AI Art and Its Limitations: Narrow Intelligence and Visual Indulgence (Master's thesis).

Singh, R. P., Hom, G. L., Abramoff, M. D., Campbell, J. P., & Chiang, M. F. (2020). Current challenges and barriers to real-world artificial intelligence adoption for the healthcare system, provider, and the patient. *Translational Vision Science & Technology, 9*(2), 45–45. DOI: 10.1167/tvst.9.2.45 PMID: 32879755

Smys, S., Chen, J. I. Z., & Shakya, S. (2020). Survey on neural network architectures with deep learning. [JSCP]. *Journal of Soft Computing Paradigm, 2*(03), 186–194. DOI: 10.36548/jscp.2020.3.006

Tang, Y., Kurths, J., Lin, W., Ott, E., & Kocarev, L. (2020). Introduction to focus issue: When machine learning meets complex systems: Networks, chaos, and nonlinear dynamics. *Chaos (Woodbury, N.Y.), 30*(6), 063151. DOI: 10.1063/5.0016505 PMID: 32611112

Vaswani, A., Shazeer, N., Parmar, N., Uszkoreit, J., Jones, L., Gomez, A. N., & Polosukhin, I. (2017). Attention is all you need. *Advances in Neural Information Processing Systems*, , 30.

Wang, Y., Wang, Y., Zhang, T., Yu, Y., Cheung, S. C., Yu, H., & Zhu, Z. (2023, November). Can machine learning pipelines be better configured? In *Proceedings of the 31st ACM Joint European Software Engineering Conference and Symposium on the Foundations of Software Engineering* (pp. 463-475). DOI: 10.1145/3611643.3616352

Wu, M., Zhou, J., Peng, Y., Wang, S., & Zhang, Y. (2023, December). Deep learning for image classification: a review. In International Conference on Medical Imaging and Computer-Aided Diagnosis (pp. 352-362). Singapore: Springer Nature Singapore.

Yilmaz, L., & Liu, B. (2022). Model credibility revisited: Concepts and considerations for appropriate trust. *Journal of Simulation, 16*(3), 312–325. DOI: 10.1080/17477778.2020.1821587

Yonck, R. (2020). *Heart of the machine: Our future in a world of artificial emotional intelligence*. Arcade.

Zhang, D., Feng, T., Xue, L., Wang, Y., Dong, Y., & Tang, J. (2025). Parameter-Efficient Fine-Tuning for Foundation Models. arXiv preprint arXiv:2501.13787.

Zhang, X., Han, N., & Zhang, J. (2024). Comparative analysis of VGG, ResNet, and GoogLeNet architectures evaluating performance, computational efficiency, and convergence rates. *Applied and Computational Engineering*, *44*(1), 172–181. DOI: 10.54254/2755-2721/44/20230676

KEY TERMS AND DEFINITIONS

Backpropagation: An algorithm used in neural networks to minimize error by adjusting weights through a process of reverse error propagation.

Convolutional Neural Networks (CNNs): A type of neural network specialized in processing grid-like data, such as images, by applying convolutional filters.

Deep Learning: A subset of machine learning that uses neural networks with multiple layers to model complex patterns and representations in data.

Neural Networks: Computational models inspired by the human brain that process information in layers of interconnected nodes to recognize patterns.

Pattern Recognition: The automated identification of regularities and structures in data, enabling machines to categorize or interpret inputs.

Supervised Learning: A machine learning technique where models are trained on labeled datasets to learn the relationship between inputs and outputs.

Transfer Learning: A method where a model developed for one task is reused as the starting point for a different but related task.

Chapter 3 Image Steganography From Classical Techniques to Deep Learning Paradigms: Exploring Hidden Communication Bridging Traditional Methods and Modern AI Innovations

Shruti
http://orcid.org/0000-0002-1958-0901
Dr. B.R. Ambedkar National Institute of Technology, India

Kunwar Pal
http://orcid.org/0009-0006-8897-8960
Dr. B.R. Ambedkar National Institute of Technology, India

ABSTRACT

Image Steganography is an approach of hiding of secret data in where secret data is inserted into digital media, including mainly images, for the purpose of ensuring secure communication. In contrast to encryption, that hides the content by making it unreadable, steganography hides the existence of the data itself, providing an additional layer of discretion. CNNs have an encoder-decoder architecture, which allows embedding information into the input data while minimizing perceptibility and robustness to various attacks such as resizing or compression. The chapter also discusses and compares CNN and GAN-based techniques with traditional ones by focusing on imperceptibility, payload capacity, and adaptability. It also

DOI: 10.4018/979-8-2600-2373-0.ch003

discusses the assessment metrics–MSE, SSIM, and PSNR–to analyze the quality and security of the stego images. In summary, this chapter provides a contribution in the field of steganography revealing a new avenue based on CNN that is secure and imperceptible with high capacity.

1. INTRODUCTION

Hiding data in digital images to enable secret communication is known as image steganography, and it can be done by hiding information in a way it is not visible for unauthorized viewers. Steganography is different from encryption, which scrambles data to be unreadable, in that it hides data inside another file, usually so that the hidden data appears just like other parts of the file, such as pixels in an image. Image steganography involves slight alterations to the pixels of a cover image to encode the secret message. Common techniques include least significant bit (LSB) methods, where the least significant (lowest order) bits in the values of the pixels are changed. This allows for sensitive information to be communicated without raising suspicion since the altered image is indistinguishable from an unaltered image. Image Steganography-Secured Communications, Copyright Protection, Digital Watermarking, Data Hiding (Li & Wang, 2024), Advances in digital technology and more specifically in machine learning, have made it possible to develop very discrete steganography methods, allowing for secure and invisible information sharing. Most of the existing steganographic algorithms have only one challenge to deal with as a problem which is that appropriate cover object selection keeps striking in some scenarios concerning security, payload or tamper resistance and sometimes even robustness and transparency are need compromise. To cater for this, the proposed algorithm tries to focus on balancing those criteria by various means of parameters harmonization (Magic Matrix and Multilevel Encryption Algorithm — MLEA) The algorithm also provides ease and convenience in selecting the cover objects. Experiments conducted on different kinds of images such as texture, aerial and RGB images to evaluate its performance proved the effectiveness and importance of this technique (Supriya & Lovesum, 2024).

1.1. Background: Steganography vs. Encryption

Steganography—the Greek for covered or concealed writing—has been employed to hide data since antiquity. Its origins are in ancient Greece, when messages were hidden on wooden tablets or covered in coats of wax, which discouraged unwelcome passersby from reading them. Another historical example is the use of invisible ink to communicate secretly during wars.Steganography evolved with technological advancements. Steganography is predominantly used today to conceal data within some type of digital file, such as photos, videos, sound files, etc. Because the file is invisible to the human eye or ear, this technique allows for secretive communication without alerting bystanders to even the existence of a message.

1.1.1 Difference Between Steganography and Encryption

Both steganography and encryption are methods of protecting data, but they're very different techniques with very different goals:

- **Encryption:** Encryption is the process of turning data into a format that cannot be understood without using a specific algorithm and key. Only someone that has the proper key can decrypt/view the original data. This approach is often used to keep sensitive data secure during transfer. Even if encrypted data is intercepted, it cannot be understood without the decryption key. But encrypted data is particularly distinctive because it looks like garbled, worthless information, which can raise suspicion in unfriendly environments (Tang et al., 2025).
- Steganography: Unlike encryption, steganography, hides the actual data sitting inside a different file, like a photo or sound file, without changing the appearance or usability of the file except for some bytes. The primary goal is to guarantee that the hidden message is not detected. For example, in the picture steganography, small modifications are made to the pixel values that remain invisible to the naked eye. Steganography, alone, fails to conceal the content of the secret message from those who do not need to read it. But the embedded data can be recovered if the carrier is found. For this reason, steganography is commonly embedded in a cover file and is even used in combination with encryption for additional protection (Rahman et al., 2025).

Steganography and encryption have diverse uses too, that can be used to increase security. The combined method first encrypts the message, and then it uses steganography to hide the message inside a file. This provides strong protection. if you know there is hidden data you need the decryption key to then pull out the original message. In short, while encryption makes data illegible, it is still obvious that data is there, encrypted. While encryption makes the data unreadable, steganography hides the data by making it undetectable without altering its appearance. You can also use the two methods together for a more secure way to protect data.

1.2. Steganography: An Overview and Applications

Steganography is the act of hiding information inside other non-secret message so that the hidden message is not obvious to the on lookers (Ahmad et al., 2024). While encryption takes data and scrambles it, so it is not easily readable, steganography takes that data and hides it from plain sight semantic meaning, typically embedding data in digital media, such as images, audio, and video files (Zhang et al., 2025). This approach allows communication to be carried out in such a manner that the message is hidden in plain sight and embedded in otherwise benign files. Steganography has drawn considerable interest from both academia and industry, particularly in the contexts of secure communication, watermarking, digital rights management, and data hiding, given the rising significance of data protection and the development of digital technology.

1.3. Applications of Steganography

- **Steganography Applications –** Secure communication: Secure communication is the main application of steganography. Organizations and individuals with more sensitive information can inject it into images or audio files in such a way that it can be transmitted over untrusted networks without attracting attention (Wang et al., 2024). Steganography is improving security alongside cryptographic methods when using with the data is being transmitted.
- **Watermarking:** Steganography is commonly used in watermarking as hidden information (such as ownership or licensing information) is embedded in a file in a way that would not be easily detected and recognised (Huo et al., 2024). It is helpful in authentication, preventing illegal copies and secure content delivery.
- **Data Hiding in Medical and Military Fields:** Hiding patient information in medical images must be done to avoid compromising clinical information while allowing patient anonymity (Liu et al., 2024). Likewise, in military settings, critical data can be hidden inside harmless-looking pictures or docs for safe transfer, minimizing chances of being intercepted.
- **Digital Forensics and Cybersecurity:** Steganography may be utilized to hide proof of cybercrimes, or to track specific digital actions without raising the alarm among likely suspects (Pramanik, 2024). This model assists in forensic analysis where obscured data could be extracted later for investigative purposes.
- **Whistleblowing and Anti-Censorship** — For people in restrictive regimes, steganography can provide a safe way to written communication.

Whistleblowers and reporters use it to secretly exchange sensitive information without raising alarms so they can avoid censorship.

1.4. Evolution of Digital Image Steganography

Adaptive steganography has emerged because of this shift, in which image characteristics like texture or complexity contextually direct data embedding. In contrast to fixed-rule techniques, adaptive steganography dynamically modifies the embedding procedure according to the cover image's content. Over the past few decades, with the progress of technology and the needs of security development, digital image steganography has experienced a great evolution (Fig. 1). Early forms of steganography were simple, mostly relegated to altering a few bits of pixel values in images. In the 1990s, early image steganography techniques, like Least Significant Bit (LSB) embedding, were proposed, which hides data by changing the least significant bits of pixel values within the image. This use case offered core capabilities but was detection-prone and easy to overcome. With the rise of digital media and increasing computing power, more sophisticated and secure steganographic techniques were devised that become increasingly difficult to detect. Subsequently, transform domain techniques, including Discrete Cosine Transform (DCT) and Discrete Wavelet Transform (DWT), gained momentum by making it possible to embed data into certain frequencies of an image. These techniques resulted in more robustness properties against compression and very simple attacks, but they still had constraints regarding payload and imperceptibility. Image steganography has experienced transformative enhancements with the introduction of machine learning and, more recently, deep learning. Adaptive, highly imperceptible steganographic methods have been developed using CNNs, autoencoders, and GANs (Li et al., 2024). Generative adversarial hiding is a more recent development that makes use of GANs to produce stego images that are statistically identical to regular images. High robustness and imperceptibility are guaranteed by the generator-discriminator design.

This permits flexible data embedding distributions which are less recognizable by classical steganalysis software's providing increased hidden information protection and reliability. As Figure 1, shows the traditional steganography workflow for example, CNN-based models can pick optimal patterns in terms of data embedding minimized impact and quality of images, and increased difficulty — to detect it by humans (Liu et al., 2025).

Figure 1. Traditional Steganography Workflow.

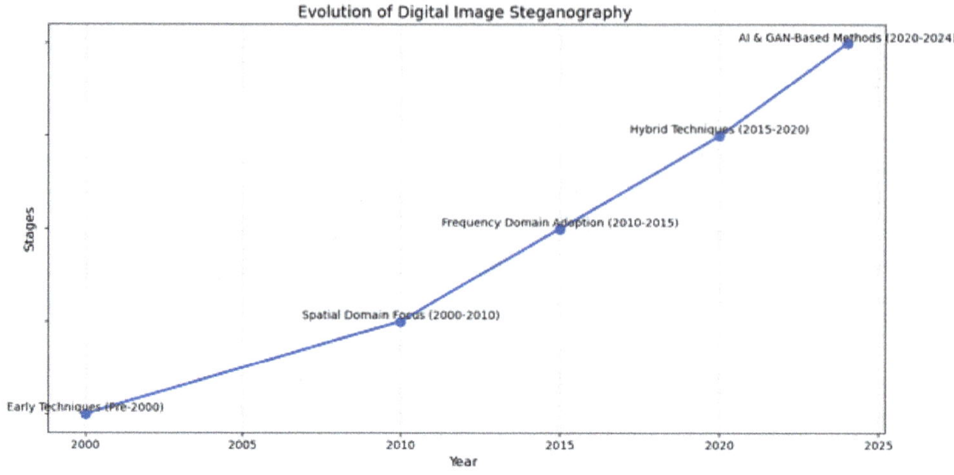

In a nutshell, we have come a long way from manipulating pixels to conceal data, to hiding data using AI-driven modern approaches of steganography in digital images. These methods are still being developed as applications such as secure communication, digital rights management, and others become possible.

1.5. Clarified Terminology

1.5.1. Least Significant Bit (LSB)

The LSB is the last bit in the binary representation of a number. of picture steganography in which the LSB method hides information within the individual least density pixels of a bitmap image. The mutation is usually invisible to the human eye, because such small pieces have not changed. For instance, modifying the final bit (to 1 from 0 or 0 from 1) on each color of an 8-bit RGB picture, which is represented with 8 bits of data for a pixel color, creates very little obvious difference while allowing great information storing capacity (Li et al., 2025).

1.5.2. Generative Adversarial Network (GAN)

In order to improve stego picture realism repeatedly, generative adversarial hiding, a steganographic technology based on GANs, uses a competitive learning process in which the discriminator assesses detectability, and the generator embeds data.A GAN is a type of deep learning model composed of two neural networks competing with each other: the discriminator and the generator. While the discriminator is the data created by real or false, the generator creates new data instances (like phony photos that imitate real photos). Because the purpose of the discriminator is to adjust and maintain the hidden information's obfuscation, GANs are widely used in image steganography for encoding secret information into an image such that it is extremely to detect (Kadem & Mohammed, 2024).

1.5.3. Frequency Domain Approaches

In Image Steganography, frequency domain approaches refer to embedding data not in the pixel values (spatial domain), but to the components of the image frequency. Using this method improves the resiliency of the embedded data against image alterations such as noise and compression. Transform methods commonly used are, Discrete Wavelet Transform (DWT) and Discrete Cosine Transform (DCT). These methods also separate the input image into frequency components and then adjust such that data is encoded to areas less visually ascertained in the image.

1.6. Importance of Security in Data Transmission

The security is also very important to the data to transmit to the network in any form. More personal, financial and organizational data gets transmitted over the internet and other networks, which have considerably increased the risks of cyber-attacks, data breaches and identity theft. It guarantees that just the specific receiver can peruse the information (Li et al., 2025), which helps to keep the information private. It also plays a role in preserving data integrity by protecting against tampering or corruption when information travels from point A to point B, verifying that whatever is received is genuinely what was sent.

In addition, Secure transmission is important for authenticity and trust in communication, such as in financial transactions, sharing medical information, and government communication (Huo et al., 2024). Using encryption, secure protocols, and authentication mechanisms assist organizations to mitigate risks, protect user privacy, and ensure compliance with regulatory requirements standards for a safer digital environment

2. FUNDAMENTALS OF DEEP LEARNING AND CONVOLUTIONAL NEURAL NETWORKS (CNNS)

Deep learning, a subset of machine learning, is based on training multi-layer (hence, the name, deep) artificial neural networks to recognize patterns and produce decisions. It is especially useful for complicated tasks such as image recognition, natural language processing and autonomous driving, where high-level feature extraction from large datasets is required (Nasr et al., 2024). Deep learning models learn in layers — the first learn to embed the input, and subsequent layers learn to embed those embeddings, and so on.

One of the most prominent types of neural networks for processing image data is the Convolutional Neural Network (CNN). CNNs is specifically meant for tasks related to image processing given the nature of spatial structure that is image, where there are significant local correlations. CNNs are made up of multiple layers:

- **Convolutional Layers –** These layers convolve, or apply filters, to input images in such a manner that they can identify edges, textures, and patterns. By applying convolutions (Dong & Yan, 2024), the network learns feature maps which accentuate certain details, allowing it to pay more attention to local patterns and structures.
- **Pooling Layers –** Pulling helps in diminutive size of feature maps but keeping important facts, and it will make modern processing more efficient and much less overdoing (Hao et al., 2024). Max pooling is the most widely used pooling method, and it picks the highest value in a region of the feature map.
- **Dense** — The network flattens the feature maps and passes them into dense layers after convolution and pooling. These layers carry out the classification or regression on the features learned in the previous layers.
- **Activation Functions:** This is usually a nonlinear function (like ReLU (Rectified Linear Unit)) applied to the output of each layer that determines the output of that layer which helps the network to learn complex nonlinear relations in data (George et al., 2024).
- **Dropout Layers (optional) —** This is used to avoid overfitting, by disabling a percentage of neurons at random, making the network to learn more robust features.

CNNs are Great for Image-related Applications CNNs are very effective at extracting features from images and are widely used for image classification, object detection and image generation, etc. (Madhu et al., 2024). This architecture is flexible in how many layers it has and can be fined-tuned for specific problems, and in fact, it's frequently used as the fundamental model in deep learning in image areas, even in domains like medical imaging or automatic driving, or in this case, almost professional image steganography.

2.1. Deep Learning: Introduction and its Importance in Steganography

Deep learning, where data is processed in similar structures to how the human brain works, is one of the machine learning-based tools within the estimated artificial intelligence parameters when several layered neural networks have been used (Lu et al., 2021). Deep learning is the paradigm that uses layers of processing that learn hierarchical representations from vast amounts of data, to accomplish or perform complex tasks like image recognition, speech recognition, and natural language understanding. Deep learning avoids feature extraction: it learns directly from raw data, which becomes richer and layered by the increased depth of the network.

One of the most widely used approaches in a deep learning is Convolutional Neural Network (CNN), especially for image Related Problems. CNNs are specifically built for processing image data, and they learn how to recognize and process pixels, spaces, textures, etc. Consequently, CNNs form the basis of deep learning-based image steganography.

2.2. Role of CNNs in Image Processing

CNNs play an important role in image processing as they can automatically learn to recognize important features in an image, that otherwise need to be hand-crafted in traditional methods (Mallet et al., 2024). Below are the main roles of CNNs in image processing.

- **Image Classification**: CNNs excel at classifying images into categories by learning hierarchical features that differentiate classes. That application crosses domains such as medical diagnosis, facial recognition and product classification.
- **Detecting and Localizing Objects in Images:** This enters CNN's golden age on work like resume with CNN based models like Faster RCNN, YOLO (You Only Look Once) for highly accurate identification of classes of objects located in the image then they are used to do many other things like driving cars autonomously or surveillance.
- **Image Segmentation:** Where each pixel of an image is classified into a desired class (e.g., road, person, bike, etc.). Semantic and instance segmentation, which are important tasks in medical imaging, robotics, and environmental analysis, have been completely transformed by CNNs.
- **Feature Extraction:** CNNs excel at extracting high-level features that capture important details within images. These characteristics are employed for

similarity matching, content-based image retrieval, and alongside other duties, including image rendering and synthesis.

- **Image Generation and Transformation:** CNNs are utilized in generative models such as GANs (Generative Adversarial Networks) and autoencoders to generate images, change styles, and make edits. Such applications are used in art, gaming and virtual reality.

CNNs are the basic building blocks of all the image processing and computer vision applications today. It is due to its capacity for automatic feature learning that convolutional neural networks have been implemented across a diverse range of industries (from healthcare to security to retail) despite the vast differences in (2.3) how they process images (Abadin et al., 2024). As research and development continue, CNNs will enable increasingly complex image processing systems and applications, revolutionizing how we view and understand visual information.

2.3. Tabular Comparison of CNNs and GAN With Traditional Methods in Steganography (shown in Table 1)

Table 1. Tabular comparison of CNNs and GAN with Traditional Methods in Steganography

Aspect	Traditional Steganography Methods	CNN-Based Steganography	GAN-Based Steganography
Approach	Rule-based; relies on fixed algorithms, like LSB (Least Significant Bit) embedding.	Data-driven; learns from patterns in training data without predefined rules.	Discriminator to refine imperceptibility, creating robust, undetectable stego images through adversarial training.
Imperceptibility	Embedding changes are often detectable with visual or statistical analysis, particularly at higher payloads.	Achieves higher imperceptibility by learning image features, allowing more seamless embedding	Offers the highest imperceptibility due to adversarial training, which minimizes detectable artifacts.
Payload Capacity	Typically limited to avoid detectable distortions; hard to increase without compromising image quality.	Higher payload capacity due to deep feature extraction, allowing more data to be embedded.	Adversarial training improves capacity while maintaining quality, as GANs generate near-indistinguishable stego images.
Robustness Against Attacks	Vulnerable to detection by statistical methods and machine learning-based steganalysis.	More resilient to attacks due to adaptive embedding in complex features but still vulnerable to advanced detection techniques.	High resilience to detection and tampering, as the discriminator in GANs enhances robustness against steganalysis attacks.

continued on following page

Table 1. Continued

Aspect	Traditional Steganography Methods	CNN-Based Steganography	GAN-Based Steganography
Processing Complexity	Lower computational requirements, making traditional methods suitable for low-resource devices.	Higher computational demands due to complex CNN architectures, requiring GPUs for optimal performance.	Most computationally intensive, as GANs require significant processing power for adversarial training and image generation.
Adaptability and Flexibility	Limited adaptability: embedding is generally fixed and rule-based, not adaptive to image content.	Highly adaptive; CNNs can learn to embed based on content features, making the embedding context aware.	Very flexible; GANs adapt dynamically through training, creating embeddings that optimize imperceptibility and robustness.
Training Requirement	Typically rule-based, with no training required, making traditional methods easy to implement.	Requires supervised or unsupervised training with labelled data, adding to development time and resource requirements.	Extensive training required with adversarial networks, increasing complexity but enhancing performance through iterative improvement.
Application Scope	Basic applications, suited for non-real-time and low-security use cases.	Suitable for high-security applications where data imperceptibility and payload capacity are priorities.	Ideal for high-security, high-capacity scenarios and dynamic environments where adaptive, robust, and undetectable data hiding is critical.

2.4. Key Advantages of a CNN-Driven Approach

Image steganography with Convolutional Neural Networks (CNNs) offers a few advantages that enhance its usefulness, safety, and flexibility for hiding data:

- **Higher Steganographic Capacity:** CNNs can learn complex and abstract features of data, which can lead to a smaller difference between original image and hidden image (Helmy, 2024). The network knows where to embed most effectively so that changes to the image are not visible to the human eye and secure data hiding is still achieved.
- **Improved Robustness to Image Tampering:** Most steganography methods are susceptible to image modifications like compression or resizing, which can corrupt or unveil the embedded data (Tabirca et al., 2025). This enables CNNs to be trained such that they are invariant under such transformations will the hidden data being embedded in some manner that is still robust and does not get lost or corrupted under such common image processing transformations.

- **More data:** CNN's allow richer feature extraction via contractive autoencoders which help you hide larger volume of data within your image without sacrificing its quality massively. This would enhance the payload capacity, which is crucial in applications, where transmission of a large amount of hidden data is required.
- **Adaptive & Self-Learning:** CNNs support adaptive steganography by learning image-specific features during training. This allows embedding strategies to be tailored to each cover image's content, improving both robustness and imperceptibility.Unlike traditional solutions, CNN driven approach is not bound by any domain specific rules and this nature and its ability to learn from raw data contribute significantly to its high efficacy. For this reason, CNNs will be able to change its embedding methods according to data type/ image content by trained on various types of images and improve steganography system both generally and specific (by increasing robustness) (Kadem & Mohammed, 2024; Tang et al., 2025).
- **Stronger Resistance to Detection:** CNNs are capable of learning to generate subtler structures and thereby making the concealed data less identifiable using steganalysis techniques. CNN-driven models can be trained to compete with various steganalysis methods, allowing the network to learn to shape the embedding strategy such that detection techniques become less effective and non-detectable embeddings can evolve even more.
- **Feature Extraction:** CNNs allow for output layers to be selected to determine useful complex features in images that are ideal for secure embedding and are largely automated (Setiadi, 2021). Such an automation spares the user from manual selection of embedding areas, hence enhancing the efficiency and effectiveness of the steganographic process.
- **Smooth Staging Functionality:** CNNs provide for combining multiple image handling processes into one framework. These chained pathways enable sophisticated manipulation such as encoding and decoding through multiple layers without interrupting the flow of data embedding and unembedding, adding to the system's cohesion and efficiency.

To summarize, a CNN-based solution achieves higher security, invisibility, and robustness in image steganography than its conventional counterparts, and appears to be a strong and versatile candidate for secure data custodianship in the era of professional-level data confidentiality attacks.

2.5. Image Steganography Techniques: A Bar Diagram Overview

Image steganography has become a substantial research area between 2010 and 2024 have three systematic approaches to either research paper strategies or even practical applications(Fig. 2) (Muralidharan et al., 2022). Spatial Domain Techniques, Frequency Domain Techniques, and Adaptive Techniques. Below is a breakdown of how they were used over that time span:

1. **Spatial Domain Techniques:** The most widely used methods are digital watermarks in the spatial domain, for example Least Significant Bit (LSB) achieving around 40% in the total usage. These are favoured for their simplicity and efficiency when embedding data directly in pixel values.
2. **Frequency Domain Techniques:**Transform-based approaches (35%): Discrete Cosine Transform (DCT) and Discrete Wavelet Transform (DWT) These techniques embed data within frequency components, making them more resilient to compression and noise.
3. **Adaptive Techniques:**The adaptive ones, for instance, the Generative Adversarial Networks (GANs) and those based on machine learning, have expanded dramatically in the last couple of years accounting for 25% of the usage. These are some of the advanced methods that increase security, and can automatically adapt to images, and whatever is embedded remains invisible.

Such distribution demonstrates the gradual shift from rudimentary approaches to advanced intelligent systems that can adjust to their environment (Hu et al., 2024), symbolizing the evolving landscape of the field's quest for efficiency, robustness, and security. As in Figure 2, demonstrates about the usage distribution of image steganography approaches in past 14 years.

Figure 2. Usage distribution of image steganography techniques (2010–2024).

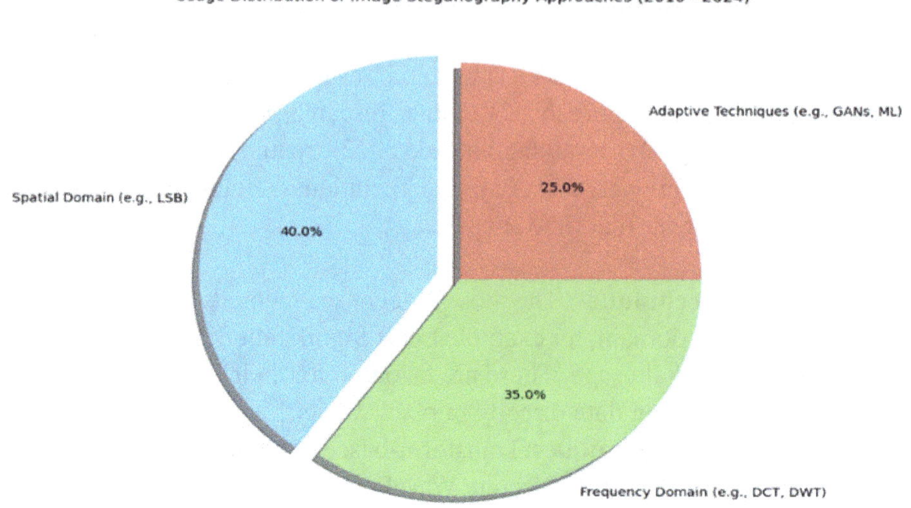

3. FOR STEGANOGRAPHY USING CNN IMAGE PROCESSING TECHNIQUES

CNN based image steganography for quality adversary or information within images using other images and running advanced image processing techniques of data digitate with strong imperceptibility and robustness embedding functions (Yao et al., 2024). Below are some of the important techniques used for this approach:

3.1. Filtering and Noise Reduction

Once the embedding is done, cover image may be processed to smoothen out visual disturbances/entry points where data is embedded through filtering and noise reduction techniques such as Gaussian and median filtering. This step also represents a pre-processing step of the image that helps get rid of minor deformations such as differentiating the background and taking a salient point without distortions.

3.2. Edge Detection and Feature Extraction

CNNs can capture the edges and textured areas where embedded data is less visible to the naked eye. Based on high complexity regions detected with layers inside CNN, the information may be concealed in non-smooth regions, so that imperceptibility and security are better.

3.3. DWT Based Frequency Domain Transformation

CNNs can perform transform on image data into a frequency domain like Discrete Cosine Transform (DCT) or Discrete Wavelet Transform (DWT) and embed data into high frequency component of image (Hu et al., 2024). This method is effective in retaining the quality of the content and provides robustness to various operations including compression.

3.4. Adaptive Blending and Masking

CNNs adjust pixel intensities where they enter data adaptively, embedding information with minimal perceptible changes based on features learned during training. Through blending and masking, the embedded information in the cover image is kept hidden and well-disguised.

3.5. Multi-Stage Feature Learning

CNN learns to extract complex features of the cover image, making the embedding adaptive and dynamic based on the specific content of each image. This applies the learning in multiple stages for the optimization of where and how in the data to embed, focusing on the trade-off between imperceptibility and payload capacity.

In steganography, the secure and high-capacity implementation of data embedding based on image processing techniques derived from CNN is more effective and robust compared to many conventional methods.

4. PREPROCESSING TECHNIQUES

Medical images are pre-processed before passing into AI models. The data cleaning and standardization process ensure the data is ready to be extracted for features or model training (Mandal et al., 2022). Data Preprocessing — We perform certain operations on images which enhances the quality of the image and gives it a needed shape for which we are going to analyze the data.

4.1. Preprocessing Goals

Preprocessing is a crucial step in medical image analysis to enhance images and prepare them for more advanced processes such as segmentation, feature extraction, and classification. The medical industry requires high-quality photos, as precise diagnosis and treatment planning depend on them. But in medical images, many noises, artifacts, and inconsistencies are often coexisted which can deteriorate the quality of subsequent analysis. Processing the data before it is being involved in the model, thus, enhances the quality and applicability of the data and ensures that the dataset is still valuable in various imaging frameworks, thus, forming the basis for reliable image interpretation. This stage directly affects the precision of later medical imaging activities like research experiments, surgical preparation, and disease diagnosis (Kunhoth et al., 2023).

Key Goals Include

There are several justifications to utilize preprocessing procedure and all of them contribute his extent to the common goal of making medical images more useful.

- **Enhancing Images Quality:**Image preprocessing is one the primary goals to visually improve the medical photographs. Medical images, whether from MRIs, CT scans, ultrasounds or X-rays, often contain distortions and noise. Noise in medical photographs can result from various factors such as sensor limits, acquisition environment, or interference from other electronic devices. Imaging systems can introduce different types of noise in an image, such as Gaussian noise, Poisson noise, or speckle noise, which may hide important anatomical structures in the image. Preprocessing techniques (contrast augmentation, denoising, filtering, etc.) are used to lessen these impacts. Histogram equalization techniques may spread the picture intensity values to get better contrast and Gaussian, or median filtering techniques can reduce noise. These improvements enable automated systems to perform segmentation, classification, etc., as well as help doctors visualize the images (Tabirca et al., 2025).
- **Heterogeneity Handling:**Medical images are often acquired with different imaging devices, in a range of conditions and may change with the patient's mobility or other conditions. Such variability, sometimes termed heterogeneity, may affect the uniformity and comparability of photographs. For example, two MRI scans from the same patient taken at different times, or with different MRI machines, might yield images that are different in brightness, contrast, or resolution. Artifact or distortion can also be introduced if

the photos are acquired at different times or if the patient moved in between photo-acquisitions; therefore, analysis of photos is often limited to tissue samples collected from a single location at the same time (Saeidi et al., 2024). It is crucial to govern this heterogeneity to ensure that data remains comparable across different imaging systems and acquisition scenarios. To address this challenge, image preprocessing methods such as image registration, normalization, and standardization are commonly employed. Normalization methods ensure that photos from different sources are comparable by scaling the intensity values of an image to a standard scale. For example, MRI intensity normalization can help standardize images from different scanners to allow consistent interpretation. Image registration techniques can reduce the influence of this noise and create a sharper image by aligning photos collected from different angles or at different times to realign any noise introduced when a patient moves or when the modalities of the imaging protocol changes.

- **Artifact Removal:** Artifacts, or undesired features or distortions in medical images, can be caused by a variety of factors, including patient motion, equipment malfunction, or incorrect scanning protocols. These artifacts can significantly affect the accuracy of image analysis because such artifacts could be mistaken for actual anatomical structures or abnormalities. Common examples of medical imaging artifacts include motion artifacts in MRIs, beam-hardening artifacts in CT scans, and speckle noise in ultrasound pictures. Preprocessing procedures aim to remove or reduce the impact of these artifacts. More advanced, low-level filtering methods can be applied to ultrasound images to reduce speckle noise, while motion correction algorithms can be employed to compensate for patient motion occurring during MRI scans. Artifact cleaning improves image quality and ensures that subsequent analysis focuses on actual anatomical structures and not irrelevant artifacts.
- **Data Preparation:**Preprocessing is also an important step to prepare medical pictures for more complicated processes such as segmentation, registration, and feature extraction. Segmentation is the process of dividing a picture into regions, usually for purposes of locating certain anatomical features/ areas of interest (e.g. tumours/organs). As a result, preprocessing methods such as denoising, contrast enhancement, and normalization increases the accuracy of segmentation algorithms by making the boundaries between different structures clearer.In a similar fashion, preprocessing is crucial for the registration of images, which involves aligning several images to a single reference frame, to ensure that the images are of similar quality and so magnificence. Preprocessing aids the feature extraction, which is the method of identifying and measuring the attributes of a picture (like graphical depiction,

form, or brightness props), as a good quality image gives much more accurate and meaningful features representation (Kaur et al., 2022).

- **Reducing Dimensionality and Computational Complexity:** Medical images are often high dimensions and contain a large amount of information, which makes processing computationally expensive. Data preprocessing helps in reducing high dimensionality of the data which can ease the analysis. Compression techniques such as down sampling or image compression can be used to further reduce images without losing important information. This allows for more manageable processing of large datasets by reducing the resources required for data analysis and increasing processing speed at the same time.
- **Improving Robustness of Algorithms:** Preprocessing also plays a crucial role in improving the robustness of deep learning and machine learning algorithms applied to medical image processing. Low-grade pictures can cause misclassifications or erroneous predictions. Preprocessing improves image quality and noise reduction, enabling algorithms to focus on the relevant aspects of the picture and thus yielding more accurate and reliable outcomes. Preparation in deep learning can also involve adding to the dataset modified images (e.g. mirrored or scaled or rotated ones) to build the capacity of the models to generalize.

4.2. Image Quality Enhancement

Noise, low-contrast, and motion artifacts are common quality-related issues in medical images. Various techniques have been deployed to mitigate these and further enhance the quality of the imagery.

- **Noise Reduction:** As the nature of imaging modalities (MRI, CT, or ultrasound) adds noise to the image itself (Subramanian et al., 2021). Techniques such as noiseless data filtering helps these algorithms to ignore the unimportant data and focus only on the required details of the image. Common methods include:
    - **Gaussian Filter:** Like moving average filter, this is slight variant that takes values of pixels in the local neighbourhood and gets a weighted average, giving higher importance to the pixels closer to filter centre (Rustad et al., 2023).
    - **Median Filter:** This is a nonlinear filter, where the value of the pixel is replaced by median of candidates (nearby) pixels, effective in salt and pepper noise removal.

- o **Bilateral Filter:** It smooths images in a way so that details are preserved using both the location of pixels of an image and contrast.

  Contrast Enhancement: Low contrast can mask relevant information in medical images and complicating diagnosis. Histogram equalization, for example, partitions contrast by redistributing the intensity values within the frame, which provides a more uniform representation of functional levels throughout the frame (Abdulla, 2024). This helps in utilizing the features and leverage more towards better diagnosis.

4.3. Standardization and Normalization

Therefore, standardization and normalization are essential preprocessing steps that eliminate variability across various patients, devices, and imaging procedures, in addition to more supervised aspects.

- **Standardization:** This is transforming a dataset such that it possesses some statistical property a mean of zero and a standard deviation of one. The standardization for comparison of single images across different datasets is therefore critical (Setiadi, 2021) and removes variability caused by differences in acquisition settings or patient characteristics.

Standardization formula:

$$X_{\text{standardized}} = \frac{(X-\mu)}{\sigma} \tag{1}$$

where X is the pixel intensity, μ is the mean, and σ is the standard deviation.

- **Normalization**: A normalization means that we scale the pixel values to a certain range. Note: this block normalizes pixel values across images. Some algorithms, for example, neural networks, are affected by the scale of the input data, and they work better with normalized input data.

Normalization formula:

$$X_{\text{normalized}} = \frac{(X - X_{\text{min}})}{(X_{\text{max}} - X_{\text{min}})} \tag{2}$$

where X_{min} and X_{max} represent the minimum and maximum intensity values of the image.

The preprocessing stage employs the standardization (eq. 1) and normalization (eq. 2) techniques to transform irregular and varied x-ray images to uniform and comparable ones, which improves the precision of analysis and boosts the reliability of the subsequent processes of segmentation, classification, and diagnosis.

4.4. Augmentation and Synthetic Data

Data augmentation and synthetic data generation can become a central unit in any medical image processing since these tend to improve model performance while also leading to generalization when data is limited.

This helps in the data augmentation process to make machine learning models and make them robust. To enlarge the number of available samples, we perform transformations to the original images; this increases the number of the dataset artificially (Kaur et al., 2022). This improves the generalization and robustness of the model. Augmentation techniques Some of the techniques commonly used for augmentation include:

- **Rotation**: It introduces variability in the orientation of images by rotating them randomly by a fixed angle.
- **Scaling**: Zooms/Objects appear larger or smaller with this operation.
- **Flipping**: Images are mirrored horizontally or vertically
- **Translation**: Shifting images in different directions to simulate variations in object positioning.
- **Brightness and Contrast Adjustments**: Modifying the intensity levels to account for varying lighting conditions.

These operations render the model more robust to the unseen changes in the data.

Synthetic Data Generation: In cases where the size of the dataset it not enough, synthetic data can be generated with different advanced techniques (e.g., Generative Adversarial Networks (GANs)). Generative adversarial networks (GANs) are composed of two neural networks (generator and discriminator) that compete against each other to produce visually plausible synthetic images (Song et al., 2024). Generator generates new data and discriminator distinguishes the real & synthetic images. As the training progresses, the generator gets better, generating images that more closely resemble the actual images. Synthetic data is particularly useful for some tasks in medicine, where obtaining labelled data is costly or even infeasible — one example is imaging for rare disease.

5. RECENT ADVANCES IN NEURAL IMAGE STEGANOGRAPHY

Advances in deep learning, adversarial training, and generative modelling have led to a considerable change in the field of image steganography in recent years. Modern methods overcome the drawbacks of imperceptibility, payload, and robustness by utilizing transformer models, diffusion models, and universal perturbation procedures, going beyond CNN- and GAN-only designs.

5.1. Transformer-Based Steganography

A revolutionary paradigm in image steganography, transformer-based architectures provide significant gains over conventional convolutional neural network (CNN) techniques, particularly for tasks requiring semantic accuracy, contextual awareness, and long-range feature representation. Models like Vision Transformer (ViT), Swin Transformer, and other variations that are excellent at capturing global dependencies within visual data are the result of the transformer architecture, which was first created for sequence modeling in natural language processing (NLP).Transformers are especially well-suited for semantic-aware embedding in the context of steganography. Their multi-head self-attention processes, which enable the network to model the connections between various parts of a picture, provide them this skill. Transformer-based models take into account the image holistically rather than just local pixel patterns, which enables contextually efficient information embedding. By aligning the embedded data with the image's semantic structure, statistical abnormalities or visual artifacts are reduced, improving imperceptibility.

- A transformer-based coverless steganography model that uses posture estimation was presented by Tan et al. (2024). This model improves concealment by removing the need for spatial pixel-level encoding.
- By creating context-aware stego-images that are guided by textual content, Li et al. (2025) presented a semantic-controlled text-to-image transformer model that permits more adaptable and high-capacity concealment.

Particularly when combined with adversarial loss or self-attention fusion mechanisms, these transformer-based systems exhibit enhanced robustness to steganalysis and greater content awareness.

5.2. Diffusion Models for Steganography

Diffusion models have found success in picture synthesis and are currently being used in steganography.Recently, diffusion models have drawn interest because to their capacity to produce incredibly lifelike images using iterative noise-based sampling. In steganography, hidden data is encoded into the denoising trajectory or latent representations using diffusion models as Stable Diffusion, DDIM, or Diffuse. Due to the indirect and stochastic nature of the embedding process, which decreases detectability, these techniques are intrinsically more resistant to steganalysis. Additionally, diffusion-based techniques surpass conventional GAN-based concealment strategies by supporting high imperceptibility scores (e.g., SSIM > 0.95 and PSNR > 40 dB). Furthermore, strong coverless steganography—where no explicit changes are made to the carrier image—is made possible by training-free frameworks like Diffuse, which offer greater stealth.

- DiffStega, a training-free diffusion-based framework that conceals information in the denoising trajectory and provides high invisibility and detection resistance, was proposed by Yang et al. in 2024.
- To provide previously unheard-of visual quality and security, Hu et al. (2024) used Stable Diffusion models to learn a mapping that reconstructs the secret data straight from the latent space of created pictures.

These models provide robust encoding routes through multi-step noise modelling and surpass conventional GAN-based techniques in terms of imperceptibility, as indicated by SSIM > 0.95 and PSNR > 40 db.

5.3. Adversarial Robustness and Steganalysis Resistance

Advanced adversarial techniques are increasingly integrated to strengthen steganography against detection:

- By using universal adversarial perturbations (UAPs) in stego-image generation, Liu et al. (2025) made embedded data impervious to transformer-based steganalysis and CNNs.
- Mallet et al. (2024) developed models that can reduce statistical divergence from natural images by relating steganographic detectability to the intrinsic regret of Gaussian feature distributions.

These methods demonstrate that steganographic models that have been adversarial trained exhibit greater generalizability across a variety of picture types and embedding tasks.

5.4. Adversarial Training and Universal Perturbations

Researchers are using adversarial robustness strategies, such as the use of universal adversarial perturbations (UAPs), to fight sophisticated steganalysis models. To trick detection algorithms, these tiny, image-agnostic disturbances are applied to stego-images. Steganographic models learn to conceal data in statistically identical distributions by being trained against cutting-edge steganalysis networks (like XceptionNet or EfficientNet). Furthermore, adversarial regularized steganography systems guarantee that hidden material is impervious to corruption or extraction, even in cases when it is suspected.

6. LIGHTWEIGHT AND REAL-TIME STEGANOGRAPHY FOR EDGE DEVICES

With the rise of IoT and mobile devices, there is an increasing interest in resource-efficient steganography models that can run in real time on edge devices. To lessen the computing footprint of steganographic models without sacrificing performance, methods including neural architecture search (NAS), quantization, knowledge distillation, and model pruning are being employed. In order to facilitate secure communication in limited settings, such as remote surveillance systems, wearable medical devices, or battlefield sensors, lightweight CNNs and Mobile Net variations are being improved.

7. DETAILED CNN ARCHITECTURE FOR IMAGE STEGANOGRAPHY: ENCODER AND DECODER

CNN-based Image Steganography image architecture usually consists of two branches namely the Encoder and the Decoder (Tan et al., 2024). The Encoder implements a secret data hiding method which embeds secret data in a cover image to generate a stego image, and then the Decoder still carries out the process to extract embedded information from the stego image. A detailed explanation of how each of these works in a CNN is below.

7.1. Encoder Network

The embedding process is then performed by the Encoder, who is responsible for encoding the secret data into the cover image without any perceptible visual difference. It learns how to change pixel values such that the hidden data becomes imperceptible to human vision and traditional steganalysis tools (Figure 3). Here's how it works:

Figure 3. Encoder algorithm using deep learning for image steganography.

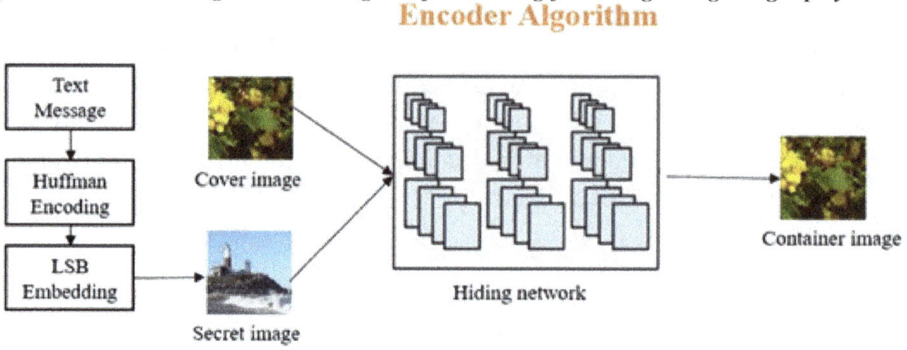

- **Input Layer:** The input to the Encoder consists of two images: the cover image (where data will be hidden) and the secret image or data (the information to be embedded). Both inputs are processed through convolutional layers.
- **Convolutional Layers for Feature Extraction:** The cover image passes through multiple convolutional layers, which analyze and extract low- and high-level features like edges, textures, and complex patterns (Yang et al., 2024). This helps identify regions where data embedding will be least noticeable, such as high-texture areas.
- **Feature Fusion Layer:** The secret data is also processed through a set of convolutional layers, transforming it into a form that can be merged with the cover image's feature map. The feature fusion layer combines the features of the cover and secret images, effectively embedding the secret data within the feature representation of the cover image.
- **Blending and Masking Layers:** Blending layers apply transparency or masking techniques to ensure that the embedding is subtle, reducing the chances of detection. For example, alpha blending combines pixel values of the cover and secret data based on weighted coefficients.
- **Reconstruction Layer:** A final convolutional layer reconstructs the stego image from the embedded features, producing an image that appears nearly identical to the original cover image to maintain imperceptibility.

The output of the Encoder is a stego image that visually resembles the cover image but contains the hidden secret data.

7.2. Decoder Network

The Decoder network's job is to accurately extract the secret data from the stego image, using a process that reverses the embedding performed by the Encoder (Figure 4) (Zhou et al., 2024). Here's how the Decoder works:

Figure 4. Decoder algorithm for extracting hidden data using a deep learning reveal network.

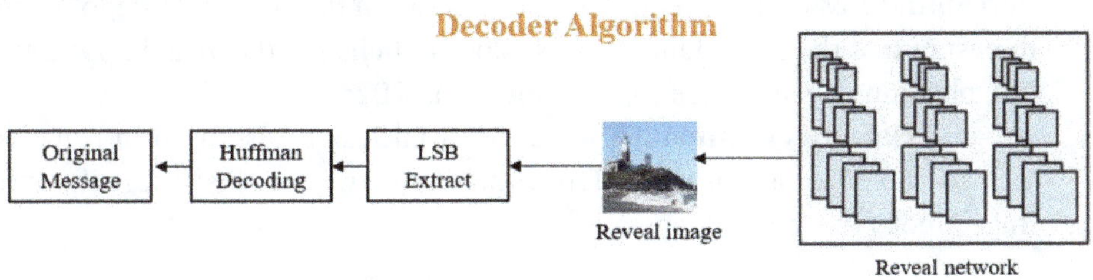

- **Input Layer:** The Decoder takes the stego image as input and begins extracting the embedded information using a series of convolutional layers.
- **Feature Extraction Layers:** The Decoder uses convolutional layers to identify and separate the hidden data from the cover image's visual features. Since the Decoder is trained alongside the Encoder, it learns to recognize embedded features within the stego image accurately.
- **Up sampling and Refinement Layers:** These layers help reconstruct the secret data from the embedded feature map. Up sampling increases the resolution of the extracted data, restoring it to its original size or clarity as much as possible (Li & Wang, 2025). Refinement layers ensure that noise or distortions introduced during encoding are minimized in the final extracted data.
- **Reconstruction Layer:** In the final layer, the Decoder reconstructs the secret data from the extracted features. This layer ensures the accuracy of the extracted data, producing an output as close as possible to the original hidden data.

The output of the Decoder is the extracted secret data, ideally identical to the original input data that was embedded.

7.3. Training Process

Both the Encoder and Decoder networks are trained together, often with a loss function those measures:

- **Reconstruction Loss**: The difference between the original and reconstructed secret data, ensuring the Decoder accurately retrieves the embedded information.
- **Perceptual Loss:** The level of similarity between the cover and stego images to ensure that the embedding process does not change the visual appearance of embedding cover image (Kuznetsov et al., 2024).
- **Adversarial Loss (Optional):** An adversarial loss is also used in some advanced implementations with a Discriminator network to make sure the stego image looks like plain images.

Image steganography using a CNN-based Encoder-Decoder architecture offers a robust approach to secure data hiding, where deep learning techniques are employed to not only enhance imperceptibility, but also fine-tune the extraction process (Yanuar et al., 2024). Extensive extent of data embedding in an image with satisfactory security, contributed to the resilience of the proposed method for contemporary steganographic use.

8. BENEFITS OF CNN-BASED STEGANOGRAPHY COMPARED TO TRADITIONAL METHODS

8.1. Enhanced Imperceptibility

Traditional steganography methods like the Least Significant Bit (LSB) method are simple, but they are detectable with advanced steganalysis techniques. These methods alter pixels in recognizable fashions, making them vulnerable to optical detection and statistical analysis. CNN-based steganography, in contrast, harnesses the ability of deep learning to learn complicated patterns in images. Using the neural net, it can identify where it would be most effective to hide data, so the changes would be less detectable by detection algorithms and the human eye. **Case Study:** If a bank uses traditional, shallow (lowest bit) LSB (least significant bit) steganography to hide the details of a transaction that is being stored to image files, attackers can determine the presence or absence of festering data by measuring pixel patterns. By using a CNN strategy the organization can reduce the danger of being distinguished from current steganalysis instruments as their hidden data stows away in the image.

8.2. Higher Payload Capacity

Traditional methods often have limited payload sizes. In other words, any changes become noticeable when merely a small amount of data is added to an image. Customary data in twin banks could be imprinted onto one another, in the region of each pixel, which together is the image data, concealing data in the image by using a CNN-based steganography, enhancing the amount of data which is concealed drastically using feature extraction techniques. Higher data can be hidden with less apparent artifacts, as a result of the capacity of the deep learning model to embed data in high-frequency areas of the image (as an example, textured sections).**Situation:** In a country with tight restrictions on what can be printed, for example, a news organization may need to send out a lot of sensitive content without alerting the authorities. Sticking existing methods, hiding it in one image may not be possible. CNN-based steganography could hide high amounts of text or even complete documents in an image, allowing them to send clearly if undetectable.

8.3. Robustness Against Attacks

Traditional methods are often vulnerable to image manipulation techniques including filtering, resizing, and compression. If you compress a picture that has hidden data, you may corrupt or lose that data. CNN-based methods are more robust as the model learns to incorporate data in a pattern that is resistant to these common transformation methods. The embedded data remains intact and intact even after compression or resizing.**Example:**A CNN-based steganography that embeds secret information was then presented to a government organization in surveillance photos sent over insecure networks. The secret data would be recoverable even if scaling or compression of the photos took place during transfer, providing for confidentiality of the data despite the transformation.

9. LOSS FUNCTION OF CNN BASED MODEL FOR IMAGE STEGANOGRAPHY

Effective steganography is shown by less distortion in the cover image. Visual fidelity is measured using metrics like SSIM and PSNR, which also reduce statistical or perceptual distortion brought on by embedding.Mean Squared Error (MSE): Represents distortion between the images; Structural Similarity (SSIM): Evaluates structural similarity between two images; Peak Signal-to-Noise Ratio (PSNR) measures image quality in decibels.

9.1. Reconstruction Loss (Mean Squared Error, MSE)

This loss measures (eq.1) a difference between the secret data and the extracted data from the stego image. The embedded information needs to be constructed in a way such that you store the embedded information accurately.

$$MSE = \frac{1}{n}\sum_{i=1}^{n}(Y_a - Y_b)^2 \tag{1}$$

The mean squared error, or MSE, computes the difference between the predicted values, or Y_b(stego-image or restored pixels) and the results, or Y_a(original image pixels). In the case of similarity measures, lower values correspond to greater similarity (Ren & Wu, 2024).

9.2. Structural Similarity Index (SSIM)

The Structural Similarity Index (SSIM) (eq. 2) is a perceptual measure of similarity between two images. Instead of metrics based on mean-square error (MSE) or peak signal-to-noise ratio (PSNR) separate measures, SSIM takes structural information, luminance, and contrast into account, making it more relevant to human visual perception (Yang et al., 2024). Image processing is one of the many fields that employs SSIM, as the quality of images is very crucial in various areas such as image compression, enhancement, and steganography.

$$SSIM(a,b) = \frac{(2\mu_a\mu_b + c1)(2\sigma_{ab} + c2)}{(\mu_a^2 + \mu_b^2 + c1)(\sigma_a^2 + \sigma_b^2 + c2)} \tag{2}$$

Where:

- $\mu_a, \mu_b$are the local means of a and b respectively.
- σ_a^2, σ_b^2 are variances,
- $\sigma_{ab}$is the correlation between x and y,
- c_1 and $c_2$be small constants to stabilize the division.

9.3. Peak Signal-to-Noise Ratio (PSNR)

The Peak Signal-to-Noise Ratio (PSNR) is a commonly used metric in image processing to assess the quality of a reconstructed or modified image with respect to the original version (Abadin et al., 2024). At its simplest level, it measures the amount of power in the signal (that is, the power in the image) compared to a measure of the power of noise that limits how closely a signal can be represented. In image-related applications like compression, enhancement, and steganography, it is important to preserve image quality, making PSNR an important metric.

$$PSNR = 20\, log_{10}\left(\frac{MAX_f}{\sqrt{MSE}}\right) \quad (3)$$

Were:

- MAX_f is the maximum pixel value of the image (e.g., 255 for 8-bit images),
- $MSE$is the square error between the produced and original image.

Here's a comparative table for images with different pixel sizes evaluated using **MSE, SSIM**, and **PSNR** metrics shown in Table 2.

Table 2. comparative table for images

Image Resolution	MSE	SSIM	PSNR (db)	Interpretation
128 x 128	10.5	0.91	37.90	High quality, minimal distortion
256 x 256	15.2	0.87	36.30	Good quality, minor differences
512 x 512	20.7	0.85	34.94	Moderate quality, noticeable but minor differences
1024 x 1024	32.1	0.80	33.04	Lower quality, visible artifacts
2048 x 2048	50.8	0.75	31.06	Significant distortion, obvious differences

10. PROPOSED ALGORITHM

Here's a proposed algorithm for a CNN-Driven Deep Learning-Based Image Steganography approach using multiple image processing operations (Martín et al., 2023). Therefore, this algorithm describes some important procedures to embed a message in a cover picture and to extract secret information within a CNN-based encoder-decoder framework as shown in Table 3

Table 3. Framework.

		Pseudocode for CNN-Driven Image Steganography
1.		Data Preprocessing
	1.1	Load the cover image C and resize it to a fixed size (e.g., 256x256 pixels).
	1.2	Normalize pixel values of C to a range [0, 1] or [-1, 1] for better CNN training.
	1.3	Convert the secret data S into a suitable format (e.g., binary array or image pixels) for embedding.
2.		Model Initialization
	2.1	Initialize the Encoder and Decoder components of the CNN-based steganography model.
	2.2	Define the required loss functions: • Reconstruction **Loss** (e.g., Mean Squared Error) for secret data recovery accuracy. • Perceptual **Loss** to maintain image imperceptibility.
	2.3	Initialize the optimizer for training the model (e.g., Adam or SGD).
3.		Training Phase (for the Encoder-Decoder CNN)
	3.1	For each training iteration:
		Input: Provide the cover image C and the secret data S to the Encoder.
	3.2	Embedding Process: • Apply image filtering techniques (e.g., Gaussian or median filters) to preprocess C for embedding. • Pass C through convolutional layers for edge detection and feature extraction, identifying suitable areas for embedding. • Embed S into C by blending it into selected high-frequency regions.
		Output: Generate the stego image C′ with embedded data.
	3.3	Extraction Process
		Pass C′ through the Decoder to reconstruct the embedded secret data S′.
	3.4	Loss Calculation: • Compute **Reconstruction Loss** between S and S′ to minimize embedding errors. • Compute **Perceptual Loss** between C and C′ to ensure imperceptibility.
	3.5	Backpropagation and Optimization: • Update the model weights to minimize the combined loss using the chosen optimizer.
4.		Embedding Process (After Training)
	4.1	Pass a new cover image C and secret data S into the trained Encoder.
	4.2	Generate the stego image C′ with the embedded data.
	4.3	Save or transmit the stego image C′.
5.		Extraction Process (After Training)
	5.1	Pass the stego image C′ through the trained Decoder.
	5.2	Extract the reconstructed secret data S′.
	5.3	Post-process S′ if necessary to match the original format of S..

11. REAL-WORLD APPLICATIONS OF STEGANOGRAPHY

11.1. Steganography in the Military

We read about military operations where command and control communication lines are made secure in order to prevent being intercepted by the enemy. Though messages encrypted may be a common red flag alerting spies, using standard methods such as encrypting a message could potentially raise suspicion as well. Military personnel could use image steganography to hide sensitive material in normal photographs. For example, steganographic methods might conceal a sensitive mission data or even command keys in an otherwise innocuous looking landscape shot. They exploited this technique to transmit strategic knowledge safely, as an opponent would not have considered anything and to reveal this type of cyber-warfare. **Example:**Traditionally covert communications in military context (e.g. World War II invisible ink and microdots) have been sent secretly, technology today can avail the same methods in digital form. Recon data can be integrated into drone photos with modern military systems. Now, these photos look normal whenever they are broadcast but it is a not real as these photos carry significant information to be accessed by authorized only.

11.2. Medical Image Steganography

The air of secrecy surrounding the product for which it was developed becomes particularly problematic in the health care industry where confidentiality of patient records must be maintained, especially when it comes to the transmission of medical photos between doctors and hospitals. Steganography is another approach in which patients' information, such as identity or medical history, can be hidden inside medical pictures (MRI scans, X-rays, etc.) and sent from one location to another. This does mean that, although the image might be taken in space and on its journey to earth, the unique patient (N = 1) will remain identifiable and not identifiable. An MRI, for example, could embed a patient's medical history in an MRI image from a hospital. To an untrained eye, nothing seems to be out of the ordinary on the MRI, but with the right tools and competent medical professionals, decoded data can be obtained. Since all data is stored in a single, unmodified image, patient privacy is maintained, and medical errors are minimized.

11.3. Digital Forensics and Cybersecurity

Digital cutters often have to sneak in and dump data from suspect devices without alerting the perps. Steganography can help hiding sizeable information or relevant forensic tracking software in plain sight files such as an image or video. This enables detectives to collect evidence without tipping off potential suspects that they are being investigated. Steganography is another type of cybersecurity technique that can be used to invisibly embed digital watermarks into private documents to determine ownership or trace leaks back to the source. For example, police could follow a suspect's movements without raising red flags by hiding surveillance data in images stored on their cell phone. In a similar fashion, companies could embed identifiers into private documents to track disclosures of sensitive information.

12. CONCLUSION

Specifically, the area of this study concentrated on image steganography, and the usage of deep learning algorithms, like the Convolutional Neural Network (CNN), to improve data hiding Technikon. In the beginning, we discuss traditional steganography techniques such as Least Significant Bit (LSB) embedding in the aspects of payload, robustness, and undetectability. The critical developments in steganography started with a nasty simple spatial domain technique and have been promoted to quite advanced transform domain approaches that are astonishingly capable data-hiding methods. Most of these methods have greatly improved with the introduction of machine learning, particularly deep learning, and a lot of the issues from previous methods have been addressed.

The CNN-guided, deep-learning-based image steganography method integrates various image-processing operations to embed data securely and imperceptibly. With the help of a well-configured CNN encoder-decoder architecture, the model is able to embed secret datum into a cover image in high Visual Quality through filtering, edge detection, and feature extraction techniques [40]. Optimized loss functions manage to achieve a trade off of imperceptibility and payload capacity, and thus storing hidden data in an imperceptible way, which can be retrieved. In conclusion, this technique demonstrates CNN's power in increasing the safety of hidden data, which may be a viable choice for image steganography techniques in securing image.

CNNs also have the other advantage of insensitivity to image manipulations, which is very important when it comes to steganography. Unlike older techniques that may be affected by loss techniques such as compressions or re-sizing's, CNN models are required to ensure that the hidden data exists after compressions or resizing, as their models depend on training. This resiliency can be essential in applications like secure communications in military or medical settings, where data could travel along erratic or untrusted networks. But even though CNN based steganography has its own advantages, but it has some drawbacks too. Deep learning suffers from one of its main disadvantages, which is that the computational resources required for the training and application of deep learning is significant. CNNs, and particularly if model like GAN would be used with them, have high data and processing power demands.This may be problematic for real-time or resource-constrained applications. In addition, although the robustness and imperceptibility of these methods have improved, deep learning-based steganographic approaches remain susceptible to strong steganalysis, especially machine-learning based methods. As these two fronts have demonstrated in recent development, adversaries on either side of the detection–confliction war can nullify technologies developed on the other side. Future research may specifically address these challenges by producing more efficient CNN architectures that demand less processing resources while preserving or improving the current level of security and imperceptibility. In addition, hybrid models that leverage the strengths of deep learning-based and traditional steganography methods can be explored.Incorporating encryption into the steganography process could add another layer of security, ensuring that, even if the hidden data is discovered, it cannot be decrypted without the appropriate key. CNN-based steganography is becoming more and more practical for real-world applications. In addition to watermarking and encrypted communications, these methods could also be helpful in areas such as digital forensics, cybersecurity, and even the arts and entertainment. As digital content production grows, we must ensure that we place a high level of trust in intellectual property through strong, virtually undetectable, watermarking.

Studies on neural network-based steganography are a valuable advancement in the domain of secure data hiding. CNNs can significantly improve both payload and imperceptibility of hidden data within images. Even if processing complexity and susceptibility to very advanced attacks persist, they can help make these techniques generally available and safe with useful research. As technology progresses, the scope of these techniques will broaden facilitating the safe transfer and safeguarding of data in a more digitized domain.Even with recent advancements, deep learning-based steganographic models still demand a lot of computing power and may need large datasets and GPU resources to train. Especially if the models are not trained with reliable or varied datasets, they are still susceptible to adversarial attacks and machine learning-based steganalysis. Furthermore, maintaining performance across a variety of image types and striking a balance between imperceptibility and payload size continue to be difficult tasks.

REFERENCES

Abadin, A. F. M., Sulaiman, R., & Hasan, M. K. (2024). Randomization strategies in image steganography techniques: A review. *Computers, Materials & Continua*, *80*(2), 1861–1896. DOI: 10.32604/cmc.2024.050834

Abdulla, A. A. (2024). Digital image steganography: Challenges, investigation, and recommendation for the future direction. *Soft Computing*, *28*(15), 8963–8976. DOI: 10.1007/s00500-023-09130-8

Ahmad, S., Ogala, J. O., Ikpotokin, F., Arif, M., Ahmad, J., & Mehfuz, S. (2024). Enhanced CNN-DCT steganography: Deep learning-based image steganography over cloud. *SN Computer Science*, *5*(4), 408. DOI: 10.1007/s42979-024-02756-x

Dong, Y., & Yan, R. (2024). A new integrated steganography scheme for quantum color images. *The Journal of Supercomputing*, *80*(16), 24758–24780. DOI: 10.1007/s11227-024-06332-1

George, R., Navanesan, L., & Thangathurai, K. (2024). Revisiting the steganography techniques with a novel region-based separation approach. *Multimedia Tools and Applications*, *83*(28), 71089–71114. DOI: 10.1007/s11042-023-17961-8

Hao, C., Yang, X., Ma, Q., Qu, D., Wang, R., & Zhang, T. (2024). Quantum audio LSB steganography with entanglement-assisted modulation. *Quantum Information Processing*, *23*(3), 106. DOI: 10.1007/s11128-024-04312-1

Helmy, M. (2024). Audio transmission based on hybrid crypto-steganography framework for efficient cyber security in wireless communication system. *Multimedia Tools and Applications*, *84*(18), 18893–18917. DOI: 10.1007/s11042-023-17921-2

Hu, K., Wang, M., Ma, X., Chen, J., Wang, X., & Wang, X. (2024). Learning-based image steganography and watermarking: A survey. *Expert Systems with Applications*, *123715*, 123715. Advance online publication. DOI: 10.1016/j.eswa.2024.123715

Hu, K., Wang, M., Ma, X., Chen, J., Wang, X., & Wang, X. (2024). Learning-based image steganography and watermarking: A survey. *Expert Systems with Applications*, *123715*, 123715. Advance online publication. DOI: 10.1016/j.eswa.2024.123715

Hu, X., Li, S., Ying, Q., Peng, W., Zhang, X., & Qian, Z. (2024). Establishing robust generative image steganography via popular stable diffusion. *IEEE Transactions on Information Forensics and Security*, *19*, 8094–8108. DOI: 10.1109/TIFS.2024.3444311

Huo, L., Chen, R., Wei, J., & Huang, L. (2024). A high-capacity and high-security image steganography network based on chaotic mapping and generative adversarial networks. *Applied Sciences (Basel, Switzerland)*, *14*(3), 1225. Advance online publication. DOI: 10.3390/app14031225

Huo, Y., Qiao, Y., & Liu, Y. (2024). A deep learning-based steganography method for high dynamic range images. *The Visual Computer*, *40*(11), 7887–7903. DOI: 10.1007/s00371-023-03214-0

Kadem, K. H., & Mohammed, M. F. (2024). OptiFusion steganography method based on masking OFDM signal in Gaussian beam intensity. *Journal of Optics*.

Kaur, S., Singh, S., Kaur, M., & Lee, H. N. (2022). A systematic review of computational image steganography approaches. *Archives of Computational Methods in Engineering*, *29*(7), 4775–4797. DOI: 10.1007/s11831-022-09749-0

Kunhoth, J., Subramanian, N., Al-Maadeed, S., & Bouridane, A. (2023). Video steganography: Recent advances and challenges. *Multimedia Tools and Applications*, *82*(27), 41943–41985. DOI: 10.1007/s11042-023-14844-w

Kuznetsov, O., Frontoni, E., & Chernov, K. (2024). Beyond traditional steganography: Enhancing security and performance with spread spectrum image steganography. *Applied Intelligence*, *54*(7), 5253–5277. DOI: 10.1007/s10489-024-05415-z

Li, F., Li, L., Zeng, Y., Yu, J., & Qin, C. (2025). Adversarial multi-image steganography via texture evaluation and multi-scale image enhancement. *Multimedia Tools and Applications*, *84*(9), 5793–5823. DOI: 10.1007/s11042-024-18920-7

Li, X., Chen, L., Fu, T., Fu, Z., & Gao, Y. (2025). Coverless image steganography based on semantic-controlled text-to-image generation. *IEEE Transactions on Circuits and Systems for Video Technology*, *35*(8), 8391–8405. DOI: 10.1109/TCSVT.2025.3545067

Li, X., Chen, L., Lai, J., Fu, Z., & Liu, S. (2024). GAN-based image steganography by exploiting transform domain knowledge with deep networks. *Multimedia Systems*, *30*(4), 224. DOI: 10.1007/s00530-024-01427-4

Li, X., & Wang, Z. (2024). Vaccine for digital images against steganography. *Scientific Reports*, *14*(1), 21340. Advance online publication. DOI: 10.1038/s41598-024-72693-5

Li, X., & Wang, Z. (2025). Image vaccine against steganography in encrypted domain. *Scientific Reports*, *15*(1), 4046. Advance online publication. DOI: 10.1038/s41598-025-88384-8

Liu, L., Liu, X., Wang, D., & Yang, G. (2024). Enhancing image steganography security via universal adversarial perturbations. *Multimedia Tools and Applications*, *84*(3), 1303–1315. Advance online publication. DOI: 10.1007/s11042-024-19122-x

Liu, L., Liu, X., Wang, D., & Yang, G. (2025). Enhancing image steganography security via universal adversarial perturbations. *Multimedia Tools and Applications*, *84*(3), 1303–1315. DOI: 10.1007/s11042-024-19122-x

Lu, S.-P.. (2021). Large-capacity image steganography based on invertible neural networks. In *Proceedings of the IEEE/CVF Conference on Computer Vision and Pattern Recognition*. IEEE. DOI: 10.1109/CVPR46437.2021.01067

Madhu, D., Vasuhi, S., & Samydurai, A. (2024). Dynamic 8-bit XOR algorithm with AES crypto algorithm for image steganography. *Signal, Image and Video Processing*, *18*(S1, Suppl 1), 429–445. DOI: 10.1007/s11760-024-03165-6

Mallet, A., Cogranne, R., & Bas, P. (2024, June). Linking intrinsic difficulty and regret to properties of multivariate Gaussians in image steganalysis. In *Proceedings of the 2024 ACM Workshop on Information Hiding and Multimedia Security* (pp. 31–39). ACM. DOI: 10.1145/3658664.3659643

Mandal, P. C., Mukherjee, I., Paul, G., & Chatterji, B. N. (2022). Digital image steganography: A literature survey. *Information Sciences*, *609*, 1451–1488. DOI: 10.1016/j.ins.2022.07.120

Martín, A., Hernández, A., Alazab, M., Jung, J., & Camacho, D. (2023). Evolving generative adversarial networks to improve image steganography. *Expert Systems with Applications*, *222*, 119841. Advance online publication. DOI: 10.1016/j.eswa.2023.119841

Muralidharan, T., Cohen, A., Cohen, A., & Nissim, N. (2022). The infinite race between steganography and steganalysis in images. *Signal Processing*, *201*, 108711. Advance online publication. DOI: 10.1016/j.sigpro.2022.108711

Nasr, M. A., El-Shafai, W., El-Rabaie, E. S. M., El-Fishawy, A. S., El-Hoseny, H. M., Abd El-Samie, F. E., & Abdel-Salam, N. (2024). A robust audio steganography technique based on image encryption using different chaotic maps. *Scientific Reports*, *14*(1), 22054. DOI: 10.1038/s41598-024-70940-3

Pramanik, S. (2024). A new method for locating data hiding in image steganography. *Multimedia Tools and Applications*, *83*(12), 34323–34349. DOI: 10.1007/s11042-023-16762-3

Rahman, S., Uddin, J., Hussain, H., Shah, S., Salam, A., Amin, F., de la Torre Díez, I., Vargas, D. L. R., & Espinosa, J. C. M. (2025). A novel and efficient digital image steganography technique using least significant bit substitution. *Scientific Reports*, *15*(1), 107. DOI: 10.1038/s41598-024-83147-3

Ren, C., & Wu, B. (2024). A robust joint coverless image steganography scheme based on two independent modules. *Cybersecurity*, *7*(1), 73. Advance online publication. DOI: 10.1186/s42400-024-00299-5

Rustad, S., Andono, P. N., & Shidik, G. F. (2023). Digital image steganography survey and investigation (goal, assessment, method, development, and dataset). *Signal Processing*, *206*, 108908. Advance online publication. DOI: 10.1016/j.sigpro.2022.108908

Saeidi, Z., Yazdi, A., Mashhadi, S., Hadian, M., & Gutub, A. (2024). High performance image steganography integrating IWT and Hamming code within secret sharing. *IET Image Processing*, *18*(1), 129–139. DOI: 10.1049/ipr2.12938

Setiadi, D. R. I. M. (2021). PSNR vs SSIM: Imperceptibility quality assessment for image steganography. *Multimedia Tools and Applications*, *80*(6), 8423–8444. DOI: 10.1007/s11042-020-10035-z

Setiadi, D. R. I. M. (2021). PSNR vs SSIM: Imperceptibility quality assessment for image steganography. *Multimedia Tools and Applications*, *80*(6), 8423–8444. DOI: 10.1007/s11042-020-10035-z

Song, B., Wei, P., Wu, S., Lin, Y., & Zhou, W. (2024). A survey on deep-learning-based image steganography. *Expert Systems with Applications*, *124390*, 124390. Advance online publication. DOI: 10.1016/j.eswa.2024.124390

Su, W., Ni, J., & Sun, Y. (2024). StegaStyleGAN: Towards generic and practical generative image steganography. [). AAAI Press.]. *Proceedings of the AAAI Conference on Artificial Intelligence*, *38*(1), 240–248. DOI: 10.1609/aaai.v38i1.27776

Subramanian, N., Elharrouss, O., Al-Maadeed, S., & Bouridane, A. (2021). Image steganography: A review of the recent advances. *IEEE Access : Practical Innovations, Open Solutions*, *9*, 23409–23423. DOI: 10.1109/ACCESS.2021.3053998

Supriya, K. S., & Lovesum, S. P. J. (2024). Review on lightweight cryptography techniques and steganography techniques for IoT environment. *International Journal of System Assurance Engineering and Management*, *15*, 4210–4228. DOI: 10.1007/s13198-024-02476-8

Tabirca, A. I., Dumitrescu, C., & Radu, V. (2025). Enhancing banking transaction security with fractal-based image steganography using Fibonacci sequences and discrete wavelet transform. *Fractal and Fractional*, *9*(2), 95. Advance online publication. DOI: 10.3390/fractalfract9020095

Tan, Y., Xiang, X., Qin, J., & Tan, Y. (2024). Robust coverless image steganography based on human pose estimation. *Knowledge-Based Systems*, *296*, 111873. Advance online publication. DOI: 10.1016/j.knosys.2024.111873

Tang, W., Rao, Y., Yang, Z., Peng, F., Cui, X., Huang, J., & Zhu, P. (2025). Reversible generative steganography with distribution-preserving. *Cybersecurity*, *8*(1), 18. DOI: 10.1186/s42400-024-00317-6

Wang, D., Liu, J., & Chen, L.. (2024). Implicit neural representation steganography by neuron pruning. *Multimedia Systems*, *30*(5), 266. DOI: 10.1007/s00530-024-01476-9

Yang, H., Xu, Y., Liu, X., & Ma, X. (2024). PRIS: Practical robust invertible network for image steganography. *Engineering Applications of Artificial Intelligence*, *133*, 108419. Advance online publication. DOI: 10.1016/j.engappai.2024.108419

Yang, Y.. (2024). Diffstega: Towards universal training-free coverless image steganography with diffusion models. arXiv. https://arxiv.org/abs/2407.10459

Yanuar, M. R., Apriono, C., & Syawaludin, M. F. (2024). Image-to-image steganography with Josephus permutation and least significant bit (LSB) 3-3-2 embedding. *Applied Sciences (Basel, Switzerland)*, *14*(16), 7119. Advance online publication. DOI: 10.3390/app14167119

Yao, Y., Wang, J., Chang, Q., Ren, Y., & Meng, W. (2024). High invisibility image steganography with wavelet transform and generative adversarial network. *Expert Systems with Applications*, *249*, 123540. Advance online publication. DOI: 10.1016/j.eswa.2024.123540

Yao, Y., Wang, J., Chang, Q., Ren, Y., & Meng, W. (2024). High invisibility image steganography with wavelet transform and generative adversarial network. *Expert Systems with Applications*, *249*, 123540. Advance online publication. DOI: 10.1016/j.eswa.2024.123540

Zhang, S., Xiao, Y., Tian, H., & Li, X. (2025). A multi-image steganography: ISS. *Cybersecurity*, *8*(1), 20. Advance online publication. DOI: 10.1186/s42400-024-00333-6

Zhou, Z., Bao, Z., Jiang, W., Huang, Y., Peng, Y., Shankar, A., Maple, C., & Selvarajan, S. (2024). Latent vector optimization-based generative image steganography for consumer electronic applications. *IEEE Transactions on Consumer Electronics*, *70*(1), 4357–4366. DOI: 10.1109/TCE.2024.3354824

Chapter 4
Computer Vision-Based Advanced Image Steganography for Secured Cyber Security

A. F. M. Saifuddin Saif
http://orcid.org/0000-0002-6163-4678
Chicago State University, USA

Zainal Rasyid Mahayuddin
http://orcid.org/0000-0002-9014-8599
Universiti Kebangsaan Malaysia, Malaysia

ABSTRACT

The lack of efficient steganography methods has been an active research concern in digital image steganography and computer vision toward efficient cyber security. This research proposes an efficient steganography method to encode and decode data from images and uses edge pixels from images. The overall method starts with detecting the edge pixel of the particular cover image using Sobel edge detector and then sorts values in descending order to get the densest edge area. The extracting process starts by detecting edge pixels of the stego image followed by sorting again similar to the embedding process. Then the sorted pixel values are read and compared to get binary values containing secret messages. Finally, secret message is retrieved from ASCII values which are derived from binary values. The proposed method achieved excellent Peak Signal Noise Ratio (PSNR) and Structural Similarity Index Metric (SSIM) results compared with the previous research indicating strong imperceptibility.

DOI: 10.4018/979-8-2600-2373-0.ch004

INTRODUCTION

The Internet revolution has become the most popular medium of digital communication. However, usage of the internet becomes a challenge for securing the information over the open network due to privacy and secrecy. In this context, Cryptology is the field of cryptography and steganography. Cryptography focuses on encrypting and decrypting the message whereas steganography focuses on hiding the message in different mediums. In this research, images are used as a medium of cryptography. Then, Steganography is the art of encoding or embedding confidential information in such a way that the information's presence is invisible within the medium (Konduru et al., 2024; Nahar and Kamal, 2024; Zhang et el., 2023). A stego-key gets used to mask the encoding mechanism to prevent the identification or retrieval of embedded data. Steganography-related watermarking and fingerprinting are primarily used to secure intellectual property. A digital watermark is a marker that is covertly inserted in a signal that tolerates noise, such as audio or image data. This is typically used by the copyright to describe ownership of such a signal. To ensure copyright security, embedded information in a watermarked item is a signature that refers to the ownership of the data. On the other hand, when any message with a communication purpose is secret, an extraction method is required which is used in this research as a significant step.

Quantum steganography is the approach that hides a secret message in a quantum shell in a medium like quantum images (Chithaluru et al., 2025; Dhar and Sahu, 2024; Varghese and Sasikala, 2023). It is the same as classical steganography, but the medium of the process is quantum image. The first step of Quantum Image Processing (QIP) (Kawasaki et al., 2025; Golchha et al., 2025; Verma and Kumar, 2025; Yang et al., 2025, Mandal et el., 2023) is to offer different algorithms for image representation using quantum mechanics. Quantum steganography uses the result of quantum mechanics like quantum computation and quantic communication to accomplish the tasks of hiding information. It can also explain that quantum steganography as the fundamental steganography in the perspective of quantum mechanics has now become an important field of quantum cryptography research. Quantum image steganography is focused on techniques of quantum image processing to remove several difficulties in classical steganography of images. Quantum image steganography covers up a hidden message such as quantum images within quantum coverings. The very first process is to represent the classical images on the quantum computers and store them. There are several representations on quantum computers for classical images including flexible representation of quantum images (FRQI) that use $2X + 1$ qubit number to display a gray image with size $2x \times 2x$ and the NEQR model to display quantum images. The Steganography algorithms for the quantum image insert binary image with a peak capacity of one bit per pixel.

Quantum image steganography algorithms have been broken to insert quantum gray images into quantum images. Previous research concentrated on developing the process of hiding images using various methods such as LSB and EMD. The Least Significant Bit (LSB) system is very common in image concealment (Panigrahi and Padhy, 2025; Rahman et al. 2025; Hameed et al., 2023). Quantum image steganography is still in its initial developmental stage.

Steganography's intent is primarily to permit communication through the channel which requires a suitable steganography method to determine how close a particular steganographic scheme gets to that target. However, prediction of the outcome gathered for steganalysis could manipulate inaccuracies in the overall methodology. High embedding capacity, invisibility, undetectability, and robustness of the original cover are the core features expected from the image steganography technique. The maximum size of a message that can be inserted in a cover image is the payload capacity normally measured with bits per pixel. Imperceptibility needs to be analyzed by means of PSNR (peak signal-to-noise ratio) and SSIM (Structural Similarity Index). Few of these expectations conflict and therefore any individual algorithm can only satisfy one or two of them. More precisely embedding capacity, robustness, and undetectability are mutually contradictory and one algorithm cannot achieve all of them. Classically, edge detection methods depend on various kinds of filtering masks to compute image gradients. In this context, classical edge detection operations are mainly based on the mathematical derivative near the original pixel image. Based on this process, inexplicable interaction can exist when two particles like atoms, photons, or electrons are entangled. In this context, entangled means the activities of particles which are attached to one another. This research proposes an efficient steganography method which is divided into two parts, i.e., embedding the secret data into the image medium and extracting that secret data from the medium successfully.

The remainder of this research is organized as follows. Critical previous research is illustrated in the background study section, comprehensive details of the proposed methodology are elaborated in the proposed methodology section, details of experimental results with analysis for validation are presented in the experimental results and analysis section and finally conclusion section presents concluding remarks.

BACKGROUND STUDY

Cryptography is one of the exciting and challenging areas for researchers to investigate to make it improved than previous methods. It keeps evolving along with time as the most secure method is yet to be found. In this modern era, as data is becoming one of the most important factors, the importance of hiding or encrypting data is getting higher day by day. The evolution of quantum computing threatens normal computer-created encryption because of its parallel task capability where it can find secret keys in a very fast way. Two forms of cryptography exist that encrypt the data or cover up the data. When the hidden message is introduced, it is linked to the stego medium (Woźniak et al. 2025; Eggers et al., 2002). Text steganography can be commonly divided into four types, i.e., format-based, random, mathematical generations, and linguistic approach. It does not alter any word or sentence, so it does not affect the cover text's "value". Random and statistical methods of generation are being used to automatically produce cover text according to the language's computational properties.

There are other approaches that have been used in previous research. The Least Significant Bit(LSB) steganography method is the easiest but most commonly used method that replaces the least significant bit of the image with message bit. LSB steganography uses message bits to explicitly replace the cover's least significant bits and block LSB to separate the cover image into blocks. Each block hides a bit of a message instead of each pixel (Jiang et al., 2016). Substitution boxes (S-boxes) play an important role in the architecture of data security strategies and a modern discrete quantum walk-based approach for generating S-boxes (QWs S-Box) which has been used as a tool to introduce a novel image steganography technique (Alexan et al., 2024; Abd EL-Latif et al., 2019). Different researchers used S-boxes differently, but the sole purpose was to hide the data from the carrier and to increase the payload.

Liu & Qiu (2002) introduced Haar DWT-based steganography where characteristics of DWT coefficients in different sub-bands result in better PSNR results. Two algorithms, i.e., quantum image edge recognition algorithm and quantum adaptive median filtering algorithm based on quantum calculation have been used in the processing of quantum digital images (Yuan et al., 2013). These methods keep this LL sub-band's coefficient unchanged and only change the threshold of the medium. But it modifies other sub-bands, i.e., LH, HL, HH. Another method to apply steganography is to follow the adaptive method. Adaptive steganography is designed to overcome this vulnerability by injecting sensitive information imperceptibly into a shielded environment without attracting any particular attention from the adversary. The system is also capable of predicting the actual edge zones of a cover image and guarantees the actual edge position after the hidden message has been embedded (Kumar et al., 2019).

Another effective way to create secret text is the Hamiltonian path because of the complexity of the Hamiltonian path (Yadav and Ojha, 2018). This method is very effective because the generation of the Hamiltonian path is very complex and that is why the pattern of embedding is almost impossible to guess. Within that method, there are two more strategies proposed so that the embedding effect is less in the stego image. Zenati et al. (2020) proposed a method based on Beta Elliptic modeling which shows very high PSNR and SSIM results. A new steganography method was proposed by Changder and Debnath (2009) where transliteration of Bengali text was used to hide information. Machine detection is risky, and this method has the lowest risk also which can be easily copped up with and applied for any other language that has alphabet of non-roman. On the other hand, it is only bound to text steganography and not applicable to others.

Vigenere Cipher and Huffman Coding methods are proven methods for steganography, and these have better Imperceptibility. These methods increase the total security of the transmission and make sure that the secret message or part of the secret message is not possible to extract without having any idea of methods of decryption. However, it is very complex and sophisticated in terms of applying in the real world (ALSAFFAWI, 2016). The inter-block coefficients scheme is capable of clustering the embedding changes and its performance is far superior to the other steganographic methods, but it is not the most secure method (Younus and Hussain, 2022).

Many frameworks were introduced to steganography techniques that exist in current research. Most of the frameworks intend to improve one or more components of the overall research, however most of them are unable to improve overall performance. One of the basic methods, where the LSB bits are replaced with the secret information bit, causes low security and integrity (Rachael et al., 2020). Then, capacity is another big issue for steganography for which various methods attempted to solve embedding (Kingsley & Barmawi, 2020) where the pixels are divided into blocks and these blocks help multiple embedding to improve the embedding capacity, PSNR value, and error correction capability. However, these methods have higher complexity. To solve this, LSB is an alternative method which led to a less secure framework (ALabaichi et al., 2020). In the LSB and secret map techniques-based framework, the secret information bit length is set to the very first two pixels and a random key is generated from the 3D Chebyshev map. This framework has higher and improved results in terms of key sensitivity, hiding capacity, quality index, MSE, PSNR, and image fidelity. However, too many keys and mappings make this framework too complex. Duan et al. (2020) imposed different approaches with image elliptic curves and deep neural networks which are highly efficient and have great capacity. The framework has a higher complexity. Besides, the semantic segmentation method was used by Pan et al. (2020) which was based on video steganography. Their experimentation shows that it has a large capacity and a certain resistance to noise attacks.

A very different and unconventional approach was made by Lee et al. (2020) where 3D magic cubes and magic matrixes for data hiding were used to ensure high capacity. EL-Latif et al, (2018) used cat maps and controlled-NOT gates caused excellent visual quality and high embedding capacity and security. Zhang et al. (2016) used the Least significant Qubit had also higher capacity due to the utilization of NEQR for quantum representation. Hadamard transformation was used by Abd-El-Atty et al. (2017) on a new Quantum Image steganography scheme but it had low capacity because of using basic embedding and extraction phase. Hastawan and Septiana (2020) used hidden multiple secret messages where they used dynamic image bit manipulation which is another form of LSB. Seven steps for the embedding process were utilized in that research. Yeh et al. (2020) focused on a high payload-based hiding method which is for AMBTC decompressed images and used a unique decodable dictionary. Zhang et al. (2020) used the MOPNA method. MOPNA (Modulus Calculations on Prime Number Algorithm) divides the cover- -image into pixel groups that include two pixels. At the next stage, a decimal value was calculated and then the confidential data was embedded. At last, they used Proof of Correctness as an extra stage. Wu et al. (2020) used state transition-binary sequence on coverless text steganography. They sorted out the frequency and added information-matching rules. After that, they established the state transition diagram and started matching the state transition diagram and binary sequence. Duan et al (2020) used GAN (Generative adversarial network) based frameworks in Steganography. They used the structure of generators and discriminators besides the information hiding and extraction process. Zhang et al. (2020) used the generative method to solve robustness issues by covering synthesis with auxiliary semantics. They used mapping rules for information to semantic Label, SSS-GAN model design, training strategies, and secret communication algorithms in their framework. Meng et al. (2020) used instance segmentation and Mask R-CNN in their research which shows greater robustness in the experimental results. Kuppusamy et al. (2020) used modified cycle generative adversarial networks and included seven steps where they used discriminators and neural networks. Kumar and Jung (2020) used a two-layer embedding strategy for a robust reversible data hiding scheme. They used scanning, sorting, and thus predicting before the two-layer embedding.

In the area of video steganography, Guan et al. (2020) proposed selective encryption of HEVC video along with various sign encryption processes. Naidu et al. (2020) proposed meaningful encryption on their research which is security-focused but lacks robustness and capacity and another area. Na (2020) proposed an unconventional and new framework for DNA steganography which may be very useful in the medical industry and very unconventional in general technology and with high-level risk factors. Sidqi (2020) proposed an efficient multi-secret approach that includes real and false data which lessens the capacity of the result. Gupta et al. (2012) used the most basic framework in their LSB-based approach where security is least concerned and keeping the simplicity and Artiemjew and Kislak-Malinowska (2020) used indiscernibility mask key but not focus on robustness and capacity. Li and Bors (2020) proposed extracting geometric features from the initial mesh in a lower resolution on their Steganalysis research which is very efficient but lacks integrity reservation and Yang et al. (2020) proposed a generator and discriminator for their framework which is based on GAN and is highly efficient in enhancing the security but creates higher complexity. Liu et al. (2020) described advancements through GAN where all types of frameworks and experiments were discussed along with their advantages and disadvantages. Liu et al. (2020) proposed different frameworks for their research-based onscreen content coding which enhances the security of video steganography but is not usable in other file formats. Mustafa (2020) proposed inserting an invisible character at the end of the block to indicate an identical character value along with multi-level complexity to avoid attackers which makes it lacking robustness and capacity. Manuilova et al. (2020) proposed a wavelet method on audio steganography where they proposed eleven phases in their framework with improved robustness and security in audio steganography where capacity was not focused. EL-Latif et al. (2019) proposed substitution boxes based on quantum walks in their framework which is highly efficient but is limited to the usage in terms of devices and Yuan et al. (2013) proposed a quantum signal processing framework that has the same problems. Wang et al. (2015) used the basic framework of quantum image steganography on LSB where they used a secret extraction procedure but still had the same problem. AL-Salhi et al. (2016) proposed a probabilistic clustering algorithm and concealing phase in their framework but yet the limitation of usage is still there. Luo et al. (2019) proposed the basic framework for their novel scheme based on ASCII which has a very efficient way of achieving information hiding but lacks security and robustness and Heidari et al. (2017) proposed Quantum red-green-blue steganography research which has high efficiency and limitation of usage. Yadav and Ojha (2018) proposed block in cover images and finding pixel sequence before rotating the blocks and bits where due to the complexity of Hamiltonian path generation, the embedding patterns become almost impossible to guess, even if the presence of secret data is observed using steganographic attacks. Kumar et al. (2019) proposed novel fuzzy edge identification in their framework which is highly efficient but low on security and unlike others Eggers et al. (2002) used STCS (spread-transform scalar Costa scheme) and histogram preserving data mappings in their framework which provides high security and integrity but lacks capacity. Random (2020) proposed two random functions with Fibonacci decomposition along with the chaotic map on their research. They used the RLE algorithm and BM along with the HMF-b vector. The results show that it ensures a high level of security while creating higher complexity.

Steganography is the art of hiding main data into fake data. There have been many methods and frameworks proposed in this technology, and it has been improved many times. The most popular method is a simple LSB method which is the most basic approach where the LSB bits are replaced with the secret information bit. But as being simple its security is low, and integrity is much lower than all the modern methods. This method is easily detectable and has no extra security to it. It does not have high capacity embedding and capacity is a big issue for steganography. Through multiple embedding, previous research attempted to solve the capacity issue where the pixels are divided into blocks and these blocks help multiple embedding which improves the embedding capacity, PSNR value, and error correction capability. However, existing frameworks have higher complexity issues, and it is based on attacking whereas steganography is mainly for lessening the attacks. To solve this, LSB can be used but it led us to a less secure framework. LSB and secret map techniques-based frameworks produce higher and improved results in terms of key sensitivity, hiding capacity, quality index, MSE, PSNR, and image fidelity. However, too many keys and mappings make this framework too complex. With an image elliptic curve and deep neural network, high-quality and capacity embedding can be achieved. Related frameworks have a higher complexity, and related unconventional approaches can ensure a very high capacity with a 3D magic cube. From the QIP (Quantum Image Processing) research area some researchers attempted to solve the capacity issues. Several researchers used cat maps and controlled-NOT gates in their research showed excellent visual quality and high embedding capacity and security. Some other research based on the Least significant Qubit has also a higher capacity as it utilized NEQR for quantum representation.

Another core problem that arises in many of that research is the lack of robustness. Synthesis with auxiliary semantics is a generative method to solve robustness issues. Related results show higher robustness parameters but had some security vulnerabilities left. Previous researchers implemented different segmentation methods for increasing robustness. Instance segmentation and Mask R-CNN showed greater robustness in the experimental results. Modified cycle generative adversarial networks produce promising results and show high robustness and security. Besides, it is observed that using a two-layer embedding strategy is a common trend for robust reversible data-hiding schemes. The experiment shows that robustness is improved higher than many other approaches. For solving robustness and capacity, previous researchers did not come up with research for solving both. Then some research was done where capacity and robustness both were focused. Some achieved improvements in terms of both capacity and robustness. On another side, A DWT-based approach for the Image steganography scheme was used and the results showed that the method improved both robustness and capacity. Then from the QIP area, several researchers used quantum image expansion and searched algorithms such as red-green-blue image steganography, and the experiments show that it can achieve good imperceptibility, security, and large capacity by virtue of quantum uncertainty and quantum non-cloning theorems. All these have a high level of complexity which is considered a significant problem. If the system complexity is too high then, the usage of the system will be difficult for general-purpose research. So, keeping the system simple and easy to use is a necessary item and the system runtime is also a big issue.

With higher robustness and capacity, the security of the system is mostly ignored though in steganography the main focus is hiding efficiency and quality. Previous research shows that the system gets highly secured as many layers of cryptography and watermarking are added to the framework. These extra layers make the whole framework too complex and upcoming research should not create higher complexity when the main idea is not leading to it and the opposite impacts. There have been many types of research which has higher complexity issues, some of them are very good for security purposes but passively contradict the steganography idea. So, this research recommends developing research methods where capacity, robustness, and efficiency will be improved, and the framework should not have higher complexity. As the future is quantum computation, researchers should be aware of that and the framework should handle that, as quantum computers have the ability of parallel computing which can destroy some high-security frameworks in the classical computers in no time. The main issue with the research from the quantum image processing domain is its usage and complexity. Though it may not exist in the future when the hardware will be ready that creates uncertainty and researchers cannot accept the impacts. Many of the QIP research included quantum circuits and other high-level algorithms made for quantum computers which can be simulated in the classical computer but that is not the way. So, researchers should try quantum image processing as it is future-proof but in such a way that it can be handled from classical computers even with some quantum circuits.

Instance segmentation and Mask R-CNN were implemented before and produced greater robustness in the experimental results. A novel approach is based on modified cycle generative adversarial networks where the results show high robustness and security. A two-layer embedding strategy was implicated for a robust reversible data hiding scheme. The experiment shows that the robustness was improved higher than many other approaches. For solving the robustness and capacity many did not come up with research for solving both. Then several research have been done where capacity and robustness both were focused. Some achieved improvements in terms of both capacity and robustness. In another field, a DWT-based approach for an Image steganography scheme was used and the results show that they improved both robustness and capacity. Then from the QIP area, previous research also used quantum image expansion and Grover search algorithms in their research as well as red-green-blue image steganography, and the experiments show that it can achieve good imperceptibility, security, and large capacity by quantum uncertainty and quantum non-cloning theorems. All these have a high level of complexity which is another significant problem. If the system complexity is too high then, the usage of the system will be difficult for general people and in urgent cases. With higher robustness and capacity, the security of the system is mostly ignored though in steganography the main focus is hiding efficiency and quality yet some research shows that the system gets highly secured as many layers of cryptography and watermarking are added to the framework. There have been many types of research which has higher complexity issues which are very good for security purposes but passively contradict the steganography idea. Image-based steganography means the cover file is an image. Here the image gets manipulated and the secret information gets hidden in the pixels of the image with different methods. The secret information can be another image or text, some binary bits, audio, GIF, or even quantum bits. The secret information gets encoded to embed it in the cover image. There are Classical methods along with Quantum steganography techniques where various types were investigated in this regard. There was audio steganography, video steganography, DNA steganography, and even MS Excel cell steganography. Researchers have been investigating to use of steganography ideas to areas that were never investigated before. From simple LSB to highly complex Quantum channel methods there are so many types of methods that have been used and could be improved or required further investigation. As the very area of research is ever evolving, the necessity of improvements will be never-ending. Due to high necessity, steganography is becoming popular and evolving vastly. There could be new possibilities with advanced AI and machine learning algorithms. The bridge between Quantum computing and classical computing where quantum computing techniques can be used without the pressure of actual hardware implementations on the general user side could be one of the breakthroughs in modern technologies. Improved Steganography will bring true secret communication ways in the upcoming days, and we hope, with new methods and frameworks, the quality will be satisfactory.

PROPOSED RESEARCH METHODOLOGY

Steganography is a branch of cryptography and there are two important divisions in cryptography, i.e., encrypting and decrypting. The same goes for steganography, which is basically divided into two parts, i.e., embedding the secret data into the medium and extracting that secret data from the medium successfully. The embedding part of the method represents the work that needs to be done at the sender end and the extraction part represents the work that needs to be done at the receiver end. These two parts are also divided into several steps. In the embedding procedure, sorting edge pixels and conversion to binary steps have to be done before coming to the step to encode the pixel. In the extraction procedure, two individual steps are created to decode the pixel steps. The proposed method by this research uses the conventional LSB method to embed data into pixels. In the proposed method, hidden data starts to embed into those columns where edge pixels are in the highest number. The reason behind this is that embedding into densely area will be less revealed than embedding random pixels.

Embedding Procedure

The proposed method starts with selecting the cover image followed by finding the edge image. Edge images can be created using several edge detection algorithms that provides edge pixel values with relative position. After getting edge pixel values, all the vertical lines that have edge values are sorted in descending order. For example, in a 4x4 image, we have x1, x2, and x4 with no vertical lines which have edge values, proposed method sorted them as in x2, x4, and x1 that x2 has the most edge pixel and x1 has the least. This sorting is for efficient embedding where the dense areas are embedded first and in such a way, the robustness of the image is improved. After getting sorted list of the vertical lines, the secret message is converted into binary. Before converting into binary value, the secret message gets converted into ASCII value first due to the difficulty of converting binary value from a string. Then the binary values are stored or embedded into the sorted pixels followed by embedding occurs on the LSB of the chosen pixels. Whenever the message binary bit is 0, the pixel value stays as it is which is 255. On the other hand, the pixel value decreases by one and forms an even value of 254 when the secret message binary bit is 1. After the embedding, the proposed research gets the stego image which consists of the secret message. The embedding procedure for the proposed method is shown in Figure 1.

Figure 1. Embedding procedure for the proposed method.

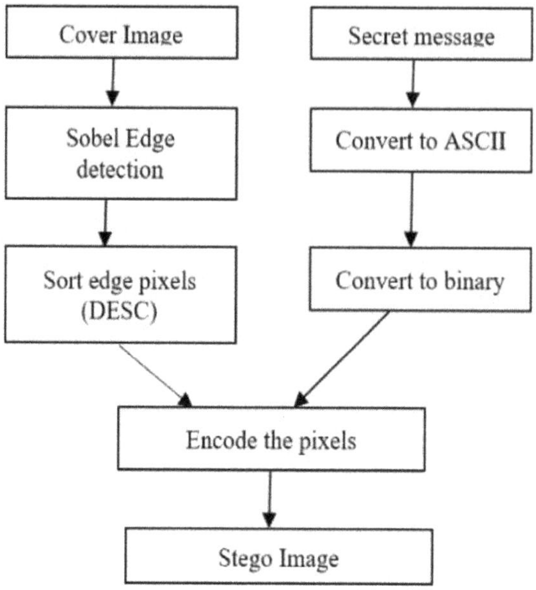

Extracting Procedure

For the extraction procedure, the Sobel edge detection algorithm is used again to stego image. Then the result of applying the Sobel algorithm provides the same edge pixel values. After that, values get sorted again and provide the pixels that are used for embedding purposes. After getting the embedded pixel list, the binary bit is extracted again by comparing the even and odd state of the pixel values. Then binary results are converted into ASCII values which show the actual secret message that was embedded in the image. The overall extraction procedure for the proposed method is shown in Figure 2. All the steps for embedding and extracting procedures are explained below.

Figure 2. Extracting procedure for the proposed method.

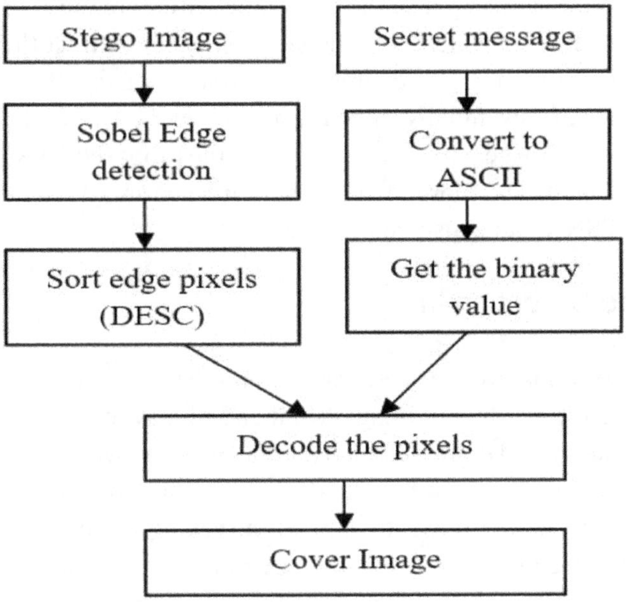

A. Cover Image

The cover image is the image that is selected to use as a medium for the information hiding. The cover image is the raw image without any data hidden in it. The steps of every steganography method start with choosing a preferable cover image. Grey image or colored image could be used as cover image. In the proposed method, the embedding procedure starts with choosing cover image which is 400x400 in this research. Then edges of the chosen cover image are produced using the Sobel edge detection algorithm (Saif and Mahayuddin, 2022; Mahayuddin and Saif, 2022). In the extraction procedure, the proposed method first starts with stego image and then after several steps of extracting the hidden message, eventually the proposed method gets the cover image back. However, because of pixel value changes, the cover image that is produced after the extracting procedure might not be the same as the actual cover image.

B. Stego Image

In the steganography technique, after embedding secret message into the cover image, the image gets changed because of the pixel value changes and then it is called a stego image. After all the steps in the embedding procedure, successfully creating the stego image is the last output of the procedure. After creating stego image, it is transferred to the receiver which uses the stego image to extract the message. So, the first step of the extracting procedure is to have stego image, then other steps are used to extract data, and eventually stego image is converted to another cover image. Comparing the cover image with the stego image, the proposed research gets PSNR value and SSIM value. The more identical both images are, the more effective the method and the PSNR value also gets increased.

C. Sobel Edge Detection Image

Sobel edge detector is an edge detection operator that uses a multi-stage algorithm to detect a wide range of edges in images (Saif and Mahayuddin, 2021). Sobel edge detector uses a filter based on the derivative of a Gaussian which reduces the effect of noise present in the image (Saif et al., 2021; Mahayuddin and Saif, 2022). Then, potential edges are thinned down to 1-pixel curves by removing non-maximum pixels of the gradient magnitude. Finally, edge pixels are kept or removed using hysteresis thresholding on the gradient magnitude. The proposed method is based on edge detection and then embedding the secret message into the edge pixels. So, to find out the edge of the cover image, the proposed method used the Sobel edge detection algorithm both in the embedding and extracting procedure to embed data edge pixels from the image and to extract data from the edge pixels.

D. Sort Edge Pixels (DESC)

The proposed method is based on hiding the hidden message in edge pixels. For that, the proposed method used the Sobel edge detection algorithm. Then, the idea is to find out the area with the most edge pixels. There are two ways to choose the most dense edge area, i.e., row-wise or column-wise. After sorting column-wise, column with most edge pixels will come out as the first column to embed the secret data. The same goes for row-wise sorting. Now, edge pixels are sorted according to ascending order, the column with the least edge pixels comes out as the first column to embed texts. The idea is to find out the column or row that has the most edge pixels using descending order. This step of both Fig. 1 and Fig. 2 does the same thing in both embedding and extraction procedures which is sorting the columns based on having the most edge pixels in the columns and sorting it.

E. Secret Message

Secret messages represent the words or sentences or any particular digits that will be passed through the cover image. The sender will send this secret message to the receiver through the image. The secret message is the same for both embedding and extraction procedures. The secret message is followed by certain words or symbols which will indicate that the message is finished. From an embedding perspective, secret message is known to the sender at first but the receiver gets the message after successfully extracting it from stego image.

F. Convert to ASCII

In the embedding procedure, after finishing the detection of the edge pixels, the next step is to embed the secret message into the edge pixels. When the proposed research gets sorted list of vertical lines or columns, secret message conversion into binary has to be done at the same time. Before converting into binary value, the secret message gets converted into ASCII value first. Because it is difficult to convert binary value from a string directly. Then binary values are stored or embedded into sorted edge pixels. In the extraction procedure, secret message is extracted from the stego image as a binary form. Then it gets converted into ASCII value and eventually, ASCII value is converted to the actual secret message that has been transferred through stego image.

G. Convert to Binary or Get the Binary Value

Secret messages can be sentences or codes or anything understandable by humans. However, the actual form of the secret message cannot be embedded into the image. In this context, the binary form of the secret message can be embedded and then transferred through the image. Because of that, the secret message needs to be converted to binary form. Direct conversion is also not possible from an actual secret message to binary form of the secret message. So, the actual secret message is converted to ASCII value and then ASCII value is converted to binary form. In the embedding procedure, conversion starts with actual secret image and ends with the binary form of the secret image. On the other hand, in the extraction procedure, the binary form of the secret message is extracted from stego image. Then binary form is converted into ASCII form and eventually into the actual secret image. In the extraction procedure, conversion occurs reversely compared with embedding procedure.

H. Encode the Pixels

In the embedding procedure, encoding the pixel step comes after sorting the edge pixel step. In sorting the edge pixel step, the edge pixel values of the stego image get sorted according to descending order to find out the column with the most pixel values. After finding out the order, the next step is to embed the secret message into the sorted edge pixel values. This step is called the encode the pixels step where basically proposed research checks edge pixel values whether they are odd or even. According to the result, binary value of the secret message is embedded into those edge pixel values in an orderly manner. Basically, the Encode the Pixel step embeds the binary value of the secret message into the ordered edge pixel values. For example, if the first 3-pixel values are 235, 120, and 199 after ordering and the first 3 binary bits of the secret message are 111. Now, Encoding the pixel step will embed 111 into those pixels by changing the last bit of those pixel values. After embedding the binary bits, the new pixel values of those pixels will be 235, 119,199 after encoding the pixel step.

I. Decode the Pixels

In the extraction procedure, decoding the pixel step comes after sorting the edge pixel step. In sorting the edge pixel step, edge pixel values of the stego image get sorted according to descending order to find out the exact same order of the embedding procedure. After finding out the order, the next step is to find out the secret message from the sorted edge pixel values. This step is called the decode the pixels step where basically proposed research checks edge pixel values whether they are odd or even and according to the result, the binary value of the secret message is found. Then, binary value gets converted to an actual human-readable secret message through several steps. Basically, decoding the pixel step finds out the hidden binary value of the secret message from the ordered edge pixel values. For example, let's assume, the first 3-pixel values are 149, 201, 240 after ordering. So, Decoding the pixel step provides binary value of 110 as the first two-pixel values are odd and the last one is even. That is how the full binary value of the secret message is created for the next step in the decode of the pixel step.

The sorted edge detection method is based on edge detection, then sorting, and finally embedding into the LSB of edge pixels. The proposed method is divided into two procedures. The embedding procedure describes or demonstrates the steps that have been used on the sender end. This procedure starts with the cover image which is the image file that is used as a medium of communication. Then, the Sobel edge detector algorithm finds the edge pixels of the cover image. Column and row of the edge pixels are stored according to descending order so that column or row with most edge pixel values come out as first column to embed data. Parallelly with these 3 steps, the secret message gets converted into ASCII form which gets converted later into binary form so that the binary bits can be embedded into the edge pixels. Finally, the secret message is embedded into the edge pixels and creates final output of the embedding procedure which is stego image. The extraction procedure starts with stego image. Then, edge pixels get detected and sorted like an embedding procedure. The secret message gets extracted from the stego image as a binary form followed by getting converted into ASCII form. The last conversion provides the actual secret message from the ASCII value. Finally, stego image is converted into the cover image so that the hidden message is no longer available in the stego image. The proposed method has the advantage of having very good PSNR value compared to previous research because the embedding procedure starts with the most densely edge pixel area. For this reason, changes between the cover image and stego image are not noticeable. The SSIM of the proposed method is also superior compared with the previous research.

EXPERIMENTAL RESULTS AND DISCUSSION

This research used the C sharp programming language for the implementation and validation of the proposed method. First, cover images were prepared in our research lab. For experimental purposes, all the images were converted to the fixed size of 400*400. All the experimental data or cover images were grayscale images. All the cover images used in the experiment are shown in Figure 3.

Figure 3. Cover images.

Results Analysis and Discussion

Experimental evaluation is divided into two parts, i.e., the embedding procedure and the extracting procedure. Overall procedures will be discussed in the subsequent sections. First, experimentation is performed based on the edge area of the cover image. Edge area is usually detected by Sobel edge detection algorithm which provides a few areas that are considered edge according to the detector. The Sobel edge detector detects edges by finding out the full value of a certain pixel. If data are embedded in those edge pixels, there is less chance of detecting hidden data. Contrarily, edge value can be changed after embedding messages into the pixels and change can be detected by comparing stego image and cover image. In this context, the cover image needs to be kept hidden to make communication secure. Cover images can also be used as a key to extract hidden messages. Edges were detected in the same way in this experiment which is gathering the highest pixel values of an image. In this research, the Sobel method was applied for the detection of the edge pixels of the cover images. In this context, there is also a hybrid method which is created by applying OR operation (Setiadi, 2022). After applying Sobel edge detection in the cover image, pixel values are stored. To find out the dense edge area of the image, previously stored pixel values are sorted in descending order. By ordering the pixel value, the new result shows the densest area of the image and secret messages start inserting into that area. Then secret message gets embedded into another less densely edged area of the image. Sample cover images along with corresponding edge images are shown in Figure 4.

Figure 4. Cover images with edges.

A. Experimental Evaluation Based on Embedding Process

After detecting the edge, the next step is to embed the secret message into the edges. First, the secret message is converted into binary ASCII value. After converting to ASCII values, these values are ready to be converted into binary using adaptive binarization. The converted binary value of the secret message gets compared with the ordered edge pixel value. When the binary bit of the secret message is 1, then the targeted edge pixel value remains unchanged which is, for example, 255. On the other hand, when the binary bit is 0, the targeted edge pixel value is decreased by

1, and the edge pixel value is changed, for example, 255 to 254. As an illustration, sample binary digits of the secret message "10111010" are shown in Table 1.

Table 1. Converted binary value gets compared with ordered pixel value

Binary bit	Edge pixel value
1	255
0	255-1 = 254
1	240-1= 239
1	179
1	200-1= 199
0	177-1 = 176
1	149
0	222

As a result, only the pixel gets changed to an even number when the secret message bit is 1, otherwise pixel value remains 255. Stego image gets created after embedding the whole secret message into the cover image. As the size of the cover images was only 512 X 512, the secret message size was smaller too. Message size can be increased by increasing the size of the cover image. For example, H denotes secret message, ASCII value = 72, and Binary Value = 01001000. For that scenario, if only 1 LSB is chosen, then edge pixel representation is shown in Table 2.

Table 2. Edge pixel value for 1 LSB

Binary bit	Edge pixel values
0	255-1=254(11111110)
1	255 (11111111)
0	123-1=122
0	152
1	198-1= 197
0	231-1= 230
0	158
0	159-1 = 158

MSE and PSNR are measurements to find out the imperceptibility of an image with embedded secret message. MSE means mean squared error which is applied on a stego image. The method to find the MSE value is to find out the difference between the sum of pixel values of the cover image and the stego image stated in Eq. (1). MSE is used to calculate Peak Signal Noise Ratio (PSNR) values. The more the PSNR values, the more the stego is imperceptible. The PSNR value is calculated from the log value of MSE.

$$MSA = \frac{1}{w \times h} \sum_{m=1}^{w} \sum_{n=1}^{h} \| S(m,n) - C(m,n) \|^2$$

$$PSNR = 10 \times Log10\left(\frac{255^2}{\sqrt{MSE}}\right) db$$

Here, h denotes the height of the image, m denotes the horizontal coordinate of the image pixel, w denotes the width of the image, n denotes the vertical coordinate of the image pixel, S denotes the stego image and C denotes the cover image.

The changes happen only in LSB (Least Significant Bit) and as a result, the overall PSNR value gets increased. On the other hand, PSNR value starts to decrease when payload capacity gets increased. Stego images after embedding secret messages are shown in Figure 5.

Figure 5. Dataset images after embedding message.

The PSNR value of the four images after embedding secret messages using the proposed method is shown in Table 3. The proposed research used these four photos as these four photos are mostly used in most of the previous research regarding steganography.

The proposed method calculated PSNR(Peak Signal to Noise Ratio) to estimate the quality of stego-image by relying on the standard value of the Human Visual System (HSV) with a value of (30 dB). If the PSNR value is greater than 30, this implies that the inserted data inside the image is invisible to the human eye. All the pictures are resized to 512 x 512 so that PSNR results can be compared for better accuracy. The PSNR results of the Lena image are the highest among all, which is 75.0991 dB. The other three images, Baboon, Cameraman, and Gold Hill have almost similar PSNR results and the results are 57.4913, 56.3789, and 56.6491 dB respectively.

Table 3. PSNR results of the proposed method

Datasets of proposed method	Average PSNR (in dB)
Dataset 1 (Lena image 512 x 512)	75.0991
Dataset 2 (Baboon image 512 x 512)	57.4913
Dataset 4(Cameraman image 512 x 512)	56.3789
Dataset 5(Gold hill image 512 x 512)	56.6491

Edge is only one feature among many more features that can be extricated from an image. Along with the edge, there are local variance and corner features. These properties are also useful for measuring the quality of an image and are very extensively used for different types of applications of image processing and pattern recognition. After creating a stego image from a cover image, embedding of secret message changes the quality of an image because there are bits that get changed which causes noise in the image as well as alteration occurs in features like edge, local variance, corners, and eventually imperceptibility decreases. SSIM or structural similarity index is another method to measure the imperceptibility of an image which is useful for the detection of alternation in structural changes, luminance, and contrast in an image after applying the steganographic method to hide secret message in the image. SSIM is calculated using Eq. (2).

$$\mathrm{SSIM(O,S)} = \frac{(2\mu_0\mu_0 + k_1)(2\sigma_{0s} + k_2)}{(\mu_0^2 + \mu_s^2 + k_1)(\sigma_0^2 + \sigma_s^2 + k_2)} \tag{2}$$

The SSIM results of the dataset after applying the proposed method are shown in Table 4.

Table 4. SSIM results of the proposed method.

Datasets of proposed method	Average SSIM
Dataset 1 (Lena image 512 x 512)	1.0000
Dataset 2 (Baboon image 512 x 512)	1.0000
Dataset 4(Cameraman image 512 x 512)	1.0000
Dataset 5(Gold hill image 512 x 512)	1.0000

The proposed method calculated SSIM (Structural Similarity Index Metric) to evaluate the likeness between the cover image and the stego-image. The results of SSIM value are limited in the range between 0 and 1. If the SSIM value is close to 1 that indicates the stego-image is like the cover image and it has high quality. The first column of the table represents the images that were used in the experimental process of the proposed method. All the pictures are resized to 400 x 400 so that SSIM results can be compared for better accuracy. The second column represents the SSIM results obtained from the experiment. The SSIM results of the second column are obtained after conducting an experiment on the images several times and the average SSIM is shown in Table 4. SSIM results of the four images are 1 which means the quality is very high and the stego image is identical to the cover image.

B. Experimental Evaluation Based on Extracting Process

Extraction procedure is necessary to retrieve the secret message after embedding the message in the cover image successfully. The process starts with detecting the edge area using the same way it was done in the embedding procedure. The steps of the extracting procedure have been demonstrated in Fig. 2. The next stage after extracting the edge area is to sort out the value same as the embedding procedure. The sorting is done in descending order and the value is stored in a place for later use. In the embedding procedure, secret data is stored by comparing the secret message binary bit value with the edge pixel value which was converted to an even value when the secret message binary bit value is 1 and the edge pixel value remained odd when the secret message binary bit is 0. As an illustration, comparing sample binary digits of the secret message "10111010" in edge pixel value is shown in Table 5.

Table 5. Edge pixels of the secret message from binary digits.

Binary bit	**Edge pixel value**
1	255
0	255-1 = 254
1	240-1= 239
1	179
1	200-1= 199
0	177-1 = 176
1	149
0	222

The comparison takes place in the extracting procedure too. Every pixel of the sorted edge value gets compared as even and odd and then the resulting value will be stored in a place as binary value. The binary value of the resulting array then gets converted into ASCII value and eventually, ASCII value is converted to the secret message that has been transferred through the stego image. In the whole procedure, LSB gets changed only as the edge pixel value changes from 255 to 254. The payload capacity can be increased by taking two LSB bits to store the value. Let's assume, the values given below are the first 8 edge pixel values after sorting according to descending order: 254, 255, 122, 152, 197, 230, 158,158. Then sorted edge values are compared as even and odd binary digits shown in Table 6. In the ASCII table, 72 is the decimal value of secret message H which remarks binary digit as 01001000. There is a certain keyword added at the end of the secret message so that the end of the extracting process can be detected.

Table 6. Sorted edge value get compared as even and odd.

Edge Pixel Values	**Binary**
254	0
255	1
122	0
152	0
197	1
230	0
158	0
158	0

Comparison With Previous Research Results

Measurements of PSNR and SSIM with previous steganographic methods are shown in Table 7 and Table 8 respectively. PSNR with the usage of Hamilton path by Yadav and Ojha (2018) was approximately 37.5435 dB which is lower than the PSNR of the proposed method by this research and the SSIM result is also little lower than the sorted edge detection technique proposed by this research. Setiadi (2022) proposed a dilated hybrid edge method where edge detection algorithms were merged and showed little better PSNR result than the proposed method by this research. However, the SSIM results of both the proposed method and the dilated hybrid edge method are almost similar. The modified LSB method achieved SSIM and PSNR results of 0.9971 and 49.35 respectively (Sahu and Swain, 2022). Although the proposed method has almost similar SSIM results, the PSNR result shows superiority over the Modified LSB method.

Table 7. Comparison of PSNR results for the proposed method with previous research.

Methods	Average PSNR(in dB)
Proposed method	61.40
Hamiltonian Path based Image Steganography Scheme (Yadav and Ojha, 2018)	37.5435
Modified LSB matching and pixel difference (Sahu and Swain, 2022)	49.35
Dilated hybrid edge detection (Setiadi, 2022)	63.6114
Exploiting modification direction (Younus and Hussain, 2022)	70.36
Beta Elliptic Modeling (Zenati et al., 2020)	86.93
Novel fuzzy edge identification (Kumar et al., 2019)	49.29
Difference expansion and modulus function (Maniriho and Ahmad, 2019)	45.6966

Table 8. Comparison of PSNR results for the proposed method with previous research.

Methods	Average SSIM
Proposed method	1.0000
Hamiltonian Path based Image Steganography Scheme (Yadav and Ojha, 2018)	0.9832
Modified LSB matching and pixel difference (Sahu and Swain, 2022)	0.9971
Dilated hybrid edge detection (Setiadi, 2022)	1.0000
Exploiting modification direction (Younus and Hussain, 2022)	0.94
Beta Elliptic Modeling (Zenati, 2020)	0.999
Novel fuzzy edge identification (Kumar et al., 2019)	0.9996

Exploiting modification direction method (Younus and Hussain, 2022) demonstrated PSNR result of 70.36 dB approximately which is higher than the proposed method, but SSIM is lower than the proposed method by this research. Exploiting modification direction method (Younus and Hussain, 2022) divided the image into different blocks and then chose specific pixel of every block to embed data. For this reason, exploiting the modification direction method (Younus and Hussain, 2022) received higher PSNR than the proposed method by this research. The payload capacity of this method is very high, and it is the reason behind achieving less SSIM value than the proposed method in this research. Zenati et al. (2020) achieved PSNR results of almost 87 DB and SSIM results of 0.999 where SSIM results are almost the same as the proposed method by this research. During experimentation, the proposed research used LSB to store the value of the secret messages which sometimes modifies pixel values to affect the imperceptibility and cause lower PSNR. In this context, previous research methods including Zenati et al. (2020) used Binary Robust Invariant Scalable Keypoints detector (BRISK) to find out the specific positions and then change the value of the LSB to identify pixels by the ith bit of the secret message to embed secret data. The proposed method by this research showed superiority in terms of achieving good imperceptibility as results show almost all the SSIM values are 1.000 and PSNR results are very good as well.

CONCLUSION

An efficient method to hide data in images using Sobel edge detection and LSB values is proposed in this research. The real motivation for this research comes from the efforts of all those researchers who are trying their best to provide different steganography methods to find out the most imperceptible technique, especially for computer vision-based image steganography towards efficient cyber security. The proposed method used Sobel edge detection to detect the edge of an image and then sort edge values to find out the most dense area in order to start embedding secret message into the selected edge pixels. The significance of the proposed method is that the proposed method chooses the densest area first to embed messages. As a result, when the secret message size is small and the dense area is bigger, PSNR becomes very high and starts decreasing when the payload size is bigger. The SSIM results show the same result for all the datasets and show superior imperceptibility. In addition, the proposed method is compared with previous methods in terms of PSNR and SSIM where the proposed method showed better results compared with previous research methods. The proposed method was experimented with using only one particular image size and format of images. In the future, investigations will be done on achieving better PSNR results using different kinds of colored images to hide data based on various edge-detecting strategies.

ACKNOWLEDGEMENT

The authors would like to thank Universiti Kebangsaan Malaysia for providing financial support under the "FTM1 - Peruntukan Dana Fakulti Teknologi dan Sains Maklumat, UKM". Besides, the author would like to thank the Department of Computing, Information and Mathematical Sciences, and Technology (CIMST), Chicago State University for various support for this research.

REFERENCES

Al-Salhi, Y. E., & Lu, S. (2016). Quantum image steganography and steganalysis based on LSQu-blocks image information concealing algorithm. *International Journal of Theoretical Physics*, *55*, 3722–3736. DOI: 10.1007/s10773-016-3001-3

Abd-El-Atty, B., Abd El-Latif, A. A., & Amin, M. (2017). New quantum image steganography scheme with Hadamard transformation. Proceedings of the International Conference on Advanced Intelligent Systems and Informatics 2016 2, Abd EL-Latif, A. A., Abd-El-Atty, B., & Venegas-Andraca, S. E. (2019). A novel image steganography technique based on quantum substitution boxes. *Optics & Laser Technology*, *116*, 92–102.

ALabaichi, A., Al-Dabbas, M. a. A. A. K., & Salih, A. (2020). Image steganography using least significant bit and secret map techniques. *International journal of electrical & computer engineering (2088-8708), 10*(1).

Alexan, W., Mamdouh, E., Aboshousha, A., Alsahafi, Y. S., Gabr, M., & Hosny, K. M. (2024). Stegocrypt: A robust tri-stage spatial steganography algorithm using TLM encryption and DNA coding for securing digital images. *IET Image Processing*, *18*(13), 4189–4206. DOI: 10.1049/ipr2.13242

ALSAFFAWI, Z. S. Y. (2016). Image steganography by using exploiting modification direction and knight tour algorithm. *Journal of Al-Qadisiyah for computer science and mathematics, 8*(1), 1-11.

Artiemjew, P., & Kislak-Malinowska, A. (2020). Indiscernibility mask key for image steganography. *Computers*, *9*(2), 38. DOI: 10.3390/computers9020038

Changder, S., & Debnath, N. C. (2009). A new approach for steganography in Bengali text. *Journal of Computational Methods in Sciences and Engineering*, *9*(s1), S111–S122. DOI: 10.3233/JCM-2009-0240

Chithaluru, P., Reddy, V. K., Narsimhulu, P., & Kumar, M. (2025). DNA computing for the smart wireless sensor networks. In *Blockchain and Digital Twin for Smart Healthcare* (pp. 395–417). Elsevier. DOI: 10.1016/B978-0-443-30300-5.00022-1

Dhar, S., & Sahu, A. K. (2024). Digital to quantum watermarking: A journey from past to present and into the future. *Computer Science Review*, *54*, 100679. DOI: 10.1016/j.cosrev.2024.100679

Duan, X., Guo, D., Liu, N., Li, B., Gou, M., & Qin, C. (2020). A new high capacity image steganography method combined with image elliptic curve cryptography and deep neural network. *IEEE Access : Practical Innovations, Open Solutions*, *8*, 25777–25788. DOI: 10.1109/ACCESS.2020.2971528

Duan, X., Li, B., Guo, D., Zhang, Z., & Ma, Y. (2020). A coverless steganography method based on generative adversarial network. *EURASIP Journal on Image and Video Processing*, *2020*(1), 1–10. DOI: 10.1186/s13640-020-00506-6

Eggers, J. J., Baeuml, R., & Girod, B. (2002). Communications approach to image steganography. Security and watermarking of Multimedia Contents IV.

Golchha, R., Sahu, M., & Bhateja, V. (2025). Quantum-based deep learning method for recognition of facial expressions. *Neural Computing & Applications*, *37*(16), 1–11. DOI: 10.1007/s00521-024-10968-8

Guan, B., Xu, D., & Li, Q. (2020). An efficient commutative encryption and data hiding scheme for HEVC video. *IEEE Access : Practical Innovations, Open Solutions*, *8*, 60232–60245. DOI: 10.1109/ACCESS.2020.2983330

Gupta, S., Goyal, A., & Bhushan, B. (2012). Information hiding using least significant bit steganography and cryptography. *International Journal of Modern Education and Computer Science*, *4*(6), 27. DOI: 10.5815/ijmecs.2012.06.04

Hameed, M. A., Abdel-Aleem, O. A., & Hassaballah, M. (2023). A secure data hiding approach based on least-significant-bit and nature-inspired optimization techniques. *Journal of Ambient Intelligence and Humanized Computing*, *14*(5), 4639–4657. DOI: 10.1007/s12652-022-04366-y

Hastawan, A. F., & Septiana, R. (2020). Hiding multiple secret information using dynamic image bit manipulation. Journal of Physics: Conference Series, Heidari, S., Pourarian, M. R., Gheibi, R., Naseri, M., & Houshmand, M. (2017). Quantum red–green–blue image steganography. *International Journal of Quantum Information*, *15*(05), 1750039.

Jiang, N., Zhao, N., & Wang, L. (2016). LSB based quantum image steganography algorithm. *International Journal of Theoretical Physics*, *55*(1), 107–123. DOI: 10.1007/s10773-015-2640-0

Kawasaki, A., Brunel, H., Ide, R., Suzuki, T., Kashiwazaki, T., Inoue, A., & Takase, K. (2025). Real-time observation of picosecond-timescale optical quantum entanglement towards ultrafast quantum information processing. *Nature Photonics*, *19*(3), 1–6. DOI: 10.1038/s41566-024-01589-7

Kingsley, K. A., & Barmawi, A. M. (2020). Improving Data Hiding Capacity in Code Based Steganography using Multiple Embedding. *J. Inf. Hiding Multim. Signal Process.*, *11*(1), 14–43.

Konduru, U. R., Nagarajan, A. P., & Sai, C. V. S. (2024). An improved performance of reversible data hiding in encrypted images using decision tree algorithm. *Engineering Applications of Artificial Intelligence*, *137*, 109100. DOI: 10.1016/j.engappai.2024.109100

Kumar, R., & Jung, K.-H. (2020). Robust reversible data hiding scheme based on two-layer embedding strategy. *Information Sciences*, *512*, 96–107. DOI: 10.1016/j.ins.2019.09.062

Kumar, S., Singh, A., & Kumar, M. (2019). Information hiding with adaptive steganography based on novel fuzzy edge identification. *Defence Technology*, *15*(2), 162–169. DOI: 10.1016/j.dt.2018.08.003

Kumar, S., Singh, A., & Kumar, M. (2019). Information hiding with adaptive steganography based on novel fuzzy edge identification. *Defence Technology*, *15*(2), 162–169. DOI: 10.1016/j.dt.2018.08.003

Kuppusamy, P., Ramya, K., Rani, S. S., Sivaram, M., & Dhasarathan, V. (2020). A novel approach based on modified cycle generative adversarial networks for image steganography. *Scalable Computing: Practice and Experience*, *21*(1), 63–72. DOI: 10.12694/scpe.v21i1.1613

Lee, C.-F., Shen, J.-J., Agrawal, S., Wang, Y.-X., & Lee, Y.-H. (2020). Data hiding method based on 3D magic cube. *IEEE Access : Practical Innovations, Open Solutions*, *8*, 39445–39453. DOI: 10.1109/ACCESS.2020.2975385

Li, Z., & Bors, A. G. (2020). Steganalysis of meshes based on 3D wavelet multiresolution analysis. *Information Sciences*, *522*, 164–179. DOI: 10.1016/j.ins.2020.02.061

Liu, T., & Qiu, Z. (2002). A DWT-based color image steganography scheme. 6th International Conference on Signal Processing, 2002., Liu, J., Ke, Y., Zhang, Z., Lei, Y., Li, J., Zhang, M., & Yang, X. (2020). Recent advances of image steganography with generative adversarial networks. *IEEE Access : Practical Innovations, Open Solutions*, *8*, 60575–60597. DOI: 10.1109/ACCESS.2020.2983175

Liu, Z., Chen, H., & Sun, S. (2020). Research on covert communication security based on screen content coding. *IEEE Access : Practical Innovations, Open Solutions*, *8*, 22275–22280. DOI: 10.1109/ACCESS.2020.2968740

Luo, J., Zhou, R.-G., Liu, X., Hu, W., & Liu, G. (2019). A novel quantum steganography scheme based on ASCII. *International Journal of Quantum Information*, *17*(04), 1950033. DOI: 10.1142/S0219749919500333

Mahayuddin, Z. R., & Saif, A. (2022). Moving object detection using semantic convolutional features. *Journal of Information Systems and Technology Management*, *7*(29), 24–41. DOI: 10.35631/JISTM.729003

Mahayuddin, Z. R., & Saif, A. (2022). Moving object detection using semantic convolutional features. *Journal of Information Systems and Technology Management*, *7*(29), 24–41. DOI: 10.35631/JISTM.729003

Mandal, A., Banerjee, S., & Panigrahi, P. K. (2023). Hybrid phase-based representation of quantum images. *International Journal of Theoretical Physics*, *62*(6), 115. DOI: 10.1007/s10773-023-05354-4

Maniriho, P., & Ahmad, T. (2019). Information hiding scheme for digital images using difference expansion and modulus function. *Journal of King Saud University. Computer and Information Sciences*, *31*(3), 335–347. DOI: 10.1016/j.jksuci.2018.01.011

Manuilova, N., Khairullina, L., Khabibullina, G., Minnegalieva, C. B., Makletsov, S., Bronskaya, V., & Kharitonova, O. (2020). Wavelet method of hiding text information in audio signals. *Journal of Physics: Conference Series*, *1515*(3), 032056. DOI: 10.1088/1742-6596/1515/3/032056

Meng, R., Cui, Q., Zhoul, Z., Yuan, C., & Sun, X. (2020). A Novel Steganography Algorithm Based on Instance Segmentation. *Computers, Materials & Continua*, *63*(1), 183–196. DOI: 10.32604/cmc.2020.05317

Mustafa, N. A. A. (2020). Text hiding in text using invisible character. *International Journal of Electrical and Computer Engineering*, *10*(4), 3550. DOI: 10.11591/ijece.v10i4.pp3550-3557

Na, D. (2020). DNA steganography: Hiding undetectable secret messages within the single nucleotide polymorphisms of a genome and detecting mutation-induced errors. *Microbial Cell Factories*, *19*(1), 1–9. DOI: 10.1186/s12934-020-01387-0 PMID: 32527315

Nahar, M., & Kamal, A. (2024). Dna steganography: Embedding the secret messages using glass stack method and detecting errors made by different attacks. *International Journal of Computers and Applications*, *46*(7), 508–525. DOI: 10.1080/1206212X.2024.2347456

Naidu, D., Tirpude, S., Kalyani, K., Bongirwar, V., & Sharma, T. (2020). Data hiding using meaningful encryption algorithm to enhance data security. *International Journal (Toronto, Ont.)*, *9*(2).

Pan, N., Qin, J., Tan, Y., Xiang, X., & Hou, G. (2020). A video coverless information hiding algorithm based on semantic segmentation. *EURASIP Journal on Image and Video Processing*, *2020*(1), 1–18. DOI: 10.1186/s13640-020-00512-8

Panigrahi, R., & Padhy, N. (2025). An effective steganographic technique for hiding the image data using the LSB technique. *Cyber Security and Applications*, *3*, 100069. DOI: 10.1016/j.csa.2024.100069

Rachael, O., Misra, S., Ahuja, R., Adewumi, A., Ayeni, F., & Mmaskeliunas, R. (2020). Image steganography and steganalysis based on least significant bit (LSB). *Proceedings of ICETIT 2019: Emerging trends in information technology* DOI: 10.1007/978-3-030-30577-2_97

Rahman, S., Uddin, J., Hussain, H., Shah, S., Salam, A., Amin, F., de la Torre Díez, I., Vargas, D. L. R., & Espinosa, J. C. M. (2025). A novel and efficient digital image steganography technique using least significant bit substitution. *Scientific Reports*, *15*(1), 107. DOI: 10.1038/s41598-024-83147-3 PMID: 39747911

Random, S. S. U. T. (2020). An effective and secure digital image steganography scheme using two random function and chaotic map. *Journal of Theoretical and Applied Information Technology*, *98*(01).

Sahu, A. K., & Swain, G. (2022). High fidelity based reversible data hiding using modified LSB matching and pixel difference. *Journal of King Saud University. Computer and Information Sciences*, *34*(4), 1395–1409. DOI: 10.1016/j.jksuci.2019.07.004

Saif, A. S., & Mahayuddin, Z. R. (2021). Crowd density estimation from autonomous drones using deep learning: Challenges and applications. *Journal of Engineering and Science Research*, *5*(6), 1–6. DOI: 10.26666/rmp.jesr.2021.6.1

Saif, A. S., Mahayuddin, Z. R., & Arshad, H. (2021). Vision-Based Efficient Collision Avoidance Model Using Distance Measurement. In *Soft Computing Approach for Mathematical Modeling of Engineering Problems* (p. 12). Taylor & Francis. DOI: 10.1201/9781003138341-12-12

Saif, F. S., & Mahayuddin, Z. R. (2022). Vision based 3D object detection using deep learning: Methods with challenges and applications towards future directions. *International Journal of Advanced Computer Science and Applications*, *13*(11), 203–214. DOI: 10.14569/IJACSA.2022.0131123

Setiadi, D. R. I. M. (2022). Improved payload capacity in LSB image steganography uses dilated hybrid edge detection. *Journal of King Saud University. Computer and Information Sciences*, *34*(2), 104–114. DOI: 10.1016/j.jksuci.2019.12.007

Sidqi, H. M. (2020). Efficient Multi-Secret Digital Images Steganography. *Egyptian Computer Science Journal*, *44*(1).

Varghese, F., & Sasikala, P. (2023). A detailed review based on secure data transmission using cryptography and steganography. *Wireless Personal Communications*, *129*(4), 2291–2318. DOI: 10.1007/s11277-023-10183-z

Verma, V., & Kumar, S. (2025). Quantum image encryption algorithm based on 3D-BNM chaotic map. *Nonlinear Dynamics*, *113*(4), 3829–3855. DOI: 10.1007/s11071-024-10403-6

Wang, S., Sang, J., Song, X., & Niu, X. (2015). Least significant qubit (LSQb) information hiding algorithm for quantum image. *Measurement*, *73*, 352–359. DOI: 10.1016/j.measurement.2015.05.038

Woźniak, K., Ogiela, M. R., & Ogiela, L. (2025). A Two-Phase Embedding Approach for Secure Distributed Steganography. *Sensors (Basel)*, *25*(5), 1448. DOI: 10.3390/s25051448 PMID: 40096275

Wu, N., Yang, Z., Yang, Y., Li, L., Shang, P., Ma, W., & Liu, Z. (2020). STBS-Stega: Coverless text steganography based on state transition-binary sequence. *International Journal of Distributed Sensor Networks*, *16*(3), 1550147720914257. DOI: 10.1177/1550147720914257

Yadav, G. S., & Ojha, A. (2018). Hamiltonian path based image steganography scheme with improved imperceptibility and undetectability. *Applied Soft Computing*, *73*, 497–507. DOI: 10.1016/j.asoc.2018.08.034

Yang, Q., Feng, X., & Wei, L. (2025). Image Similarity Quantum Algorithm and Its Application in Image Retrieval Systems. *Entropy (Basel, Switzerland)*, *27*(2), 137. DOI: 10.3390/e27020137 PMID: 40003134

Yang, Z., Wei, N., Liu, Q., Huang, Y., & Zhang, Y. (2020). GAN-TStega: Text steganography based on generative adversarial networks. Digital Forensics and Watermarking: 18th International Workshop, IWDW 2019, Chengdu, China, November 2–4, 2019, Revised Selected Papers 18

Yeh, J.-Y., Chen, C.-C., Liu, P.-L., & Huang, Y.-H. (2020). High-payload data-hiding method for AMBTC decompressed images. *Entropy (Basel, Switzerland)*, *22*(2), 145. DOI: 10.3390/e22020145 PMID: 33285920

Younus, Z. S., & Hussain, M. K. (2022). Image steganography using exploiting modification direction for compressed encrypted data. *Journal of King Saud University. Computer and Information Sciences*, *34*(6), 2951–2963. DOI: 10.1016/j.jksuci.2019.04.008

Yuan, S., Mao, X., Chen, L., & Xue, Y. (2013). Quantum digital image processing algorithms based on quantum measurement. *Optik (Stuttgart)*, *124*(23), 6386–6390. DOI: 10.1016/j.ijleo.2013.05.063

Zenati, A., Ouarda, W., & Alimi, A. M. (2020). SSDIS-BEM: A new signature steganography document image system based on beta elliptic modeling. *Engineering Science and Technology, an International Journal*, *23*(3), 470–482. DOI: 10.1016/j.jestch.2019.09.002

Zhang, H., Sun, S., Hu, L., & Meng, F. (2023). A novel data hiding scheme based on improved diamond encoding in IWT domain. *Multimedia Tools and Applications*, *82*(12), 18727–18745. DOI: 10.1007/s11042-022-14235-7 PMID: 36250182

Zhang, T., Abd-El-Atty, B., Amin, M., & El-Latif, A. (2016). QISLSQb: A quantum image steganography scheme based on Least Significant Qubit. *International Conference on Mathematical, Computational and Statistical Sciences and Engineering*.

Zhang, Y., Wang, S., Li, T., Liu, B., & Pan, D.-B. (2020). Modulus calculations on prime number algorithm for information hiding with high comprehensive performance. *IEEE Access : Practical Innovations, Open Solutions*, *8*, 85309–85320. DOI: 10.1109/ACCESS.2020.2992690

Zhang, Z., Fu, G., Ni, R., Liu, J., & Yang, X. (2020). A generative method for steganography by cover synthesis with auxiliary semantics. *Tsinghua Science and Technology*, *25*(4), 516–527. DOI: 10.26599/TST.2019.9010027

Chapter 5
AI-Driven Biostatistics in Healthcare:
From Predictive Modeling to Real-World Applications – Improving Outcomes With Intelligent Data Analysis

Amrutha Jose
http://orcid.org/0000-0002-1192-2217
Indian Council of Medical Research - National Institute of Immunohaematology (ICMR-NIIH), Mumbai, India

Rohith Mohan
State Health Agency, Kerala, India

Seena Thomas Kaithathara
http://orcid.org/0000-0002-8503-1468
King Abdulla International Medical Research Center (KAIMRC), Riyadh, Saudi Arabia

ABSTRACT

Artificial intelligence (AI) is transforming biostatistics and epidemiology by providing advanced tools to manage the increasing complexity and scale of healthcare data. This chapter examines how AI techniques – such as machine learning, deep learning, and probabilistic modeling – are reshaping traditional statistical methods. With the growing use of electronic health records, genomic data, and real-world evidence, AI-driven approaches enable more accurate disease prediction, public health monitoring, clinical decision-making, and personalized treatment. It explores the

DOI: 10.4018/979-8-2600-2373-0.ch005

shift from conventional statistical models to AI-integrated frameworks, highlighting applications in early diagnosis, risk stratification, and outcome forecasting. The chapter also addresses ethical and regulatory concerns, including algorithmic bias, data privacy, and model transparency. Emphasizing explainability, fairness-aware algorithms, and federated learning, it outlines the future of AI in biostatistics as both innovative and ethically grounded.

1. INTRODUCTION

1.1 Overview of AI in Healthcare and Biostatistics

Artificial intelligence (AI) refers to the ability of machines to mimic human cognitive functions like learning, reasoning, and decision-making. The rapid evolution of AI has ushered in a new era in healthcare and medical research. Historically rooted in computer science, AI has progressively found transformative applications across clinical and public health domains, fundamentally altering how data is interpreted, decisions are made, and interventions are deployed (Alowais et al., 2023). In the context of healthcare, AI is not merely a computational tool; it is a catalyst for a paradigm shift that integrates sophisticated algorithms with diverse medical data sources to generate insights that were previously inaccessible through traditional methodologies (Karalis, 2024).

The emergence of data science as a core discipline within healthcare has played a pivotal role in facilitating this transition. With the proliferation of electronic health records (EHRs), medical imaging, wearable sensor data, and genomic databases, the healthcare sector is inundated with complex, high-dimensional data. Biostatistics, traditionally the cornerstone of health data analysis, has evolved in parallel, adopting and integrating machine learning (ML) and AI techniques to enhance the granularity, speed, and predictive power of statistical inference (Rajkomar et al., 2019). This convergence opens a new path where AI expands the capabilities of traditional biostatistics, allowing flexible and large-scale analysis of diverse data.

Moreover, the synergy between AI, biostatistics, and epidemiology is reshaping our approach to population health (Meder et al., 2025; Wang & Li, 2024). In the realm of disease surveillance and outbreak prediction, for instance, ML models can detect subtle signals and trends that might avoid conventional epidemiological tools. Similarly, AI models trained on diverse demographic, clinical, and social determinants of health data can improve the identification of at-risk populations and inform targeted interventions. This triad of AI, biostatistics, and epidemiology forms a powerful foundation for advancing precision public health and evidence-based policymaking (Goldstein et al., 2020; Olawade et al., 2023; Wang & Li, 2024).

1.2 The Role of AI in Modern Medical Research

In the landscape of modern medical research, AI has evolved from an experimental innovation to an indispensable instrument for scientific discovery. One of its most impactful contributions is in hypothesis generation and validation. By examining through enormous datasets using unsupervised learning methods, AI can uncover hidden patterns, associations, and anomalies that may form the basis of new scientific inquiries. These data-driven hypotheses can then be validated through experimental designs or traditional statistical analysis, creating a dynamic feedback loop between computational discovery and empirical verification (Rashid & Kausik, 2024; Trezza et al., 2024).

Furthermore, AI serves as a complement – not a replacement – to traditional statistical methods. Where classical biostatistics relies on predefined models and assumptions, AI excels at adapting to complex, non-linear relationships and interacting variables. This hybridization is particularly effective in modeling multifactorial diseases such as cancer, cardiovascular disease, and diabetes, where pathophysiology is influenced by a myriad of genetic, behavioral, and environmental factors (Rashid & Kausik, 2024). Techniques such as regularized regression (Fridgeirsson et al., 2024), ensemble learning (Alsadi et al., 2024) and neural networks (Nasarudin et al., 2024) enhance model flexibility and robustness, allowing researchers to derive more nuanced interpretations from health data (Javed et al., 2025; Naderalvojoud & Hernandez-Boussard, 2024).

AI is also revolutionizing practical applications within healthcare delivery. Diagnostic systems powered by deep learning now challenging or surpass expert clinicians in fields such as radiology and dermatology (Alowais et al., 2023; Javed et al., 2025). Natural language processing (NLP) algorithms are being used to extract structured information from unstructured clinical notes, thereby streamlining documentation and facilitating better decision support (Hossain et al., 2023). In treatment planning, AI models can simulate various therapeutic pathways and predict outcomes, enabling personalized medicine approaches tailored to the patient's unique risk profile and response probabilities (Serrano et al., 2024).

Moreover, AI plays a critical role in real-time decision-making in clinical settings. From intensive care units employing AI-based monitoring systems to telehealth platforms using predictive analytics for remote triaging, AI is integrated at multiple levels of healthcare infrastructure (Tsvetanov, 2024). These applications reflect a fundamental shift from reactive to proactive care models, where decisions are increasingly informed by predictive insights rather than retrospective analysis.

1.3 Why AI-Driven Biostatistics Matters

The integration of AI into biostatistics is not simply an academic exercise – it addresses core limitations of conventional statistical methods and meets the evolving needs of modern healthcare systems. Traditional models often struggle with high-dimensional, noisy, and incomplete datasets. They are typically constrained by linear assumptions and may not scale effectively with the massive influx of real-world data. AI-driven biostatistics offers a robust alternative by leveraging data-adaptive algorithms that can accommodate missing values, handle complex data structures, and dynamically adjust to new patterns without the need for manual model revision.

Importantly, AI bridges significant gaps in health data analysis, especially in low-resource settings or among underserved populations (Tsvetanov, 2024). By connecting unstructured data from clinical narratives, social media, or mobile health apps, AI models can generate insights even in environments with sparse structured datasets. This capacity is particularly valuable in global health initiatives and epidemiological surveillance, where traditional data collection and analysis infrastructure may be lacking.

One of the most compelling reasons for adopting AI in biostatistics is its potential to enhance predictive accuracy and improve health outcomes (Meder et al., 2025). Whether it's forecasting hospital readmissions, identifying patients at high risk of adverse drug reactions, or optimizing screening protocols, AI models consistently outperform baseline statistical approaches in terms of sensitivity, specificity, and overall accuracy (Michailidis et al., 2022). In oncology, for example, AI-assisted models have demonstrated superior performance in predicting tumor progression, guiding radiotherapy, and stratifying patients for clinical trials, thereby contributing to more effective and individualized care pathways. Furthermore, AI-driven biostatistics is integral to achieving the broader goals of value-based healthcare. By delivering actionable insights in real time, these models support more efficient resource allocation, reduce unnecessary interventions, and ultimately contribute to better patient satisfaction and clinical efficiency. The ethical imperative to provide equitable, effective, and evidence-based care makes the integration of AI into biostatistics not just a technical advancement but a moral and strategic necessity.

This chapter aims to provide a comprehensive exploration of how artificial intelligence is reshaping the field of biostatistics and its applications in healthcare. The central objective is to explain the theoretical foundations, methodological innovations, and practical implementations of AI in biostatistical analysis, while critically examining the ethical, regulatory, and practical challenges involved. By navigating the continuum from algorithmic development to clinical and public health deployment, the chapter seeks to illuminate the multifaceted impacts of AI-driven biostatistics on both research and real-world decision-making.

Several key research themes guide the discourse in this chapter: i) the integration of AI and biostatistics to improve the modeling of disease prediction, risk assessment, and outcome forecasting; ii) the ways in which AI techniques enhance or replace conventional statistical methodologies in healthcare research; iii) the most promising applications of AI-driven biostatistics in clinical trials, public health policy, and precision medicine; and iv) the limitations, ethical concerns, and potential risks associated with the deployment of AI in biostatistical contexts. The scope of this chapter spans various healthcare analytics domains, including but not limited to disease surveillance, clinical trial design, personalized medicine, and population health monitoring. Special emphasis is placed on case studies and real-world implementations, highlighting the translational value of AI-driven insights from research settings to clinical practice. The content also extends to regulatory perspectives and future directions, offering a holistic view of where the field stands today and where it is heading.

2. THE FOUNDATIONS OF AI IN BIOSTATISTICS

2.1 Basics of AI and ML in Biostatistics

Artificial intelligence, particularly ML and deep learning (DL), has transformed the landscape of biostatistics by introducing new methodologies for pattern recognition, predictive modeling, and decision support. Traditionally, biostatistics has relied on established probabilistic and inferential techniques to draw conclusions from data. However, the influx of high-dimensional biomedical data has necessitated the use of algorithms capable of uncovering complex, nonlinear patterns – a domain where AI thrives.

ML refers to algorithms that learn from data by identifying statistical patterns without being explicitly programmed. In healthcare biostatistics, ML is now extensively used for risk stratification, outcome prediction, and image-based diagnostics (Sarker, 2021). DL, a subfield of ML modeled after the human brain's neural architecture, offers exceptional performance in tasks such as image classification, speech recognition, and genomics due to its hierarchical representation learning (Rahman et al., 2024; Zafar et al., 2023).

The transition from rule-based analytical frameworks to AI-powered systems marks a significant shift in biostatistics. Traditional statistical models often require strong assumptions regarding data distribution and variable relationships. AI, on the other hand, is more data-driven, capable of adapting to diverse data structures and detecting subtle trends. This flexibility enhances analytical power, particularly in complex or noisy datasets such as EHRs, sensor data, or high-throughput sequencing outputs (Serrano et al., 2024).

2.2 Key Statistical Methods and AI Techniques

2.2.1 Regression Models vs. AI-Based Predictive Models

Regression analysis has long been a fundamental tool in biostatistics for modeling relationships between variables. Linear regression is suited for continuous outcomes, while logistic regression is applied to binary outcomes. These models are interpretable, statistically rigorous, and effective when data adhere to linearity and homoscedasticity assumptions (Hosmer Jr. et al., 2013). However, with the explosion of high-dimensional and non-linear healthcare data, the limitations of traditional regression have become apparent. AI-based predictive models such as random forests, support vector machines, and gradient boosting methods offer alternatives that are non-parametric and highly flexible (Imam et al., 2024). These models excel in capturing complex interactions and higher-order relationships without prior specification, thereby improving predictive accuracy in clinical settings. While traditional regression emphasizes interpretability and inference, AI models focus on predictive performance (Freiesleben et al., 2024). Notably, for instance, an XGBoost classifier may outperform logistic regression in predicting hospital readmissions, but its inner workings are often less transparent, raising concerns about explainability.

2.2.2 Supervised, Unsupervised, and Reinforcement Learning

Supervised learning remains the most widely applied branch of ML in healthcare biostatistics. It involves training algorithms on labeled datasets where the target variable is known. This method is particularly useful for diagnostic classification (e.g., disease presence) or prognosis estimation (e.g., survival time). Examples include neural networks for breast cancer detection from mammograms or support vector machines for sepsis prediction (Bilal et al., 2024; Quazi, 2022). Unsupervised learning, in contrast, discovers intrinsic patterns in data without prior labels. This is valuable for segmenting patient populations, uncovering phenotypes, or identifying comorbidity clusters. Furthermore, clustering algorithms such as k-means or hierarchical clustering have been instrumental in discovering subtypes of diseases like diabetes or asthma (Lopez et al., 2018). Similarly, reinforcement learning, although less prevalent, is gaining attention for sequential decision-making problems in clinical environments. It enables adaptive learning through rewards and penalties, which is suitable for optimizing treatment strategies over time (Jayaraman et al., 2024).

For example, reinforcement learning has been explored for dosing adjustments in critical care or personalized chemotherapy scheduling.

2.3 Data Types and Sources in AI-Driven Biostatistics

2.3.1 Electronic Health Records (EHRs)

EHRs represent one of the richest sources of real-world data in healthcare. They include structured data (e.g., lab values, ICD codes) and unstructured narratives (e.g., clinical notes, radiology reports). AI has enhanced the usability of EHRs by enabling the extraction and interpretation of unstructured data using NLP. These algorithms can convert clinical notes into quantifiable features, facilitating their integration into predictive models (Sheikhalishahi et al., 2019). Notably, NLP-based algorithms have been used to identify early signs of deterioration in hospitalized patients by analyzing temporal sequences in EHR data. This augments the capacity of biostatisticians to construct more nuanced risk prediction tools using unstructured sources (Scharp et al., 2024).

2.3.2 Wearable and Sensor Data

The increasing availability of wearable technologies and IoT-enabled sensors has opened new frontiers in real-time health monitoring. Devices that track heart rate, oxygen saturation, glucose levels, and physical activity produce longitudinal, high-resolution datasets. These datasets are invaluable for chronic disease monitoring, behavioral interventions, and personalized healthcare. AI techniques, particularly time-series analysis and DL, have been employed to detect anomalies in physiological signals, predict acute exacerbations in chronic illnesses, or even detect atrial fibrillation before onset (Kwon et al., 2025). The biostatistical challenge lies in managing data volume, signal noise, and temporal correlations – issues AI algorithms are increasingly adept at addressing.

2.3.3 Genomic and Omics Data

The integration of genomics, proteomics, metabolomics, and other "omics" technologies has greatly expanded the analytical complexity in biomedical research. These high-dimensional datasets present multicollinearity, sparsity, and batch effects that traditional biostatistical methods may struggle to address. AI algorithms have shown significant promise in decoding complex biological data. For example, CNNs have been applied to predict gene expression profiles, while autoencoders assist in dimensionality reduction of single-cell RNA-seq data (Brendel et al., 2022).

Furthermore, ensemble learning models have been used for polygenic risk score calculations and drug response predictions, providing more refined risk stratification in precision medicine contexts.

2.4 Strengths and Limitations of AI in Biostatistics

One of the most celebrated strengths of AI in biostatistics is its scalability. ML models can process vast datasets with numerous variables, identifying patterns that are often imperceptible to human analysts. This has been transformative for big data applications in public health surveillance, imaging, and genomics (Quazi, 2022). AI also facilitates automation in repetitive analytic tasks, reducing manual workload and enabling real-time updates in dynamic systems like ICU monitoring dashboards or telehealth platforms. Furthermore, AI models often yield superior predictive performance compared to conventional methods, especially in classification and regression problems with complex, non-linear relationships (Abdeljaber et al., 2025; Varnosfaderani & Forouzanfar, 2024). However, limitations persist. AI models are often criticized for their "black box" nature, which can obscure understanding of how predictions are made. This compromises their acceptability in clinical settings where explainability is paramount. Moreover, the performance of AI models heavily depends on the quality and diversity of training data. Biases in data – such as underrepresentation of minority populations – can lead to skewed predictions and exacerbate health disparities (Norori et al., 2021). Ethical and regulatory concerns also arise, particularly regarding data privacy, informed consent, and algorithmic accountability. The potential for overfitting, data leakage, and misuse of AI outputs underscores the need for robust validation, transparency, and interdisciplinary oversight.

3. AI-POWERED STATISTICAL MODELING IN HEALTHCARE

3.1 AI in Disease Prediction and Risk Assessment

3.1.1 ML Models for Disease Screening

AI-powered models are revolutionizing disease screening by enhancing the sensitivity and specificity of early detection systems across a wide range of conditions, including cancer, diabetes, and neurological disorders. Traditional statistical approaches in screening programs rely heavily on risk factor-based stratification and clinical scoring systems. However, ML introduces the capacity to learn intricate patterns from multimodal datasets, significantly improving predictive accuracy. In oncology, supervised learning models have been successfully deployed to detect malignancies from mammographic, cytologic, and genomic data. For example, convolutional neural networks (CNNs) have demonstrated performance comparable to expert radiologists in detecting breast cancer from mammograms (Jiang et al., 2023; Nasir et al., 2025). The study by Perez et al. highlights how multimodal data - including EHRs, wearable data, and telehealth - enhances predictive modeling, particularly in rural and resource-limited settings (Perez et al., 2025). Similarly, AI models trained on liquid biopsy data can identify early-stage pancreatic and colorectal cancers, which are typically diagnosed at advanced stages using conventional methods (Ginghina et al., 2022).

In diabetes care, AI models have been developed to predict the onset of type 2 diabetes using EHRs, incorporating time-series data and lifestyle variables (Khokhar et al., 2025). Algorithms like random forests and gradient boosting machines efficiently capture nonlinear interactions between metabolic markers, socioeconomic indicators, and medication use, enabling proactive interventions. Neurological screening has also benefited from AI innovations. Notably, DL algorithms have been applied to MRI and PET imaging to detect early signs of Alzheimer's disease years before the clinical manifestation of symptoms. Remarkably, such approaches facilitate pre-symptomatic diagnosis, enabling timely therapeutic planning and potentially altering disease trajectories (Mohammed et al., 2024).

3.1.2 AI-Based Early Warning Systems

Early warning systems (EWS) are critical in preventing adverse events such as clinical deterioration, ICU admissions, and in-hospital mortality. Traditional scoring systems like MEWS or APACHE are often constrained by static parameters and linear associations (Sena et al., 2024). AI models, however, offer dynamic, real-time risk estimation using complex clinical data streams. For instance, predictive modeling for sepsis detection – an area marked by high morbidity and mortality – has seen major improvements with AI. DL models using temporal EHR data can identify subtle precursors of sepsis up to 40 hours before clinical diagnosis, outperforming conventional algorithms in sensitivity and timeliness (Islam et al., 2023). Furthermore, in cardiovascular medicine, AI-based risk stratification models integrate variables from wearable sensors, imaging data, and genomics to predict outcomes such as myocardial infarction and stroke. Neural networks and ensemble methods can analyze electrocardiogram (ECG) signals, detect arrhythmias, and assess left ventricular function with remarkable precision, providing personalized risk scores that inform preventive strategies (Ansari et al., 2023; Gupta et al., 2024). Such applications not only enhance clinical decision-making but also support the development of autonomous systems capable of triggering alerts, optimizing triage, and allocating resources in critical care settings.

3.2 AI in Epidemiology: Surveillance and Outbreak Prediction

3.2.1 AI for COVID-19 and Infectious Disease Monitoring

The COVID-19 pandemic underscored the need for agile, accurate, and scalable epidemiological tools. AI proved instrumental in real-time surveillance, contact tracing, and outbreak prediction. Early in the pandemic, NLP and ML were employed to monitor news sources, social media, and mobility data to forecast disease spread – a practice that continues in global disease surveillance systems (Al-Garadi et al., 2022). AI has also been used to predict COVID-19 case trends based on human mobility data, lockdown measures, and vaccination coverage. Recurrent neural networks (RNNs) and long short-term memory (LSTM) networks excel at modeling temporal dynamics, making them ideal for forecasting epidemic curves (Uppalaiah et al., 2025). Furthermore, AI-enabled contact tracing apps and automated symptom checkers have empowered population-level risk management while preserving user anonymity through federated learning approaches. Beyond COVID-19, similar AI frameworks are being adapted to monitor emerging infectious diseases such as Zika, Ebola, and antimicrobial-resistant pathogens, strengthening global health preparedness.

3.2.2 Predictive Models for Non-Communicable Diseases

While infectious diseases benefit from outbreak-based modeling, chronic non-communicable diseases (NCDs) require long-term surveillance systems capable of identifying at-risk individuals and population-level trends. AI plays a crucial role in aggregating diverse datasets – such as clinical records, lifestyle data, and environmental exposures – to predict the onset and progression of conditions like cardiovascular disease, diabetes, and neurodegenerative disorders. For example, predictive models developed using ensemble learning and DL have been applied to large-scale epidemiological cohorts to forecast cardiovascular events over a 10-year horizon. Notably, these models leverage longitudinal variables, including systolic blood pressure trajectories, HbA1c levels, and behavioral factors like smoking or physical activity (Stevens et al., 2021).

Moreover, in neuroepidemiology, ML algorithms have been trained on MRI, proteomic, and cognitive test data to classify different types of dementia, including Alzheimer's and vascular dementia, with high diagnostic precision. By modeling prodromal changes, these systems enable preclinical detection, a critical step in delaying or preventing disease progression (Aghdam et al., 2025; Aljuhani et al., 2024). AI's integration with geographic information systems (GIS) further enhances its utility in public health surveillance, enabling spatiotemporal mapping of NCD hotspots and identifying social determinants of health disparities.

3.3 AI for Patient Outcome Prediction

3.3.1 Survival Analysis and Prognostic Models

Survival analysis has been a cornerstone of biostatistics in clinical trials and longitudinal studies. Traditional approaches like the Cox proportional hazards model assume linear, proportional relationships over time. AI-based survival models, such as DeepSurv and random survival forests, overcome these constraints by learning complex covariate interactions and adapting to non-linear hazard functions (Wiegrebe et al., 2024). In oncology, AI-enhanced survival models have been trained on multidimensional datasets – including imaging, genomics, and treatment protocols – to predict patient-specific survival probabilities and recurrence risks. These models are particularly valuable in tailoring follow-up strategies, identifying high-risk patients, and informing adjuvant therapy decisions.

Furthermore, critical care medicine also benefits from AI-driven prognosis. Algorithms analyzing ICU data streams – like oxygen saturation trends, ventilator settings, and medication administration – can predict in-hospital mortality or transitions to palliative care. Such tools assist clinicians in making timely decisions, balancing aggressive care with quality-of-life considerations. Moreover, survival models incorporating NLP-derived data from clinical notes provide context-aware risk estimation, offering richer insights than structured data alone. This multimodal approach marks a significant advance in individualized patient care.

3.3.2 Personalized Risk Scores in Healthcare

Personalized medicine is predicated on the ability to accurately assess an individual's risk of disease or poor outcomes. AI significantly enhances the precision and personalization of risk scoring systems by dynamically adjusting predictions based on evolving data inputs. Cardiovascular risk calculators, traditionally based on pooled cohort equations, are being supplanted by AI models that incorporate biomarkers, imaging findings, and genetic profiles. DL models trained on echocardiographic data can automatically assess cardiac function and predict heart failure exacerbations with high reliability (Jiang et al., 2025). In mental health, AI-based predictive analytics utilize data from EHRs, wearable sensors, and mobile apps to assess suicide risk, forecast depressive episodes, and monitor treatment adherence.

Notably, NLP techniques analyze linguistic cues from therapy session transcripts or online communications, offering early warning signals for relapse in mood or psychotic disorders (Malgaroli et al., 2023). Such applications highlight the growing role of AI in preventive care, empowering clinicians with tools that not only predict outcomes but also enable timely, individualized interventions that improve health trajectories.

4. APPLICATIONS OF AI-DRIVEN BIOSTATISTICS IN MEDICINE

4.1 AI in Public Health Research

4.1.1 AI-Powered Policy Decisions

In an era where data volumes are expanding exponentially, AI has emerged as a critical tool for informed policy decision-making in public health. By leveraging ML (ML) and advanced analytics, AI enables health policymakers to optimize resource allocation, forecast disease outbreaks, and tailor interventions based on population-specific health needs. Predictive models trained on demographic, clinical, and environmental data help simulate scenarios for healthcare burden under varying policy frameworks. For example, during the COVID-19 pandemic, AI-powered simulations played a vital role in evaluating the effectiveness of containment strategies and vaccination rollouts, offering governments timely evidence to adjust public health responses (Gawande et al., 2025; Hyun Lim et al., 2024).

Moreover, AI algorithms are also being applied in modeling the burden of noncommunicable diseases (NCDs), including diabetes and cardiovascular disorders, to project long-term health and economic impacts. These models assist health authorities in planning preventive strategies such as screening programs and lifestyle interventions in high-risk groups (Stevens et al., 2021). Moreover, AI tools are now integral to surveillance systems in tracking antibiotic resistance patterns and vaccine coverage across regions, providing near-real-time data to guide responsive health actions.

4.1.2 Real-World Data for Public Health Strategies

The utility of AI in public health is amplified by its capacity to integrate and analyze real-world data (RWD) from various sources, including EHRs, environmental monitoring, census data, and social media. In environmental health research, AI models are employed to evaluate the impact of air pollution, water quality, and climate change on population-level health outcomes. For instance, CNNs have been used to predict asthma exacerbations based on pollution and weather data, supporting community-based health warnings (Lopez et al., 2018).

Furthermore, social determinants of health (SDOH) such as income, housing, education, and neighborhood safety significantly influence health equity. AI has facilitated the integration of SDOH into predictive models to identify vulnerable populations and target them for tailored interventions. Recent advances include NLP applied to social service records and EHRs, enabling automated extraction of socio-economic indicators that were previously difficult to quantify (Olawade et al., 2023; Wang & Li, 2024). These advances are instrumental in designing inclusive health programs, addressing disparities in access, and measuring intervention effectiveness.

4.2 AI in Precision Medicine

4.2.1 AI-Driven Biomarker Discovery

Precision medicine aspires to provide individualized care by considering a patient's genetic, environmental, and lifestyle variability. At the core of this vision is biomarker discovery – identifying molecular indicators that can predict disease susceptibility, prognosis, or therapeutic response. Traditional methods are limited by dimensionality and noise in high-throughput datasets, but AI techniques, particularly DL, offer a powerful means of uncovering patterns in complex 'omics' data.

For example, support vector machines (SVMs), random forests, and deep neural networks (DNNs) have been utilized to identify genomic, proteomic, and metabolomic signatures associated with cancer subtypes, autoimmune disorders, and metabolic syndromes (Ali, 2023; Huang et al., 2018). In oncology, AI has been instrumental in analyzing single-cell RNA sequencing data to detect rare tumor clones, guiding personalized immunotherapies. A notable instance is the use of unsupervised learning to cluster molecular features of glioblastomas, leading to distinct biological classifications that inform therapeutic targeting (Zhan et al., 2025).

Moreover, integration of multi-modal data sources, including genomic and clinical data, enhances the predictive performance of AI models. Ensemble learning approaches combining transcriptomic profiles with imaging biomarkers have achieved high accuracy in identifying Alzheimer's disease stages, demonstrating the transformative potential of AI in biomarker-driven diagnostics.

4.2.2 Predicting Drug Response Using ML

Drug response prediction is another key area in precision medicine that has seen remarkable progress through AI. Pharmacogenomics, which studies how genes affect an individual's response to drugs, benefits from ML algorithms capable of modeling gene-drug interactions. ML has enabled the stratification of patients based on their predicted drug response, supporting the design of personalized treatment plans and avoiding adverse drug reactions. For example, gradient boosting models have been used to predict resistance to chemotherapeutic agents in breast cancer based on genomic signatures and prior treatment histories. Importantly, reinforcement learning is gaining traction in optimizing treatment regimens over time, particularly in chronic disease management. These models adapt to dynamic patient responses and side effects, guiding clinicians toward more effective, patient-centric care pathways.

4.3 AI in Clinical Trials and Drug Development

4.3.1 AI for Adaptive Trial Designs

Clinical trials are the cornerstone of evidence-based medicine, yet they are often constrained by high costs, prolonged durations, and recruitment challenges. AI has revolutionized clinical trial methodologies, particularly through adaptive trial designs that allow modifications based on interim data. ML algorithms are now utilized to optimize patient stratification, ensuring that subgroups with the highest likelihood of treatment response are adequately represented (Kim et al., 2020)

Similarly, Bayesian adaptive models, in particular, benefit from AI by incorporating real-time data streams into trial simulations. These models continuously learn and adjust treatment allocation probabilities, reducing the time to determine efficacy or futility and improving ethical allocation of interventions. AI also facilitates virtual control arms – synthetic cohorts constructed from historical or observational data – which reduce the number of patients required for placebo groups and enhance recruitment efficiency (Askin et al., 2023; Lee & Lee, 2020).

Moreover, NLP has further streamlined trial operations by extracting eligibility criteria from unstructured documents and matching them with EHRs for automated patient screening. These innovations lower trial costs and increase diversity in enrollment, promoting generalizability of findings.

4.3.2 Predicting Patient Dropout and Treatment Success

One of the under-addressed challenges in clinical research is patient adherence and retention. Dropouts can compromise statistical power and introduce bias, ultimately affecting the trial's validity. AI models now offer predictive analytics to identify patients at high risk of discontinuation based on sociodemographic data, health history, and behavioral patterns. For instance, AI-based adherence predictive model could identify high-risk patients for dropout in a clinical trial by analyzing early adherence patterns. The model achieved high accuracy in predicting nonadherence, enabling timely interventions to improve retention (Kanyongo & Ezugwu, 2023).

Besides, recurrent neural networks (RNNs) and long short-term memory (LSTM) networks, which handle sequential data, are particularly effective in modeling patient engagement over time. These models have been applied to predict dropout in mental health trials, where attrition rates are notably high. Factors such as appointment adherence, medication pickup, and wearable device usage patterns are analyzed to flag at-risk individuals, enabling timely intervention (Stech et al., 2020; Zantvoort et al., 2023). Furthermore, predictive modeling of treatment success enhances trial efficiency by focusing efforts on patients likely to benefit, facilitating adaptive dose adjustments and minimizing unnecessary exposure to ineffective therapies. AI-guided monitoring systems are increasingly incorporated into remote and decentralized trials, offering real-time alerts and feedback loops that keep patients engaged and compliant.

5. CASE STUDIES: AI-DRIVEN INSIGHTS IN HEALTHCARE DECISION-MAKING

5.1 AI in Cancer Prediction and Treatment Optimization

5.1.1 AI-Assisted Radiomics and Tumor Segmentation

Radiomics involves the extraction of high-dimensional quantitative features from medical images such as CT, MRI, and PET scans, transforming these visual data into mineable biomarkers. AI, particularly DL, has significantly advanced radiomics by automating tumor detection, classification, and segmentation processes with high accuracy and speed (Papadimitroulas et al., 2021). AI-driven radiomic tools help oncologists analyze tumor heterogeneity, vascularity, and cellular density – features often imperceptible to human interpretation but vital for personalized treatment planning (Jiang et al., 2023; Zhang et al., 2023).

CNNs, for instance, have demonstrated high efficacy in tumor segmentation across cancer types, including brain, lung, and liver cancers. One notable example is the U-Net architecture, widely adopted in biomedical imaging, which delineates tumor boundaries with pixel-level precision (Alwadee et al., 2024; Avazov et al., 2024). Automated segmentation reduces inter-observer variability and facilitates reproducible quantitative analysis, crucial for longitudinal treatment response assessments.

In non-small cell lung cancer (NSCLC), radiomics combined with AI has enabled the extraction of texture features predictive of gene mutations such as EGFR or ALK, guiding the selection of targeted therapies (Chen et al., 2023). AI also supports radiation therapy planning by mapping organs-at-risk (OARs) and optimizing dose distributions to balance efficacy and safety.

5.1.2 AI in Immunotherapy Response Prediction

Immunotherapy has transformed oncology by harnessing the immune system to target cancer, yet predicting which patients will respond remains a challenge. AI algorithms are increasingly being developed to identify immunotherapy responders using multi-modal datasets, including histopathological slides, genomics, and immunoprofiling data (Xie et al., 2023).

A pioneering application involves AI-assisted digital pathology, where whole-slide images are analyzed using DL to quantify immune cell infiltration, tumor architecture, and expression of markers such as PD-L1 (Hijazi et al., 2024). For example, attention-based neural networks have been shown to predict survival and immunotherapy response in melanoma and lung cancer by evaluating spatial arrangements of immune-tumor interactions (Saltz et al., 2018).

Moreover, ML models trained on genomic signatures (e.g., tumor mutation burden, neoantigen load) can stratify patients likely to benefit from checkpoint inhibitors. In a study involving urothelial cancer, a gradient boosting model integrating tumor mutational burden and immune gene expression profiles achieved >85% accuracy in predicting response to atezolizumab (Cristescu et al., 2018). By identifying non-responders early, AI enhances clinical decision-making, minimizing unnecessary toxicity and enabling alternative therapies. These predictive frameworks also contribute to the design of adaptive trials for novel immunotherapies, making treatment development more efficient.

5.2 AI in Cardiovascular Disease Risk Stratification

5.2.1 AI-Based ECG Interpretation and Arrhythmia Detection

Electrocardiograms (ECGs) are foundational to cardiovascular diagnostics, yet manual interpretation is time-consuming and prone to variability. AI-powered ECG interpretation systems now rival expert cardiologists in detecting subtle waveform abnormalities and diagnosing complex arrhythmias (Hannun et al., 2019).

DL models, such as those developed by the Mayo Clinic and Stanford University, have demonstrated superior performance in recognizing conditions like atrial fibrillation (AF), long QT syndrome, and left ventricular hypertrophy from raw ECG signals (Hannun et al., 2019). These models are trained on millions of labeled ECG recordings and can detect fleeting paroxysmal episodes that traditional reviews may miss.

Notably, AI-augmented ECG has expanded beyond arrhythmia detection. Researchers have developed algorithms that predict asymptomatic left ventricular dysfunction or future heart failure from normal-appearing ECGs, facilitating earlier intervention (Attia, Friedman, et al., 2019; Attia, Noseworthy, et al., 2019). Integration into wearable devices and mobile apps has democratized access to cardiovascular screening, empowering individuals and expanding outreach in underserved areas. Furthermore, continuous learning from real-time ECG streams enables personalized risk monitoring and alerts, especially beneficial for high-risk patients under remote care or post-discharge surveillance.

5.2.2 ML in Heart Failure Management

Heart failure (HF) is a complex condition requiring nuanced management decisions. ML models have been employed to stratify patients based on clinical risk, predict readmissions, and recommend evidence-based treatments. These models leverage EHR data, lab values, medication histories, and echocardiographic findings to predict adverse outcomes with greater precision than traditional risk scores like the Seattle Heart Failure Model.

Gradient boosting machines (GBMs), random forests, and recurrent neural networks (RNNs) have been particularly effective in forecasting short-term and long-term mortality in HF patients (Mpanya et al., 2021). Another innovative application involves reinforcement learning, where AI dynamically learns optimal medication adjustments and dosage changes. In the CHAMPION trial, such AI-driven systems helped optimize beta-blocker titration and diuretic management, resulting in improved functional outcomes (Costanzo et al., 2016). Importantly, these models are being incorporated into clinical decision support systems (CDSS), offering physicians real-time guidance tailored to individual patient trajectories, thus enhancing both safety and efficacy in HF care.

5.3 AI in Rare Disease Diagnosis and Patient Identification

5.3.1 AI-Driven Phenotyping for Rare Genetic Disorders

Rare diseases often present with complex, heterogeneous symptoms that defy conventional diagnostic pathways. AI is proving transformative in this field by enabling phenotypic clustering, anomaly detection, and genotype-phenotype correlation analysis. Facial recognition algorithms powered by DL, such as DeepGestalt, have achieved over 90% accuracy in identifying syndromic features associated with more than 200 genetic conditions using patient photos (Gurovich et al., 2019). These tools assist pediatricians and geneticists in flagging potential disorders during routine assessments, accelerating referrals for confirmatory testing.

NLP techniques are also utilized to mine unstructured EHR narratives for clinical descriptions suggestive of rare disorders. By converting free-text clinical notes into structured phenotypic profiles, AI tools like Phenotips and PheRS facilitate matchmaking against known disease ontologies and aid in diagnosis (Girdea et al., 2013). In genomics, AI enhances variant prioritization by integrating inheritance patterns, evolutionary conservation, and predicted pathogenicity scores. This enables faster and more accurate interpretation of whole exome and genome sequencing results, reducing the diagnostic odyssey for patients and families.

5.3.2 Use of Federated Learning in Rare Disease Research

One major barrier in rare disease research is the limited availability of large, centralized datasets due to privacy concerns and patient dispersion across multiple sites. Federated learning (FL), a privacy-preserving AI paradigm, addresses this challenge by enabling decentralized model training across multiple institutions without sharing patient data. In FL frameworks, local models are trained on-site using patient-level data and only model parameters (not raw data) are shared with a central server, where they are aggregated to improve a global model. This approach preserves confidentiality and regulatory compliance, particularly under data protection laws like GDPR and HIPAA.

Federated learning has been successfully applied in rare diseases such as amyotrophic lateral sclerosis (ALS), Huntington's disease, and pediatric cancers. A prominent case study by Sheller et al. (2020) demonstrated that FL models trained on distributed brain tumor data across multiple centers achieved comparable performance to models trained on pooled data, without compromising patient privacy. This paradigm shift not only fosters cross-institutional collaborations but also improves algorithm generalizability by exposing models to diverse populations and imaging modalities, ultimately enhancing diagnostic accuracy for rare conditions. Notably, the study by Zhang et. al illustrates novel federated learning techniques for rare disease data, addressing scalability challenges in existing analysis and reinforcing the utility of decentralized AI in biostatistics (Zhang et al., 2024).

6. CHALLENGES AND ETHICAL CONSIDERATIONS

The integration of AI-driven biostatistics into healthcare offers transformative potential but also raises complex ethical, legal, and practical challenges. Ensuring that AI models are fair, secure, explainable, and respectful of patient autonomy is essential for trustworthy deployment. This section explores critical ethical dimensions of AI in healthcare, focusing on bias and fairness, privacy and data security, interpretability and explainability, and regulatory considerations.

6.1 Bias and Fairness in AI-Driven Biostatistics

6.1.1 Addressing Algorithmic Bias

Sources of Bias in AI Models: Bias in AI systems often originates from historical data that reflects existing inequalities in healthcare access, diagnosis, and treatment. For instance, training datasets may underrepresent minority populations or reflect systemic biases in clinical documentation and diagnostic labeling (Cross et al., 2024). These imbalances can lead to skewed model performance, where AI algorithms underperform for certain demographic groups, exacerbating existing health disparities. Algorithmic bias can also stem from data preprocessing methods, feature selection, and the lack of contextual sensitivity in model design. For example, the use of race as a proxy for biological differences can reinforce inequities rather than address them (Cross et al., 2024). Moreover, biases may be inadvertently introduced during the development pipeline through subjective annotation by clinical experts or due to limited validation across population subgroups.

Strategies for Bias Detection and Mitigation: To address bias, it is essential to incorporate fairness-aware ML frameworks that assess model outcomes across diverse population segments. Bias detection can be carried out using statistical fairness metrics, such as demographic parity, equalized odds, or disparate impact ratios (Castelnovo et al., 2022). Additionally, bias audits should be embedded as standard practice in model evaluation. Mitigation strategies include data augmentation to ensure balanced representation, reweighting or re-sampling of underrepresented classes, adversarial de-biasing, and fairness constraints during model optimization. Furthermore, participatory model development – engaging patients, clinicians, and community stakeholders in design – can help align model objectives with ethical goals and community values.

6.1.2 Ensuring Equitable AI Models

Representation of Diverse Populations in AI Training Data: Ensuring equity in AI requires the inclusion of data from racially, ethnically, and socioeconomically diverse populations. Unfortunately, many AI models are trained using data from tertiary centers or high-income countries, limiting their generalizability to underserved communities (Cross et al., 2024). However, the study by Yang et al examines fairness disparities across healthcare settings, offering empirical insights into mitigating bias in diverse populations - strengthening the analysis of equitable AI model design (Cross et al., 2024; Yang et al., 2024). This lack of diversity may lead to lower accuracy in populations with different disease prevalence, comorbidities, or healthcare-seeking behavior. Global efforts to promote data equity include the creation of diverse, representative biobanks and the adoption of data governance frameworks that prioritize inclusivity. Multinational collaborations are also promoting open-source AI benchmarks across geographies to democratize access to diverse data.

AI for Reducing Health Disparities: Paradoxically, when designed ethically, AI has the potential to reduce disparities by improving access to diagnostic tools in resource-limited settings. Mobile AI applications for skin cancer detection, portable ultrasound interpretation, and automated diabetic retinopathy screening have expanded care to rural areas (Perez et al., 2025). AI models trained on diverse datasets can provide decision support for primary care physicians, bridging gaps in specialist availability. However, deploying these tools equitably requires culturally appropriate design, transparent communication with communities, and mechanisms for ongoing model refinement based on real-world outcomes.

6.2 Privacy and Data Security Issues

6.2.1 Ethical AI in Healthcare Data Usage

Challenges in Obtaining Informed Consent for AI Research: AI models are often trained on large-scale retrospective datasets, where traditional informed consent may not be feasible. Furthermore, future uses of data in AI applications may not be known at the time of collection, complicating ethical approval and patient understanding (Khalifa & Albadawy, 2024). Broad consent models, while administratively convenient, may fail to uphold autonomy if not coupled with continuous patient engagement and governance transparency. Dynamic consent frameworks, which allow participants to adjust their data-sharing preferences over time through digital platforms, offer a promising alternative. These models enhance agency and trust but require infrastructural investment and digital literacy support.

Ethical Dilemmas in Automated Healthcare Decision-Making: AI systems capable of autonomous or semi-autonomous decision-making raise ethical concerns regarding accountability and the potential dehumanization of care (Farhud & Zokaei, 2021). In cases where AI recommends or overrides clinical judgments—such as ICU triage or cancer treatment planning—the lines of responsibility become blurred (Nord-Bronzyk et al., 2025). Clear documentation of AI recommendations, shared decision-making with patients, and clinician oversight are essential to maintain ethical integrity. Regulatory standards must ensure that AI tools support, rather than replace, human empathy and professional expertise.

6.2.2 Balancing Data Sharing and Patient Confidentiality

Privacy-Preserving AI Techniques: To facilitate AI development while preserving patient privacy, novel computational techniques have been introduced. Federated learning enables model training across decentralized datasets – such as data from different hospitals – without transferring sensitive patient information (F. Zhang et al., 2024). Each institution trains the model locally and only shares model updates, preserving confidentiality. Differential privacy adds statistical noise to individual data contributions, making re-identification nearly impossible while allowing aggregate insights. These techniques are critical for compliance with privacy regulations and public trust, especially when data are shared across institutional or national boundaries.

Regulatory Frameworks (GDPR, HIPAA): Compliance with legal frameworks such as the General Data Protection Regulation (GDPR) in Europe and the Health Insurance Portability and Accountability Act (HIPAA) in the U.S. (Pantanowitz et al., 2024) is mandatory for ethical AI deployment. These regulations require transparency in data usage, data minimization, and patient control over personal health information. Emerging regulations, such as the EU Artificial Intelligence Act, are likely to classify many medical AI systems as high-risk, requiring robust documentation, risk management, and post-market surveillance. Thus, ethical AI must be embedded in both technological design and regulatory compliance.

6.3 Interpretability and Explainability of AI Models

6.3.1 Making AI Models Understandable for Clinicians and Policymakers

Explainable AI (XAI) Techniques in Healthcare: Black-box models such as deep neural networks often lack interpretability, hindering their adoption in clinical settings. Explainable AI (XAI) aims to make model outputs understandable and justifiable to end users. Techniques such as SHAP (SHapley Additive exPlanations), LIME (Local Interpretable Model-Agnostic Explanations), and attention mechanisms offer insight into feature contributions and decision pathways (Nambiar et al., 2023). Interpretable models enhance trust, facilitate regulatory approval, and enable clinicians to evaluate the clinical plausibility of AI-generated recommendations. XAI is particularly important in high-stakes decisions such as cancer diagnosis, where model transparency can guide second opinions and patient counseling.

The Importance of Human-AI Collaboration: AI systems should augment rather than replace human decision-making. Clinical workflows that integrate AI suggestions while preserving clinician autonomy result in better acceptance and patient outcomes. Human-AI collaboration promotes accountability, contextual reasoning, and moral judgment – dimensions that AI alone cannot replicate (Vaccaro et al., 2024). Building interfaces that present AI insights alongside clinical indicators and supporting evidence allows for informed decision-making. Equally important is training healthcare professionals to understand AI limitations and interpret model outputs critically.

6.3.2 Regulatory Challenges for AI in Healthcare

FDA and EMA Perspectives on AI-Driven Medical Devices: Regulatory agencies such as the U.S. Food and Drug Administration (FDA) and the European Medicines Agency (EMA) are adapting to the dynamic nature of AI. The FDA has introduced a framework for Software as a Medical Device (SaMD), with specific provisions for continuously learning algorithms. These frameworks require transparent documentation, risk categorization, and a predefined change control plan (European Medicines Agency, 2024; U.S. Food & Drug Administration, 2021). The EMA has similarly issued guidelines emphasizing data quality, performance metrics, and bias risk assessments in AI-based medical products. Regulatory harmonization and international collaboration are needed to facilitate cross-border adoption of AI tools in global health.

Ethical Implications of Autonomous Decision-Making in Healthcare: As AI systems evolve toward greater autonomy – such as robotic surgery, remote diagnostics, or autonomous drug dosing – the ethical stakes intensify. Concerns arise regarding patient safety, consent, liability, and the potential displacement of human roles. Determining when it is ethically acceptable for AI to make or recommend critical healthcare decisions is an ongoing debate. The principle of "meaningful human control" must be upheld, where humans retain the final authority in life-altering decisions. Moreover, interdisciplinary governance frameworks involving ethicists, clinicians, data scientists, and patients are necessary to navigate the responsible evolution of healthcare AI.

7. THE FUTURE OF AI-INTEGRATED BIOSTATISTICS

As the convergence of AI and biostatistics reshapes the healthcare landscape, future developments will depend not only on technological progress but also on ethical governance, equitable access, and interdisciplinary cooperation. Looking ahead, several emerging trends, innovative research directions, and policy implications will shape the trajectory of AI-integrated biostatistics.

7.1 Emerging Trends in AI and Biostatistics

7.1.1 AI for Causal Inference in Healthcare Research

Traditionally, biostatistical models have more focused on associations rather than causality. However, the rise of AI has opened new avenues for integrating ML techniques with causal inference frameworks. Methods such as causal forests, Bayesian networks, and targeted maximum likelihood estimation (TMLE) are being increasingly employed to estimate treatment effects and uncover underlying mechanisms from observational data (Luque-Fernandez et al., 2018). Furthermore, the study by Meder et al demonstrates how AI refines causal inference in cardiovascular outcomes research, providing practical examples of translating observational data into actionable causal insights (Meder et. al, 2025).

Unlike classical regression-based causal models, modern AI-driven approaches can accommodate high-dimensional and non-linear relationships without strict parametric assumptions. This is particularly useful in real-world data analyses where confounding and selection bias are prevalent. For instance, in pharmacoepidemiology, AI-based causal modeling is being applied to estimate comparative effectiveness of treatments across diverse subpopulations using EHRs. In the near future, we can expect broader adoption of counterfactual prediction models and hybrid systems that combine ML with structural causal models. These innovations will enable more nuanced understanding of healthcare interventions, particularly in precision medicine, where the goal is to personalize causal inferences at the patient level.

7.1.2 Integration of AI With Blockchain for Secure Health Data Management

As data privacy remains a pressing issue in healthcare AI, the fusion of AI and blockchain technology is gaining momentum. Blockchain offers decentralized, tamper-proof data storage, making it a promising partner for secure and transparent health data management. By leveraging smart contracts, healthcare systems can facilitate controlled access to patient data for AI model training without compromising confidentiality. Blockchain-integrated AI systems can enhance data provenance, ensuring that every data access or modification is traceable. This is especially relevant in biostatistics applications involving multi-center collaborations, where data integrity and auditability are critical. Federated AI training combined with blockchain further ensures that no raw data leaves the local site, supporting privacy-preserving analytics at scale. In the future, we may see AI-powered digital twins or personalized health records anchored in blockchain ecosystems, enabling real-time, secure analysis across institutions, particularly for chronic disease management and population health surveillance.

7.2 Future Research Directions and Innovations

7.2.1 AI-Driven Meta-Analyses for Evidence Synthesis

Systematic reviews and meta-analyses form the cornerstone of evidence-based healthcare, but they are time-consuming and prone to human subjectivity. AI is poised to transform this space through automation and intelligent synthesis. NLP techniques are now being developed to automate literature screening, data extraction, and quality assessment of studies (Badalotti et al., 2024). More innovatively, ML-based meta-analysis models can account for study heterogeneity, detect reporting bias, and update effect estimates in real time as new evidence emerges. For example, Bayesian meta-analytical approaches augmented by ML can model uncertainty and detect publication bias patterns, providing a more robust basis for clinical guidelines. In the next decade, AI-driven evidence synthesis could support living meta-analyses, which automatically incorporate new trial results and continuously update estimates, offering clinicians up-to-date information at the point of care. These tools will be particularly useful during public health emergencies, where rapid evidence integration is crucial.

7.2.2 AI for Global Health and Low-Resource Settings

While AI advancements have predominantly benefited high-income countries, there is growing interest in deploying AI-based solutions tailored to low-resource environments. Innovations such as mobile AI applications, offline-compatible diagnostic algorithms, and solar-powered diagnostic tools are expanding healthcare reach in remote areas. In biostatistics, AI models trained on minimal inputs (e.g., symptoms, demographic data) can enable risk stratification and triage in places where laboratory diagnostics are unavailable. AI has also shown promise in epidemic forecasting, resource allocation, and vaccine distribution modeling in underserved populations. To truly empower global health, AI tools must be contextualized – designed with cultural sensitivity, validated using local data, and co-created with community stakeholders. Open-source platforms, international research consortia, and capacity-building initiatives will be pivotal in ensuring that the benefits of AI-driven biostatistics extend across geographical and economic divides.

7.3 Policy and Regulatory Considerations for AI in Healthcare

7.3.1 Ethical AI Governance Frameworks

As AI systems become deeply embedded in healthcare delivery and research, there is a growing demand for robust ethical governance. Policymakers are increasingly advocating for frameworks that ensure transparency, accountability, and fairness across the AI lifecycle – from data collection and model development to deployment and monitoring.

Key elements of such frameworks include *impact assessments* that evaluate ethical risks and benefits, *bias audits* to monitor performance across demographic groups, *ethical review boards* inclusive of technical experts, ethicists, and patient representatives, and post-deployment surveillance for detecting unintended consequences or model drift. Recent policy developments, such as the WHO's guidance on ethical AI in health and the European Union's proposed AI Act, underscore the importance of risk-based regulation, requiring higher scrutiny for AI systems that impact human health. Future governance will likely adopt adaptive regulatory models, where AI tools undergo continuous evaluation rather than a one-time approval.

7.3.2 The Role of Interdisciplinary Collaboration in AI Policymaking

Effective AI policy cannot be crafted in isolation by technologists or regulators. Interdisciplinary collaboration is essential to ensure that AI policies are practically feasible, clinically relevant, and ethically grounded. Biostatisticians play a critical role in this dialogue by providing methodological insights into model validation, uncertainty quantification, and population-level impacts. Moreover, involving clinicians, patients, public health experts, and social scientists ensures that policies reflect the lived experiences of those affected by AI technologies. Policymaking should also be informed by empirical research on AI implementation, examining real-world barriers and facilitators to adoption. Academic institutions and professional societies are encouraged to develop policy labs or multidisciplinary think tanks where innovation and regulation can co-evolve. These collaborations will be key to shaping AI policies that are anticipatory rather than reactive, enabling safe, equitable, and responsible AI integration into health systems worldwide.

8. CONCLUSION

8.1 The Potential of AI to Transform Medical Decision-Making

The fusion of AI with biostatistics marks a significant paradigm shift in how data is harnessed to improve human health. This chapter has explored the transformative potential of AI in reshaping biostatistical applications across healthcare domains, from disease prediction and early diagnostics to precision medicine, public health surveillance, and clinical trial optimization. A key contribution of AI lies in its ability to process large, complex, and often unstructured datasets – such as imaging, genomic sequences, and EHRs – with a level of speed and depth not previously possible. ML algorithms, particularly DL models, have enabled early detection of diseases like cancer and cardiovascular disorders, offering improved accuracy in prediction and diagnosis over conventional statistical methods. AI has also empowered healthcare providers with real-time insights into patient risk, allowing for timely interventions and resource optimization, especially in critical care environments like ICUs.

Importantly, AI has augmented traditional biostatistical methods by introducing adaptive modeling, non-linear inference capabilities, and real-time learning from incoming data. These advancements are pivotal in modern epidemiology, enabling faster detection of outbreaks and more precise estimation of disease burdens. In the realm of drug development, AI-driven biostatistics has accelerated clinical research by enhancing adaptive trial designs, predicting patient dropouts, and identifying subgroups likely to respond to targeted therapies. Furthermore, the application of AI in public health has broadened the scope of biostatistical insights beyond clinical settings. From modeling environmental exposures to identifying social determinants of health, AI tools are informing population-level strategies with greater precision and agility. AI's role in health equity is also beginning to take shape, with applications aimed at identifying and addressing disparities in care delivery. However, this integration is not without complexity. The adoption of AI in biostatistics and healthcare requires careful consideration of ethical, regulatory, and operational issues. The challenges of algorithmic bias, model explainability, data privacy, and equitable access to AI technologies underscore the need for responsible innovation guided by interdisciplinary collaboration.

8.2 The Road Ahead for AI in Biostatistics and Healthcare

As we stand on the rim of a new era in healthcare analytics, it is evident that AI will continue to play a central role in transforming medical decision-making and research methodologies. However, realizing the full potential of AI in biostatistics depends on addressing several critical challenges and embracing a collaborative, forward-thinking approach. One of the foremost challenges is ensuring fairness and inclusivity in AI models. Training datasets must adequately represent diverse populations across age, gender, ethnicity, and geography to prevent reinforcing existing health disparities. Algorithmic transparency and rigorous bias audits should become standard practices to build trust among stakeholders, including clinicians, patients, and policymakers. Another significant hurdle lies in bridging the gap between AI model development and clinical implementation. While academic prototypes demonstrate promising accuracy, the translation of these models into everyday clinical workflows often encounters resistance due to concerns over reliability, interpretability, and integration with existing health information systems. Collaborative efforts between AI developers, biostatisticians, healthcare professionals, and IT specialists are essential to ensure usability and contextual relevance of AI solutions. Moreover, the interpretability of AI models remains a priority area for future research. The emergence of explainable AI techniques offers a pathway for demystifying complex algorithms, enabling clinicians and decision-makers to understand the rationale behind model outputs. This is particularly important in high-stakes environments, where trust and transparency are crucial for patient safety.

From a regulatory perspective, national and international bodies must evolve their frameworks to accommodate the dynamic nature of AI technologies. The traditional linear approval processes for medical devices are often incompatible with AI systems that continuously learn and adapt. Adaptive regulatory models, periodic post-deployment evaluations, and the inclusion of ethical review boards can help ensure that AI tools remain safe, effective, and aligned with societal values. Looking ahead, the intersection of AI with other emerging technologies – such as blockchain for secure data sharing, Internet of Things for real-time health monitoring, and quantum computing for complex simulations – will further redefine the scope of biostatistics. These convergences hold immense promise for developing scalable, secure, and globally accessible AI solutions in healthcare. Crucially, the future of AI in biostatistics is inherently interdisciplinary. The collaboration of biostatisticians, data scientists, clinicians, epidemiologists, ethicists, and policymakers will be fundamental in shaping the trajectory of AI-driven healthcare. Educational institutions and professional societies must also adapt by embedding AI literacy into biostatistical training, thereby equipping the next generation of researchers with the skills needed to navigate this evolving landscape.

In conclusion, AI-integrated biostatistics stands at the frontier of a healthcare revolution. With responsible innovation, inclusive design, and interdisciplinary synergy, AI has the potential not only to enhance statistical precision and efficiency but also to fundamentally reimagine how we understand, prevent, and treat disease. The journey ahead is complex but promising – and the thoughtful application of AI in biostatistics will be instrumental in creating a future of equitable, data-driven, and patient-centered healthcare.

REFERENCES

Abdeljaber, A., Al Smadi, S., Talib, M. A., & Abdallah, M. (2025). Comparative Analysis of Machine Learning and Conventional Methods for Waste Generation Forecasting. *Cleaner Engineering and Technology*, *27*, 100992. Advance online publication. DOI: 10.1016/j.clet.2025.100992

Aghdam, M. A., Bozdag, S., & Saeed, F. (2025). Machine-learning models for Alzheimer's disease diagnosis using neuroimaging data: Survey, reproducibility, and generalizability evaluation. *Brain Informatics*, *12*(8), 8. Advance online publication. DOI: 10.1186/s40708-025-00252-3

Al-Garadi, M. A., Yang, Y. C., & Sarker, A. (2022). The Role of Natural Language Processing during the COVID-19 Pandemic: Health Applications, Opportunities, and Challenges. *Healthcare (Basel)*, *10*(2270), 2270. Advance online publication. DOI: 10.3390/healthcare10112270

Ali, H. (2023). Artificial intelligence in multi-omics data integration : Advancing precision medicine, biomarker discovery and genomic-driven disease interventions. *International Journal of Science and Research Archive*, *08*(01), 1012–1030. DOI: 10.30574/ijsra.2023.8.1.0189

Aljuhani, M., Ashraf, A., & Edison, P. (2024). Use of Artificial Intelligence in Imaging Dementia. *Cells*, *13*(1965). DOI: 10.62486/latia202492

Alowais, S. A., Alghamdi, S. S., Alsuhebany, N., Alqahtani, T., Alshaya, A. I., Almohareb, S. N., Aldairem, A., Alrashed, M., & Saleh, K. (2023). Revolutionizing healthcare: The role of artificial intelligence in clinical practice. *BMC Medical Education*, *23*(1), 689. DOI: 10.1186/s12909-023-04698-z

Alsadi, B., Musleh, S., Al-Absi, H. R. H., Refaee, M., Qureshi, R., El Hajj, N., & Alam, T. (2024). An ensemble-based machine learning model for predicting type 2 diabetes and its effect on bone health. *BMC Medical Informatics and Decision Making*, *24*(144), 144. Advance online publication. DOI: 10.1186/s12911-024-02540-0

Alwadee, E. J., Sun, X., Qin, Y., & Langbein, F. C. (2024). LATUP-Net: A Lightweight 3D Attention U-Net with Parallel Convolutions for Brain Tumor Segmentation. *Computers in Biology and Medicine*, *184*(109353), 109353. Advance online publication. DOI: 10.1016/j.compbiomed.2024.109353

Ansari, Y., Mourad, O., Qaraqe, K., & Serpedin, E. (2023). Deep learning for ECG Arrhythmia detection and classification: An overview of progress for period 2017–2023. *Frontiers in Physiology*, *14*(1246746), 1246746. Advance online publication. DOI: 10.3389/fphys.2023.1246746

Askin, S., Burkhalter, D., Calado, G., & El Dakrouni, S. (2023). Artificial Intelligence Applied to clinical trials: Opportunities and challenges. *Health and Technology*, *13*(2), 203–213. DOI: 10.1007/s12553-023-00738-2

Attia, Z. I., Friedman, P. A., Noseworthy, P. A., Lopez-Jimenez, F., Ladewig, D. J., Satam, G., Pellikka, P. A., Munger, T. M., Asirvatham, S. J., Scott, C. G., Carter, R. E., & Kapa, S. (2019). Age and Sex Estimation Using Artificial Intelligence from Standard 12-Lead ECGs. *Circulation: Arrhythmia and Electrophysiology*, *12*(9), e007284. Advance online publication. DOI: 10.1161/CIRCEP.119.007284

Attia, Z. I., Noseworthy, P. A., Lopez-Jimenez, F., Asirvatham, S. J., Deshmukh, A. J., Gersh, B. J., Carter, R. E., Yao, X., Rabinstein, A. A., Erickson, B. J., Kapa, S., & Friedman, P. A. (2019). An artificial intelligence-enabled ECG algorithm for the identification of patients with atrial fibrillation during sinus rhythm: A retrospective analysis of outcome prediction. *Lancet*, *394*(10201), 861–867. DOI: 10.1016/S0140-6736(19)31721-0

Avazov, K., Mirzakhalilov, S., Umirzakova, S., Abdusalomov, A., & Cho, Y. I. (2024). Dynamic Focus on Tumor Boundaries: A Lightweight U-Net for MRI Brain Tumor Segmentation. *Bioengineering (Basel, Switzerland)*, *11*(1302), 1302. Advance online publication. DOI: 10.3390/bioengineering11121302

Badalotti, D., Agrawal, A., Pensato, U., Angelotti, G., & Marcheselli, S. (2024). Development of a Natural Language Processing (NLP) model to automatically extract clinical data from electronic health records: Results from an Italian comprehensive stroke center. *International Journal of Medical Informatics*, *192*(105626), 105626. Advance online publication. DOI: 10.1016/j.ijmedinf.2024.105626

Bilal, A., Imran, A., Baig, T. I., Liu, X., Abouel Nasr, E., & Long, H. (2024). Breast cancer diagnosis using support vector machine optimized by improved quantum inspired grey wolf optimization. *Scientific Reports*, *14*(10714), 10714. Advance online publication. DOI: 10.1038/s41598-024-61322-w

Brendel, M., Su, C., Bai, Z., Zhang, H., Elemento, O., & Wang, F. (2022). Application of Deep Learning on Single-cell RNA Sequencing Data Analysis: A Review. *Genomics, Proteomics & Bioinformatics*, *20*(5), 814–835. DOI: 10.1016/j.gpb.2022.11.011

Castelnovo, A., Crupi, R., Greco, G., Regoli, D., Penco, I. G., & Cosentini, A. C. (2022). A clarification of the nuances in the fairness metrics landscape. *Scientific Reports*, *12*(4209), 4209. Advance online publication. DOI: 10.1038/s41598-022-07939-1

Chen, M., Copley, S. J., Viola, P., Lu, H., & Aboagye, E. O. (2023). Radiomics and artificial intelligence for precision medicine in lung cancer treatment. *Seminars in Cancer Biology*, *93*, 97–113. DOI: 10.1016/j.semcancer.2023.05.004

Costanzo, M. R., Stevenson, L. W., Adamson, P. B., Desai, A. S., Heywood, J. T., Bourge, R. C., Ms, J. B., & Abraham, W. T. (2016). Interventions Linked to Decreased Heart Failure Hospitalizations During Ambulatory Pulmonary Artery Pressure Monitoring. *JACC. Heart Failure*, *4*(5), 333–344. DOI: 10.1016/j.jchf.2015.11.011

Cristescu, R., Mogg, R., Ayers, M., Albright, A., Murphy, E., Sher, X., Liu, X. Q., Lu, H., Nebozhyn, M., Lunceford, J. K., Joe, A., Cheng, J., Webber, A. L., Ibrahim, N., Plimack, E. R., Ott, P. A., Seiwert, T. Y., Mcclanahan, T. K., Tomassini, J. E., & Kaufman, D. (2018). Pan-tumor genomic biomarkers for PD-1 checkpoint blockade– based immunotherapy. *Science*, *362*(6411), eaar3593. Advance online publication. DOI: 10.1126/science.aar3593

Cross, J. L., Choma, M. A., & Onofrey, J. A. (2024). Bias in medical AI: Implications for clinical decision-making. *PLOS Digital Health*, *3*(11), e0000651. Advance online publication. DOI: 10.1371/journal.pdig.0000651

European Medicines Agency. (2024). *Reflection paper on the use of Artificial Intelligence (AI) in the medicinal product lifecycle*. https://www.ema.europa.eu/en/documents/scientific-guideline/draft-reflection-paper-use-artificial-intelligence-ai-medicinal-product-lifecycle_en.pdf

Farhud, D. D., & Zokaei, S. (2021). Ethical issues of artificial intelligence in medicine and healthcare. *Iranian Journal of Public Health*, *50*(11), i–v. DOI: 10.18502/ijph.v50i11.7600

U.S. Food & Drug Administration. (2021). *Artificial Intelligence/Machine Learning (AI/ML)-Based Software as a Medical Device (SaMD) Action Plan*. DOI: 10.1145/3447548.3470823

Freiesleben, T., König, G., Molnar, C., & Tejero-Cantero, Á. (2024). Scientific Inference with Interpretable Machine Learning: Analyzing Models to Learn About Real-World Phenomena. In *Minds and Machines* (Vol. 34, Issue 32). Springer Netherlands. DOI: 10.1007/s11023-024-09691-z

Fridgeirsson, E. A., Williams, R., Rijnbeek, P., Suchard, M. A., & Reps, J. M. (2024). Comparing penalization methods for linear models on large observational health data. *Journal of the American Medical Informatics Association : JAMIA*, *31*(7), 1514–1521. DOI: 10.1093/jamia/ocae109

Gawande, M. S., Zade, N., Kumar, P., Gundewar, S., Weerarathna, I. N., & Verma, P. (2025). The role of artificial intelligence in pandemic responses: From epidemiological modeling to vaccine development. *Molecular Biomedicine*, *6*(1), 1. Advance online publication. DOI: 10.1186/s43556-024-00238-3

Ginghina, O., Hudita, A., Zamfir, M., Spanu, A., Mardare, M., Bondoc, I., Buburuzan, L., Georgescu, S. E., Costache, M., Negrei, C., Nitipir, C., & Galateanu, B. (2022). Liquid Biopsy and Artificial Intelligence as Tools to Detect Signatures of Colorectal Malignancies: A Modern Approach in Patient's Stratification. *Frontiers in Oncology*, *12*(856575), 856575. Advance online publication. DOI: 10.3389/fonc.2022.856575

Girdea, M., Dumitriu, S., Fiume, M., Bowdin, S., Boycott, K. M., Chénier, S., Chitayat, D., Faghfoury, H., Meyn, M. S., Ray, P. N., So, J., Stavropoulos, D. J., & Brudno, M. (2013). PhenoTips: Patient phenotyping software for clinical and research use. *Human Mutation*, *34*(8), 1057–1065. DOI: 10.1002/humu.22347

Goldstein, N. D., Levasseur, M., & Mcclure, L. A. (2020). On the Convergence of Epidemiology, Biostatistics, and Data Science. *Harvard Data Science Review*, *2*, 2. DOI: 10.1162/99608f92.9f0215e6

Gupta, U., Paluru, N., Nankani, D., Kulkarni, K., & Awasthi, N. (2024). A comprehensive review on efficient artificial intelligence models for classification of abnormal cardiac rhythms using electrocardiograms. *Heliyon*, *10*(5, e26787), e26787. Advance online publication. DOI: 10.1016/j.heliyon.2024.e26787

Gurovich, Y., Hanani, Y., Bar, O., Nadav, G., Fleischer, N., Gelbman, D., Basel-Salmon, L., Krawitz, P. M., Kamphausen, S. B., Zenker, M., Bird, L. M., & Gripp, K. W. (2019). Identifying facial phenotypes of genetic disorders using deep learning. *Nature Medicine*, *25*(1), 60–64. DOI: 10.1038/s41591-018-0279-0

Hannun, A. Y., Rajpurkar, P., Haghpanahi, M., Tison, G. H., Bourn, C., Turakhia, M. P., & Ng, A. Y. (2019). Cardiologist-Level Arrhythmia Detection and Classification in Ambulatory Electrocardiograms Using a Deep Neural Network. *Nature Medicine*, *25*(1), 65–69. DOI: 10.1038/s41591-018-0268-3

Hijazi, A., Bifulco, C., Baldin, P., & Galon, J. (2024). Digital Pathology for Better Clinical Practice. *Cancers, 16*(1686). DOI: 10.3390/cancers16091686

Hosmer, D. W., Jr., Lemeshow, S., & Sturdivant, R. X. (2013). Applied Logistic Regression. In *John Wiley & Sons, Hoboken, NJ.* DOI: 10.1002/9781118548387

Hossain, E., Rana, R., Higgins, N., Soar, J., Barua, P. D., Pisani, A. R., & Turner, K. (2023). Natural Language Processing in Electronic Health Records in relation to healthcare decision-making: A systematic review. *Computers in Biology and Medicine*, *155*, 106649. Advance online publication. DOI: 10.1016/j.compbiomed.2023.106649

Huang, S., Nianguang, C. A. I., Penzuti Pacheco, P., Narandes, S., Wang, Y., & Wayne, X. U. (2018). Applications of support vector machine (SVM) learning in cancer genomics. *Cancer Genomics & Proteomics*, *15*(1), 41–51. DOI: 10.21873/cgp.20063

Hyun Lim, S., Hersi, M., Krishnan, R., Montroy, J., Rook, B., Farrah, K., Chung, Y. E., Stevens, A., Zafack, J., Wong, E., Forbes, N., Killikelly, A., Young, K., & Tunis, M. (2024). COVID-19 vaccine evidence monitoring assisted by artificial Intelligence: An emergency system implemented by the Public Health Agency of Canada to capture and describe the trajectory of evolving pandemic vaccine literature. *Vaccine: X*, *21*(100575), 100575. Advance online publication. DOI: 10.1016/j.jvacx.2024.100575

Imam, F., Musilek, P., & Reformat, M. Z. (2024). Parametric and Nonparametric Machine Learning Techniques for Increasing Power System Reliability: A Review. *Information (Basel)*, *15*(37), 37. Advance online publication. DOI: 10.3390/info15010037

Islam, K. R., Prithula, J., Kumar, J., Tan, T. L., Reaz, M. B. I., Sumon, M. S. I., & Chowdhury, M. E. H. (2023). Machine Learning-Based Early Prediction of Sepsis Using Electronic Health Records: A Systematic Review. *Journal of Clinical Medicine*, *12*(5658), 5658. Advance online publication. DOI: 10.3390/jcm12175658

Javed, H., El-Sappagh, S., & Abuhmed, T. (2025). Robustness in deep learning models for medical diagnostics: Security and adversarial challenges towards robust AI applications. *Artificial Intelligence Review*, *58*(12), 12. Advance online publication. DOI: 10.1007/s10462-024-11005-9

Jayaraman, P., Desman, J., Sabounchi, M., Nadkarni, G. N., & Sakhuja, A. (2024). A Primer on Reinforcement Learning in Medicine for Clinicians. *NPJ Digital Medicine*, *7*(337), 337. Advance online publication. DOI: 10.1038/s41746-024-01316-0

Jiang, L., Zuo, H. J., & Chen, C. (2025). Artificial intelligence in echocardiography: Applications and future directions Luying. *Fundamental Research (Beijing)*. Advance online publication. DOI: 10.1016/j.fmre.2025.01.020

Jiang, X., Hu, Z., Wang, S., & Zhang, Y. (2023). Deep Learning for Medical Image-Based Cancer Diagnosis. *Cancers (Basel)*, *15*(3608), 3608. Advance online publication. DOI: 10.3390/cancers15143608

Kanyongo, W., & Ezugwu, A. E. (2023). Machine learning approaches to medication adherence amongst NCD patients: A systematic literature review. *Informatics in Medicine Unlocked*, *38*(101210), 101210. Advance online publication. DOI: 10.1016/j.imu.2023.101210

Karalis, V. D. (2024). The Integration of Artificial Intelligence into Clinical Practice. *Applied Biosciences*, *3*(1), 14–44. DOI: 10.3390/applbiosci3010002

Khalifa, M., & Albadawy, M. (2024). Artificial Intelligence for Clinical Prediction: Exploring Key Domains and Essential Functions. *Computer Methods and Programs in Biomedicine Update*, *5*(100148), 100148. Advance online publication. DOI: 10.1016/j.cmpbup.2024.100148

Khokhar, P. B., Gravino, C., & Palomba, F. (2025). Advances in artificial intelligence for diabetes prediction: Insights from a systematic literature review. *Artificial Intelligence in Medicine*, *164*(103132), 103132. Advance online publication. DOI: 10.1016/j.artmed.2025.103132

Kim, J., Greenberg, D. E., Pifer, R., Jiang, S., Xiao, G., Shelburne, S. A., Koh, A., Xie, Y., & Zhan, X. (2020). VaMPR: VAriant Mapping and Prediction of antibiotic resistance via explainable features and machine learning. *PLoS Computational Biology*, *16*(1), e1007511. Advance online publication. DOI: 10.1371/journal.pcbi.1007511

Kwon, D., Kang, H., Lee, D., & Kim, Y. C. (2025). Deep learning-based prediction of atrial fibrillation from polar transformed time-frequency electrocardiogram. *PLoS One*, *20*(3), e0317630. Advance online publication. DOI: 10.1371/journal.pone.0317630

Lee, C. S., & Lee, A. Y. (2020). How artificial intelligence can transform randomized controlled trials. *Translational Vision Science & Technology*, *9*(2), 9. Advance online publication. DOI: 10.1167/tvst.9.2.9

Lopez, C., Tucker, S., Salameh, T., & Tuckera, C. (2018). An unsupervised machine learning method for discovering patient clusters based on genetic signatures. *Journal of Biomedical Informatics*, *85*, 30–39. DOI: 10.1016/j.jbi.2018.07.004

Luque-Fernandez, M. A., Schomaker, M., Rachet, B., & Schnitzer, M. E. (2018). Targeted maximum likelihood estimation for a binary treatment: A tutorial. *Statistics in Medicine*, *37*(16), 1–17. DOI: 10.1002/sim.7628

Malgaroli, M., Hull, T. D., Zech, J. M., & Althoff, T. (2023). Natural language processing for mental health interventions: A systematic review and research framework. *Translational Psychiatry*, *13*(309), 309. Advance online publication. DOI: 10.1038/s41398-023-02592-2

Meder, B., Asselbergs, F. W., & Ashley, E. (2025). Artificial intelligence to improve cardiovascular population health. *European Heart Journal*, *00*(20), 1–10. DOI: 10.1093/eurheartj/ehaf125

Michailidis, P., Dimitriadou, A., Papadimitriou, T., & Gogas, P. (2022). Forecasting Hospital Readmissions with Machine Learning. *Healthcare (Basel)*, *10*(981), 981. Advance online publication. DOI: 10.3390/healthcare10060981

Mohammed, E. M., Fakhrudeen, A. M., & Alani, O. Y. (2024). Detection of Alzheimer's disease using deep learning models: A systematic literature review. *Informatics in Medicine Unlocked*, *50*(101551), 101551. Advance online publication. DOI: 10.1016/j.imu.2024.101551

Mpanya, D., Celik, T., Klug, E., & Ntsinjana, H. (2021). Predicting mortality and hospitalization in heart failure using machine learning: A systematic literature review. *International Journal of Cardiology. Heart & Vasculature*, *34*(100773), 100773. Advance online publication. DOI: 10.1016/j.ijcha.2021.100773

Naderalvojoud, B., & Hernandez-Boussard, T. (2024). Improving machine learning with ensemble learning on observational healthcare data. *AMIA ... Annual Symposium Proceedings - AMIA Symposium. AMIA Symposium*, •••, 521–529.

Nambiar, A., Harikrishnaa, S., & Sharanprasath, S. (2023). Model-agnostic explainable artificial intelligence tools for severity prediction and symptom analysis on Indian COVID-19 data. *Frontiers in Artificial Intelligence*, *6*(1272506), 1272506. Advance online publication. DOI: 10.3389/frai.2023.1272506

Nasarudin, N. A., Al Jasmi, F., Sinnott, R. O., Zaki, N., Al Ashwal, H., Mohamed, E. A., & Mohamad, M. S. (2024). A review of deep learning models and online healthcare databases for electronic health records and their use for health prediction. *Artificial Intelligence Review*, *57*(9), 249. Advance online publication. DOI: 10.1007/s10462-024-10876-2

Nasir, F., Rahman, S., & Nasir, N. (2025). Breast Cancer Detection Using Convolutional Neural Networks : A Deep Learning-Based Approach. *Cureus*, *17*(5). Advance online publication. DOI: 10.7759/cureus.83421

Nord-Bronzyk, A., Savulescu, J., Ballantyne, A., Braunack-Mayer, A., Krishnaswamy, P., Lysaght, T., Ong, M. E. H., Liu, N., Menikoff, J., Mertens, M., & Dunn, M. D. (2025). Assessing Risk in Implementing New Artificial Intelligence Triage Tools—How Much Risk is Reasonable in an Already Risky World? *Asian Bioethics Review*, *17*(1), 187–205. DOI: 10.1007/s41649-024-00348-8

Norori, N., Hu, Q., Aellen, F. M., Faraci, F. D., & Tzovara, A. (2021). Addressing bias in big data and AI for health care: A call for open science. *Patterns (New York, N.Y.)*, *2*(10), 100347. Advance online publication. DOI: 10.1016/j.patter.2021.100347

Olawade, D. B., Wada, O. J., David-Olawade, A. C., Kunonga, E., Abaire, O., & Ling, J. (2023). Using artificial intelligence to improve public health: A narrative review. *Frontiers in Public Health*, *11*(1196397), 1196397. Advance online publication. DOI: 10.3389/fpubh.2023.1196397

Pantanowitz, L., Hanna, M., Pantanowitz, J., Lennerz, J., Henricks, W. H., Shen, P., Quinn, B., Bennet, S., & Rashidi, H. H. (2024). Regulatory Aspects of Artificial Intelligence and Machine Learning. *Modern Pathology*, *37*(100609), 100609. Advance online publication. DOI: 10.1016/j.modpat.2024.100609

Papadimitroulas, P., Brocki, L., Christopher Chung, N., Marchadour, W., Vermet, F., Gaubert, L., Eleftheriadis, V., Plachouris, D., Visvikis, D., Kagadis, G. C., & Hatt, M. (2021). Artificial intelligence: Deep learning in oncological radiomics and challenges of interpretability and data harmonization. *Physica Medica*, *83*, 108–121. DOI: 10.1016/j.ejmp.2021.03.009

Perez, K., Wisniewski, D., Ari, A., Lee, K., Lieneck, C., & Ramamonjiarivelo, Z. (2025). Investigation into Application of AI and Telemedicine in Rural Communities: A Systematic Literature Review. *Healthcare (Basel)*, *13*(324), 324. Advance online publication. DOI: 10.3390/healthcare13030324

Quazi, S. (2022). Artificial intelligence and machine learning in precision and genomic medicine. *Medical Oncology (Northwood, London, England)*, *39*(120), 120. Advance online publication. DOI: 10.1007/s12032-022-01711-1

Rahman, A., Debnath, T., Kundu, D., Khan, M. S. I., Aishi, A. A., Sazzad, S., Sayduzzaman, M., & Band, S. S. (2024). Machine learning and deep learning-based approach in smart healthcare: Recent advances, applications, challenges and opportunities. *AIMS Public Health*, *11*(1), 58–109. DOI: 10.3934/publichealth.2024004

Rajkomar, A., Dean, J., & Kohane, I. (2019). Machine Learning in Medicine. *The New England Journal of Medicine*, *380*(14), 1347–1358. DOI: 10.1056/NEJMra1814259

Rashid, A., & Kausik, M. D. A. K. (2024). AI revolutionizing industries worldwide: A comprehensive overview of its diverse applications. *Hybrid Advances*, *7*(100277), 100277. Advance online publication. DOI: 10.1016/j.hybadv.2024.100277

Saltz, J., Gupta, R., Hou, L., Kurc, T., Singh, P., Nguyen, V., Samaras, D., Shroyer, K. R., Zhao, T., Batiste, R., Van Arnam, J., Caesar-Johnson, S. J., Demchok, J. A., Felau, I., Kasapi, M., Ferguson, M. L., Hutter, C. M., Sofia, H. J., Tarnuzzer, R., & Thorsson, V. (2018). Spatial Organization and Molecular Correlation of Tumor-Infiltrating Lymphocytes Using Deep Learning on Pathology Images. *Cell Reports*, *23*(1), 181–200. DOI: 10.1016/j.celrep.2018.03.086

Sarker, I. H. (2021). Machine Learning: Algorithms, Real-World Applications and Research Directions. *SN Computer Science*, *2*(160), 160. Advance online publication. DOI: 10.1007/s42979-021-00592-x

Scharp, D., Hobensack, M., Davoudi, A., & Topaz, M. (2024). Natural Language Processing Applied to Clinical Documentation in Post-acute Care Settings: A Scoping Review. *Journal of the American Medical Directors Association*, *25*(1), 69–83. DOI: 10.1016/j.jamda.2023.09.006

Sena, J., Mostafiz, M. T., Zhang, J., Davidson, A. E., Bandyopadhyay, S., Nerella, S., Ren, Y., Ozrazgat-Baslanti, T., Shickel, B., Loftus, T., Schwartz, W. R., Bihorac, A., & Rashidi, P. (2024). Wearable sensors in patient acuity assessment in critical care. *Frontiers in Neurology*, *15*(1386728), 1386728. Advance online publication. DOI: 10.3389/fneur.2024.1386728

Serrano, D. R., Luciano, F. C., Anaya, B. J., Ongoren, B., Kara, A., Molina, G., Ramirez, B. I., Sánchez-Guirales, S. A., Simon, J. A., Tomietto, G., Rapti, C., Ruiz, H. K., Rawat, S., Kumar, D., & Lalatsa, A. (2024). Artificial Intelligence (AI) Applications in Drug Discovery and Drug Delivery: Revolutionizing Personalized Medicine. *Pharmaceutics*, *16*(1328), 1328. Advance online publication. DOI: 10.3390/pharmaceutics16101328

Sheikhalishahi, S., Miotto, R., Dudley, J. T., Lavelli, A., Rinaldi, F., & Osmani, V. (2019). Natural language processing of clinical notes on chronic diseases: Systematic review. *JMIR Medical Informatics*, *7*(2), e12239. Advance online publication. DOI: 10.2196/12239

Sheller, M. J., Edwards, B., Reina, G. A., Martin, J., Pati, S., Kotrotsou, A., Milchenko, M., Xu, W., Marcus, D., Colen, R. R., & Bakas, S. (2020). Federated learning in medicine: Facilitating multi-institutional collaborations without sharing patient data. *Scientific Reports*, *10*(12598), 12598. Advance online publication. DOI: 10.1038/s41598-020-69250-1

Stech, E. P., Grierson, A. B., Chen, A. Z., Sharrock, M. J., Mahoney, A. E. J., & Newby, J. M. (2020). Intensive one-week internet-delivered cognitive behavioral therapy for panic disorder and agoraphobia: A pilot study. *Internet Interventions : the Application of Information Technology in Mental and Behavioural Health, 20*(100315), 100315. Advance online publication. DOI: 10.1016/j.invent.2020.100315

Stevens, D., Lane, D. A., Harrison, S. L., Lip, G. Y. H., & Kolamunnage-Dona, R. (2021). Modelling of longitudinal data to predict cardiovascular disease risk: A methodological review. *BMC Medical Research Methodology, 21*(283), 283. Advance online publication. DOI: 10.1186/s12874-021-01472-x

Trezza, A., Visibelli, A., Roncaglia, B., Spiga, O., & Santucci, A. (2024). Unsupervised Learning in Precision Medicine: Unlocking Personalized Healthcare through AI. *Applied Sciences (Basel, Switzerland), 14*(9305), 9305. Advance online publication. DOI: 10.3390/app14209305

Tsvetanov, F. (2024). Integrating AI Technologies into Remote Monitoring Patient Systems. *Engineering Proceedings, 70*(54), 54. Advance online publication. DOI: 10.3390/engproc2024070054

Uppalaiah, B., Mallikarjuna Reddy, D., Rajalakshmi, K., Vignesh, P., Govindan, V., & Donganont, S. (2025). Hybrid modeling approaches for predicting COVID-19 mortality: A comparative study across USA, France, and India. *Results in Engineering, 26*(105092), 105092. Advance online publication. DOI: 10.1016/j.rineng.2025.105092

Vaccaro, M., Almaatouq, A., & Malone, T. (2024). When Are Combinations of Humans and AI Useful: A systematic review and meta-analysis. *Nature Human Behaviour, 8*(12), 2293–2303. https://arxiv.org/abs/2405.06087. DOI: 10.1038/s41562-024-02024-1

Varnosfaderani, S. M., & Forouzanfar, M. (2024). The Role of AI in Hospitals and Clinics: Transforming Healthcare in the 21st Century. *Bioengineering (Basel, Switzerland), 11*(337), 337. Advance online publication. DOI: 10.3390/bioengineering11040337

Wang, J., & Li, J. (2024). Artificial intelligence empowering public health education: Prospects and challenges. *Frontiers in Public Health, 12*(1389026), 1389026. Advance online publication. DOI: 10.3389/fpubh.2024.1389026

Wiegrebe, S., Kopper, P., Sonabend, R., Bischl, B., & Bender, A. (2024). Deep learning for survival analysis: a review. In *Artificial Intelligence Review* (Vol. 57, Issue 65). Springer Netherlands. DOI: 10.1007/s10462-023-10681-3

Xie, J., Luo, X., Deng, X., Tang, Y., Tian, W., Cheng, H., Zhang, J., Zou, Y., Guo, Z., & Xie, X. (2023). Advances in artificial intelligence to predict cancer immunotherapy efficacy. *Frontiers in Immunology, 13*(1076883), 1076883. Advance online publication. DOI: 10.3389/fimmu.2022.1076883

Yang, J., Dung, N. T., Thach, P. N., Phong, N. T., Phu, V. D., Phu, K. D., Yen, L. M., Thy, D. B. X., Soltan, A. A. S., Thwaites, L., & Clifton, D. A. (2024). Generalizability assessment of AI models across hospitals in a low-middle and high income country. *Nature Communications, 15*(8270), 8270. Advance online publication. DOI: 10.1038/s41467-024-52618-6

Zafar, I., Anwar, S., Kanwal, F., Yousaf, W., Un Nisa, F., Kausar, T., ul Ain, Q., Unar, A., Kamal, M. A., Rashid, S., Khan, K. A., & Sharma, R. (2023). Reviewing methods of deep learning for intelligent healthcare systems in genomics and biomedicine. *Biomedical Signal Processing and Control, 86*(105263), 105263. Advance online publication. DOI: 10.1016/j.bspc.2023.105263

Zantvoort, K., Scharfenberger, J., Boß, L., Lehr, D., & Funk, B. (2023). Finding the Best Match — a Case Study on the (Text-)Feature and Model Choice in Digital Mental Health Interventions. In *Journal of Healthcare Informatics Research* (Vol. 7). DOI: 10.1007/s41666-023-00148-z

Zhan, Y., Hao, Y., Wang, X., & Guo, D. (2025). Advances of artificial intelligence in clinical application and scientific research of neuro-oncology: Current knowledge and future perspectives. *Critical Reviews in Oncology/Hematology, 209*(104682), 104682. Advance online publication. DOI: 10.1016/j.critrevonc.2025.104682

Zhang, F., Kreuter, D., Chen, Y., Dittmer, S., Tull, S., Shadbahr, T., Schut, M., Asselbergs, F., Kar, S., Sivapalaratnam, S., Williams, S., Koh, M., Henskens, Y., de Wit, B., D'Alessandro, U., Bah, B., Secka, O., Nachev, P., Gupta, R., & Schönlieb, C. B. (2024). Recent methodological advances in federated learning for healthcare. *Patterns (New York, N.Y.), 5*(6), 101006. Advance online publication. DOI: 10.1016/j.patter.2024.101006

Zhang, Y.-P., Zhang, X.-Y., Cheng, Y.-T., Li, B., Teng, X.-Z., Zhang, J., Lam, S., Zhou, T., Ma, Z.-R., Sheng, J.-B., Tam, V. C. W., Lee, S. W. Y., Ge, H., & Cai, J. (2023). Artificial intelligence-driven radiomics study in cancer: The role of feature engineering and modeling. *Military Medical Research, 10*(22), 22. Advance online publication. DOI: 10.1186/s40779-023-00458-8

Chapter 6
Comparative Analysis of AI-Driven Traffic Light Optimization:
Impacts on Traffic Flow, Transportation System Efficiency, and Sustainable Traffic Mobility

Poshan Yu
http://orcid.org/0000-0003-1069-3675
Soochow University, China

Yuan Gao
Independent Researcher, China

ABSTRACT

This study explores how AI - driven traffic light optimization differs across urban contexts and affects traffic flow, transportation efficiency, and sustainable mobility. Using CiteSpace for literature analysis and case studies of Beijing, Shenzhen, and Hangzhou, it analyzes related trends. Beijing's use of machine learning and IoT sensors cut travel time and emissions. Shenzhen's automated system and digital upgrade yielded good results, while Hangzhou's "City Brain" improved traffic via real - time analysis and dynamic adjustments. The research shows that AI - driven traffic light optimization can enhance traffic flow, boost transportation efficiency, and promote sustainable mobility. Key to success is using real - time data for dynamic changes. This study enriches academic knowledge, offers practical urban solutions, and helps policymakers develop better traffic management policies.

DOI: 10.4018/979-8-2600-2373-0.ch006

1. INTRODUCTION

1.1 Research Area Overview

In the modern age, urbanization has been progressing rapidly, bringing about a profound transformation in urban transportation. The continuous growth of urban populations and the increasing popularity of private vehicles have led to a sharp rise in the number of vehicles on the roads (Haydari & Yilmaz, 2022). This has given rise to a series of complex problems in urban traffic, with traffic congestion emerging as a particularly prominent issue (Abduljabbar et al., 2019). Congestion not only extends travel times for commuters but also raises the operational costs of freight transportation, thereby imposing a heavy economic burden on both individuals and society (Zhu et al., 2022).

Simultaneously, the increase in vehicle emissions due to traffic congestion has become a major environmental concern (Liu et al., 2022). The exhaust gases from vehicles are a significant contributor to air pollution, having a negative impact on air quality and posing potential threats to public health.

To address these challenges, Intelligent Transportation Systems (ITS) have emerged as a crucial solution. Among the various elements of ITS, AI-driven traffic light optimization has attracted substantial attention (Chen et al., 2021). By leveraging AI algorithms, this technology can analyze real-time traffic data, including information on traffic volume, vehicle speeds, and road conditions. Based on this analysis, it can dynamically adjust traffic light timings, aiming to optimize traffic flow and improve transportation efficiency (Noaeen et al.,, 2022). The development of advanced sensor technologies and machine learning algorithms has further enhanced the capabilities of AI-driven traffic light optimization, enabling more accurate traffic prediction and control.

1.2 Research Problem Definition

Despite the growing interest in AI-driven traffic light optimization, there are several notable gaps in the existing research. Firstly, existing studies often focus on the technical aspects of AI-driven traffic light optimization in isolation, without fully considering the diverse characteristics of different urban contexts (Alotaibi, 2025). Each city has its own unique urban layout, population density distribution, and traffic patterns, all of which can significantly influence the effectiveness of optimization strategies. However, the differences in optimization requirements across various urban scenarios have not been adequately explored.

Secondly, the long-term impact of AI-driven traffic light optimization on sustainable traffic mobility remains unclear. Sustainable traffic mobility involves not only short-term improvements in traffic flow but also long-term considerations such as environmental sustainability and the overall development of the transportation system (Leonardi et al,, 2025). While some short-term benefits have been observed in certain applications, the long-term implications of these optimization efforts on sustainable traffic development have not been comprehensively studied.

Finally, the relationship between AI-driven traffic light optimization and urban traffic management policies has not been thoroughly investigated. Policies play a crucial role in guiding the implementation and development of new technologies. However, there is a lack of in-depth research on how to effectively integrate AI-driven traffic light optimization with existing and future urban traffic policies to maximize their impact.

This research aims to bridge these gaps by conducting a comprehensive comparative analysis of AI-driven traffic light optimization in different urban contexts. It will explore how various optimization practices influence traffic flow, transportation system efficiency, and sustainable traffic mobility, and also examine the role of policies in this process.

1.3 Paper Structure

This paper is structured systematically to achieve its research objectives. The Literature Review section will begin by analyzing previous publications. Key words will be extracted and categorized to identify major themes and trends in the existing literature. CiteSpace will be utilized to map the relationships between these key words, helping to visualize the knowledge structure of the literature and precisely identify research gaps.

The Methodology section will then detail the specific research methods employed. For the CiteSpace analysis, data sources and analysis parameters will be specified. Regarding case studies, the selection criteria for cases, data collection methods, and the integration of policy analysis will be explained.

The Discussion section is the core of the paper. It will present and analyze case-based findings, explore trends in relevant policies, apply relevant theories to interpret the results, and use tables to clearly present data and key findings for deep analysis.

Finally, the Conclusion section will summarize the main research findings, highlight the research contributions in terms of academic knowledge and practical applications, and provide suggestions for future research based on the limitations of the current study and new research questions that have emerged.

2. LITERATURE REVIEW

2.1 Keyword Analysis and Theme Identification

In academic research, extracting and analyzing keywords from relevant literature titles is a crucial method for discerning core themes and trends (Yigitcanlar & Cugurullo, 2020). After extracting these keywords, using CiteSpace for co-occurrence and co-citation analysis can vividly illustrate the literature's knowledge structure and research hotspots.

In the field of AI-driven traffic light optimization, common keywords such as “Artificial Intelligence (AI)”, “Traffic Light Optimization”, “Intelligent Transportation Systems”, “Urban Traffic Management”, and “Sustainable Mobility” are frequently encountered. Through co-occurrence analysis of these keywords, several prominent research themes have emerged.

(1) AI-powered Traffic Light Adjustment: Many studies concentrate on leveraging AI techniques like machine learning and deep learning to optimize traffic light timings. By processing real-time traffic data, these technologies can adapt traffic light cycles to changing traffic conditions, aiming to enhance traffic flow and reduce congestion. For example, machine learning algorithms can predict traffic volumes based on historical data and real-time sensor information, enabling more efficient traffic light control (Singh, Sahana & Bhattacharjee, 2022).

(2) Integration within Intelligent Transportation Systems: Research also delves into integrating AI-driven traffic light optimization with other components of intelligent transportation systems (Said, 2025). This includes incorporating IoT sensors for data collection and real-time traffic monitoring systems for comprehensive traffic management. The goal is to create a seamless and intelligent transportation ecosystem that can respond dynamically to various traffic scenarios.

(3) Sustainable Urban Traffic Management: There is a growing focus on the environmental and long-term impacts of AI-driven traffic light optimization. This involves studying how it can contribute to reducing vehicle emissions and energy consumption, thus promoting sustainable urban development. By minimizing traffic jams, the technology can help cut down on pollutant emissions, improving air quality and making cities more livable (Tao et al., 2024).

(4) Policy-Technology Interaction: Another key theme is the relationship between urban traffic policies and AI technology (Xie et al., 2023). Research analyzes how existing policies affect the implementation of AI-driven traffic light optimization and how new policies can be formulated to better support its development. This

includes exploring how to balance regulatory requirements with technological innovation to maximize the benefits of intelligent traffic management.

2.2 Identification of Research Gaps

Despite the progress in these research areas, there are still significant gaps that need to be addressed:

- Context-specific Optimization: Most existing studies emphasize technical aspects but overlook the diverse optimization needs of different cities. Each city has unique characteristics, such as population density, traffic patterns, and infrastructure. These differences can greatly influence the effectiveness of optimization strategies (Bohra et al., 2025). For example, a strategy that works well in a large, grid-patterned city may not be suitable for a small, hilly town. However, there is a lack of in-depth research on adapting optimization strategies to specific urban contexts.
- Long-term Sustainability: While short-term traffic improvements are well-studied, the long-term impact of AI-driven traffic light optimization on sustainable traffic development remains unclear (Lin et al., 2025). This includes aspects like long-term environmental benefits, social equity, and the overall evolution of the transportation system. For instance, it is unknown whether the technology can maintain its environmental advantages as traffic demands change over time or if it benefits all social groups equally.
- Policy-Technology Synergy: There is a lack of systematic research on integrating AI-driven traffic light optimization with urban traffic management policies. Understanding how to align technology development with policy goals is essential for effective implementation (Nigam, Singh & Choudhary, 2023). Without proper integration, the potential of AI in traffic management may not be fully realized. For example, policies may not be updated in a timely manner to support new AI-based traffic solutions, or technology development may not consider policy requirements, leading to inefficiencies.

2.3 Determination of Research Questions

The identified research gaps in the field of AI-driven traffic light optimization set the stage for the formulation of the main research question and sub-questions.

Main Research Question: How do differences in AI-driven traffic light optimization practices in various urban contexts affect urban traffic flow, transportation system efficiency and sustainable traffic mobility?

Sub-Questions

- How have researchers in different types of urban areas studied the relationship between AI-driven traffic light optimization and urban traffic flow, and what are the emerging trends in this area as per CiteSpace analysis?
- How has the research on improving transportation system efficiency in the context of sustainable traffic mobility through AI-driven traffic light optimization evolved in different urban areas, as analyzed by CiteSpace and specific cases?
- What are the key strategies of AI-driven traffic light optimization in promoting sustainable traffic mobility in urban contexts, and how do they compare according to specific cases and policy?

3. METHODOLOGY

This research employs a mixed-method approach, combining Citespace analysis, case studies and policy analysis.

3.1 CiteSpace Analysis

The application of AI in urban management, especially in traffic-related aspects, has drawn significant attention. In this study, it is of theoretical and practical significance to use bibliometric methods to systematically sort out the research focal points and developmental trajectories in this field (Liang et al., 2024). We collected 500 articles on the utilization of AI-Driven Traffic Light Optimization from the "Web of Science Core Database" in 2021-2025. We explore research hotspots and development trends by keyword co-occurrence analysis.

Figure 1.

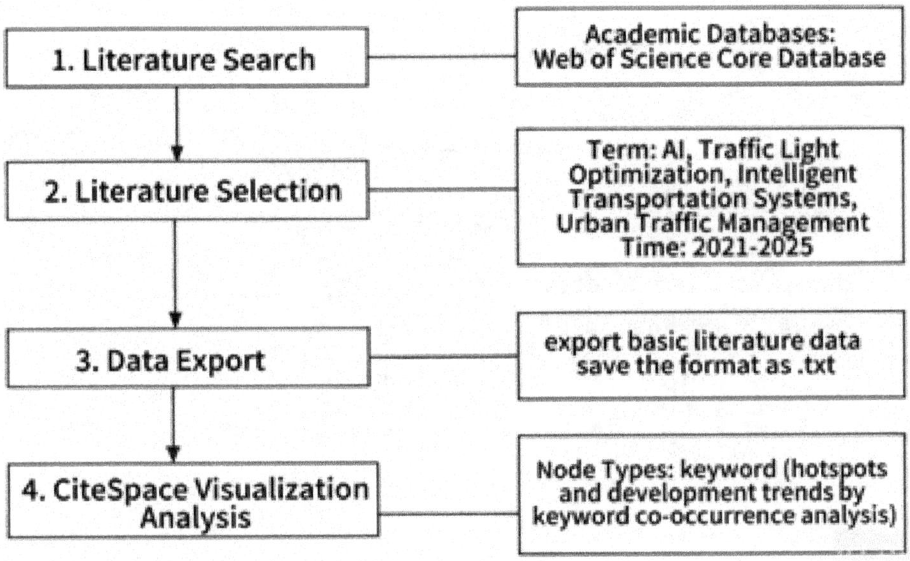

(Source: Web of Science Core Database)

The authors of an article use keywords to encapsulate the essence of the core content of the literature. In this paper, the keywords appearing in each one-year time slice are selected and used to create co-occurrence maps.

Figure 2.

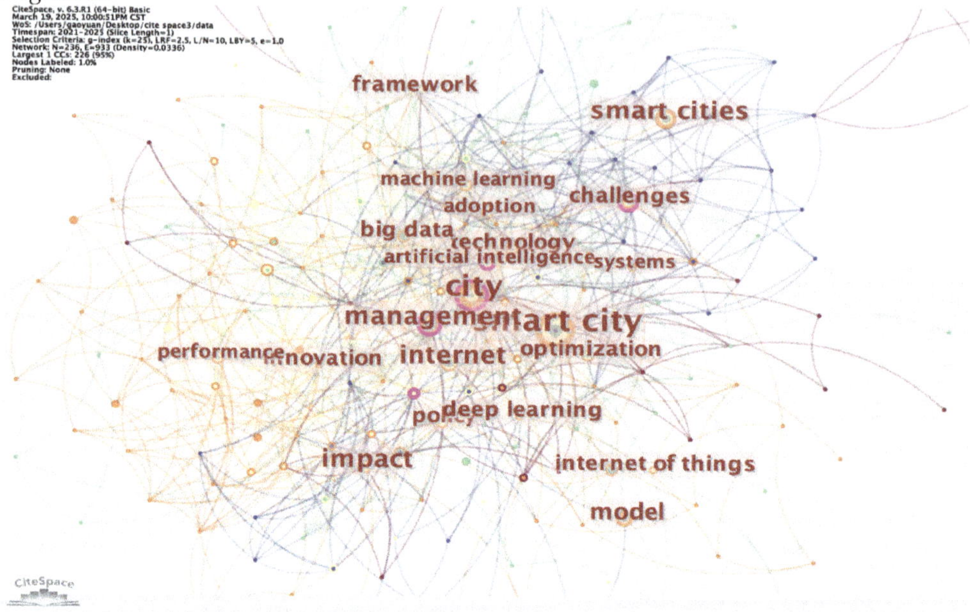

(Source: CiteSpace)

The size of each node in the graph directly reflects the frequency of keyword occurrences. In the content of this CiteSpace graph regarding AI in the field of smart cities, we can observe a rich network consisting of 236 nodes (N = 236) and 933 line segments (E = 933), with a connection density of 0.0336 (Density = 0.0336). This demonstrates a relatively close interaction among the concepts represented by the keywords. Prominent keywords such as "smart cities", "artificial intelligence", "machine learning", and "urban management" are central in the research on AI applications in urban scenarios.

Among them, "smart cities", as the core theme in the visualization, emphasizes the broad urban environment where AI-driven optimizations take place. Elements like "management" and "optimization" are directly related to the improvement of traffic light systems. By leveraging these technological and conceptual elements, we can conduct a more deep analysis of how AI-driven traffic light optimization impacts traffic flow, enhances transportation system efficiency, and contributes to sustainable traffic mobility. This not only helps us understand the current research status but also paves the way for future research on refining and implementing optimization strategies.

3.2 Case Study Analysis

Figure 3.

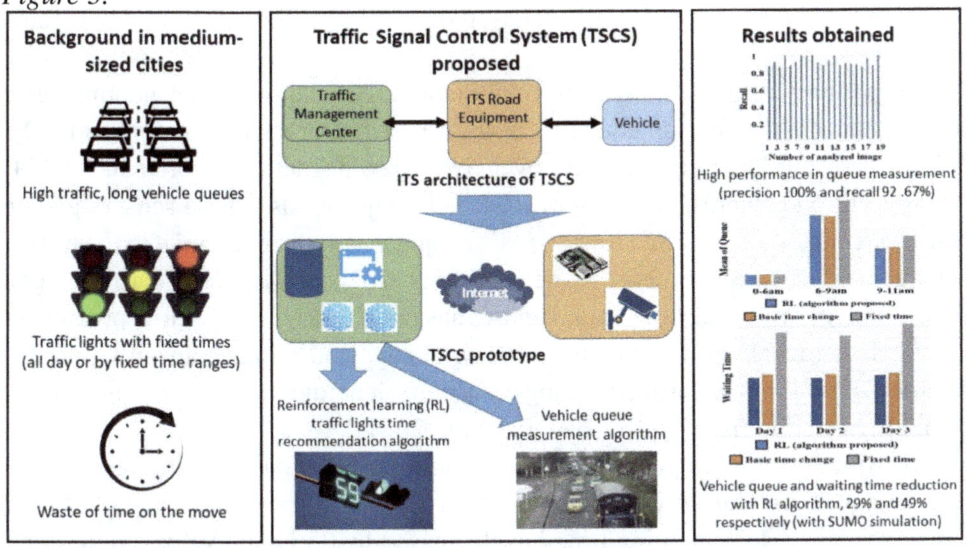

(Source: Traffic Signal Control System Based on Intelligent Transportation System and Reinforcement Learning)

To explore how AI-driven traffic light optimization improves transportation efficiency for sustainable mobility in different cities, case studies of Beijing and Shenzhen were done, yielding practical insights. An image shows a related Traffic Signal Control System (TSCS).

In medium-sized cities (left of the image), issues like heavy traffic, long queues, fixed-time lights, and wasted travel time are common. The TSCS architecture (middle) includes a Traffic Management Center, ITS Road Equipment, and vehicles (Sadaf et al., 2023). Its prototype uses a Reinforcement Learning (RL) algorithm for traffic light timing and vehicle queue measurement, similar to Beijing and Shenzhen's tech-based traffic management (Ghasemieh & Kashef, 2024).

The results (right) show high-performance queue measurement (100% precision, 92.67% recall) and RL-driven reductions in vehicle queue (29%) and waiting time (49%) in SUMO simulation. These, like the case-study findings, prove AI-driven methods boost traffic flow and system efficiency for sustainable mobility (Hurtado-Gómez et al., 2021).

3.2.1 Case Study of Beijing

Beijing, a major Chinese first-tier city, has long faced traffic congestion. To ease traffic and boost transportation efficiency, it has actively adopted AI for traffic light optimization.

Beijing has installed numerous intelligent traffic sensors, like geomagnetic sensors and high-definition cameras, in its core urban areas and major roads. By 2023, Chaoyang District alone had over 5,000 geomagnetic sensors and 3,000+ high-definition cameras, covering over 90% of major roads. These sensors gather real-time traffic data, such as flow, speed, and queue length, and send it to the traffic management center every few seconds (Mohsen, 2024). Using deep-earning algorithms and massive real-time data, Beijing has developed a traffic flow prediction model. This model can forecast traffic flow changes 30 minutes ahead with 92% accuracy. For instance, during morning rush hours, it predicts congestion and adjusts traffic light timings in advance (Estrada et al., 2021).

The AI-driven traffic light optimization system in Beijing has been highly effective. In Zhongguancun, during weekday morning rush hours, the average vehicle speed has increased by 18%, waiting time has decreased by 25%, and vehicle emissions have dropped by about 12%, improving air quality. On the East 3rd Ring Road, optimizing traffic light timings has increased the road section's traffic capacity by around 20%, reducing congestion. (Vaca-Recalde et al., 2024).

3.2.2 Case Study of Shenzhen

Shenzhen, a frontrunner in China's technological landscape, has been at the vanguard of leveraging AI for traffic management. In recent years, the city has made remarkable strides in implementing AI-driven traffic light optimization strategies, aiming to revolutionize urban mobility and foster sustainable transportation (Mon et al., 2022).

Shenzhen has installed over 10,000 high-definition cameras, 8,000 geomagnetic sensors, and 5,000 radar devices on major roads and intersections by 2023. These sensors, covering about 80% of the main road network, collect real-time data rapidly (cameras capture 30 frames/s, sensors transmit every 2-5 s), like in Futian CBD.

Using advanced machine-learning algorithms, Shenzhen analyzes and predicts traffic patterns. Its big-data platform processes over 100 terabytes of data daily (Shulajkovska et al., 2024). Deep-learning models can forecast traffic flow with over 90% accuracy 30 minutes ahead, helping adjust traffic lights on key routes like Shennan Boulevard during peak hours.

The city's intelligent traffic signal control system optimizes traffic effectively. At the Yitian Road-Shennan Boulevard intersection, vehicle waiting time dropped

35% during peak hours. The system analyzes multi-source real-time data, adjusts green-light duration in 3-5-second increments, and allocates more time to congested directions when needed.

3.2.3 Case Analysis Based on CiteSpace

The CiteSpace visualization offers a comprehensive overview of research trends in the context of smart cities and sustainable traffic mobility, which can be fruitfully connected to the cases of Beijing and Shenzhen.

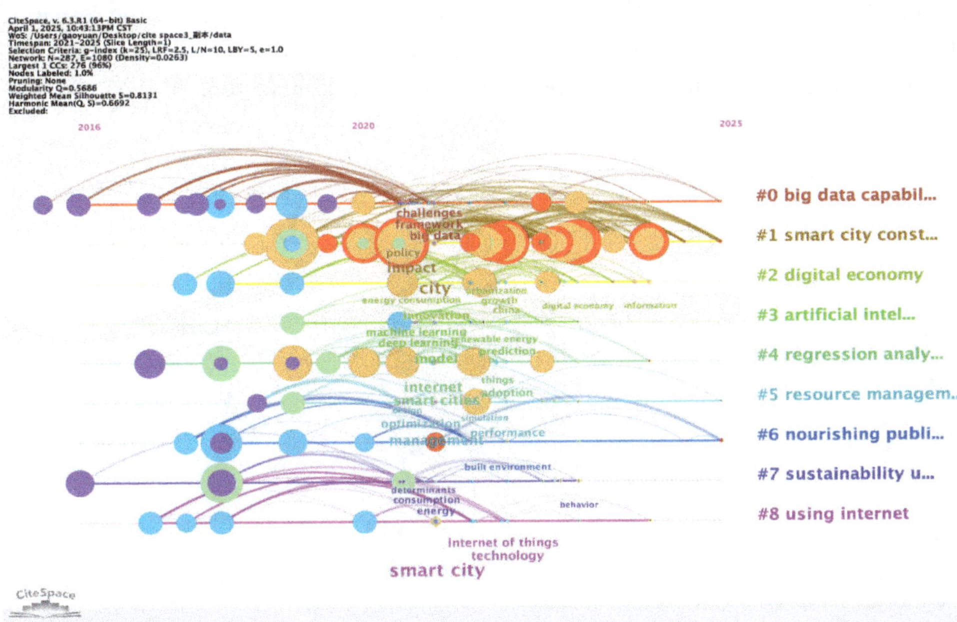

(Source: CiteSpace)

Keywords such as "big data", "machine learning" and "internet of things" are prominently featured, indicating their centrality in contemporary research on urban transportation optimization. In the case of Beijing, the utilization of machine learning models and IoT sensors, as evidenced by the revision of over 5,000 traffic light regulations, aligns seamlessly with this research focus. The real-time data collection and analysis enabled by these technologies, as suggested by the emphasis on data-related keywords in the CiteSpace map, are crucial for predicting traffic patterns and dynamically adjusting traffic light timings, thereby reducing peak-hour travel time and vehicle emissions.

For Shenzhen, the launch of an automated traffic management system, which relies on AI algorithms analyzing data from various sensors, also resonates with the technological trends depicted in the CiteSpace output. The planned expansion of this system and the digital upgrade of the bus system reflect a broader trend towards resource management and optimization in smart cities, as indicated by keywords like “optimization” and “resource management” in the visualization.

The overarching theme of sustainable traffic mobility, a key concern in both cities' initiatives, is mirrored in the CiteSpace map through related keywords such as “sustainability”. This emphasizes the interconnectedness of technological advancements with the goal of creating more sustainable urban transportation systems (Noveski & Bohanec, 2024). Overall, the CiteSpace analysis not only highlights the research hotspots but also validates the practical applications and significance of AI-driven traffic optimization strategies in cities like Beijing and Shenzhen.

3.3 Analysis of Technical Principles

Figure 5. Decentralized FL architecture

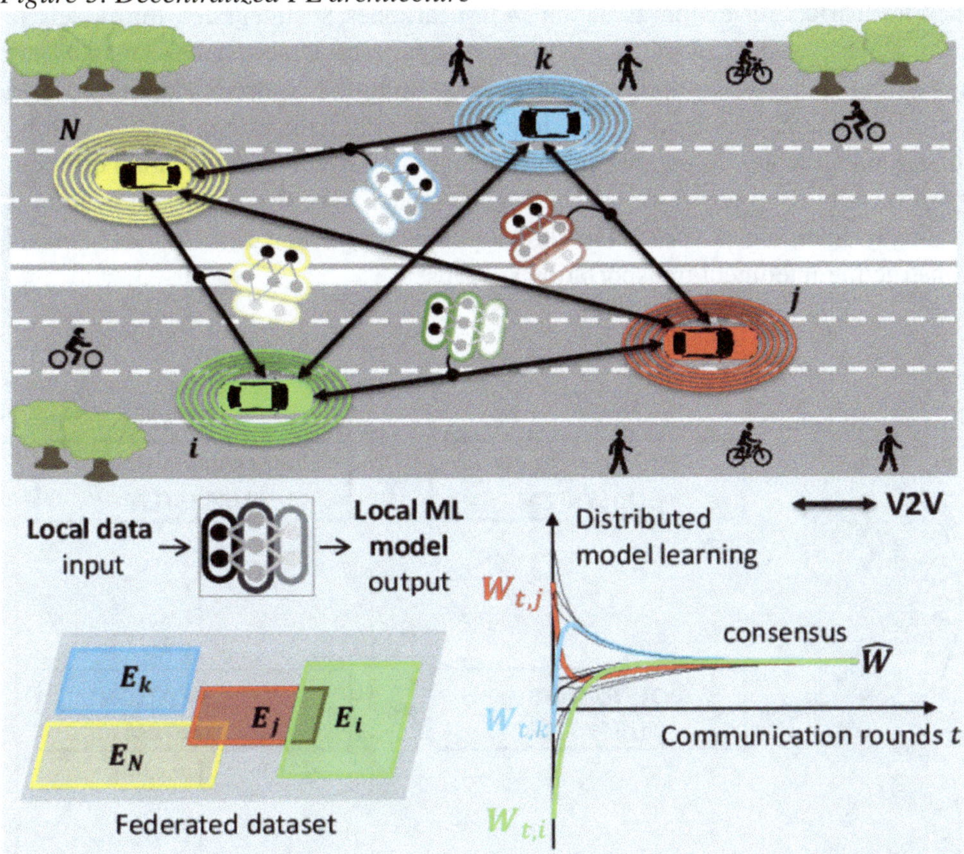

(Source: Decentralized Federated Learning for Road User Classification in Enhanced V2X Networks)

In the realm of AI-Driven Traffic Light Optimization, different city areas serve as independent nodes, equipped with a network of intelligent sensors that continuously and accurately collect local traffic data, including traffic volume, vehicle speed, and driving direction. Each node is furnished with a dedicated local machine-learning model. This model employs advanced data-mining algorithms to conduct in-depth analyses of the collected data, generating targeted traffic light adjustment strategies that adapt to real-time traffic conditions. The mechanism of distributed model learning plays a pivotal role. It breaks down the information barriers between regions, enabling seamless information sharing and collaborative learning among local models. By aggregating the local data from each node into a federated dataset, researchers can leverage large-scale data samples and cutting-edge techniques such as deep learning to train models that are better suited to complex traffic scenarios and offer more accurate predictions (Ang et al., 2022).

For example, when peak-hour data from diverse functional areas, including commercial districts, residential areas, and industrial zones, are integrated, the model can comprehensively learn a wide variety of traffic patterns. Based on these insights, the system can dynamically optimize traffic light timings. This optimization leads to a significant increase in road traffic flow, a substantial reduction in vehicle waiting times, and ultimately, a notable enhancement in the overall transportation efficiency of the city (Barbieri et al., 2021). This approach to traffic light optimization is gradually emerging as a crucial method for alleviating urban traffic congestion and constructing intelligent transportation systems.

Figure 6. Road actor classificator subsystems

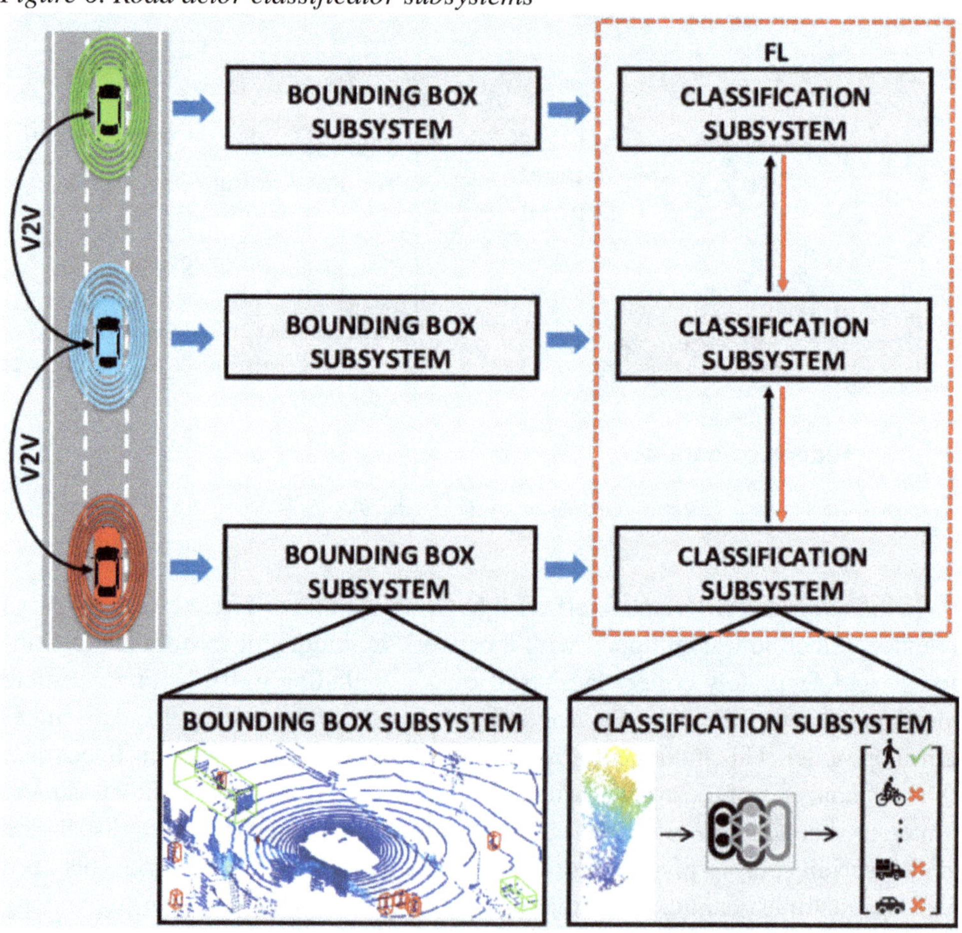

(Source: Decentralized Federated Learning for Road User Classification in Enhanced V2X Networks)

In complex traffic scenarios, a state-of-the-art computer vision-based system, often incorporating advanced deep learning architectures like convolutional neural networks (CNNs) and recurrent neural networks (RNNs), is utilized to identify and classify various traffic participants, encompassing vehicles, pedestrians, and non-motor vehicles. The system meticulously processes high-resolution image or video data captured by strategically placed cameras at intersections and along roadways. Through a series of operations such as feature extraction, object detection, and pattern recognition, it precisely draws bounding boxes around each detected object. This not only allows for the accurate determination of the position and size of different targets but also enables detailed classification based on their unique visual characteristics and movement patterns.

This in-depth identification process generates highly detailed and comprehensive traffic information for the AI system. For example, it can accurately determine the number of vehicles in different directions at a specific intersection, analyze the speed and density of traffic flows, and assess the travel demand and movement intentions of pedestrians (Zuluaga-Gomez et al., 2023). Leveraging this rich dataset, the AI system can implement sophisticated dynamic traffic light control strategies. When it detects that one road is severely congested with a long queue of vehicles while another adjacent road has significantly lighter traffic, it can intelligently and adaptively extend the green light time of the congested road. This adjustment not only helps ensure the rapid passage of vehicles, reducing waiting times and minimizing emissions caused by idling, but also significantly improves road utilization. By optimizing traffic flow in this manner, the system plays a crucial role in achieving sustainable traffic mobility, aligning with the overarching goals of modern intelligent transportation systems (Barbieri, 2021).

4. DISCUSSIONS

4.1 Case-Based Analysis From Hotspot Perspective

From the perspective of industry hotspots, the Hangzhou City Brain Project stands out as a remarkable initiative in leveraging AI-driven traffic light optimization for sustainable traffic mobility. In an era where urban congestion is a pressing global issue and the integration of advanced technologies like big data, cloud computing, and artificial intelligence into urban management is a key trend, this project has become a notable example.

What makes the Hangzhou case unique is its comprehensive and integrated approach. By collaborating with Alibaba, the city was able to build an intelligent traffic management system that taps into multiple data-collecting devices to gather real-time traffic data, such as vehicle flow and speed. This real-time data-driven approach is a key strategy in AI-driven traffic light optimization. For instance, in Xiaoshan District, the immediate increase in traffic speed by 15% in the initial stage showcases the potency of this data-informed strategy (Yin et al., 2022). The utilization of artificial intelligence algorithms to deeply analyze the data and accurately simulate intersection traffic dynamics is another distinctive feature. This allows for the generation of optimized traffic light timing plans in real-time, directly addressing the research problem of how to effectively promote sustainable traffic mobility (Han et al., 2024). In terms of the research problem, the Hangzhou City Brain Project reveals that a combination of real-time data collection, advanced algorithm-based analysis, and dynamic traffic light adjustment is crucial. This not only reduces vehicle waiting time and improves road traffic efficiency, effectively alleviating congestion, but also extends its benefits to traffic safety, emergency rescue, and urban planning (Zhou et al., 2022). The system's ability to automatically detect accidents and plan routes for emergency vehicles demonstrates how AI-driven traffic light optimization can contribute to a more holistic and sustainable urban traffic ecosystem. Compared to other cases, this all-encompassing approach that goes beyond mere traffic flow improvement and integrates with various aspects of urban management sets the Hangzhou initiative apart, offering valuable insights into key strategies for promoting sustainable traffic mobility in urban contexts (Liu et al,, 2023).

4.2 Key Policies Trend Analysis

4.2.1 Policy Analysis Based on Case Studies

In the process of urban development, sustainable transportation is a key goal, and the optimization of traffic lights driven by artificial intelligence has become a powerful means to achieve this goal (Vieira et al., 2024). The Hangzhou City Brain Project is a model in this regard.

Table 1.

Issue Time	Policy	Main Contents	Potential Implications from Stakeholders
2016	"Three-Year Action Implementation Plan for 'Internet +' Artificial Intelligence"	Promote the in-depth integration of artificial intelligence with various industries, with a focus on urban management and transportation. It laid the foundation for the subsequent research and development of traffic signal optimization systems and encouraged local governments to explore intelligent transportation solutions.	Local governments, enterprises related to the transportation field, scientific research institutions, and urban residents.
2017	"New Generation Artificial Intelligence Development Plan"	Clearly proposed to accelerate the construction of intelligent transportation systems and use artificial intelligence technology to improve traffic management efficiency.	Traffic management departments, the general public traveling on the roads, and enterprises upstream and downstream of the intelligent transportation industry.
2018	"Intelligent Transportation System Development Strategy"	Emphasized accelerating the construction of intelligent transportation infrastructure, promoting the informatization and intelligence of transportation.	Transportation infrastructure construction enterprises, traffic operation management departments, and urban residents.
2019	"Implementation Plan for the Construction of Hangzhou City Brain"	Utilize big data and artificial intelligence technology to improve urban traffic management. The traffic signal optimization system in this plan adjusts traffic signals dynamically through real-time data analysis, improving traffic smoothness.	Hangzhou traffic management departments, enterprises and institutions participating in the "City Brain" construction, Hangzhou citizens, and relevant technology researchers and developers.
2020	"Guiding Opinions on Promoting the Development of Intelligent Transportation"	Emphasized using artificial intelligence and big data technology to improve the intelligence level of traffic signal control systems.	Enterprises developing traffic signal control systems, transportation scientific research institutions, traffic management department, and the traveling public.
2021	"Overall Layout Plan for the Construction of Digital China"	Accelerate the construction of digital infrastructure and promote the in-depth integration of digital technology with the real economy.	Digital technology enterprises, real economy enterprises in the transportation field, urban planning and management departments, and urban residents.
2022	"Guidelines for the Construction of Intelligent Transportation Systems"	Strengthen the intelligent transformation of traffic signal control systems and promote the artificial intelligence-based traffic management model.	Intelligent transportation system construction enterprises, traffic signal control equipment manufacturers, traffic management departments, and travelers.

continued on following page

Table 1. Continued

Issue Time	Policy	Main Contents	Potential Implications from Stakeholders
2023	"Intelligent Transportation System Development Action Plan (2023-2025)"	Continue to promote the application of intelligent transportation technology, with a focus on optimizing traffic signal control, improving the efficiency and safety of urban traffic management, encouraging local governments and enterprises to innovate in traffic signal optimization, and promoting the construction of intelligent transportation infrastructure.	Local governments, intelligent transportation technology enterprises, transportation infrastructure construction enterprises, traffic management departments, and urban residents.
2024	"National Intelligent Transportation System Construction Plan (2024-2030)"	Define the construction goals of intelligent transportation systems in the next few years, including specific measures for traffic signal optimization, intelligent scheduling, etc., and plan the development direction of intelligent transportation systems.	Traffic planning departments, intelligent transportation construction enterprises, scientific research institutions, traffic management departments, and the general public traveling on the roads.

(Source: Government Departments)

Since the launch of the Hangzhou City Brain Project in 2016, a series of policies have provided all-round support for its development in the transportation field (Yin & Song, 2023).

The "Internet +" Artificial Intelligence Three-Year Action Implementation Plan issued in 2016 emphasized the integration of artificial intelligence with various industries, especially in the fields of urban governance and transportation, laying the foundation for Hangzhou to explore intelligent transportation solutions and prompting the Hangzhou City Brain Project to focus on the research and development of traffic signal optimization systems. Subsequently, the New-Generation Artificial Intelligence Development Plan released by the State Council in 2017 clearly proposed to use artificial intelligence technology to accelerate the construction of intelligent transportation systems and improve transportation management efficiency, providing core guidance for the strategic formulation of the Hangzhou City Brain Project and guiding it to use data and algorithms for traffic signal optimization. In 2018, the Intelligent Transportation System Development Strategy of the Ministry of Transport called for accelerating the construction of intelligent transportation infrastructure and promoting informatization and intelligent development, urging the Hangzhou City Brain Project to deploy data-collection equipment and integrate traffic data to adjust signal timings in real time. The Hangzhou City Brain Construction Implementation Plan of the Hangzhou Municipal Government in 2019 emphasized the use of big data and artificial intelligence to strengthen urban traffic management. By analyzing real-time data, traffic signals were dynamically adjusted, significantly improving traffic fluidity.

The Guidance on Promoting the Development of Intelligent Transportation of the National Development and Reform Commission in 2020, the Overall Layout Plan for Digital China Construction of the State Council in 2021, the Intelligent Transportation System Construction Guide of the Ministry of Transport in 2022, and the relevant policies in 2023 that continuously promoted the development of intelligent transportation systems have, respectively, from the aspects of improving the intelligent level of traffic signal control systems, integrating digital technologies, constructing intelligent transportation infrastructure, and innovating traffic signal optimization, continuously promoted the continuous improvement and expansion of the application of the Hangzhou City Brain Project in traffic signal optimization. The National Intelligent Transportation Construction Plan (2024-2030) and the Implementation Plan for the Intelligent Development of Urban Transportation in 2024 further clarify the construction goals and measures, providing directions for the continuous optimization of the traffic signal system of the project (Zhang & Fan, 2023).

These policies, from the introduction of concepts, strategic planning to specific implementation details, have formed a complete policy support system, comprehensively promoting the continuous innovation and improvement of the Hangzhou City Brain Project in the optimization of traffic lights (Mao et al., 2024).

4.2.2 Policy Trend Analysis

The policies related to intelligent transportation show an obvious evolution trend. Early policies such as the "Internet +" Artificial Intelligence Three-Year Action Implementation Plan in 2016 mainly focused on introducing the concept of integrating artificial intelligence with industries, laying the foundation for subsequent development. As time goes by, the policies have gradually transitioned to the specific implementation level. The Intelligent Transportation System Development Strategy in 2018 and the Hangzhou City Brain Construction Implementation Plan in 2019 emphasized infrastructure construction and the implementation of intelligent transportation at the local level. After that, the attention of policies to the improvement of intelligent level and the integration of digital technologies has increased day by day, as exemplified by the Guidance on Promoting the Development of Intelligent Transportation in 2020 and the Overall Layout Plan for Digital China Construction in 2021 (Wang et al., 2021). The Intelligent Transportation System Construction Guide in 2022 highlighted the intelligent transformation of the traffic signal control system, and in 2023, the innovation of traffic signal optimization and infrastructure construction were continuously promoted. The policies in 2024 are more specific in construction goals and detailed measures.

This evolution process shows that the policies have gradually deepened from the introduction of macro-concepts to the practical operation level, putting forward higher and more specific requirements for technical application, system optimization, and construction goals, continuously promoting the development of intelligent transportation from initial exploration to in-depth development and comprehensive application, and effectively promoting the upgrade of the Hangzhou City Brain Project in traffic light optimization from basic construction to refined and intelligent regulation (Han et al., 2023).

4.2.3 Comparison with Other Cities

Compared to other cities, Hangzhou's City Brain Project excels in AI-driven traffic light optimization. It integrates advanced tech, large-scale data handling, and robust policy support, forming a comprehensive and efficient system. Policy-guided, it deploys many data-collection devices to gather real-time traffic data, uses AI algorithms for in-depth analysis, and dynamically adjusts traffic lights (Paiva et al., 2021). This real-time data-driven approach eases traffic congestion and benefits traffic safety and urban planning.

The project's accident detection and emergency vehicle route-planning functions ensure traffic safety and response efficiency, and its accumulated data supports urban planning (Ding, Du & Xia, 2025). Other cities can draw on the Hangzhou model, adjusting policy-making, technical application, and data use based on local conditions. Cities with similar traffic and tech can adopt Hangzhou's data-related methods and local-policy-integrated intelligent transportation systems to enhance traffic management.

4.3 Theory Analysis

4.3.1 Network Economics Theory

The Hangzhou City Brain Project is a typical case of using artificial intelligence to optimize traffic lights and promote sustainable traffic mobility. By applying the three key concepts of network externality, network structure and connections, and synergistic effect in the Network Economics Theory (Moreno-Vozmediano et al., 2025), we can analyze this project from different perspectives and understand its impact in the transportation field and its relationship with the overall research.

- From the Perspective of Network Externality: Network externality means that the value of a product to users increases as the number of other users of the product increases. This theory is clearly reflected in the Hangzhou City Brain Project. As more traffic data collection devices, such as a large number of sensors and cameras deployed on the roads, are connected to the City Brain system within the project-covered area, the real-time traffic data collected becomes richer and more comprehensive (Guo & Yuan, 2021). These data not only provide more accurate basis for optimizing traffic lights, but also as more vehicles and roads are incorporated into the system, each part interacts with others, enhancing the efficiency of the entire traffic network. For example, after the traffic lights at a certain intersection are adjusted according to real-time data, the traffic pressure on the surrounding roads is also relieved, which further promotes the traffic improvement in other related areas, thus generating a positive network externality (Khan & Park, 2024). From the perspective of the overall research, network externality indicates that the AI-driven traffic light optimization system has the characteristics of self-reinforcement and expansion. Urban traffic management can take advantage of this characteristic to continuously expand the project coverage and improve the overall traffic efficiency.
- From the Perspective of Network Structure and Connections: The Hangzhou City Brain Project has constructed a complex and efficient network structure. In this network, traffic data collection devices, artificial intelligence algorithm processing centers, traffic light control systems, and various traffic nodes (such as intersections and road sections) in the city are interconnected. Different types of data collection devices are responsible for collecting multi-dimensional information such as vehicle flow, speed, and congestion. This information is transmitted to the algorithm processing center through the network (Arunkumar, 2024). After the algorithm processing center analyzes and processes the data, it sends instructions to the traffic light control system to achieve dynamic adjustment of traffic lights. Each traffic node realizes information sharing and collaborative work through this network connection. This tight network structure and connection method ensure the rapid and accurate transmission and processing of traffic information within the system, improving the real-time and precision of traffic management (Zaim, 2021). From the research perspective, it provides a practical example for understanding how to improve the efficiency of the traffic system by optimizing the network structure and connections, indicating that a reasonable network structure design can better play the role of AI in traffic light optimization.
- From the Perspective of Synergistic Effect: The synergistic effect means that the overall effect generated by the collaboration of all components of a sys-

tem is greater than the sum of the individual effects of each component (Ren, 2024). The Hangzhou City Brain Project integrates multiple links such as traffic management, data analysis, and intelligent control, achieving a significant synergistic effect. In terms of traffic management, the project not only optimizes traffic lights but also can automatically detect accidents and plan routes for emergency vehicles, improving traffic safety and emergency response efficiency (Su et al., 2024). The data analysis link provides strong support for traffic light adjustment and other traffic decisions. Intelligent control ensures that traffic lights can be adjusted accurately according to real-time situations. These links cooperate with each other, enabling the project to relieve traffic congestion and increase road traffic speed, while also having a positive impact on urban planning. From the perspective of the overall research, the synergistic effect reflects the importance of combining AI-driven traffic light optimization with other aspects of the urban traffic system, providing a comprehensive solution for achieving sustainable traffic mobility and also offering a reference for studying how to integrate different elements to improve the overall performance of the traffic system.

4.3.2 Principle Application Explanation

Figure 7.

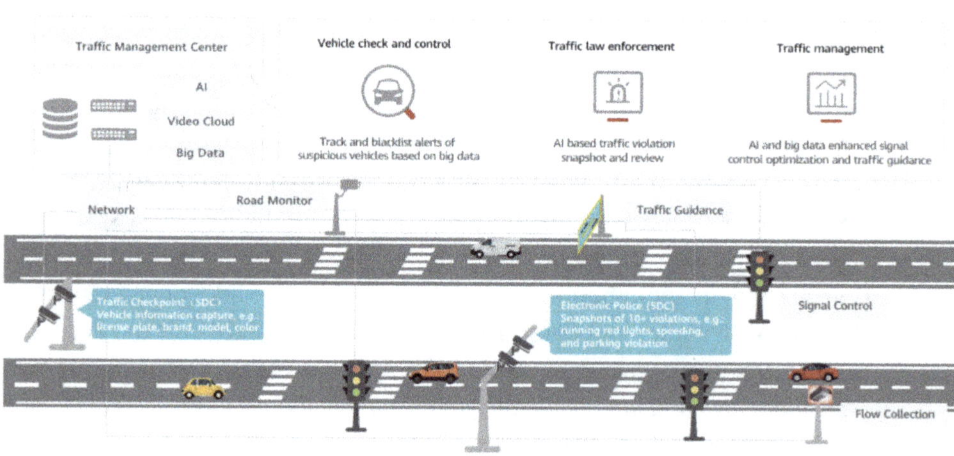

(Source: Official Website of Huawei Traffic Management Department)

This picture shows the operational architecture of an intelligent traffic management system, emphasizing the key roles of AI-Driven Traffic Light Optimization and its network. The system's core, the Traffic Management Center, combines AI, Video Cloud, and Big Data technologies, connecting to Road Monitors via a network for information interaction (Lee et al., 2023).

For AI-Driven Traffic Light Optimization, the center uses multi-source data and AI algorithms to optimize traffic lights (Gagliardi et al., 2024). When road monitors detect increased traffic, data goes to the center, is processed by AI, and then instructions adjust traffic light durations for smooth traffic flow. In the system's network, Traffic Checkpoints and Electronic Police act as nodes. Checkpoints gather vehicle info, and Electronic Police catch traffic violations. Their data is sent to the center, which also sends instructions to modules for vehicle inspection, control, and traffic law enforcement. All components are network-connected, working together to boost traffic management efficiency and intelligence (Damadam et al., 2022).

5. CONCLUSION

5.1 Main Findings and Answers to Research Questions

AI-driven traffic light optimization practices vary across different urban contexts, which have significant impacts on urban traffic flow, transportation system efficiency, and sustainable traffic mobility (Ragab et al., 2023). Given the diverse urban layouts, population densities, and traffic patterns, Beijing, Shenzhen, and Hangzhou have adopted different optimization strategies. These strategies have achieved positive results in their respective cities, such as improving traffic flow, enhancing transportation system efficiency, and promoting sustainable traffic mobility, demonstrating the feasibility and effectiveness of AI-driven traffic light optimization in different urban contexts.

Researchers mainly focus on the application of AI technology in traffic light optimization, its integration with intelligent transportation systems, its impact on sustainable transportation, and the interaction between policies and technology. CiteSpace analysis shows that keywords such as “Artificial Intelligence”, “Machine Learning”, and “Internet of Things” stand out, indicating that using real-time data and advanced technologies for traffic light optimization is the main trend. Although research focuses may vary according to the characteristics of different cities, overall, they are all moving towards a more precise, efficient, and sustainable direction.

CiteSpace analysis and specific cases indicate that different cities have effectively improved traffic conditions by using AI technology to achieve dynamic adjustment of traffic lights. Beijing revised its traffic light regulations, utilized machine learning models and IoT sensors, and adjusted traffic light timings based on real-time traffic data, reducing peak-hour travel time and vehicle emissions. Shenzhen launched an automated traffic management system, used AI algorithms to analyze traffic data and adjust traffic lights, and promoted the digital upgrade of its specific system, enhancing traffic flow and promoting the use of public transportation. These practices reflect a shift from traditional fixed traffic light settings to AI-based dynamic optimization, with an increasing emphasis on sustainable transportation development.

Key strategies include dynamic adjustment using real-time data, integrating multi-source data with advanced algorithms, and collaborative optimization with other parts of the urban traffic system. Hangzhou's City Brain project is a typical example. Through multi-source data collection, artificial intelligence algorithm analysis, and dynamic traffic light adjustment, it has significantly improved traffic conditions and also played a positive role in traffic safety, emergency rescue, and urban planning. Compared with other cities, Hangzhou's advantage lies in its complete policy support system and the in-depth integration of technology, data, and policies. Beijing focuses on the combination of regulation revision and technology, while Shenzhen is characterized by its automated system and system upgrade. The strategies of different cities have different focuses, all of which provide experiences for sustainable traffic mobility.

5.2 Contributions to the Academic Field and Suggestions for Future Research

This research significantly enriches the academic landscape. In the realm of new knowledge, it meticulously explores how AI-driven traffic light optimization functions across diverse urban settings. By analyzing cities with varying layouts, population densities, and traffic patterns, it uncovers unique applications. For instance, in large grid-patterned cities, AI might focus on optimizing traffic flow across multiple intersections simultaneously, while in smaller, more compact cities, it could prioritize reducing congestion at key bottlenecks. This not only broadens the scope of intelligent transportation system research but also provides in-depth insights into context-specific applications.

Regarding relationship comprehension, this study delves deep into the intricate connections between AI technology, urban traffic traits, sustainable traffic development, and traffic policies. It elucidates how AI algorithms adapt to different traffic characteristics, such as peak-hour traffic in commercial areas versus residential areas. Additionally, it clarifies how traffic policies can either support or hinder the implementation of AI-based traffic light optimization. For example, some policies might promote the use of certain AI-enabled traffic management systems, while others could pose regulatory challenges. Practically, this research is a valuable resource. It gives policymakers data-driven insights to craft effective traffic policies. By understanding the unique needs of each city, they can design AI-based traffic optimization strategies that are both efficient and sustainable. Moreover, the multiple case studies from different cities offer practical blueprints for the transportation industry. These cases can inspire the development of innovative technologies, the optimization of existing systems, and the widespread adoption of sustainable practices, thereby facilitating a seamless transition from traditional to intelligent and sustainable urban traffic management. Based on the limitations of the current study and the emerging issues during the research process, the following suggestions for future research can be proposed.

The current research insufficiently addresses the diverse optimization needs of different cities. Future research should deeply analyze the unique factors of each city, such as population density, traffic patterns, and infrastructure (Pandey & Kumari, 2025). For example, in mountainous cities with steep roads and narrow streets, studies could focus on how to optimize traffic lights to adapt to such special road conditions by developing optimization models highly tailored to specific urban contexts.

The existing research on the long-term sustainability of AI-driven traffic light optimization is incomplete. Future research should primarily focus on its long-term environmental benefits (Reis, 2025), such as whether the technology can continuously reduce pollutant emissions over an extended period. It should also assess the impact on social equity to ensure that all social groups can benefit from it equally, and explore its role in the overall evolution of the transportation system, including its influence on the development of future traffic patterns.

There is a lack of systematic research on the integration of AI-driven traffic light optimization and urban traffic management policies in current studies. Future research should strive to establish a theoretical framework and practical model for their coordinated development (Son et al., 2025). This involves deeply exploring how to guide technology research and development according to policy goals, enabling technology development to better meet policy requirements. At the same time, it is necessary to study how to adjust and improve traffic policies in a timely manner based on the dynamics of technology development, so as to fully unleash the potential of AI in traffic management.

REFERENCES

Abduljabbar, R., Dia, H., Liyanage, S., & Asadi Bagloee, S. (2019). Applications of Artificial Intelligence in Transport: An Overview. *Sustainability (Basel)*, *11*(1), 189. DOI: 10.3390/su11010189

Alotaibi, J. (2025). Enhancing Traffic Accident Severity Prediction: Feature Identification Using Explainable AI. *Vehicles (Basel)*, *7*(2), 38. DOI: 10.3390/vehicles7020038

Ang, K. L. M., Seng, J. K. P., Ngharamike, E., & Ijemaru, G. K. (2022). Emerging Technologies for Smart Cities' Transportation: Geo-Information, Data Analytics and Machine Learning Approaches. *ISPRS International Journal of Geo-Information*, *11*(2), 85. DOI: 10.3390/ijgi11020085

Barbieri, L., Savazzi, S., & Nicoli, M. (2021). Decentralized Federated Learning for Road User Classification in Enhanced V2X Networks. *2021 IEEE International Conference on Communications Workshops (ICC Workshops)*, 1-6. https://www.semanticscholar.org/paper/Decentralized-Federated-Learning-for-Road-User-in-Barbieri-Savazzi/3ecf7fa75f06b14a37756fa1d9fe42920efa3a91

Bohra, N., Kumari, A., Mishra, V. K., Soni, P. K., & Balyan, V. (2025). Intelligence-Based Strategies with Vehicle-to-Everything Network: A Review. *Future Internet*, *17*(2), 79. DOI: 10.3390/fi17020079

Chen, C., Liu, B., Wan, S. H., Qiao, P., & Pei, Q. Q. (2021). An edge traffic flow detection scheme based on deep learning in an intelligent transportation system. *IEEE Transactions on Intelligent Transportation Systems*, *22*(3), 1840–1852. DOI: 10.1109/TITS.2020.3025687

Damadam, S., Zourbakhsh, M., Javidan, R., & Faroughi, A. (2022). An Intelligent IoT Based Traffic Light Management System: Deep Reinforcement Learning. *Smart Cities*, *5*(4), 1293–1311. DOI: 10.3390/smartcities5040066

Ding, H., Du, Y., & Xia, Z. (2025). Urban Road Anomaly Monitoring Using Vision-Language Models for Enhanced Safety Management. *Applied Sciences (Basel, Switzerland)*, *15*(5), 2517. DOI: 10.3390/app15052517

Estrada, M., Mension, J., & Salicrú, M. (2021). Operation of transit corridors served by two routes: Physical design, synchronization, and control strategies. *Transportation Research Part C, Emerging Technologies*, *130*, 103283. DOI: 10.1016/j.trc.2021.103283

Gagliardi, G., Gallelli, V., Violi, A., Lupia, M., & Gario, G. (2024). Optimal Placement of Sensors in Traffic Networks Using Global Search Optimization Techniques Oriented towards Traffic Flow Estimation and Pollutant Emission Evaluation. *Sustainability (Basel), 16*(9), 3530. DOI: 10.3390/su16093530

Ghasemieh, A., & Kashef, R. (2024). Advanced Monocular Outdoor Pose Estimation in Autonomous Systems: Leveraging Optical Flow, Depth Estimation, and Semantic Segmentation with Dynamic Object Removal. *Sensors (Basel), 24*(24), 8040. DOI: 10.3390/s24248040 PMID: 39771776

Guo, A., & Yuan, C. (2021). Network Intelligent Control and Traffic Optimization Based on SDN and Artificial Intelligence. *Electronics (Basel), 10*(6), 700. DOI: 10.3390/electronics10060700

Han, Y., Cai, J., Ma, E., Du, S., & Lin, J. (2023). Understanding smart city practice in urban china: A governance perspective. *Sustainability (Basel), 15*(9), 7034. DOI: 10.3390/su15097034

Han, Y. W., Du, X., Zhang, H. M., Ni, J. F., & Fan, F. Y. (2024). Does smart home adoption reduce household electricity-related CO2 emissions? Evidence from Hangzhou city, China. *Energy, 289*, 129890. DOI: 10.1016/j.energy.2023.129890

Haydari, A., & Yilmaz, Y. (2022). Deep reinforcement learning for intelligent transportation systems: A survey. *IEEE Transactions on Intelligent Transportation Systems, 23*(1), 11–32. DOI: 10.1109/TITS.2020.3008612

Hurtado-Gómez, J., Romo, J. D., Salazar-Cabrera, R., Pachón de la Cruz, Á., & Madrid Molina, J. M. (2021). Traffic Signal Control System Based on Intelligent Transportation System and Reinforcement Learning. *Electronics (Basel), 10*(19), 2363. DOI: 10.3390/electronics10192363

Khan, M. A., & Park, H. (2024). Exploring Explainable Artificial Intelligence Techniques for Interpretable Neural Networks in Traffic Sign Recognition Systems. *Electronics (Basel), 13*(2), 306. DOI: 10.3390/electronics13020306

Lee, H., Chatterjee, I., & Cho, G. (2023). AI-Powered Intelligent Seaport Mobility: Enhancing Container Drayage Efficiency through Computer Vision and Deep Learning. *Applied Sciences (Basel, Switzerland), 13*(22), 12214. DOI: 10.3390/app132212214

Leonardi, S., Distefano, N., & Gruden, C. (2025). Advancing Sustainable Mobility: Artificial Intelligence Approaches for Autonomous Vehicle Trajectories in Roundabouts. *Sustainability (Basel), 17*(7), 2988. DOI: 10.3390/su17072988

Liang, Y., You, J., Wang, R., Qin, B., & Han, S. (2024). Urban Transportation Data Research Overview: A Bibliometric Analysis Based on CiteSpace. *Sustainability (Basel), 16*(22), 9615. DOI: 10.3390/su16229615

Lin, C. H., Yu, C. T., Chen, Y. L., Lin, Y. Y., & Chiao, H. T. (2025). Simulated Adversarial Attacks on Traffic Sign Recognition of Autonomous Vehicles. *Engineering Proceedings, 92*(1), 15. DOI: 10.3390/engproc2025092015

Liu, J. M., Li, J. Y., Chen, Y., Lian, S., Zeng, J. Q., Geng, M. S., Zheng, S. J., Dong, Y. A., He, Y., Huang, P., Zhao, Z., Yan, X., Hu, Q., Wang, L., Yang, D., Zhu, Z., Sun, Y., Shang, W., Wang, D., & Chen, X. M. (2023). Multi-scale urban passenger transportation CO2 emission calculation platform for smart mobility management. *Applied Energy, 331*, 120407. DOI: 10.1016/j.apenergy.2022.120407

Liu, S., Li, H., Kun, W., Zhang, Z., & Wu, H. (2022). How do transportation influencing factors affect air pollutants from vehicles in china? Evidence from threshold effect. *Sustainability (Basel), 14*(15), 9402. DOI: 10.3390/su14159402

Mao, F. F., Wei, Y. F., & Ren, J. Y. (2024). Are Smart Cities Smarter? The Impact of Smart City Policy on Digital Autonomy of Cities in China. *Polish Journal of Environmental Studies, 33*(3), 2209–2222. DOI: 10.15244/pjoes/174837

Mohsen, B. M. (2024). Al-Driven Optimization of Urban Logistics in Smart Cities: Integrating Autonomous Vehicles and loT for Efficient Delivery Systems. *Sustainability (Basel), 16*(24), 11265. DOI: 10.3390/su162411265

Mon, E. E., Ochiai, H., Komolkiti, P., & Aswakul, C. (2022). Real - world sensor dataset for city inbound-outbound critical intersection analysis. *Scientific Data, 9*(1), 357. Advance online publication. DOI: 10.1038/s41597-022-01448-6

Moreno-Vozmediano, R., Huedo, E., Montero, R. S., & Llorente, I. M. (2025). Al-Driven Resource Allocation and Auto-Scaling of VNFs in Edge-5G-loT Ecosystems. *Electronics (Basel), 14*(9), 1808. DOI: 10.3390/electronics14091808

Nigam, N., Singh, D. P., & Choudhary, J. (2023). A Review of Different Components of the Intelligent Traffic Management System (ITMS). *Symmetry, 15*(3), 583. DOI: 10.3390/sym15030583

Noaeen, M., Naik, A., Goodman, L., Crebo, J., Abrar, T., Abad, Z. S. H., Bazzan, A. L. C., & Far, B. (2022). Reinforcement learning in urban network traffic signal control: A systematic literature review. *Expert Systems with Applications, 199*, 116830. DOI: 10.1016/j.eswa.2022.116830

Paiva, S., Abdul Ahad, M., Tripathi, G., Feroz, N., & Casalino, G. (2021). Enabling Technologies for Urban Smart Mobility: Recent Trends, Opportunities and Challenges. *Sensors (Basel), 21*(6), 2143. DOI: 10.3390/s21062143 PMID: 33803903

Pandey, S. C., & Kumari, P. V. (2025). Adaptive Al-Driven Toll Management: Enhancing Traffic Flow and Sustainability Through Real-Time Prediction, Allocation, and Task Optimization. *Future Transportation, 5*(1), 21. DOI: 10.3390/futuretransp5010021

Ragab, M., Abdushkour, H. A., Maghrabi, L., Alsalman, D., Fayoumi, A. G., & AL-Ghamdi, A. (2023). Improved Artificial Rabbits Optimization with Ensemble Learning-Based Traffic Flow Monitoring on Intelligent Transportation System. *Sustainability (Basel), 15*(16), 12601. DOI: 10.3390/su151612601

Reis, M. J. C. S. (2025). Internet of Things and Artificial Intelligence for Secure and Sustainable Green Mobility: A Multimodal Data Fusion Approach to Enhance Efficiency and Security. *Multimodal Technologies and Interaction, 9*(5), 39. DOI: 10.3390/mti9050039

Sadaf, M., Iqbal, Z., Javed, A. R., Saba, I., Krichen, M., Majeed, S., & Raza, A. (2023). Connected and Automated Vehicles: Infrastructure, Applications, Security, Critical Challenges, and Future Aspects. *Technologies, 11*(5), 117. DOI: 10.3390/technologies11050117

Shulajkovska, M., Smerkol, M., Noveski, G., Bohanec, M., & Gams, M. (2024). Artificial Intelligence-Based Decision Support System for Sustainable Urban Mobility. *Electronics (Basel), 13*(18), 3655. DOI: 10.3390/electronics13183655

Shulajkovska, M., Smerkol, M., Noveski, G., & Gams, M. (2024). Enhancing Urban Sustainability: Developing an Open-Source Al Framework for Smart Cities. *Smart Cities, 7*(5), 2670–2701. DOI: 10.3390/smartcities7050104

Singh, V., Sahana, S. K., & Bhattacharjee, V. (2022). Nature-inspired Cloud-Crowd computing for intelligent transportation system. *Sustainability (Basel), 14*(23), 16322. DOI: 10.3390/su142316322

Son, H., Jang, J., Park, J., Balog, A., Ballantyne, P., Kwon, H. R., Singleton, A., & Hwang, J. (2025). Leveraging Advanced Technologies for (Smart) Transportation Planning: A Systematic Review. *Sustainability (Basel), 17*(5), 2245. DOI: 10.3390/su17052245

Su, S., Liu, J., Wang, Y., & Dong, K. (2024). Research on topological characteristics of spatial network based on complex network theory and its applications. *Mathematics, 12*(23), 3746. DOI: 10.3390/math12233746

Tao, X. Y., Cheng, L., Zhang, R. H., Chan, W. K., Chao, H., & Qin, J. (2024). Towards Green Innovation in Smart Cities: Leveraging Traffic Flow Prediction with Machine Learning Algorithms for Sustainable Transportation Systems. *Sustainability (Basel), 16*(1), 251. DOI: 10.3390/su16010251

Vaca-Recalde, M. E., Marcano, M., Matute, J., Hidalgo, C., Martinez-Rodriguez, B., Bilbao-Arechabala, S., Jorge-Hernandez, F., Murgoitio, J., Rastelli, J. P., & Santaella, J. (2024). Connected and Intelligent Framework for Vehicle Automation in Smart-Ports. *IEEE Access : Practical Innovations, Open Solutions, 12*, 120347–120361. DOI: 10.1109/ACCESS.2024.3434628

Vieira, M., Galváo, G., Vieira, M. A., Véstias, M., Vieira, P., & Louro, P. (2024). Integration of Visible Light Communication, Artificial Intelligence, and Rerouting Strategies for Enhanced Urban Traffic Management. *Vehicles (Basel), 6*(4), 2106–2132. DOI: 10.3390/vehicles6040103

Wang, K., Zhao, Y., Gangadhari, R. K., & Li, Z. (2021). Analyzing the Adoption Challenges of the Internet of Things (loT) and Artificial Intelligence (Al) for Smart Cities in China. *Sustainability (Basel), 13*(19), 10983. DOI: 10.3390/su131910983

Xie, Q. W., Shi, K., Wu, X., Huang, W. L., Zheng, X. L., & Li, Y. J. (2023). Transportation Efficiency Evaluation Under the Policies of Energy Savings and Emissions Reduction. *IEEE Intelligent Transportation Systems Magazine, 15*(6), 192–211. DOI: 10.1109/MITS.2023.3301877

Yigitcanlar, T., & Cugurullo, F. (2020). The Sustainability of Artificial Intelligence: An Urbanistic Viewpoint from the Lens of Smart and Sustainable Cities. *Sustainability (Basel), 12*(20), 8548. DOI: 10.3390/su12208548

Yin, J. H., & Song, H. Y. (2023). Does the perception of smart governance enhance commercial investments? Evidence from Beijing, Shanghai, Guangzhou, and Hangzhou. *Heliyon, 9*(8), e19024. DOI: 10.1016/j.heliyon.2023.e19024 PMID: 37609407

Yin, J. H., Song, H. Y., & Zeng, K. X. (2022). Does a smart business environment promote corporate investment? a case study of Hangzhou. *PLoS One, 17*(7), e0269089. DOI: 10.1371/journal.pone.0269089 PMID: 35793371

Zhang, X. F., & Fan, D. C. (2023). Collaborative emission reduction research on dual - pilot policies of the low-carbon city and smart city from the perspective of multiple innovations. *Urban Climate, 47*, 101364. DOI: 10.1016/j.uclim.2022.101364

Zhou, X. L., Jia, Y. W., Bai, C., Zhu, H. P., & Chan, S. X. (2022). Multi-object tracking based on attention networks for Smart City system. *Sustainable Energy Technologies and Assessments, 52*(C), 102216. DOI: 10.1016/j.seta.2022.102216

Zhu, H. Y., Shen, L. Y., & Ren, Y. T. (2022). How can smart city shape a happier life? The mechanism for developing a Happiness Driven Smart City. *Sustainable Cities and Society*, *80*, 103791. DOI: 10.1016/j.scs.2022.103791

Zuluaga-Gomez, J., Nigmatulina, I., Prasad, A., Motlicek, P., Khalil, D., Madikeri, S., Tart, A., Szoke, I., Lenders, V., Rigault, M., & Choukri, K. (2023). Lessons Learned in Transcribing 5000 h of Air Traffic Control Communications for Robust Automatic Speech Understanding. *Aerospace (Basel, Switzerland)*, *10*(10), 898. DOI: 10.3390/aerospace10100898

Chapter 7
AI in Higher Education: Personalizing Learning With Machine Learning

Mustafa Kayyali
http://orcid.org/0000-0003-3300-262X
Maaref University of Applied Sciences, Syria

ABSTRACT

The integration of artificial intelligence (AI) in higher education is not just a technological shift—it marks a fundamental transformation in how we understand and design learning experiences. This chapter explores how machine learning technologies are enabling deeply personalized approaches to education, reshaping the traditional, one-size-fits-all model into a more fluid, responsive, and student-centered system. By analyzing the mechanisms through which machine learning processes data to adapt instruction in real time, the chapter unpacks the promise of personalization: increased engagement, improved learning outcomes, and more inclusive educational pathways. Through case studies and grounded reflections, we examine the tensions between automation and human guidance, and the implications of algorithmic decision-making in educational spaces. As we move from research into real-world integration, the chapter calls for a balanced approach that champions transparency, empathy, and shared responsibility in shaping the future of AI-powered learning.

INTRODUCTION

The landscape of higher education is undergoing a seismic transformation—one not driven solely by policy shifts, curriculum reforms, or even globalization, but by a rapidly evolving technological frontier: artificial intelligence. At the heart of this shift lies a powerful and often misunderstood concept—personalization

DOI: 10.4018/979-8-2600-2373-0.ch007

(Oinas-Kukkonen et al, 2022). For decades, educators have spoken of the need to tailor instruction to individual learners, but the scale and complexity of such efforts have historically made true personalization more aspirational than practical. Today, however, the capabilities of machine learning technologies are bringing that aspiration within reach. In traditional learning environments, the pace, content, and style of instruction are largely uniform. While this model may suffice for some, it often fails to account for the diversity of learners—differences in background knowledge, learning styles, motivation, and cognitive processing. What results is a widening gap between what is taught and what is learned. Machine learning offers a bridge across that gap (Qraitem et al, 2020). By continuously analyzing data—from quiz scores and participation patterns to more nuanced indicators like time spent on tasks or response latency—AI systems can adapt content delivery in real time, providing learners with targeted feedback, custom learning paths, and timely interventions. It's not just about using data to inform instruction; it's about creating an ongoing dialogue between the learner and the system—one that learns from the learner to improve the learning process itself.

This chapter is not a celebration of AI for its own sake, nor is it an unquestioning embrace of algorithmic solutions. Rather, it is an exploration of how machine learning technologies can be meaningfully integrated into higher education to create more human-centered learning environments. The personalization enabled by AI is not meant to replace teachers, but to support them—to offload repetitive tasks, to surface insights about student needs, and to expand what is pedagogically possible within the constraints of time and scale (Rane et al, 2023). In short, AI, when thoughtfully applied, becomes a collaborator in the educational process. Yet the integration of AI into higher education also demands a pause for reflection. Who decides what an algorithm should optimize for? What biases might be embedded in the data on which these systems are trained? How do we ensure that personalization does not become surveillance? And how can we balance the efficiencies of automation with the need for human judgment, empathy, and ethical discernment?

Throughout this chapter, we will examine not only the technical mechanics of machine learning in education but also the broader questions it raises. We will explore case studies that illustrate both the promise and pitfalls of AI-powered personalization. We will look at the kinds of data being collected, the ways in which algorithms make decisions, and the implications of those decisions for equity, access, and autonomy in learning. And, perhaps most importantly, we will consider how to design AI systems that reflect the values we hold as educators, researchers, and members of a democratic society. The integration of AI into higher education is not a distant future—it is already happening. But whether this integration leads to deeper learning or deeper divides depends not on the technology itself, but on the choices we make about how we use it. This chapter is a call to engage with those choices critically, creatively, and collaboratively.

RETHINKING LEARNING IN THE AGE OF AI

It's an interesting moment to be an educator—or a learner, for that matter. Higher education is in the midst of a quiet revolution. Unlike past transformations sparked by grand reforms or sweeping ideological shifts, this one is being shaped subtly, sometimes invisibly, by technologies that work behind the scenes (Bessant, 2018). Artificial Intelligence, once a distant idea confined to labs and science fiction, has moved into the everyday lives of students and educators alike. It's in our search engines, our learning platforms, our feedback tools. It anticipates the next word we type, the next article we should read, the next concept we might struggle to grasp. And yet, in all its pervasiveness, AI doesn't arrive with loud declarations. It slips in, reshaping our experience of learning in ways that are both powerful and quietly profound. To rethink learning in the age of AI means we must step back and ask ourselves what learning has always meant—and what it could mean now (Markauskaite et al, 2022). For much of modern history, education in its formal sense has been organized around a system designed for scalability and standardization. It's a system that assumes relative uniformity across learners: that they will benefit from the same materials, move through content at the same pace, and demonstrate understanding in similar ways. There's an efficiency to that model, and to some extent, it has worked. But it has also left countless students behind—students whose learning styles don't align with traditional teaching, whose cultural or linguistic backgrounds go unrecognized, whose strengths emerge in non-traditional contexts, and whose progress doesn't always fit neatly into standardized metrics.

AI, especially through machine learning, has introduced a completely different paradigm—one that starts not with the assumption of sameness, but with a recognition of difference (Fitz & Romero, 2021). It doesn't treat learners as static recipients of knowledge but as dynamic participants in a fluid and ongoing process. Through AI, learning can begin to look more like a dialogue than a broadcast. And that changes everything. Consider, for a moment, what happens when a student engages with a learning platform powered by AI. Behind the interface, algorithms are silently observing patterns—how long the student spends on a particular question, which concepts they revisit, how quickly they answer, and what mistakes they repeatedly make. None of these data points mean much in isolation. But when gathered and analyzed over time, they begin to tell a story—a highly individualized story about how that particular student learns. Based on that story, the system adjusts. It slows down, speeds up, offers hints, reshuffles the content, or introduces new concepts in more digestible formats. The learning experience, in short, begins to adapt to the learner, rather than forcing the learner to adapt to a one-size-fits-all structure (Yang et al, 2019). This isn't just a technical development. It's a philosophical one. For the first time, we are seeing a shift from education as mass instruction to education as personal experience. And while that shift may be powered by algorithms, its implications are deeply human. If education has always been about unlocking human potential, then AI offers a way to do that with more precision, empathy, and relevance than ever before.

But this rethinking also demands that we reconsider the role of the teacher. There's a common fear, especially in discussions around automation, that AI will replace educators. But the reality is more nuanced. In truth, AI doesn't diminish the role of the teacher—it expands it. When machines can handle tasks like grading quizzes, monitoring engagement, or identifying at-risk students, educators are freed to focus on the things only humans can do: mentoring, motivating, building relationships, fostering curiosity, and guiding students through uncertainty. Teaching, at its best, has always been about more than delivering content—it's about helping students make meaning of their experiences (Churchill et al, 2024). AI can't do that. But it can create the space and support for teachers to do it more deeply. That said, not all is rosy. This shift, like any major change, comes with its complications. There is a real risk that we become so enamored with the efficiency of AI systems that we lose sight of the messy, unpredictable, and beautifully human nature of learning. Algorithms are only as good as the data they're trained on—and educational data is never neutral. It reflects the biases, assumptions, and inequalities of the systems from which it's drawn. If left unchecked, AI could reinforce those patterns rather than challenge them. A platform might "learn" that certain groups of students struggle more often and begin to lower its expectations for them, offering easier content or fewer challenges. Personalization, in that case, becomes a kind of soft discrimination—well-intentioned, perhaps, but ultimately harmful.

So, rethinking learning in the age of AI also means rethinking how we define success. What do we want our students to gain from their education? Is it mastery of content? Critical thinking? Creativity? Resilience? Some of these are measurable; others are not. AI thrives on what can be quantified—but education thrives on what can't (Pedro et al, 2019). The danger is that in optimizing for what's easy to track, we might neglect what truly matters. This tension—the one between data and meaning, between efficiency and depth—is at the heart of the conversation. And it's not one we can resolve with more sophisticated technology alone. It requires us to be thoughtful and deliberate about the values we embed in our systems, the goals we set for our institutions, and the kind of learners—and citizens—we hope to nurture. What AI offers is not a silver bullet, but a mirror. It reflects back to us the assumptions and priorities we bake into our educational design. If we program our systems to reward speed, they will. If we teach them to value curiosity and persistence, they can do that too. The technology is flexible—but our vision must be clear.

And that vision must include equity. True personalization is not just about tailoring content; it's about creating pathways for every student to succeed, regardless of where they start (Kayyali, 2024 A). It means designing systems that recognize and respond to difference—not as a deficit, but as a strength. It means using AI to identify gaps in opportunity, not just performance. And it means inviting students to be co-creators in their learning journey, not passive subjects of an algorithm's recommendation. Perhaps the most profound shift AI brings to education is not in what we teach or how we teach it—but in how we understand learning itself (Felix, 2020). Learning is no longer seen as a linear progression through a fixed curriculum, but as a dynamic, iterative process shaped by feedback, reflection, and growth. AI can help make that process visible. It can give students insight into how they learn, not just what they know. It can surface patterns they didn't see, reveal strengths they didn't recognize, and show progress in ways that go beyond grades. There's something quietly radical in that. In a world where students are often reduced to numbers, rankings, and metrics, AI can paradoxically humanize education—if we let it (Kayyali, 2020). If we use it not to sort and standardize, but to illuminate and empower. And yet, we must proceed with care. This is not a race to adopt the latest tool or integrate the flashiest algorithm. It's a slow and ongoing process of reflection, experimentation, and adaptation. We must remain skeptical of hype, critical of bias, and steadfast in our commitment to student wellbeing (Kayyali, 2024 D). AI can transform education, yes—but only if we remain committed to the humanity at its core. Rethinking learning in the age of AI is not a one-time effort (Collins & Halverson, 2018). It's a continuous conversation—about what matters, who gets to decide, and how we build systems that reflect our highest ideals. It's about re-centering the learner in a world of data, and remembering that behind every interaction, every insight, and every outcome, there is a person trying to learn, grow, and find their place in the world. In the end, the promise of AI in higher education is not about technology. It's about possibility. And possibility, more than anything else, is what education has always been about.

THE MECHANICS OF PERSONALIZATION: HOW MACHINE LEARNING WORKS IN EDUCATION

Personalized learning has always been the dream (Kallick & Zmuda, 2017). Long before technology entered the picture, educators intuitively knew that no two students learned in exactly the same way. In classrooms around the world, teachers have modified lesson plans, created alternative assignments, and offered extra help to ensure that each student has the chance to succeed. But doing this consistently and at scale—especially in higher education environments with large, diverse student populations—has often proven difficult, if not impossible. This is where machine learning steps in, not as a replacement for human understanding, but as an assistant capable of making sense of the enormous complexity of individual learning journeys. At its core, machine learning is not magic. It is a method—a set of techniques that allows computers to identify patterns in large datasets and make predictions or decisions based on those patterns. In the context of education, what this means is that we now have tools that can observe how students interact with content, how they perform over time, and how their behaviors and choices relate to their outcomes. And more importantly, we have systems that can use that information to make adjustments—automatically and in real time—so that each learner gets what they need, when they need it.

But to truly understand how personalization happens, we need to go beyond the buzzwords and dig into the human logic behind the algorithms. Think of a classroom where a teacher notices that one student frequently looks puzzled during math lessons, another rushes through assignments, and a third rarely asks questions but scores well on tests (Clement, 2018). A good teacher adapts. She slows down for one student, challenges another with extra problems, and checks in quietly with the third. Machine learning, in many ways, tries to mimic this kind of adaptive response—but instead of relying on observation alone, it processes a vast stream of data to draw conclusions that would be nearly impossible for a single teacher to capture, especially at scale. The process begins with data—lots of it. Every click, pause, quiz response, video replay, note taken, or forum post in an online learning environment generates a data point (Yoon, 2021). Over time, this adds up to a digital footprint that reflects how a student engages with the material. The job of machine learning is to sift through this footprint to detect trends, anomalies, and signals of progress or struggle. For example, if a student repeatedly revisits certain video segments, the system might infer that those concepts are challenging. If the student consistently scores well on certain types of questions but poorly on others, the system can adjust the difficulty level or provide targeted feedback. One of the most transformative aspects of machine learning in education is its capacity to deliver real-time responsiveness (Valaboju, 2024). In traditional models, feedback often comes too late—after an exam, after a missed assignment, after disengagement has already taken root. Machine learning changes that by flagging issues early (Kallis et al, 2019). It doesn't just record performance; it interprets it. When a student's behavior begins to deviate from patterns associated with success, the system can intervene—nudging the student to review a topic, alerting an instructor, or offering a different explanation or format. This creates a kind of just-in-time support system that is highly sensitive to each student's evolving needs.

But personalization isn't just about catching students when they fall. It's also about knowing when to challenge them. One of the hidden problems in education is that students who grasp material quickly often become bored or disengaged. Machine learning helps prevent this by identifying mastery and pushing learners forward with more advanced or in-depth content. In this way, it supports not just struggling students, but high performers as well, ensuring that everyone is learning at a level that matches their abilities. Of course, none of this works without thoughtful design. Algorithms don't operate in a vacuum; they reflect the choices of their creators (Finn, 2017). What data is collected? How is it interpreted? What outcomes are prioritized? These questions shape the experience of personalization. For instance, an algorithm that rewards speed may disadvantage students who are reflective or methodical. One that focuses solely on test scores might miss improvements in critical thinking or creativity. The art of personalization lies in balancing these trade-offs—making sure that what we're optimizing for aligns with what we actually value in education.

Another key element of machine learning–driven personalization is the idea of continuous improvement (Song et al, 2024). Unlike static systems, machine learning models evolve. As they gather more data, they refine their predictions and recommendations. This makes the system more accurate over time—but it also introduces new complexities. For one, the system's logic becomes less transparent. Even designers may not fully understand why the algorithm made a particular recommendation. This "black box" nature of some machine learning models raises important questions about trust, accountability, and explainability in education (Hassija et al, 2024). If a student is placed on a certain learning path by an algorithm, they deserve to know why. Teachers and institutions must be able to interpret and, when necessary, override algorithmic decisions (Levantis & Sgora, 2024). And then there's the matter of consent. Personalization works because it knows the learner—but how much should a system know? To what extent should students' behaviors be tracked, and what safeguards should be in place to protect their privacy? These are not just technical questions. They are ethical ones, and they speak to the broader relationship between students and the institutions that serve them. It's not enough for personalization to be effective; it must also be respectful.

Still, when implemented with care and clarity, machine learning can bring us closer to an educational experience that genuinely reflects the individuality of each student. It can help educators identify not just who is succeeding or failing, but why. It can support students in understanding their own learning patterns, encouraging them to become more self-aware and self-directed. And it can make the learning process more flexible, more responsive, and ultimately more humane. It's worth remembering that personalization is not new. Educators have always strived to know their students, to adapt their teaching, to connect in ways that foster growth (Mohamed & Nadia, 2024). What machine learning offers is a way to extend that philosophy across larger, more diverse populations. It takes the core values of good teaching—attentiveness, responsiveness, empathy—and gives them technological expression. This doesn't mean we should automate care or replace intuition with code. It means we should use these tools to enhance what we already do well, and to fill in the gaps where the system falls short.

In practice, the most effective implementations of machine learning in education are those that maintain a human-in-the-loop approach. The technology supports decisions, but people make them. Teachers use the insights provided by algorithms to inform their instruction—not to surrender their judgment (Schouten, 2017). Students are given agency, with personalization tools offering options and suggestions rather than rigid prescriptions (Kayyali, 2025). In this way, the mechanics of machine learning become part of a broader ecosystem of learning that honors both data and dialogue. There's no denying that we are still early in this journey. The systems are improving, but they are far from perfect. There will be missteps, blind spots, and unintended consequences. But the direction is promising. We are moving toward a vision of education that is less about conformity and more about possibility—one where every learner is seen, supported, and challenged in a way that respects their unique trajectory. To understand how machine learning works in education is to recognize that personalization is both a technical and a philosophical project. It's about building systems that can respond to complexity without reducing learners to numbers. It's about using data to deepen our understanding, not narrow it. And it's about never forgetting that behind every line of code is a student trying to make sense of the world—and a teacher trying to help them do it.

FROM DATA TO DESIGN: BUILDING ADAPTIVE LEARNING ENVIRONMENTS

The notion of a classroom as a fixed space—a place with four walls, a whiteboard, a row of chairs, and a lecturer at the front—is fading. In its place, we are witnessing the rise of something far more dynamic: adaptive learning environments. These are not simply digital classrooms or online platforms. They are complex ecosystems designed to respond to individual learners in real time, shifting content, feedback, pacing, and pathways according to what each student needs at any given moment. But this responsiveness doesn't come from nowhere. It begins with data—an ever-growing stream of it—and evolves through thoughtful design rooted in pedagogy, empathy, and care.

In many ways, the building of adaptive learning environments starts with a fundamental question: How do people learn best when they are seen, heard, and understood? The answer is never straightforward, because learning is never linear. Some students need more time. Others need more context. Some thrive on visual input. Others need hands-on examples or a guiding narrative to make sense of what they're absorbing. What adaptive environments seek to do is to take this messiness—the inherent variability of how humans learn—and turn it into a strength, not a problem. The journey from data to design is not mechanical. It's interpretive. It requires not only collecting information about students but also knowing what to do with it—when to act on it, when to wait, and when to override it altogether (Simkins & Maier, 2023). In a well-built adaptive system, everything a student does is a form of communication. Every time they pause on a difficult question, every time they replay a video segment, every time they skip a reading or excel on a challenge—it all means something. These signals become inputs for systems that are constantly recalibrating what comes next. The design, then, is less about dictating a path and more about preparing for a multitude of possible paths.

But let's not confuse data with understanding. Numbers alone don't tell us much. What matters is how we interpret those numbers—what patterns we recognize, what assumptions we challenge, what actions we decide to take (Lindebaum et al, 2020). For instance, if a student scores poorly on an assessment, the data might suggest they don't understand the material. But is that always true? Maybe they were tired. Maybe the assessment format didn't align with their strengths. Maybe they knew the content but couldn't recall it under pressure. This is where design becomes essential. An adaptive learning environment worth its name doesn't just respond to performance; it tries to understand the reasons behind that performance and offers flexible ways for students to demonstrate learning.

Designing these environments, then, is an act of educational empathy. It requires imagining the experience of the learner—what it feels like to be lost in a lesson, to get stuck on a concept, to finally have something click. The best systems are not the ones that react the fastest, but the ones that respond with care. They offer second chances, alternate explanations, visual aids, interactive exercises, or even a gentle nudge to take a break and come back later. They understand that learning isn't just cognitive—it's emotional, psychological, and deeply human. A big part of what makes adaptive learning environments work is their ability to connect small pieces of information into a coherent whole (Shute & Towle, 2018). This is where machine learning plays its role, identifying patterns across thousands—even millions—of learners to anticipate what might help any one individual. If a student's learning profile matches the profile of others who struggled with a particular topic, the system might suggest a different approach, one that proved effective for similar learners. Over time, the system doesn't just react to what's happening; it begins to anticipate what's likely to happen next. But anticipation is not enough. Real adaptation requires choice. Students must be part of the loop. The best environments don't just push recommendations—they offer options. They allow students to reflect on their own progress, to choose how they want to move forward, to make decisions about their learning journey. In this way, the adaptive environment becomes a partnership. It's not just something that happens to the student—it's something they shape and influence.

Building such environments requires collaboration across disciplines. Educators bring the pedagogical insight. Data scientists bring the technical expertise (Williamson, 2017). Designers ensure that the interface is intuitive and humane. And most importantly, students bring their lived experience—their frustrations, their triumphs, their feedback. Without that, the environment risks becoming a cold, mechanical system that serves efficiency more than learning. It's also important to acknowledge the potential pitfalls. Not every adaptive system is created with the same care. Some are overly prescriptive, locking students into rigid tracks based on early performance. Others focus too narrowly on test scores, ignoring broader indicators of growth. And some simply lack the transparency to explain why certain decisions are being made, leaving students and instructors in the dark. Good design, in this space, means more than clever algorithms. It means transparency, flexibility, and a willingness to keep listening—to data, yes, but also to people (Schildt, 2017). One of the overlooked challenges in building adaptive learning environments is the invisible labor behind the scenes. These systems need to be maintained, updated, and improved. They require ongoing monitoring to ensure they're working as intended, and not drifting into harmful or biased behaviors. They need educators to stay involved—not just as users, but as co-creators. This is not a set-it-and-forget-it kind of technology. It's a living system, one that must evolve in dialogue with its users.

In the classroom, the effects of a well-designed adaptive environment can be transformative (Vezhbovska et al, 2024). A student who previously struggled in silence might now receive timely support. Another, who felt unchallenged, might discover new levels of depth in the material. Over time, the entire tone of learning can shift—from passive reception to active engagement, from anxiety to confidence. The student is no longer just following a curriculum; they're inhabiting it, shaping it, making it their own. But for all its power, adaptive learning is not a cure-all. It doesn't eliminate the need for good teaching. It doesn't replace the value of discussion, community, or mentorship. What it does is extend the reach of those things—helping each learner connect more deeply with the material, and helping educators better understand how to support them. It complements the human elements of education, rather than competing with them. It also invites us to reconsider some of our most basic assumptions. For instance, what if learning goals didn't have to be bound by time? What if a semester wasn't a fixed unit, but a flexible framework? What if assessments weren't final judgments, but opportunities to understand more deeply? Adaptive environments open up these possibilities—not by abandoning structure, but by making structure more responsive. They give us a chance to design for real learning, not just surface-level performance.

Ultimately, building adaptive learning environments is about imagining what education could look like if it truly met students where they are—not just in theory, but in practice (Regan et al, 2022). It's about moving from data to design, not through mechanical processes, but through human insight. It's about using the tools we have—powerful, yes, but still just tools—to build something more humane, more flexible, and more inclusive. These environments will continue to evolve. They will become more sophisticated, more intuitive, and hopefully, more equitable. But they will only do so if we stay involved—if we ask hard questions, push for transparency, and insist on designs that prioritize learning over metrics, students over systems. In the end, adaptive learning is not about creating smarter machines. It's about creating smarter, more compassionate learning experiences—experiences that remind us why we teach, why we learn, and what it means to grow.

CHALLENGES AND ETHICAL CONSIDERATIONS IN AI-POWERED EDUCATION

When we talk about AI in education, the conversation often begins with excitement—about efficiency, personalization, real-time feedback, and the potential to transform learning at scale. It's hard not to be drawn to the possibilities. But for all the promise AI brings, there are difficult, sometimes uncomfortable questions that we must not avoid. These questions aren't peripheral. They lie at the heart of what it means to learn, to teach, and to trust the systems that increasingly mediate those experiences. One of the first challenges we must face is the illusion of objectivity (Smail, 2018). There's a widespread assumption that machines don't carry the same biases humans do—that they process information neutrally, logically, and without prejudice. But the truth is, AI systems in education are trained on data generated by human institutions (Kayyali, 2025 B). That data reflects real-world disparities—gaps in access, differences in performance shaped by socio-economic background, language, race, gender, and so much more. When an algorithm learns from that data, it doesn't magically erase these inequities. It can, and often does, entrench them further. Imagine a predictive system that identifies students at risk of failure based on past performance metrics. If those metrics already reflect systemic inequalities—such as under-resourced schools, linguistic disadvantages, or cultural disconnects—the system may flag the very students who most need encouragement as poor prospects. It may steer them away from more challenging paths. It may offer them fewer opportunities under the guise of personalization. And if these decisions happen quietly, invisibly, as they often do in algorithmic systems, we may never realize the subtle discrimination at play.

This leads us into a second, deeply ethical concern: transparency. In traditional education, even when decisions are imperfect, they're visible. A student knows who graded their paper. An instructor knows why they adjusted a student's final grade. But with AI-powered systems, the logic behind decisions can become obscure. Why was a student shown a particular recommendation? Why was another nudged to review certain material while others were not? The algorithms that drive these decisions are often complex, sometimes proprietary, and rarely fully understood—even by those who implement them. This "black box" nature raises serious issues about accountability. If a student is harmed by an AI-driven decision, who takes responsibility?

And it's not just students who are affected. Educators, too, face a shifting landscape. On one hand, AI can lighten their workload—handling administrative tasks, flagging students in need, suggesting differentiated resources. On the other hand, it can erode professional autonomy. What happens when a system begins to suggest which students are "worth investing in," or which teaching strategies are "most effective," based on cold data rather than human judgment? There is a risk that educators become implementers of algorithmic suggestions, rather than critical thinkers and compassionate professionals. The more we rely on data-driven tools, the more pressure there is to trust their outputs, even when they conflict with gut feeling or nuanced understanding (Gade, 2021). Then there is the issue of consent. In most AI-powered educational platforms, data is collected passively. Students log in, complete activities, and the system quietly records everything—clicks, pauses, keystrokes, even facial expressions in some experimental settings. But how many students truly understand the extent to which they are being observed? How many have given meaningful consent for their data to be used in this way? And how do we ensure that this consent is informed, ongoing, and voluntary—not something buried in a terms-of-use agreement no one reads?

Privacy, too, becomes a pressing concern. Educational data is deeply personal (Reidenberg & Schaub, 2018). It contains not just academic performance, but also behavioral patterns, learning preferences, emotional responses, and sometimes even biometric data. Who has access to this data? How is it stored? Who decides how long it is kept, or whether it can be sold, shared, or reused for purposes beyond education? In an era where data is a valuable commodity, educational institutions must be especially vigilant. Students are not consumers—they are individuals engaged in a vulnerable and formative process. Their data should never be treated as a product. A further complication lies in the global nature of AI. Many educational tools are developed by companies based in specific cultural contexts, often in the Global North (Titarenko & Little, 2017). Yet these tools are used in vastly different settings—across countries, languages, belief systems, and pedagogical traditions. The risk here is subtle but real: cultural assumptions baked into algorithms can shape how learning is defined, measured, and rewarded. What counts as "participation"? What is considered a "correct" answer? How is curiosity recognized? If systems are not designed with cultural sensitivity, they may promote narrow visions of success and marginalize students who don't conform to those norms. And let's not forget the psychological impact of AI-mediated learning. When students interact with systems that monitor and adapt to them constantly, how does that affect their sense of agency? Some may feel empowered, but others may feel surveilled, manipulated, or reduced to a data profile. There's a fine line between helpful nudging and coercive guidance. When a student is told what to study next, not by a teacher but by a machine that "knows" their patterns, it can create a subtle dependence on external validation. Instead of fostering self-directed learners, we risk creating users who look to the system for every next move.

This concern ties into broader questions about what education is for. If we're not careful, AI can push us toward a narrow definition of learning—one that emphasizes measurable outcomes over deeper understanding. After all, machines are best at tracking what can be quantified: time on task, test scores, completion rates. But many of the most important aspects of learning are messy, slow, and difficult to measure—curiosity, resilience, critical thinking, ethical reasoning, and the ability to ask new questions rather than simply answer existing ones. If we design systems that focus only on what's easy to measure, we may inadvertently sideline what matters most (Manheim, 2023). There's also a question of pace. AI moves quickly. Educational systems do not. Universities and schools are slow by design—deliberate, layered, and often resistant to fads. That resistance, though frustrating at times, is also a safeguard. It ensures that change is debated, tested, and rooted in values. The danger is that AI systems may be adopted too quickly, outpacing our ability to understand or regulate them. A school might implement a predictive analytics platform without fully grasping its implications. A university might adopt an automated grading tool without adequate review. In the rush to innovate, we risk losing control over the very systems meant to serve us.

So, what do we do with all these challenges? Do we abandon AI in education? No. That's neither realistic nor wise. The potential benefits—especially in terms of accessibility, responsiveness, and scale—are too significant to ignore. But we must approach this work with humility, vigilance, and a commitment to values that place people above performance metrics. We need transparency—about how systems work, what data they use, and how decisions are made. We need accountability—clear lines of responsibility when harm occurs. We need inclusivity—design processes that involve students, educators, ethicists, and communities from diverse backgrounds. We need adaptability—mechanisms for challenging, revising, or shutting down systems that fail to serve their purpose. And most of all, we need a renewed focus on the human heart of education. Because in the end, AI is not a neutral force. It reflects the priorities we encode into it. If we value speed, it will optimize for speed. If we value conformity, it will reward conformity. But if we value growth, diversity, equity, and depth, then we can build systems that honor those values. The technology is only as ethical as the people who design and deploy it (Baldini et al, 2018). The real challenge of AI-powered education is not technological—it's moral. It asks us to decide what kind of learning environments we want to create, what kind of learners we want to nurture, and what kind of society we want to build. And those are questions no machine can answer for us.

CASE STUDIES AND REAL-WORLD APPLICATIONS IN HIGHER EDUCATION

It's one thing to talk about the transformative potential of AI in higher education. It's quite another to see it in action—tested in real classrooms, used by real students, and shaped by the messy realities of institutional life. While much of the discourse surrounding AI in education still hovers around possibilities and projections, a growing number of universities and colleges around the world are already experimenting with machine learning–driven systems that aim to personalize, support, and sometimes even rethink the learning experience (Kayyali, 2024 B). These experiments, these early applications, provide something crucial: context. They show us what works, what stumbles, and what it truly takes to bring AI beyond theory and into practice. They remind us that no matter how intelligent or adaptive a system may be, its value is ultimately measured by how it is received, trusted, and used by the people it is meant to serve.

Take Georgia State University in Atlanta, for example. A public institution serving a large and highly diverse student population, GSU had long struggled with high dropout rates, especially among first-generation college students (Green & Wright, 2017). Instead of accepting attrition as a statistical inevitability, the university made a bold move: it implemented a predictive analytics platform to track over 800 markers of student performance and behavior—things like missed assignments, poor performance in key courses, or even reduced logins to the university portal. The system flagged these indicators in real time, allowing advisors to reach out proactively—sometimes before the students even realized they were in academic trouble. This wasn't about replacing human advisors with technology (Kayyali, 2021). It was about giving those advisors better tools, better timing, and better insight. The results were striking. Over several years, graduation rates increased, and achievement gaps between student groups narrowed significantly. But perhaps the most telling success was this: students reported feeling seen, supported, and cared for—not surveilled or micromanaged. That speaks volumes about how the thoughtful use of AI can enhance, rather than undermine, human connection in education.

Then there's Arizona State University, which has invested heavily in adaptive courseware—particularly in large, high-enrollment courses like introductory biology and math, where traditionally, failure rates were high and personalized instruction was hard to scale. Using adaptive learning platforms like ALEKS (Assessment and LEarning in Knowledge Spaces), ASU began to individualize the pace and sequence of content delivery based on each student's performance (Harati et al, 2021). These platforms adjust in real time, identifying gaps in knowledge and re-routing students through prerequisite material when needed, while accelerating progress for those who demonstrate mastery. The impact was not just academic. Students who might have otherwise dropped out of these foundational courses began to persist, and faculty reported that the adaptive systems helped them focus their attention where it was needed most. It's worth noting that these systems didn't diminish the role of instructors. On the contrary, they allowed instructors to shift from delivering uniform lectures to offering more targeted guidance, hosting small group discussions, and engaging in meaningful mentorship. In this way, the technology didn't replace the teacher—it freed the teacher to teach more effectively.

In the United Kingdom, the Open University has taken a slightly different route. As a leader in distance education, OU has long been interested in learning analytics and their potential to improve student retention. One of its more innovative systems, OU Analyse, uses historical data combined with machine learning models to predict which students are at risk of failing or dropping out of a module. What makes the OU approach stand out is its sensitivity to student context. The system does not merely flag poor performance—it also considers life circumstances, enrollment patterns, and even the time students engage with the platform (night owls, for instance, are often juggling study with full-time jobs or parenting). By feeding this data back to both students and tutors in a transparent and user-friendly way, the university creates a shared awareness of progress and risk. Tutors can offer support, students can self-correct, and interventions can be made early. Crucially, OU continues to emphasize the role of the student as an active participant—not just a subject of analysis. Students are invited to reflect on their own patterns, to question the system's feedback, and to set their own learning goals accordingly. This reinforces agency, rather than diminishing it.

Not all applications of AI in higher education revolve around academic performance (Altememy et al, 2023). Some focus on access, equity, and student wellbeing. At Deakin University in Australia, for instance, the university has implemented a virtual student advisor powered by natural language processing and machine learning. Known as "Genie," the system answers questions from students around the clock—about enrollment, deadlines, library services, and even mental health resources. While this might seem basic, its impact is anything but. For students who feel overwhelmed or isolated—especially first-years or those studying remotely—having immediate, judgment-free access to help can be the difference between persistence and withdrawal. Genie doesn't try to do everything. It doesn't offer academic counseling or deep emotional support. But it plays a crucial triage role—pointing students in the right direction, reducing friction in everyday tasks, and freeing up staff to focus on more complex needs. The key here is intentional design. The system was built not to dazzle or automate, but to genuinely help—and to do so in ways that respect the dignity and diversity of the student body.

Of course, these successes are not without complications. Institutions that have embraced AI-powered tools often face pushback—sometimes from faculty wary of data-driven teaching, sometimes from students concerned about privacy, and sometimes from administrators grappling with ethical questions (Murgatroyd, 2024). For example, how much data is too much? Should students be required to opt in to learning analytics platforms? What happens if an algorithm is wrong—and a student is labeled at risk unfairly? The University of Edinburgh has taken a proactive approach to these questions, developing a set of guiding principles for the ethical use of learning analytics. These principles emphasize transparency, student agency, and the importance of context. Rather than treating AI as a back-end function, the university brings it into the open—discussing its use with students, training staff to interpret analytics responsibly, and ensuring that no algorithm operates without human oversight. This culture of openness helps build trust, which in turn makes the technology more effective.

In some cases, the most powerful real-world applications come not from elite universities or well-funded pilots, but from smaller institutions experimenting with grassroots solutions. At Minerva University—a relatively new institution with a global, fully online model—adaptive learning is built into the very structure of the curriculum. Students engage in live, synchronous seminars supported by AI tools that track participation, prompt reflection, and analyze engagement patterns over time. This doesn't just help instructors adjust in the moment—it creates a feedback-rich environment in which students become more aware of their own learning behaviors and are encouraged to grow through self-observation. Across these diverse case studies, a few patterns begin to emerge. First, the most successful applications of AI in higher education are not those that focus on replacing human roles but those that support them—making the invisible visible, making the complicated manageable, and making the learning experience more tailored, humane, and responsive. Second, transparency matters. Systems that explain what they're doing, and why, tend to be more trusted and more effective (Bess et al, 2023). And third, context is everything. AI systems must be designed and adapted with an awareness of the unique needs, cultures, and values of the institutions and communities they serve. What these examples collectively show is that AI is not a single technology but a wide array of tools and practices—each with its own strengths, limitations, and ethical considerations. There is no one-size-fits-all solution (Kayyali, 2024 C). But there is a growing body of evidence that, when used with care and intention, these tools can improve student outcomes, reduce inequalities, and enrich the educational experience for all involved. Still, we must remain clear-eyed. AI can be useful, even transformative—but only when we keep humans at the center of the system. These case studies remind us that technology is not destiny. It is design. And design is always a reflection of values, choices, and the people who make them.

LOOKING AHEAD: SHAPING THE FUTURE OF PERSONALIZED LEARNING

We often talk about the future as if it's some far-off, intangible horizon. But in education—especially when it comes to personalized learning powered by AI—that future is already unfolding around us. It's present in the quiet evolution of course design, in the subtle interventions that guide students through difficult content, in the ways our learning platforms observe, interpret, and respond. We are no longer wondering whether education will change. It already has. The real question now is what kind of future we are building, who gets to shape it, and how we ensure that, in our pursuit of innovation, we don't lose sight of the values that brought us here in the first place. Personalized learning, as a concept, is not new (Brass & Lynch, 2020). Educators have long sought to meet students where they are—to differentiate instruction, to allow for different paces and paths, to respect the uniqueness of each learner. What's different now is the scale at which this can be done. Machine learning, big data, and advanced analytics give us the tools to make personalization not only possible but sustainable across entire institutions, across thousands—sometimes millions—of learners (Regan & Jesse, 2019). But the speed and scale of this transformation bring both extraordinary potential and sobering responsibility. Looking ahead, the challenge is not just to make systems more intelligent, but to make them more humane. The risk with any technological movement is that it can drift into efficiency for its own sake—optimizing for speed, completion, or surface-level performance while neglecting the deeper, slower work of human growth. The future of personalized learning cannot be a future of automation alone. It must be a future of intention—one where every design decision, every algorithmic tweak, every data point is held up to the light of our highest educational values: equity, curiosity, care, and agency.

In this envisioned future, learners are not passive recipients of algorithmic recommendations (Elwarraki et al, 2023). They are active participants in shaping their own learning journeys. They understand how systems work, they are given meaningful choices, and they are encouraged to reflect on their own patterns, preferences, and progress. Personalization, in its most empowered form, becomes a partnership—a dialogue between the learner and the system, guided by trust and shared purpose. Students learn to ask not only "What should I study next?" but also "Why is this being suggested to me?" and "What kind of learner do I want to be?"

That vision requires more than good software. It requires a cultural shift—one in which institutions commit not just to adopting new tools, but to rethinking the structures, timelines, and assumptions that define how education is delivered. In a truly personalized learning environment, semesters may become more flexible, assessments more formative, and progress less about keeping pace and more about meaningful mastery. These changes challenge long-held traditions, and they won't happen overnight. But they're necessary if we want technology to serve the learner, rather than force the learner to adapt to the technology. Another important shift on the horizon is the growing recognition of data as a relational asset. For too long, data in education has been treated as something extracted—collected from students, analyzed behind closed doors, and returned in the form of grades or dashboards. But this extractive model is beginning to give way to a more relational one—where data is shared, discussed, co-owned. Students are invited into the conversation. They learn to interpret their own learning data, to see it not as a judgment but as a mirror, a tool for self-awareness and growth. In this model, personalization is no longer something done to the student—it's something done with them. The future also demands that we confront the biases and blind spots embedded in our systems. As machine learning models become more complex, so too do the risks of unintentional harm (Tan et al, 2022). Bias in training data, narrow definitions of success, and a lack of transparency in algorithmic decision-making can all reinforce inequalities rather than reduce them. If left unexamined, these systems could become self-fulfilling prophecies—tracking students into certain paths based on incomplete or flawed assumptions about their potential. That's why building the future of personalized learning must include rigorous, ongoing reflection. Ethics must be baked into the design process from the very beginning, not tacked on as an afterthought. We will also need new kinds of collaboration—across disciplines, sectors, and communities. Technologists cannot build these systems in isolation. Educators, psychologists, ethicists, students, and even parents must be part of the design conversation (Bar-on, 2018). This is not just a matter of input—it's about perspective. Those closest to the learning experience bring insights that no algorithm can replicate. They see the nuances, the context, the complexity. They ask questions that data alone cannot answer. If we want personalized learning to reflect real human lives, it must be shaped by real human voices.

At the same time, we must prepare educators to navigate this new landscape. The shift toward personalized, AI-supported learning changes the role of the teacher—not by diminishing it, but by evolving it. Educators become more like learning architects, curators, facilitators, and mentors. They interpret data not as cold statistics but as part of a rich story about each student's path. This requires support, training, and a culture that values both innovation and critical thinking. It also requires time—time to explore new tools, to reflect on practice, to collaborate with peers. If the future of learning is to be truly personalized, then the professional development of teachers must be personalized as well. One of the most exciting, and perhaps most radical, possibilities lies in the idea of co-created curricula (Stoddard et al, 2024). In a world where learning is increasingly adaptive, there is room for students to help design not only how they learn, but what they learn. Personalized learning doesn't have to be limited to adjusting pre-set pathways. It can mean expanding those pathways, creating space for passion projects, interdisciplinary exploration, and real-world problem-solving. It can mean turning education from a transmission model into a creation model—where learners are not just consumers of content but producers of knowledge. This isn't just about engagement. It's about agency. And agency, more than anything, is what makes learning meaningful.

As we look to the future, we must also think globally. The promise of personalized learning is not limited by geography, but its accessibility often is. Many of the most advanced systems are developed in contexts with high levels of connectivity, stable infrastructure, and institutional investment (Markolf et al, 2018). But education is a global project, and the tools we build must reflect global realities. That means designing for low-bandwidth environments, supporting multiple languages, respecting diverse pedagogies, and ensuring that personalization does not become a luxury afforded only to the privileged. Equity cannot be a feature; it must be the foundation. And finally, we must remember that not everything in education can—or should—be personalized. There is value in shared experiences, in common texts, in collective discussion. Learning is not only about individual mastery; it's also about encountering other ways of thinking, participating in a community, and learning to live with complexity and difference. The future we shape must leave room for these things. It must honor the balance between individual paths and shared purpose.

So what does it take to build that future? It takes imagination and humility. It takes experimentation and patience. It takes a willingness to ask hard questions, to learn from failure, and to keep learners—not metrics—at the center of the conversation. It takes people who care deeply about what education can be, and who are willing to challenge what it has always been. Personalized learning, in its most authentic form, is not about catering to preference or convenience (Bernacki et al, 2021). It's about recognizing potential. It's about creating environments where students are seen for who they are and supported as they become who they might be. It's about holding the tension between structure and freedom, between data and story, between innovation and care. And it's about hope. The belief that, with the right tools, the right design, and the right intentions, we can build learning experiences that are more inclusive, more responsive, and more meaningful than ever before. The future of personalized learning is not something we wait for. It's something we shape—day by day, choice by choice, with eyes wide open and hearts fully engaged.

CONCLUSION

As we stand at the intersection of pedagogy and technology, it is clear that the conversation about AI in higher education is not just about machines—it is fundamentally about people. Personalization through machine learning technologies offers a compelling vision: a learning experience that recognizes the uniqueness of every student, responds to their evolving needs, and empowers them to take ownership of their educational journey. Yet, realizing this vision requires more than technical sophistication; it requires a reimagining of the values and structures that underpin higher education. Throughout this chapter, we have seen that AI holds immense potential to support more responsive, data-informed, and individualized teaching and learning practices. We have explored how machine learning algorithms can detect patterns invisible to the human eye, providing real-time feedback and adaptive pathways that were once unthinkable in traditional classroom settings. The ability of AI systems to continuously learn from student interactions and refine instructional delivery offers a powerful tool to close achievement gaps, identify struggling learners before they fall behind, and offer enrichment opportunities to those ready to go further.

However, with such power comes a heightened responsibility. The same algorithms that can personalize learning can also inadvertently reinforce existing inequities, if they are trained on biased data or used without a clear understanding of their limitations. The very act of collecting and analyzing student data raises important ethical questions around consent, privacy, and autonomy. If not handled with care, the promise of personalization could morph into a regime of hyper-monitoring, where students are reduced to data points and learning becomes a path determined more by prediction than possibility. Educators must remain central to this conversation. No algorithm, no matter how advanced, can replace the intuition, empathy, and contextual judgment of a skilled teacher. Instead, the goal should be to create symbiotic systems in which AI and educators work together—where machines handle routine tasks and surface insights, and teachers use that information to craft richer, more meaningful learning experiences. This partnership, when built on trust and transparency, can elevate the entire educational experience.

Looking ahead, the future of personalized learning in higher education will be shaped by our collective decisions—about what we value, who we include, and how we define success. Will we use AI to merely optimize existing systems, or will we allow it to help us imagine new possibilities for teaching and learning? Will we build technologies that serve all learners equitably, or only those who fit a certain profile? And will we remain vigilant about the human dimensions of education—curiosity, creativity, connection—even as we embrace the tools of automation? In the end, AI is neither a threat nor a panacea. It is a mirror that reflects our priorities and amplifies our decisions. If we are thoughtful, collaborative, and courageous in how we approach its integration, we can ensure that the era of AI in higher education is not one of disconnection and depersonalization, but one of deeper understanding, greater inclusion, and transformative growth.

REFERENCES

Altememy, H. A., Mohammed, B. A., Hsony, M. K., Hassan, A. Y., Mazhair, R., Dawood, I. I., & Sharif, H. R. (2023). The influence of the artificial intelligence capabilities of higher education institutions in Iraq on students' academic performance: The role of AI-based technology application as a mediator. *Eurasian Journal of Educational Research*, *104*(104), 267–282.

Baldini, G., Botterman, M., Neisse, R., & Tallacchini, M. (2018). Ethical design in the internet of things. *Science and Engineering Ethics*, *24*(3), 905–925. DOI: 10.1007/s11948-016-9754-5 PMID: 26797878

Baron, P. R. (2018). Ethical inclusive curricula design: Conversational teaching and learning. *South African Journal of Higher Education*, *32*(6), 326–350. DOI: 10.20853/32-6-2987

Bernacki, M. L., Greene, M. J., & Lobczowski, N. G. (2021). A systematic review of research on personalized learning: Personalized by whom, to what, how, and for what purpose (s)? *Educational Psychology Review*, *33*(4), 1675–1715. DOI: 10.1007/s10648-021-09615-8

Bess, J. L., Johnstone, D. B., & Dee, J. R. (2023). Understanding college and university organization: Theories for effective policy and practice: Volume II—Dynamics of the system. Routledge.

Bessant, J. (2018). *The great transformation: History for a techno-human future*. Routledge. DOI: 10.4324/9781315643533

Brass, J., & Lynch, T. L. (2020). Personalized learning: A history of the present. *Journal of Curriculum Theorizing*, *35*(2). Advance online publication. DOI: 10.63997/jct.v35i2.807

Churchill, R., Apps, T., Batt, J., Beckman, K., Grainger, P., Holloway, J., & Shaw, K. (2024). *Teaching: Making a difference*. John Wiley & Sons.

Clement, M. C. (2018). *What successful teachers do: a dozen things to ensure student learning*. Rowman & Littlefield.

Collins, A., & Halverson, R. (2018). *Rethinking education in the age of technology: The digital revolution and schooling in America*. Teachers College Press.

Elwarraki, O., Aammou, S., Jdidou, Y., & Lahiassi, J. (2023). Toward the future of personalized learning: Emerging trends and challenges in recommendation systems. ICERI2023 Proceedings, 7226-7235.

Felix, C. V. (2020). The role of the teacher and AI in education. In *International perspectives on the role of technology in humanizing higher education* (pp. 33–48). Emerald Publishing Limited. DOI: 10.1108/S2055-364120200000033003

Finn, E. (2017). What algorithms want: Imagination in the age of computing. mit Press.

Fitz, S., & Romero, P. (2021). Neural networks and deep learning: A paradigm shift in information processing, machine learning, and artificial intelligence. The Palgrave handbook of technological finance, 589-654.

Gade, K. R. (2021). Data-driven decision making in a complex world. *Journal of Computational Innovation*, *1*(1).

Green, S. L., & Wright, C. F. (2017). Retaining first generation underrepresented minority students: A struggle for higher education. *The Journal of Educational Research*, *11*(3).

Harati, H., Sujo-Montes, L., Tu, C. H., Armfield, S. J., & Yen, C. J. (2021). Assessment and learning in knowledge spaces (ALEKS) adaptive system impact on students' perception and self-regulated learning skills. *Education Sciences*, *11*(10), 603. DOI: 10.3390/educsci11100603

Hassija, V., Chamola, V., Mahapatra, A., Singal, A., Goel, D., Huang, K., Scardapane, S., Spinelli, I., Mahmud, M., & Hussain, A. (2024). Interpreting black-box models: A review on explainable artificial intelligence. *Cognitive Computation*, *16*(1), 45–74. DOI: 10.1007/s12559-023-10179-8

Kallick, B., & Zmuda, A. (2017). *Students at the center: Personalized learning with habits of mind*. Ascd.

Kallis, R., Di Sorbo, A., Canfora, G., & Panichella, S. (2019, September). Ticket tagger: Machine learning driven issue classification. In *2019 IEEE International Conference on Software Maintenance and Evolution (ICSME)* (pp. 406-409). IEEE. DOI: 10.1109/ICSME.2019.00070

Kayyali, M. (2020). Pros and Cons of University Rankings. *Online Submission*, *1*(1), 1–6.

Kayyali, M. (2021). Positive impact of high technology on higher education.

Kayyali, M. (2024). B). Future possibilities and challenges of AI in education. In *Transforming education with generative AI: Prompt engineering and synthetic content creation* (pp. 118–137). IGI Global Scientific Publishing. DOI: 10.4018/979-8-3693-1351-0.ch006

Kayyali, M. (2024 C). Immersive Technologies: Virtual and Augmented Reality in Higher Education. In Reshaping learning with next generation educational technologies (pp. 99-114). IGI Global.

Kayyali, M. (2024 A). Global Perspectives on Personalized Learning: Case Studies and Best Practices. In Transforming Education for Personalized Learning (pp. 66-84). IGI Global.

Kayyali, M. (Ed.). (2024 D). Building Resiliency in Higher Education: Globalization, Digital Skills, and Student Wellness: Globalization, Digital Skills, and Student Wellness. IGI Global.

Kayyali, M. (2025). A). The Impact of Personalized Learning on Student Engagement and Achievement in STEAM. In *Integrating Personalized Learning Methods Into STEAM Education* (pp. 51–78). IGI Global Scientific Publishing. DOI: 10.4018/979-8-3693-7718-5.ch003

Kayyali, M. (2025 B). The Future of AI in Education: Predictions and Emerging Trends. Next-Generation AI Methodologies in Education, 367-406.

Levantis, N., & Sgora, A. (2024, May). Algorithmic Decision Making in Education: Challenges and Opportunities. In *2024 IEEE Global Engineering Education Conference (EDUCON)* (pp. 1-7). IEEE. DOI: 10.1109/EDUCON60312.2024.10578645

Lindebaum, D., Vesa, M., & Den Hond, F. (2020). Insights from "the machine stops" to better understand rational assumptions in algorithmic decision making and its implications for organizations. *Academy of Management Review*, *45*(1), 247–263. DOI: 10.5465/amr.2018.0181

Manheim, D. (2023). Building less-flawed metrics: Understanding and creating better measurement and incentive systems. *Patterns (New York, N.Y.)*, *4*(10), 100842. DOI: 10.1016/j.patter.2023.100842 PMID: 37876897

Markauskaite, L., Marrone, R., Poquet, O., Knight, S., Martinez-Maldonado, R., Howard, S., Tondeur, J., De Laat, M., Buckingham Shum, S., Gašević, D., & Siemens, G. (2022). Rethinking the entwinement between artificial intelligence and human learning: What capabilities do learners need for a world with AI? *Computers and Education: Artificial Intelligence*, *3*, 100056. DOI: 10.1016/j.caeai.2022.100056

Markolf, S. A., Chester, M. V., Eisenberg, D. A., Iwaniec, D. M., Davidson, C. I., Zimmerman, R., Miller, T. R., Ruddell, B. L., & Chang, H. (2018). Interdependent infrastructure as linked social, ecological, and technological systems (SETSs) to address lock-in and enhance resilience. *Earth's Future*, *6*(12), 1638–1659. DOI: 10.1029/2018EF000926

Mohamed, K. I. E. S., & Nadia, K. I. E. S. (2024). Adapting to the Transformation of Education: New Challenges for Teachers. *Journal of Languages and Translation*, *4*(1), 80–88. DOI: 10.70204/jlt.v4i1.310

Murgatroyd, S. (2024). *The future of higher education in an age of artificial intelligence*. Ethics International Press.

Oinas-Kukkonen, H., Pohjolainen, S., & Agyei, E. (2022). Mitigating issues with/of/for true personalization. *Frontiers in Artificial Intelligence*, *5*, 844817. DOI: 10.3389/frai.2022.844817 PMID: 35558170

Pedro, F., Subosa, M., Rivas, A., & Valverde, P. (2019). Artificial intelligence in education: Challenges and opportunities for sustainable development.

Qraitem, M., Kularatne, D., Forgoston, E., & Hsieh, M. A. (2020). Bridging the gap: Machine learning to resolve improperly modeled dynamics. *Physica D. Nonlinear Phenomena*, *414*, 132736. DOI: 10.1016/j.physd.2020.132736

Rane, N., Choudhary, S., & Rane, J. (2023). Education 4.0 and 5.0: Integrating artificial intelligence (AI) for personalized and adaptive learning.

Regan, L., Hopson, L. R., Gisondi, M. A., & Branzetti, J. (2022). Creating a better learning environment: A qualitative study uncovering the experiences of Master Adaptive Learners in residency. *BMC Medical Education*, *22*(1), 141. DOI: 10.1186/s12909-022-03200-5 PMID: 35241060

Regan, P. M., & Jesse, J. (2019). Ethical challenges of edtech, big data and personalized learning: Twenty-first century student sorting and tracking. *Ethics and Information Technology*, *21*(3), 167–179. DOI: 10.1007/s10676-018-9492-2

Reidenberg, J. R., & Schaub, F. (2018). Achieving big data privacy in education. *Theory and Research in Education*, *16*(3), 263–279. DOI: 10.1177/1477878518805308

Schildt, H. (2017). Big data and organizational design–the brave new world of algorithmic management and computer augmented transparency. *Innovation (North Sydney, N.S.W.)*, *19*(1), 23–30. DOI: 10.1080/14479338.2016.1252043

Schouten, G. (2017). On meeting students where they are: Teacher judgment and the use of data in higher education. *Theory and Research in Education*, *15*(3), 321–338. DOI: 10.1177/1477878517734452

Shute, V., & Towle, B. (2018). Adaptive e-learning. In *Aptitude* (pp. 105–114). Routledge.

Simkins, S., & Maier, M. (Eds.). (2023). *Just in Time Teaching: Across the Disciplines, and Across the Academy*. Taylor & Francis.

Smail, D. (2018). *Illusion and reality: The meaning of anxiety*. Routledge. DOI: 10.4324/9780429475733

Song, C., Shin, S. Y., & Shin, K. S. (2024). Implementing the dynamic feedback-driven learning optimization framework: A machine learning approach to personalize educational pathways. *Applied Sciences (Basel, Switzerland)*, *14*(2), 916. DOI: 10.3390/app14020916

Stoddard, H. A., Lee, A. C., & Gooding, H. C. (2024). Empowerment of learners through curriculum co-creation: Practical implications of a radical educational theory. *Teaching and Learning in Medicine*, , 1–7. PMID: 38332636

Tan, S., Taeihagh, A., & Baxter, K. (2022). The risks of machine learning systems. arXiv preprint arXiv:2204.09852.

Titarenko, L., & Little, C. B. (2017). International cross-cultural online learning and teaching: Effective tools and approaches. *American Journal of Distance Education*, *31*(2), 112–127. DOI: 10.1080/08923647.2017.1306767

Valaboju, V. K. (2024). The Synergy of Just-in-Time Learning and Artificial Intelligence: Revolutionizing Personalized Education. [IJCET]. *International Journal of Computer Engineering and Technology*, *15*(5), 707–715.

Vezhbovska, L., Boltenkov, A., Vaskialite, V., Lopukhova, N., & Dementovych, T. (2024). Global trends in educational environment design: From cultural dimensions to innovations. Research Journal in Advanced Humanities, 5(1).

Williamson, B. (2017). Who owns educational theory? Big data, algorithms and the expert power of education data science. *E-Learning and Digital Media*, *14*(3), 105–122. DOI: 10.1177/2042753017731238

Yang, S., Tian, H., Sun, L., & Yu, X. (2019, June). From one-size-fits-all teaching to adaptive learning: The crisis and solution of education in the era of AI. [). IOP Publishing.]. *Journal of Physics: Conference Series*, *1237*(4), 042039. DOI: 10.1088/1742-6596/1237/4/042039

Yoon, M., Lee, J., & Jo, I. H. (2021). Video learning analytics: Investigating behavioral patterns and learner clusters in video-based online learning. *The Internet and Higher Education*, *50*, 100806. DOI: 10.1016/j.iheduc.2021.100806

Chapter 8
A Computational Study on Text Quality and Citation Frequency in Research Papers

Manoj Himmatrao Devare
http://orcid.org/0000-0002-9530-3914
Amity University, Mumbai, India

Debesh Das
http://orcid.org/0009-0004-0548-0418
Amity University, Mumbai, India

Anita Manoj Devare
http://orcid.org/0009-0009-4159-6289
Amity University, Mumbai, India

Pravin Laxmikant Yannawar
http://orcid.org/0000-0002-3398-0565
Dr. Babasaheb Ambedkar Marathwada University, India

ABSTRACT

The abstract and conclusions are the important sections of the published paper. Based on the comprehension of the content written in these sections, other sections of the paper are read by researchers. Various factors, such as the number of citations, social transformations, and intellectual property rights, are considered indicators of research impact. This study utilizes Natural Language Processing techniques to analyze a dataset of 50 highly cited research papers from 2020, aiming to understand the relationship between text quality and citation count. The correlation coefficient

DOI: 10.4018/979-8-2600-2373-0.ch008

indicates that high-citation papers tend to have longer abstracts and shorter conclusions. The results show that when the citation of the paper is low, the words used in the abstract and conclusion have high similarity. As citations are increasing, the similarity of the words used in the abstract and conclusion is reducing. This indicates that those articles with a higher Type Token Ratio (TTR) in the abstract and a unique number of words used in conclusion have high citations.

INTRODUCTION

The content and quality factors, such as novelty and originality, which include new ideas, theories, or data not previously published, are important factors influencing the researcher's decision to cite published research work. Additionally, the relevance of the problem in the field, which addresses current and trending issues, is also important. The scientific rigor is mentioned through the effective language in the published indicating the use of sound methodology, proper statistical analysis, and reproducible results. The clarity and structure of the manuscript have characteristics such as well-organization, clear arguments, well-written text, helpful visuals, meaningful tables, and figures. It also includes a comprehensive literature review provided through background, and its link to the references for context.

High-impact-factor journals tend to attract researchers and further cite the published paper as a reference. The visibility, free and open accessibility, and indexing in the major databases such as Scopus, Web of Science, or Google Scholar improve discoverability, as more likely to be cited. The social network, affiliation with the established researcher or institution, may imply the author's reputation, indicating more citations. International and interdisciplinary collaboration tends to increase reach for impact. The promotion and sharing of research work at conferences, social media, and academic forums increases visibility. The proven, practical, reusable methodological tools, models, and datasets are cited often. The foundational survey papers that serve as key theoretical bases or comprehensive overviews tend to become highly cited.

There are some specific linguistic requirements while writing a research paper. Different sections of the research paper are required to fulfill certain criteria to ensure better comprehension by the readers. The abstract is expected to avoid references, citations, figures, or footnotes in the abstract. The abstract section is required to clearly state the purpose of the research, methodology, key findings, and implications. Abstract should be written in the past tense, except for conclusions. The various publishers put the minimum and maximum word count limits during the abstract writing. The key results are expected in the abstract. For example, the abstract of book chapters in IGI Global has a minimum of 500 characters and a maximum of 1100 characters.

Figure 1. Shows the minimum to maximum number of words in the abstract as per the requirement of the publishers.

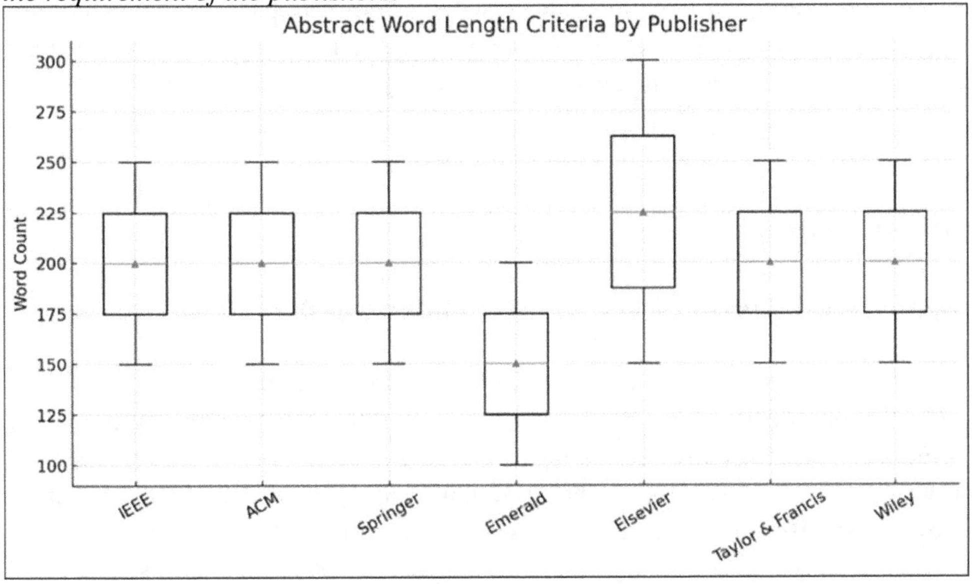

The abstract and conclusions are the important sections of the published paper. The researcher observes, and then the focus moves to the other sections of the paper based on the impression of the content written in these sections. Further decision to refer to the analysis of the published paper in the ongoing research work as a citation. Citations are one of the criteria to evaluate the impact of the existing published paper. It is important to understand the relationship between the linguistic characteristics of the two sections, the abstract and conclusion of the published papers, and their relationship with the citation count. To carry out this research work, the PDF files of the published research papers are used as the dataset. Further, the dataset is prepared by extracting the abstract and conclusion text sections. This research work uses natural language processing and text analysis after the extraction of linguistic features from abstracts and conclusions sections of research papers. These features span word frequency distributions, vocabulary richness indicators, complexity measures, sentiment analysis scores, and other pertinent linguistic attributes. This chapter outlines the use of techniques such as text preprocessing, feature extraction, model training, and evaluation.

To effectively classify research paper abstracts and conclusions as high-quality or standard, it is crucial to identify and extract relevant linguistic features that serve as indicators of quality. While the literature on this specific task is limited, related studies in the field of academic writing and discourse analysis are of major interest. Word frequency distributions and vocabulary richness metrics have been explored as potential indicators of writing quality, with high-quality papers often exhibiting a more diverse and sophisticated vocabulary. Additionally, complexity measures, such as readability scores and syntactic complexity indices, have been examined as potential markers of academic writing quality.

BACKGROUND

Evaluation Criteria in the Recognized English Proficiency Test

In the reputed benchmark exam Test of English as a Foreign Language (TOEFL), the Evaluation Criteria for writing skills are important to evaluate the text quality, including coherence and organization, logical flow, paragraph structure, and clear progression of ideas. In addition, the range and accuracy of vocabulary and grammar also carry significant importance. Spelling, punctuation, and grammar accuracy are important aspects of the evaluation of writing skills. There are two tasks, such as integrated Writing including summary writing and analysis. There are independent essays with opinions written clearly.

In International English Language Testing System (IELTS) has evolved as completeness and relevance of answers. In IELTS, Well-developed ideas and examples along with coherence and cohesion are important. The sentence should have logical sequencing and use of linking. The lexical resources such as Range, sentence variety, tenses, subject-verb agreement, and accuracy of vocabulary. In the case of the Graduate Record Examination (GRE), Analytical Writing requires articulation of complex Ideas, with clarity and depth of reasoning and argument. This requires the use of examples, logical progression, and evidence. The clear structure of writing with introductions, transitions, and conclusions. It also includes Vocabulary, syntax variety, and grammar.

TYPE TOKEN RATIO

The study of the words, their meaning, and the relationship between them is called a lexical analysis of the given text. It also includes the analysis of the structure of words called morphology and their meanings called semantics within a given language. Lexica is a plural form of lexicon, which means the vocabulary of the language. The words in a sentence are separated by spaces or punctuation marks, are called tokens. Punctuation is also considered a token.

Type-Token Ratio (TTR) is a measure of the lexical diversity in a text. TTR ranges between o to 1, excluding zero. A token in each sentence, paragraph, or document is any instance of a word or punctuation mark. The Types can be a unique word. Lexical diversity is an indicator that there is enough pool of words available to the individual to express the ideas precisely. The high TTR implies a greater variety of words used, indicating potentially richer vocabulary. Low TTR implies more repetition of words indicates possibly simpler or more focused text. TTR is also useful in the text complexity & readability measurement. It is used in educational settings to assess writing complexity or development in second language learners. The automated readability analysis can be performed using the simple formula of TTR as the ratio of unique tokens divided by the total number of tokens. TTR can help in identifying or verifying the authorship of anonymous texts. It has been found that fiction or narrative texts may have higher TTR due to varied vocabulary. The domain-specific papers or documents can have a lower TTR. It is found that TTR decreases as the length of the text increases. That is, more tokens imply more repetition is likely. There is also a variation to the TTR as Moving-Average TTR (MATTR), Root TTR, or Corrected TTR are also useful.

MATTR is a measure of lexical diversity, that is, how varied the vocabulary is in a text. It is a more stable alternative to the traditional TTR, which is sensitive to text length. In the case of TTR, when the text length varies, it becomes unreliable. MTTR has a sliding window of a fixed length, moving one word at a time, averaging the TTR across the windows. MATTR is consistent across texts of different lengths and captures local fluctuations in vocabulary diversity.

Root TTR (RTTR) is another measure of lexical diversity, designed to reduce the influence of text length on the traditional Type-Token Ratio (TTR). (1)

Corrected Type-Token Ratio (CTTR) is a variant of the traditional Type-Token Ratio (TTR) that adjusts for text length, aiming to provide a more stable measure of lexical diversity. The correction involves dividing by the square root of twice the number of tokens. This dampens the natural decrease of TTR with longer texts, making CTTR. (2)

Heap's Law is an empirical law that describes the relationship between the number of tokens and the number of types in a corpus. The number of unique words in each corpus can be calculated as the k and β value lies between 0.4 to 0.6. N can be the number of tokens. TTR is inversely related to the number of tokens. The Heap's law states that as N, i.e. number of tokens, increases, TTR decreases.

$$V(N)=k \cdot N^{\beta} \quad (3)$$

Zipf's Law is an empirical law stating that in any natural language corpus, the frequency of a word at rank r is inversely proportional to its rank in the frequency table. Here, r is the rank of the word by frequency. The rank 1 indicates the most frequent word. Here value of s is nearly 1 in natural languages. Lots of rare words occur just once or twice.

f(r) ∝

$$\mathbf{Attn}\left(Q, K, V\right) = \mathbf{Softmax}\left(\frac{QK}{\sqrt{d}}\right)V \tag{4}$$

CONTEXTUALIZED SENTENCES

A paragraph-level contextualized sentence is a sentence that derives its full meaning from the surrounding paragraph. In other words, its interpretation depends on the context provided by other sentences around it, rather than standing alone. Sentences using pronouns such as he, she, it, or general phrases like this, that, the event, the plan often rely on earlier sentences for meaning. Contextualized sentences often build on previous information. To find out whether the sentence is contextualized or not, generally, if the sentence is removed from the paragraph and the paragraph becomes confusing or ambiguous, then the sentence is considered contextualized. Words like however, therefore, meanwhile, in contrast indicate the contextualized sentences. To understand the impact of the contextualized sentence, Wright & Augenstein (2021) used the dataset developed by CiteWorth, a large, contextualized dataset for cite-worthiness detection from scientific documents. The methodology used has introduced a paragraph-level contextualized sentence labelling model based on Longformer to detect cite-worthiness. Results show that the model outperformed existing approaches, achieving improvement over SciBERT. It concludes that fine-tuning language models with cite-worthiness detection enhances performance in scientific document understanding tasks.

The intent in the sentence is to know the purpose or goal behind the sentence. What the speaker is trying to achieve or communicate. The intent can be informative, directive, expressive, committing something, i.e., commissive, or declarative. Mercier et al. (2020) used the publicly available citation analysis datasets, including the CSC-Clean corpus, for citation sentiment classification. Benchmarked language models like BERT, ALBERT, and XLNet for citation sentiment and intent classification are used in this research work. Results show that ImpactCite, based on XLNet, achieved state-of-the-art performance, outperforming existing approaches by 3.44% and 1.33% in F1-score for sentiment and intent classification, respectively. It concludes that advanced language models effectively analysed the qualitative aspects of citations, aiding in a better understanding of scientific impact. The improvement of text quality can be achieved by utilizing cloud-based computational power and innovations, as highlighted by Devare (2019a). The principles of resource convergence between cloud and IoT outlined by Devare (2019b) can be adapted for scalable text quality enhancement, leveraging distributed cloud resources for higher efficiency. Cloud resources play a vital role in enhancing text quality and data processing efficiency (Devare & Devare, 2026).

Contextual embeddings of the word in a sentence represent the words that capture the meaning from the surroundings. Gosangi et al. (2021) used the dataset of the researchers to compile a benchmark dataset containing over two million sentences from scholarly articles, labelled for citation worthiness. A hierarchical BiLSTM model was employed to predict citation worthiness, treating the task as a sequence labelling problem. The model incorporated contextual information by preserving sentence order and performing document-level train and test splits.[REMOVED HYPERLINK FIELD] The results show that incorporating context and contextual embeddings significantly improved the model's ability to predict citation worthiness. The study highlights the importance of contextual information in accurately determining the citation worthiness of sentences in scholarly articles.

Teplitskiy et al. (2020) used the dataset with surveyed 12,670 authors across 15 academic fields, analysing approximately 25,000 referencing decisions. The research work has conducted a survey with an embedded experiment to assess how citation counts influence perceptions of quality and impact. The results showed that exposure to citation counts led to perceptions of lower quality for all but the top 10% cited papers. Additionally, 54% of references had minimal influence on citing authors. This research work concludes that Citation counts can misrepresent the actual quality and impact of research articles.[REMOVED HYPERLINK FIELD]

Lei et al. (2021) used the dataset in the study to analyse the English research articles on COVID-19 medical empirical studies, published in journals with varying impact factors. It has used the methodology as feature engineering techniques, 25 micro-level linguistic features were extracted from the Corpus of English Journal Articles. Supervised machine learning methods, including random forest models, were applied to assess the relationship between these features and academic impact. The results show that twenty-four linguistic features, such as content word overlap, use of third-person pronouns, auxiliary verbs, tense, and emotional words, consistently predicted the academic impact of journal articles. The auxiliary verb helps the main verb to express tense, mood, voice, or aspect. The common auxiliary verbs are, am, is, are, was, were, being, have, do, does, did, can, could, may, might, must, shall, should, will, and would. In a sentence, the auxiliary verb comes before the main verb and helps indicate time, form questions or negatives, or add emphasis. The random forest model demonstrated the best performance in fitting the relationship between these features and article impact. The findings suggest that specific linguistic features can serve as indicators of a research article's academic impact, providing insights for academic writing and evaluation systems.

Nazir et al. (2022) analysed a dataset comprising scientific articles with in-text citations, focusing on sentiment and section-wise citation weights. Employed sentiment analysis and section-wise in-text citation weighting to identify important citations. Utilized machine learning techniques to assess the influence of citations based on their contextual placement and sentiment. The results show that combining sentiment analysis with section-wise citation weights improves the identification of significant citations, enhancing the understanding of an article's impact. It is concluded that integrating sentiment and contextual information provides a more nuanced approach to evaluating citation importance, contributing to a better assessment of research impact.

Vyas et al. (2020) used the dataset developed eight datasets comprising citation sentences, manually annotated into positive, negative, and neutral sentiments, with three datasets considering the full context of citations. The sentiment analysis of the text has opened many opportunities as the niche areas have been advanced beyond the positive, negative, and neutral. The methodology used is an ensemble feature engineering method combining word embeddings, parts-of-speech tags, and dependency relationships. Applied deep learning and support vector machine classifiers to assess citation sentiment. Results show that context-based samples are more effective for citation sentiment analysis. Deep learning models performed better with larger datasets, while support vector machines excelled with smaller datasets. It is concluded that incorporating contextual information enhances the accuracy of citation sentiment analysis, providing deeper insights into the qualitative aspects of scientific literature.

Sunar and Khalid emphasize research analyzing over 1,300 articles across six journals to assess the impact of publication language on citation rates. Controlling for variables such as journal, publication year, and paper length, the study found that articles published in English received significantly more citations than those in other languages. For instance, 33.7% of English articles remained uncited compared to 46.3% of non-English articles, highlighting the advantage of publishing in English for wider dissemination and impact. This study explored the use of semantic analysis to predict the future citation impact of scientific articles. By representing abstracts as vectors in a semantic space, the researchers developed a classification system that distinguished between highly cited and less cited papers with approximately 80% accuracy. The findings suggest that the semantic content and clarity of English texts are strong predictors of their future citation performance.

This research examined whether syntactic complexity features could effectively predict the writing quality of English research articles. Analyzing various syntactic metrics, the study found that certain features, such as the use of complex noun phrases and subordinate clauses, were positively correlated with higher writing quality scores. These findings underscore the importance of syntactic sophistication in enhancing the perceived quality and, potentially, the citation impact of English academic texts.

McCannon (2019) analyzed articles published in the *American Economic Review* from 2000 to 2009 to assess the impact of writing quality on research influence. Using a standardized readability metric applied to the introductions of these papers, the study found that less readable papers received significantly fewer citations. Specifically, papers with readability scores one standard deviation above the mean experienced approximately 155 fewer citations. This suggests that clearer writing enhances a paper's visibility and impact within the academic community.

Lu et al. (2019) investigated the relationship between linguistic complexity and scientific impact by analyzing 36,400 biology and 1,797 psychology articles. They examined 12 variables of linguistic complexity, including syntactic and lexical features, and compared these with citation counts. The study concluded that there was no practically significant relationship between linguistic complexity and citation frequency, suggesting that textual complexity plays a limited role in determining a paper's scientific impact.

Callaham et al. (2006) examined 448 original research articles published in four psychiatric journals to assess whether statistical reporting quality influenced citation counts. They found that while inadequate reporting of research questions and outcomes did not significantly affect citations, a thorough description of statistical methods was associated with increased citations in two of the journals studied. The study highlights that clear methodological reporting can enhance a paper's visibility and impact.

CITATION NETWORK ANALYSIS

Concerns regarding how some researchers misuse citations to unfairly increase their academic reputation have been gaining traction in recent times. Liu et al. (2022) identified and analyzed this problem and proposed a novel deep graph learning framework, Graph Learning for Anomaly Detection (GLAD), which uses advanced computer techniques. It utilizes deep learning with graphs to find unusual or suspicious citation patterns in research papers. Their method can fill the critical gap of identifying whether the citations are being used unethically, which the present available detection techniques have failed to do.

Citation analysis has always been central to researchers as a way to measure the importance of research papers and authors using measures like the h-index and Journal Impact Factor. However, as Liu et al. (2022) noted, these metrics have increasingly been taken advantage of through practices such as self-citation such as citing their work too much. It has also been found that there is the formation of journal cartels, i.e., groups of journals citing each other. There is also coercive citation, which has the forcing authors to add citations. While past studies have explored and examined these issues, there remains a lack of automated methods to detect such unusual or unethical citation patterns. This kind of citation leads to the illusion of the increased impact of the research carried out by the researcher. However, the research topic undertaken will not be useful for the benefit of society and humanity in large. The scientific inventions claimed in such research papers will perhaps not cause any disruption, or even a small change for the betterment of the livelihood of the people, animals, or planet. To provide a solution to these limitations, Liu and his team created a method called GLAD. It uses a powerful AI technique called Graph Neural Networks (GNNs), which uniquely integrates node and edge attributes within a citation graph to identify and examine how papers and citations are connected to each other. The uniqueness of the GLAD method is that it examines both the structure of citation networks, i.e., who cites whom, and the meaning of the citation and why something was cited. GLAD utilized a dedicated Citation Purpose (CPU) classifier, which uses SCIBERT embeddings and SVMs to categorize citation intents. These intents can be identified as comparison, support, or criticism.

The authors tested GLAD by constructing a simulated dataset made from known cases of citation abuse, such as journal cartels and inflated citation behaviors. Following the testing, GLAD was compared against models like DeepWalk, GraphSAGE, DGI, and CARE-GNN. GLAD performed better than the other models in accuracy, precision, and F1-score parameters. The result supports GLAD's robustness in capturing complex patterns of citation misuse.

Moreover, Liu et al. (2022) contribute significantly to the methodological landscape of citation analysis. Their paper underlines the limitations of the present available graph-based anomaly detection methods, which are that the methods often do not account for the fact of the relationship between papers. It means the parameters, like whether the authors know each other or if the citation had any real purpose about the paper, are often ignored. The authors suggest that a more context-aware and semantically enriched approach is needed instead of the traditional one-class classification model.

The authors combine different fields such as citation tracking, language understanding, and graph-based machine learning, offering a practical tool to protect the fairness of academic research. The inclusion of edge features like journal similarity, self-citation indicators, and co-authorship history is used to improve upon the traditional models.

EFFECTIVE DIAGRAMS AND EXPLANATION

Marshall et al. (2021) conducted a study analyzing diagrams in 195 papers from the ACL 2017 conference. They found that the inclusion of system diagrams correlated with higher citation counts after three years. However, papers with more than three diagrams tended to receive fewer citations, suggesting that excessive use of diagrams might be counterproductive. The study also assessed the quality of neural network system diagrams based on compliance with established diagramming guidelines. Papers featuring diagrams that adhered closely to these guidelines were more likely to be highly cited. Interestingly, classifications based on visual or mental model types did not significantly correlate with citation numbers, but they did help quantify diagram diversity. The authors concluded that effective diagramming practices are associated with increased scholarly impact and emphasized the need for better support in developing diagrammatic literacy among researchers.

Lee et al. (2016) introduced the concept of "viziometrics," focusing on the analysis of visual information in scientific literature. By classifying over 8 million figures from PubMed into categories like diagrams, visualizations, and photographs, they discovered that higher-impact papers tend to include more diagrams. This suggests a significant correlation between the use of visual information and scientific impact, highlighting the importance of visual elements in scholarly communication.

Stokes et al. (2022) explored how the integration of text and charts affects reader comprehension and preferences. Their study involved 302 participants who evaluated line charts with varying amounts of textual annotations. Findings indicated that charts with more textual annotations were preferred and led to better information retention. This underscores the value of effectively combining textual descriptions with visual elements to enhance understanding, which could, in turn, influence citation rates.

A study published in the *Artificial Intelligence Review* examined various factors influencing citation counts, including readability. The researchers found that articles with higher readability scores, as measured by the Flesch readability score, tended to receive more citations. This suggests that clearer and more accessible writing, including diagram descriptions, may positively impact a paper's citation frequency.

While direct research on the specific impact of English language quality in diagram descriptions on citation counts is scarce, existing studies indicate that both the quality of diagrams and their integration with textual explanations play significant roles in a paper's scholarly impact. Effective visual communication, supported by clear and concise language, enhances reader comprehension and may lead to increased citations. These findings highlight the importance of developing strong diagrammatic and linguistic skills in academic writing.

COMPOUND COMPLEX SENTENCES

The compound sentences have coordinating conjunctions as for, and, nor, but, or, yet, and so (FANBOYS). The complex sentences are formed by " because, although, since, if, and when. The sophisticated thinking, thoughtful, and nuanced in layers can be reflected using compound complex sentences. If these sentences are written very well, then they enhance the clarity. It explains the complex relationship between the ideas. However, it may increase the length of the sentences. Few readers prefer to use the atomic sentences of shorter length. If the sentences consist of compound and complex in nature and are overused, then it can make the reader tired and confused. In this context, Porwal & Devare (2024) used a dataset having collected titles, abstracts, and conclusions from 1,000 articles authored by scientists with an H-index ≥ 40 in computer science and electronics. It analysed linguistic properties such as sentence length and paragraph structure to assess their correlation with citation counts. The results show that certain linguistic features, like longer sentences and paragraphs, are associated with higher citation counts. It concludes that, linguistic properties of scientific papers can influence their citation impact, suggesting the importance of writing style in research dissemination.

Textual complexity has important criteria, such as reading and understanding. It is influenced by Qualitative features such as language clarity, such as vocabulary is simple or sophisticated. The sentence structure is short, straightforward, or long and complex. It has multiple layers of meaning, such as symbolism or irony. The organization of text structure is such that ideas are clear or unconventional. Complex sentences have one main independent clause and at least one subordinate or dependent clause. The subordinating conjunctions are used in complex sentences such as because, although, since, unless, while, if, etc. The complex sentences show relationships such as cause and effect, contrast, condition, or time. Symbolism in English is a literary device where a word, object, character, or event represents a deeper meaning beyond its literal one. It's often used in literature, poetry, and everyday language to convey complex ideas, emotions, or themes indirectly. Symbolism helps writers communicate abstract ideas through more concrete images or actions. Irony in English is a figure of speech where the intended meaning is different from or even the opposite of the literal meaning of the words. It is often used for humor, criticism, or dramatic effects. The qualitative features of the text are calculated using formulas such as word length and frequency, sentence length, readability scores calculated using Lexile levels, or Flesch-Kincaid. The textual complexity is evaluated by Lu et al. (2019) using the dataset prepared from 36,400 full-text Biology articles and 1,797 full-text Psychology articles from arXiv. There are 12 linguistic complexity variables, such as sentence length, syntactic depth are assessed to determine their relationship with citation counts. It is found that there is no significant relationship between linguistic complexity and citation strata in either discipline. It is concluded that Textual complexity appears to play little role in scientific impact within the analysed datasets.

The compound sentences have coordinating conjunctions as for, and, nor, but, or, yet, and so (FANBOYS). The complex sentences are formed by " because, although, since, if, and when. The sophisticated thinking, thoughtful, and nuanced in layers can be reflected using compound complex sentences. If these sentences are written very well, then they enhance the clarity. It explains the complex relationship between the ideas. However, it may increase the length of the sentences. Few readers prefer to use the atomic sentences of shorter length. If the sentences consist of compound and complex in nature and are overused, then it can make the reader tired and confused. In this context, Porwal & Devare (2024) used a dataset having collected titles, abstracts, and conclusions from 1,000 articles authored by scientists with an H-index $\geq$ 40 in computer science and electronics. It analysed linguistic properties such as sentence length and paragraph structure to assess their correlation with citation counts. The results show that certain linguistic features, like longer sentences and paragraphs, are associated with higher citation counts. It concludes that, linguistic properties of scientific papers can influence their citation impact, suggesting the importance of writing style in research dissemination.

Purba et al. (2023) conducted a syntactic analysis of scientific articles, focusing on the use of clauses and phrases. They identified various sentence structures, including compound, complex, and compound-complex sentences, emphasizing the role of subordinate clauses in conveying detailed information. Their study highlights that complex sentence constructions are prevalent in scientific literature, facilitating the expression of intricate ideas and relationships between concepts.

Similarly, Saragih (2023) analyzed sentence complexity in students' scientific papers, particularly in abstract sections. The study found that complex sentences were the most used (26.25%), followed by compound sentences (25.97%), simple sentences (24.58%), and compound-complex sentences (23.19%). This distribution suggests a preference for complex sentence structures in academic writing to articulate nuanced arguments and findings. The general trend indicates that complex and compound sentences are integral to academic writing in this field. The use of such sentence structures allows authors to present multifaceted information, elaborate on methodologies, and discuss results comprehensively. The prevalence of complex sentences in scientific writing underscores their importance in effectively communicating sophisticated ideas. Authors aiming for high citation impact should consider employing varied sentence structures to enhance clarity and depth in their writing.

The research paper titled "*The Anatomy of the Grid: Enabling Scalable Virtual Organizations*" by Ian Foster, Carl Kesselman, and Steven Tuecke, published in 2001, is a seminal work in the field of grid computing. The authors employ a formal academic tone, utilizing precise terminology pertinent to computer science and distributed systems. The use of well-defined sections and subsections aids in guiding the reader through the intricate details of grid architecture and its components. In terms of sentence structure, the authors predominantly use complex sentences to convey detailed information and elucidate relationships between various components of grid systems. For instance, sentences often contain multiple clauses to explain the functionality and interdependence of different system elements. This approach facilitates a comprehensive understanding of the subject matter, catering to readers with a background in the field. The clarity and depth of the writing have made it a foundational reference for subsequent research in the domain. The meticulous writing style, characterized by structured organization and the use of complex sentences, has significantly contributed to the paper's influence and widespread citation. By effectively communicating sophisticated ideas in a coherent manner, the authors have ensured that the paper remains a critical resource for researchers and practitioners in the field of computer science.

The Physiology of the Grid: An Open Grid Services Architecture for Distributed Systems Integration by Ian Foster, Carl Kesselman, Jeffrey M. Nick, and Steven Tuecke, published in 2002, is a foundational paper in the field of grid computing. The use of complex sentence structures is prevalent throughout the paper. This sentence integrates multiple clauses to convey the multifaceted nature of OGSA, illustrating the complexity of the subject matter. The paper utilizes compound sentences to connect related ideas, enhancing the logical flow of information.

AVAILABILITY OF THE DATASET

Tschalzev et al. (2025) examine the implications of utilizing tabular datasets from repositories like OpenML without critical evaluation. The authors identify common pitfalls, including suboptimal model selection strategies, neglect of robust baselines, and inappropriate preprocessing techniques. These issues can compromise the integrity of research findings and, consequently, affect the study's credibility and citation potential. The paper advocates for enhanced guidelines and metadata standards to ensure the responsible use of tabular data in research.

Colavizza et al. (2019) analyzes over 500,000 articles to assess the impact of including data availability statements with direct links to datasets. Their findings reveal that articles providing accessible data links experience a citation increase of up to 25.36%. This underscores the significance of transparency and data accessibility in enhancing a publication's reach and influence.

Avula and Tummala (2021) focus on the healthcare sector, evaluating how data quality dimensions—accuracy, completeness, and timeliness—affect predictive analytics using Electronic Health Records (EHRs). The study highlights that deficiencies in these areas can lead to unreliable predictive models, adversely impacting clinical decisions and patient outcomes. Implementing robust data governance and real-time validation techniques is recommended to enhance data quality and, by extension, research credibility and citations.

Nieminen, P. (2006) et al, in a study of 448 psychiatric research articles, the authors investigated whether the quality of statistical reporting correlates with citation frequency. The results indicate that while inadequate reporting of research questions and outcomes does not significantly affect citations, detailed descriptions of statistical procedures are associated with higher citation counts. This suggests that meticulous data presentation, including tabular formats, can enhance a study's visibility and impact.

Wang et al. (2023) provide a comprehensive overview of data quality dimensions, including accuracy, completeness, consistency, and timeliness. The paper discusses how these dimensions influence decision-making and research outcomes. High-quality data is linked to improved research reliability and increased citations, emphasizing the need for rigorous data quality assessment in research practices.

IMPACT OF THE LENGTH OF THE ARTICLE TITLE

The use of a question mark in the title of a research paper can significantly affect how the paper is perceived, interpreted, and discovered. A question in the title can spark curiosity and draw attention. Often used in qualitative, theoretical, or early-stage research where the aim is to explore rather than conclude. The metadata of the paper, such as keywords, is important, along with the number of authors, author contact details, and author names. Multiple regression can provide the relationship between the various factors considered in the metadata and their relation to the citations. Graf-Vlachy et al. (2022) analysed metadata from 16,131 software engineering articles published between 1990 and 2020 across 20 venues. The Methodology employed multiple regression analyses to examine the relationship between article metadata characteristics and citation counts. It is found that factors like the number of authors, keywords, abstract length, and presence of question marks in titles significantly relate to citation frequency. It concludes that various metadata characteristics are linked to how frequently articles are cited, highlighting the importance of these features in scientific communication.

Jacques and Sebire (2010) conducted a study to explore the relationship between article title characteristics and citation frequency in medical journals. They analysed the 25 most cited and 25 least cited articles published in 2005 across general and specialist medical journals, including *The Lancet*, *BMJ*, and *Journal of Clinical*

Pathology. The study focused on title length, the presence of punctuation such as colons, the use of acronyms, and geographical references. Their findings revealed that longer titles, titles containing colons, and those including acronyms were positively correlated with higher citation rates. Conversely, titles referencing specific countries were associated with lower citation frequencies. The authors hypothesized that these patterns might be linked to how electronic searches are conducted, suggesting that certain title structures enhance discoverability and, consequently, citations. This study underscores the significance of thoughtful title construction in academic publishing. By optimizing title features, authors can potentially increase the visibility and impact of their research.

Habibzadeh and Yadollahie (2010) investigated whether shorter article titles are associated with higher citation rates. They analysed 9,031 articles published in 2005 across 22 English-language journals, examining the correlation between title length and the number of citations received by 2008. The study found a positive correlation between title length and citation frequency, indicating that longer titles were associated with more citations. This trend was particularly evident in journals with higher impact factors. The authors suggested that longer titles might provide more descriptive information, enhancing the article's visibility and appeal to potential readers. These findings challenge the conventional preference for concise titles, suggesting that more detailed titles could improve an article's discoverability and citation potential.

Letchford et al. (2015) analysed the relationship between title length and citation rates across a large dataset of scientific articles. They examined the titles of the 20,000 most cited papers published each year from 2007 to 2013, totalling 140,000 articles, to determine if shorter titles were associated with higher citation counts. Contrary to some previous studies, their analysis revealed that papers with shorter titles tended to receive more citations. The authors proposed that shorter titles might be easier to comprehend and more engaging, thereby attracting a broader readership and increasing citation rates. This study highlights the potential benefits of concise titles in enhancing the impact of scientific publications, suggesting that brevity may be advantageous in certain contexts.

Paiva et al. (2012) explored how the structure and content of article titles influence citation rates. They analyzed 423 original articles published in open-access journals, categorizing titles based on length and whether they described methods, results, or were neutral. The study found that articles with shorter titles that explicitly described the study's results were cited more frequently than those with longer, method-focused titles. The authors suggested that result-oriented titles might better capture the attention of readers and researchers, leading to increased citations. These findings emphasize the importance of crafting titles that succinctly convey the main findings of a study to enhance its visibility and impact.

Yitzhaki (2014) examined how various title characteristics affect citation rates by analysing 302 articles published in the *Addictive Behaviors* journal. The study assessed factors such as title length, presence of colons or hyphens (indicative of combinational titles), inclusion of acronyms, and references to specific locations. The analysis revealed that articles with combinational titles (using colons or hyphens to separate ideas) and those with diverse keywords do not present in the title received more citations. However, there was no significant correlation between title length and citation frequency. Additionally, titles referencing specific countries were associated with lower citation rates. This study suggests that certain structural elements in titles, such as the use of punctuation to combine concepts and the strategic selection of keywords, can enhance an article's citation potential.

METHODOLOGY

Corpus Acquisition

As the published papers are in Portable Document Format (PDF), the extraction of the section is performed using the Python library. Through this acquisition process, a robust and representative corpus of 50 highly cited research papers from 2020 was compiled. This dataset provides a solid foundation for analyzing the factors that contribute to the citation impact of research papers, offering valuable insights into the elements that enhance a paper's visibility and influence within the academic community. This chapter will be a lesson for those who wish to process the PDF documents for the textual analysis using Python code. Similarly, the analysis of the textual features is done using the programming approach. This work also tries to perform the clustering of the documents based on the words and the quality of words and find the Silhouette Score to check its effectiveness.

The corpus for this study is designed to ensure the inclusion of highly impactful research papers, thereby facilitating a robust analysis of the factors influencing citation counts. The first step involved establishing stringent selection criteria to guarantee the relevance and impact of the papers. Specifically, the criteria mandated that only papers published in the year 2020 were considered to maintain temporal consistency, and each paper had to have more than 100 citations to ensure they were recognized and influential within their respective academic communities.

The primary sources included Web of Science, known for its extensive indexing and reliable citation data; Google Scholar, valued for its broad coverage across various disciplines; IEEE Xplore, particularly useful for engineering and technology-related papers; and PubMed, essential for biomedical and life sciences research. Using these databases, a comprehensive search strategy was implemented. Relevant keywords central to the research domain, such as "machine learning," "data analysis," and "artificial intelligence," were utilized. Advanced search filters were applied to limit the results to papers published in 2020 with citation counts exceeding 100.

The initial search yielded a substantial number of potential papers, which then underwent a rigorous screening process. Titles and abstracts were reviewed to assess their relevance to the research topic. For the shortlisted papers, the full text was evaluated to ensure they met all selection criteria, including the quality and comprehensiveness of the abstracts and conclusions. Citation counts were verified using multiple databases to ensure accuracy and reliability, further validating the impact of the selected papers.

To facilitate easy identification and organization of the corpus, each paper was uniquely identified by a filename in the format `Paper{number}Cited{number}.pdf`. The first number denotes the sequence in the dataset, and the second number represents the citation count. For example, `Paper1Cited150.pdf` indicates the first paper with 150 citations. This systematic naming convention ensured that the papers could be efficiently managed and referenced throughout the study.

The abstracts and conclusions were then extracted from each paper for subsequent analysis. Abstracts provided summaries of key objectives, methods, and findings, offering crucial insights into the research focus and scope. Conclusions summarized the results and implications, highlighting the main contributions and potential future directions indicated by the authors. This extraction was essential for understanding the detailed content and thematic elements of each paper.

Efforts were made to ensure that the selected papers represented a diverse range of subfields and research interests within the domain. This diversity was achieved by including papers from various sub-disciplines, capturing a wide spectrum of research themes, and ensuring geographic and institutional diversity to reflect a broad range of perspectives. This approach was crucial in ensuring that the corpus provided a comprehensive snapshot of the field.

The final step involved a thorough verification process to ensure the reliability and integrity of the corpus. This included cross-referencing citation counts from multiple sources, checking for any discrepancies or inconsistencies in the data, and ensuring that the abstracts and conclusions were correctly extracted and accurately represented the content of the papers.

The PyPDF2 Python library and regular expressions are used to prepare the data set having the abstract and conclusion of the published research paper. Libraries such as PyMuPDF or PDFPlumber, for instance, can be used to extract text content from PDF documents while maintaining the structure of the document.

The start and finish of the abstract and conclusion parts can then be indicated by patterns or keywords that can be found using regular expressions or rule-based parsers. As an alternative, parsing libraries like Beautiful Soup or lxml can be used to browse the document tree and extract the appropriate portions based on their tags or structural markers for research papers in HTML or XML formats.

To guarantee correct and consistent extraction of the abstract and conclusion sections throughout the corpora, it is imperative to manage various document formats as well as variances in section labeling or formatting patterns. To make sure that the analyses only concentrate on these important areas, the research papers' abstracts and conclusions will be taken out of the complete text and separated. Research paper abstracts and conclusions are frequently extracted by parsing the documents' structure and using formatting signals or metadata to precisely locate the pertinent portions. For this task, a variety of methods can be used, including rule-based parsers, machine learning models particularly trained for section extraction, and regular expressions.

The extracted text will undergo a thorough cleaning process to remove irrelevant characters, special symbols, and formatting artifacts that could potentially interfere with the analyses. Text cleaning is a crucial step in NLP pipelines as it ensures that the data is in a consistent and standardized format, free from noise and extraneous elements that could adversely affect the performance of subsequent processing tasks. The cleaning process typically involves a series of operations, including removing control characters, such as newline characters, tabs, and other non-printable characters, to ensure a clean and consistent text stream. Special elements such as mathematical symbols, currency symbols, or other Unicode characters that are not part of the standard alphanumeric character set are either removed or normalized to their closest ASCII equivalent, depending on their relevance to the task at hand. In addition, stripping formatting artifacts such as Hyper Text Markup Language (HTML) tags, Extensible Markup Language (XML) markup, or LaTeX commands is removed, as they do not contribute to the semantic content of the text. Multiple consecutive whitespace characters are normalized to a single space character to ensure consistent handling of word boundaries and sentence segmentation. These cleaning operations can be performed using a combination of regular expressions, string manipulation functions, and dedicated text cleaning libraries.

The cleaned text will be tokenized, turning the continuous stream of characters into a series of meaningful units, such as words, subwords, or character-level tokens. A crucial stage in NLP pipelines is tokenization, which converts unstructured text input into a representation that is structured and suitable for processing by machine learning models. Since the tokenization technique defines how the text is separated and represented, it can have a big effect on how well downstream operations are executed.

The most popular method is word-level tokenization, in which the text is divided into separate words using other delimiters or blank characters. The basic string splitting algorithms and advanced tokenizers that handle complex scenarios like contractions, abbreviations, and multi-word expressions can be used. As an alternative, subword tokenization, also called word-piece tokenization, separates words into smaller units like byte-pair encodings (BPE) or character n-grams. It enables a more flexible and compact representation of the vocabulary. This technique is especially helpful for managing uncommon words, out-of-vocabulary terms, or morphologically rich languages. Another method is character-level tokenization, in which the text is handled like a string of individual characters. This method captures fine-grained patterns at the character level, which makes it useful for tasks like text production or language modeling. Popular NLP libraries and frameworks, such as NLTK, spaCy, or the tokenizers provided by the library, offer various tokenization strategies and utilities to handle different use cases and languages.

Normalization techniques such as case folding, i.e., converting all text to lowercase or uppercase, are used to ensure that text is treated consistently throughout the corpus. Normalization is an important step in the NLP pipeline because it helps mitigate the effects of variations in text that do not affect semantic meaning, such as differences between case or encoding formats. Case folding is one of the most common normalization techniques, where all text is converted to lowercase or uppercase. This step is especially important for tasks where capitalization does not matter or where capitalization does not contain significant information. For example, when analyzing summaries and conclusions of research papers, capitalization is unlikely to be a significant differentiator between high-quality and standard papers. By converting the entire text to a single font, models can focus on more significant linguistic features without being affected by superficial differences in capitalization. Case folding can be implemented using built-in string manipulation functions in most programming languages or through.

Few abstracts and conclusions and performed a thorough linguistic analysis of them using sophisticated NLP techniques. Lexical density, grammatical complexity, sentiment polarity, and readability ratings were among the language characteristics. The percentage of content words of total words, or lexical density, was shown to be significantly higher in high-quality publications. This suggests a more nuanced and illuminating use of language, which enhances the communication's accuracy and clarity.

High lexical density indicates that well-written articles eliminate superfluous filler words and communicate important information succinctly. The use of subordination and a variety of sentence patterns, or syntactic complexity, was another important characteristic that set superior works apart. More advanced command of language, which indicates a deeper involvement with the research issue, is often demonstrated in papers with higher syntactic complexity, which also articulates ideas more clearly and eloquently. The nuances of cutting-edge research can only be fully communicated through more nuanced and thorough explanations, which are made possible by this complexity.

The Gunning Fog Index and Flesch Reading Ease are two measures considered as techniques to calculate readability scores. These metrics demonstrate that even with complicated syntactic structures, high-quality publications are easier to read. This paradox is explained by the language's accuracy and clarity, which successfully conveys complicated ideas without the need for superfluous jargon or long, complicated sentences. A research paper with a high reading level makes it accessible to a wider readership, including those who are not directly involved in the subject of study.

The distinction between superior papers was also based on the usage of active versus passive voice. Active voice was a common technique in excellent research papers, which made the story more interesting and dynamic. The purposeful use of passive voice was to draw attention to the research process and conclusions rather than the researchers themselves. The content can become simpler to read and more engaging with this deliberate use of voice.

High-quality articles employed hedging language words like "suggests," "may indicate," and "potentially" more skillfully than other types of writing that weaken claims. In academic writing, it is essential to use language like this to carefully present findings and acknowledge the limitations of the research. Scholarly communication values the deliberate and balanced presentation of research findings, which can be demonstrated through the effective use of hedging language.

The analysis's conclusions offer insightful advice to scholars who want to improve the calibre of their writing. The language elements that have been found function as standards for efficient communication in scholarly research. Researchers can enhance the overall quality, impact, and clarity of their articles by implementing these techniques. These linguistic characteristics might be used as further standards by reviewers and evaluators to gauge the Caliber of research articles. The evaluation process should consider the effectiveness and clarity of communication, even while content and methodological rigor continue to be of utmost importance.

The abstracts of each paper, summarizing the key objectives, methods, and findings, were extracted for analysis. Abstracts are crucial for understanding the research focus and scope of each paper. The conclusions, summarizing the results and implications of the research, were also extracted. These sections highlight the main contributions and potential future directions indicated by the authors.

The lexical features capture the characteristics of individual words and their distributions within the text, providing insights into the vocabulary richness, complexity, and specificity of the language used in research paper abstracts and conclusions. The word frequency distributions having term frequency-inverse document frequency (TF-IDF) vectors were computed to capture the distribution of word frequencies across the corpora. Additionally, pre-trained word embeddings, Word2Vec, and

GloVe were employed to obtain dense vector representations of words, capturing semantic and syntactic relationships.

The vocabulary richness metrics, such as type-token ratio, Honoré's statistics, and Maas' log metrics, were computed to assess the diversity and sophistication of the vocabulary employed in the research paper abstracts and conclusions. Measures of lexical diversity, including the proportion of unique words and the Squared Vocabulary Use (SVU) index, were calculated to quantify the breadth and depth of the language used.

The domain-specific terminologies, such as the presence and distribution of technical jargon, were quantified by leveraging domain-specific lexicons and ontologies, serving as potential indicators of subject matter expertise and research rigor. The readability metrics established readability metrics, such as the Flesch-Kincaid Grade Level, Gunning Fog Index, and Dale-Chall Readability Formula, can be computed to assess the complexity and comprehensibility of the language used in the research paper abstracts and conclusions.

The analysis of these lexical features revealed several notable patterns and trends. High-quality research papers exhibited a more diverse and sophisticated vocabulary, as evidenced by higher scores on vocabulary richness metrics and lexical diversity measures. Additionally, the presence of domain-specific terminology was more pronounced in the high-quality corpus, suggesting a deeper immersion in the subject matter and a more technical writing style.

RESULTS

The readability metrics showed a nuanced relationship with research quality. While some high-quality papers exhibited higher complexity scores, indicating a more advanced and technical writing style, others demonstrated a balanced approach, employing clear and concise language to convey complex ideas effectively. There are 50 research papers, and have meaning of a citation count of 1077, a standard deviation of 1108, a minimum citation of 9, and a maximum citation of 4449. The first quartile is at 193 citations, the second quartile is at 745 citations, and the third quartile is at 1637 citations.

Figure 2. Distribution of Citation Count

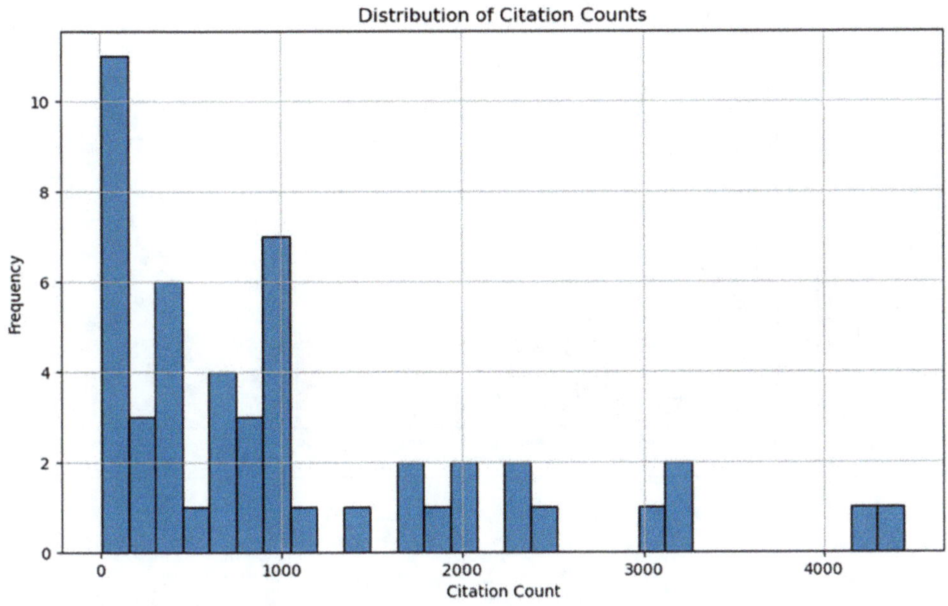

The distribution of the citations of the dataset is shown in Figure 2.

Figure 3. Box Plot Citation Count

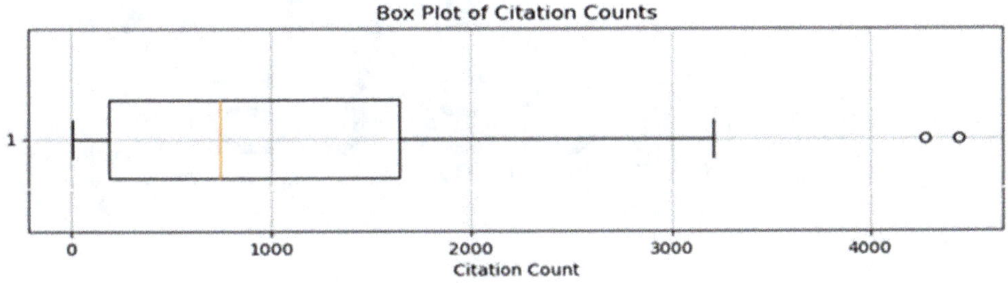

Figure 3 shows the box plot of the citation count of the papers taken into the dataset. Figure 4 shows the distribution of the number of words in the conclusion section of the dataset.

Figure 4. Distribution of Conclusion Word Counts

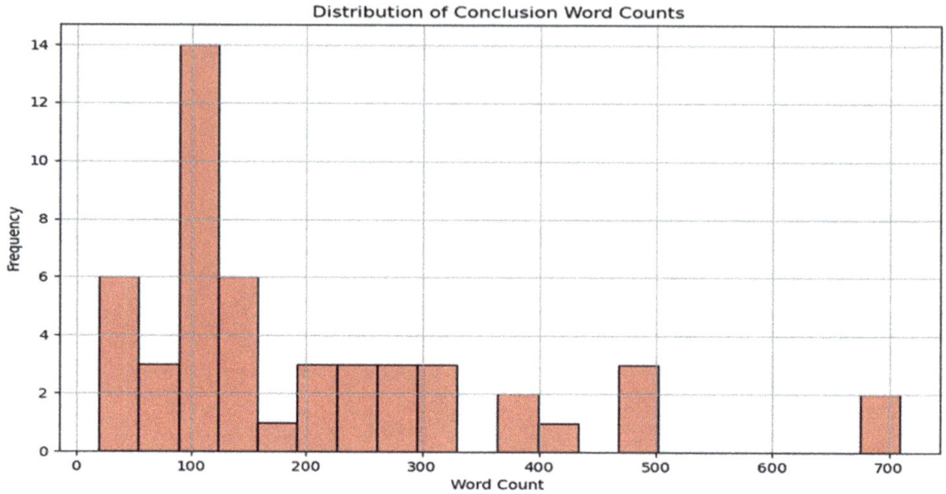

Figure 5. Word Cloud of Conclusions

Figure 5 shows that the maximum number of words appearing in the dataset is "network," and then the word appearing is "data," and other lesser numbers of times the words appear in the conclusion section of the paper. This gives the idea that the domain of the papers selected for the research work is computer science, with the domain of computer networks.

Figure 6. The Silhouette Plot for the various clusters.

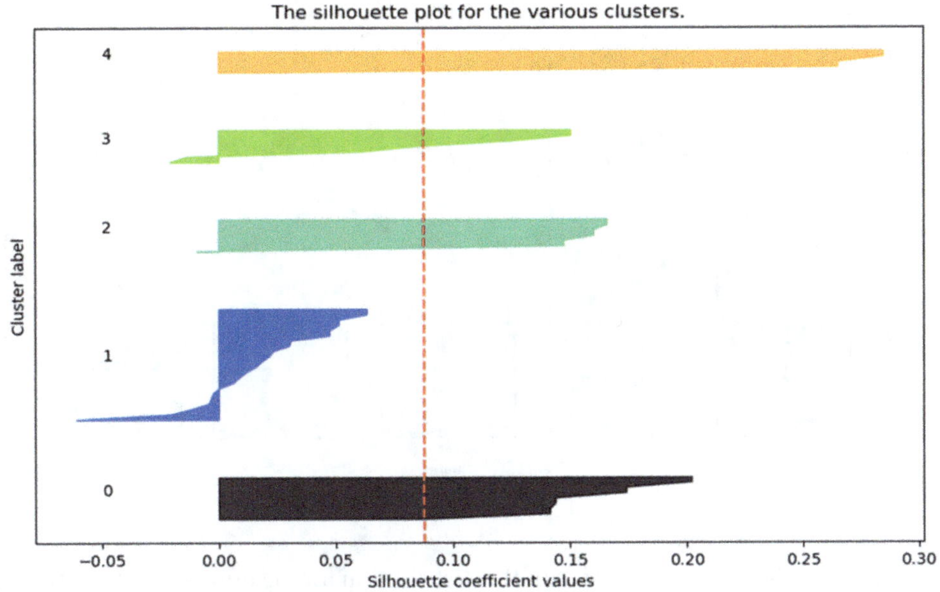

Figure 6 shows the silhouette coefficient values with a Score of 0.08775077405254668. The silhouette score is an evaluation metric that helps gauge the consistency within clusters compared to the separation between clusters. This metric essentially provides an insight into how well each data point has been assigned to its corresponding cluster. The score shows the week clustering. There are five clusters created for unique word creations. There are topics according to five clusters. The cluster number is zero of the nine papers. The number one cluster has twenty-one papers. Cluster five has more unique words. The red line is a vertical line of average.

Figure 7. Cluster Size of Distribution

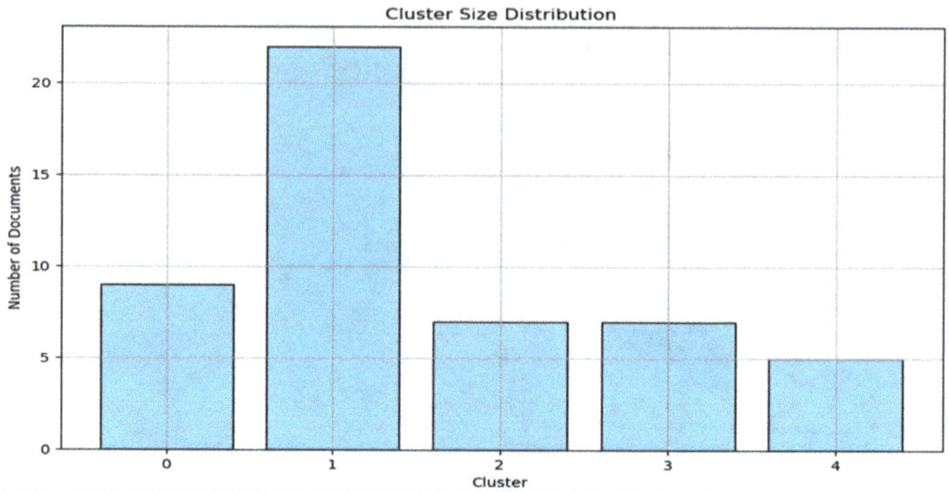

Figure 7 is about the cluster size of the distribution for the number of documents. Cluster number one has a greater number of documents, as compared to cluster zero, two, three, and four. Figure 8 shows the two-dimensional visualization of the clusters using principal component analysis.

Figure 8. 2D Visualization of Clusters

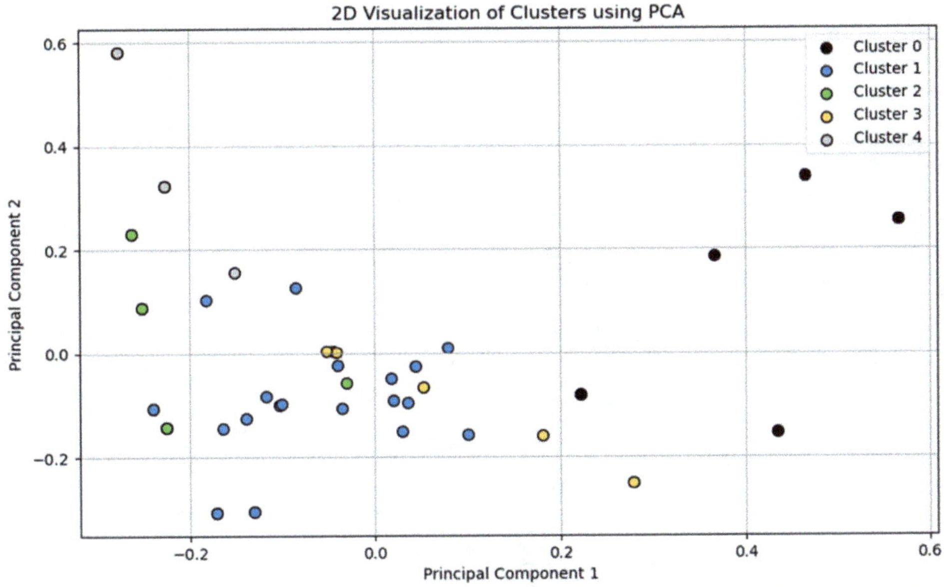

The efficiency of the clustering created using PCA is having Mean Squared Error is 1129204, R-Squared value is 0.10. The linear regression is applied to predict the value of the number of citations based on the length of the number of words in the conclusion section of the documents used. As per Figure 9, the citations prediction is performed having an MSE prediction as 881927, and the R-Squared value is 0.14.

Figure 9. Linear Regression to fit the line from the actual to the predicted citations.

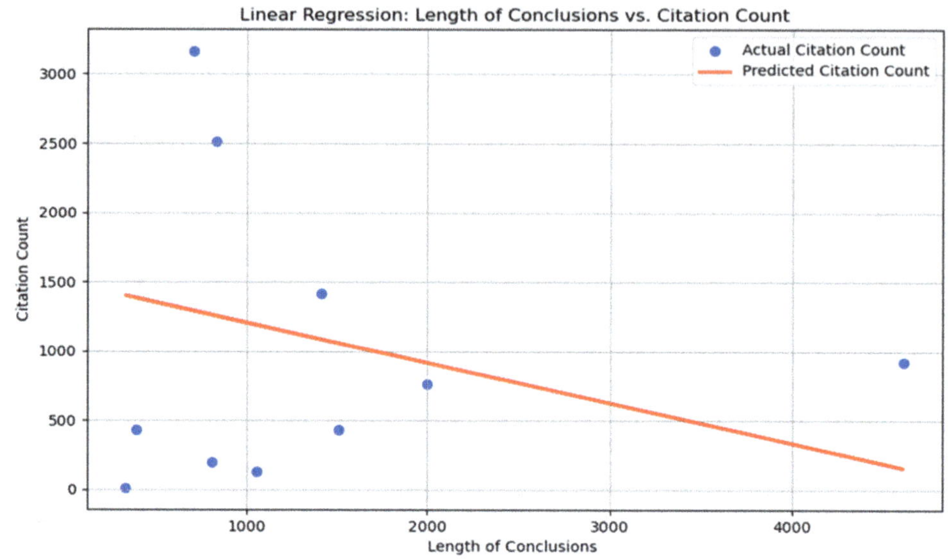

Figure 9 shows the actual versus the predicted citation values. This indicates that there is no linear relationship between the length of the conclusion and the citations.

Figure 10. Word Cloud of the Conclusion section of the dataset

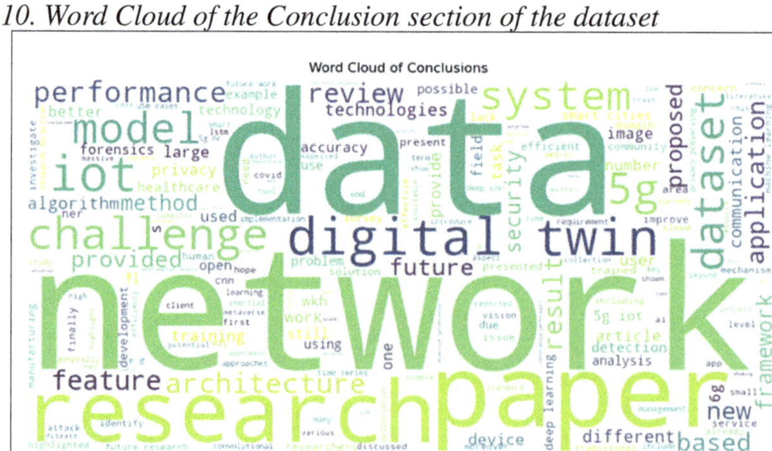

Figure 10 shows that the papers are from the computer science domain. The major words are data, network, research paper, digital twin, and IOT, etc.

Figure 11. Topic Distribution across documents 1

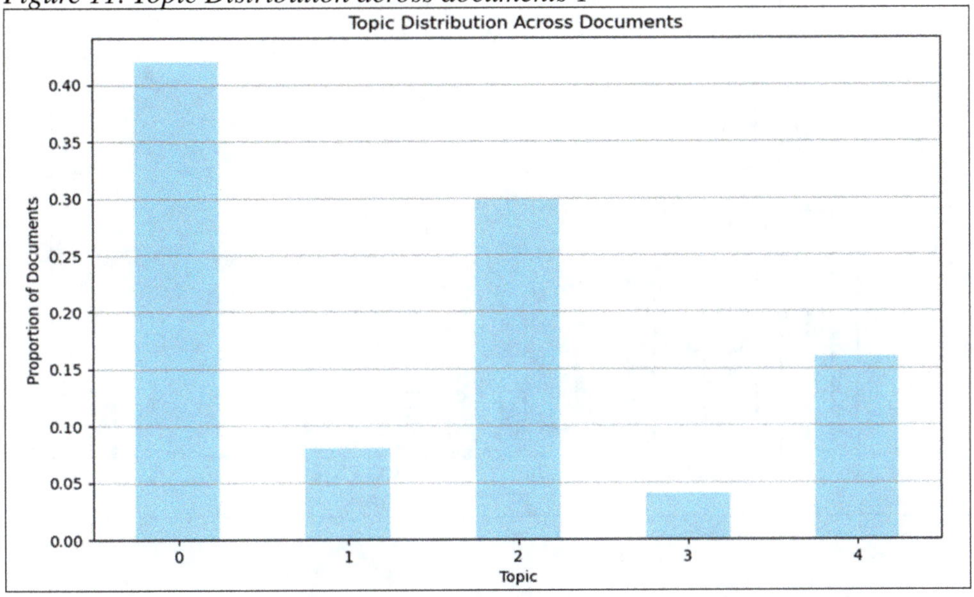

Figure 11 is about the distribution across the topics and the proportion of the documents. Topic zero is found more in the proportion of the documents. Topics one and three are found less frequently in the proportion of documents.

Figure 12. Distribution of Abstract-Conclusion Similarity Scores

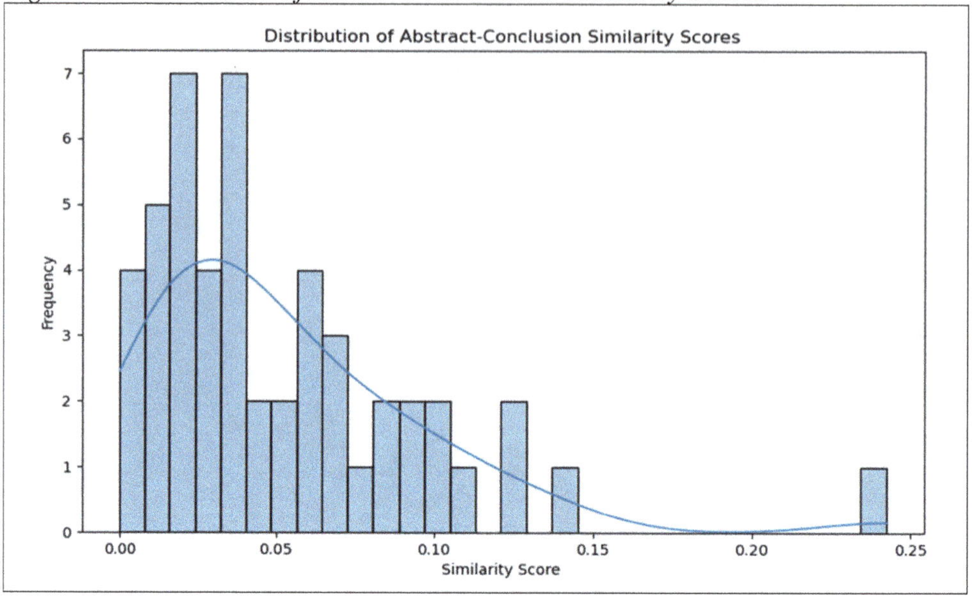

Figure 12 shows the similarity score of the distribution of the abstract and conclusion sections. For the 1000-2000 citations, here the similarity of words is high. When citation increases, then the similarity of the words is reduced, i.e., unique words are used.

Figure 13. Correlation with Citation Count

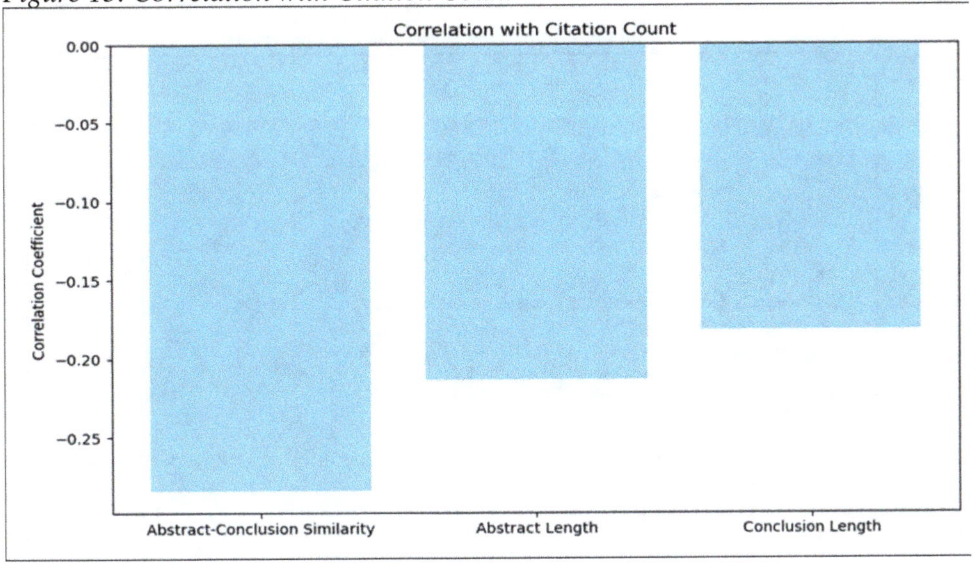

Figure 13 shows that there is a correlation coefficient with a negative relation with the abstract-conclusion similarity, abstract length, and conclusion length. High citation papers have a high length of abstract and low length of conclusion.

Figure 14. Sentiment Comparison in the abstract and the conclusion.

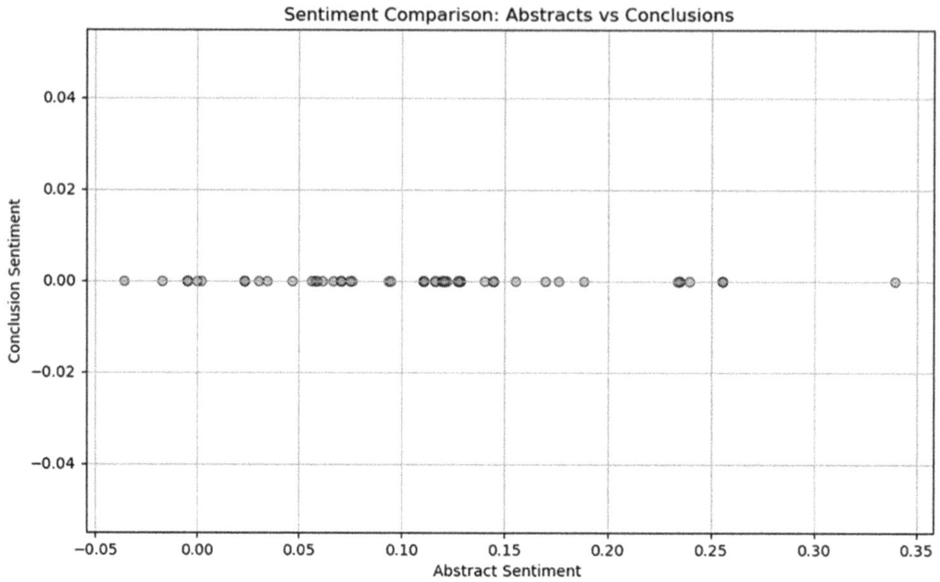

Figure 14 shows the comparison of the abstract and the conclusion section. This indicates that there are neural sentiments in the sentences written in these two sections.

Figure 15. Distribution of Sentiment Scores

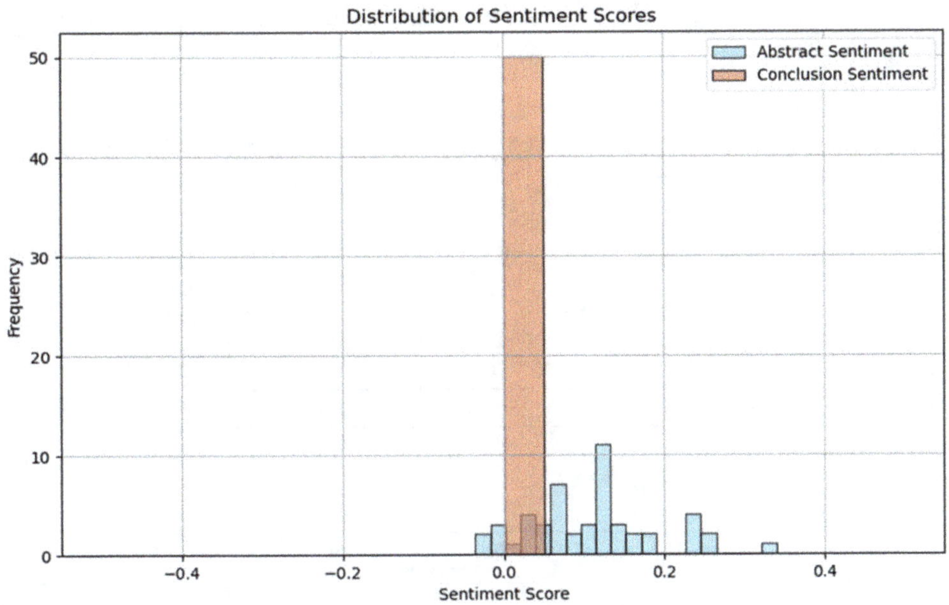

Figure 15 shows the distribution of sentiment scores. The conclusion sentiment is very close to zero. The abstract sentiments are in the range from 0.05 to 0.35. This indicates the sentiments are not polarized.

Figure 16. Box Plot of Word Count comparison to abstracts and conclusions.

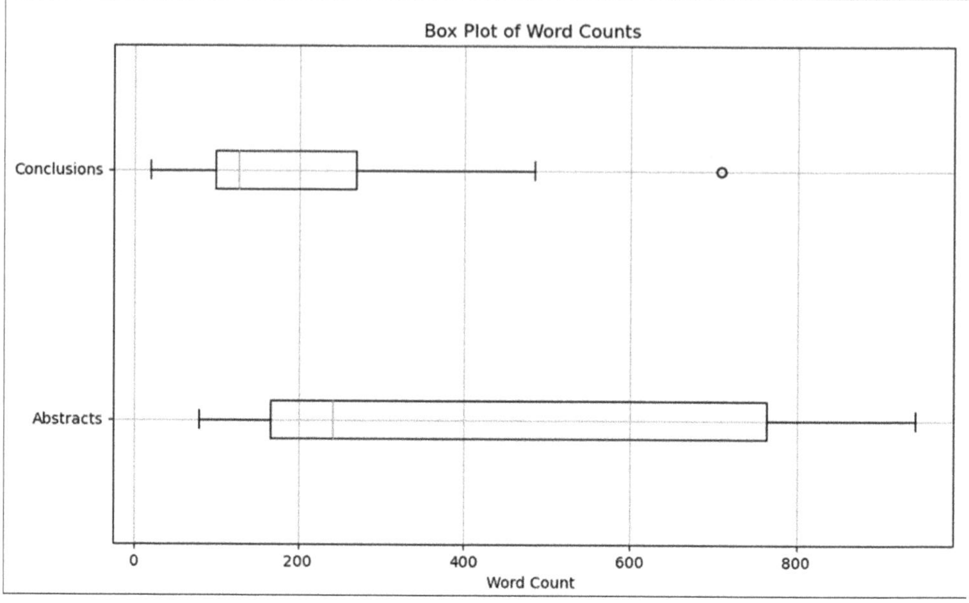

As shown in Figure 4.17, the number of words in the abstract are minimum of 180 and a maximum of 980. The box plot shows that the number of words in the abstract is more than the number of words in the conclusion section of the dataset under consideration. It is concluded that the authors of the paper do not use many words in the conclusion.

CONCLUSION

The results show that when the citation of the papers is low as per the dataset, then it is observed that the words used in the abstract and conclusion have high similarity. As citations are increasing, the similarity of the words used in the abstract and conclusion is reducing. This indicates that those authors have a high Type token ratio (TTR) in the abstract and a unique number of words used in conclusion, resulting in high citations.

Hence, the researchers should take care while writing the abstract of the manuscript that the essence and curiosity of the paper are maintained through the proper choice of the vocabulary. Although the abstract is available at the beginning of the document, it is the first and foremost referred by the readers, before going through the entire manuscript. Generally, abstract is written at the end in timeline, once all the other sections of the manuscript are written. However, some researchers write the abstract section of the paper in the initial stage, and then again do not revisit to rewrite it in the revised manner. Author should calculate the TTR of the abstract and conclusion. Before calculation of the TTR, the stop words should not be considered. The correct choice of words in the abstract can impact on the reader to consider its contribution of the paper to refer and cite during their extended research work. Similarly, the conclusion of the paper should be written by calculating the TTR. Most of the time, due to the deadline of the manuscript submission, the conclusion section is ignored by the author while writing a paper. TTR is not the only measurement to consider, but comparing the similarity of the conclusion with the abstract of the paper will help the author to project it as quality research work. The abstract section generally highlights the research problem, objective, methodology, and the results achieved from the research work.

It has been observed from the result of this research work that the number of words in the conclusion is less as compared to the number of words in the abstract. The box whisker plot shows that the number of words in the conclusion is less, as compared to the number of words in the abstract. The minimum number of words in the conclusion is less than the minimum number of words in the abstract. Similarly, the maximum number of words in the conclusion is less than the minimum number of words in the abstract.

Generally, the restrictions are imposed by the publisher on the minimum and maximum number of words or characters in an abstract of the paper. However, there are no restrictions on the maximum number of words in the conclusions section of a paper. Hence, giving careful attention to the detailed writing of the conclusion section can have a proper impact on the reader. The essence of the conclusion section required to be different as it implies the conclusion based on the results. The conclusion is to interpret the findings and emphasize the significance of the findings. The interpretation of the key findings is written in the conclusion section. Conclusion reflects what the results mean and how they contribute to the field. It has been observed that, in most of the research papers, a major part of the conclusion is like what is written in the abstract section. Hence, the similarity of the words picked to write conclusion is also same. Author can use the similarity checking between the abstract and conclusion of the manuscript before the final submission to the venue.

REFERENCES

Avula, R., & Tummala, S. (2021). Assessing the impact of data quality on predictive analytics in healthcare: Strategies, tools, and techniques for ensuring accuracy, completeness, and timeliness in electronic health records. *Sage Science Review of Applied Machine Learning*, *4*(2), 31–47.

Callaham, M., Wears, R. L., & Weber, E. (2006). The relationship between quality of research and citation frequency. *BMC Medical Research Methodology*, *6*(1), 42. DOI: 10.1186/1471-2288-6-42 PMID: 16948835

Colavizza, G., Hrynaszkiewicz, I., Staden, I., Whitaker, K., & McGillivray, B. (2019). The citation advantage of linking publications to research data. *arXiv preprint arXiv:1907.02565*.

Devare, M. H. (2019a). Cloud computing and innovations. In Kecskemeti, G. (Ed.), *Applying integration techniques and methods in distributed systems and technologies* (pp. 1–33). IGI Global Scientific Publishing., DOI: 10.4018/978-1-5225-8295-3.ch001

Devare, M. H. (2019b). Convergence of manufacturing cloud and industrial IoT. In Kecskemeti, G. (Ed.), *Applying integration techniques and methods in distributed systems and technologies* (pp. 49–78). IGI Global Scientific Publishing., DOI: 10.4018/978-1-5225-8295-3.ch003

Devare, M. H., & Devare, A. M. (2026). Predictive Maintenance Using Sensor Data Processing. In Habib, M. (Ed.), *AI-Driven Smart Industrial Technologies* (pp. 175–210). IGI Global Scientific Publishing., DOI: 10.4018/979-8-3693-7994-3.ch008

Foster, I., Kesselman, C., Nick, J. M., & Tuecke, S. (2002). *The physiology of the grid: An open grid services architecture for distributed systems integration*. Global Grid Forum.

Foster, I., Kesselman, C., & Tuecke, S. (2001). The Anatomy of the Grid: Enabling Scalable Virtual Organizations. *International Journal of High Performance Computing Applications*, *15*(3), 200–222. DOI: 10.1177/109434200101500302

Gosangi, R., Arora, R., Gheisarieha, M., Mahata, D., & Zhang, H. (2021). *On the Use of Context for Predicting Citation Worthiness of Sentences in Scholarly Articles*. arXiv preprint arXiv:2104.08962 DOI: 10.18653/v1/2021.naacl-main.359

Graf-Vlachy, L., Graziotin, D., & Wagner, S. (2022). *Text and Team: What Article Metadata Characteristics Drive Citations in Software Engineering?* arXiv preprint arXiv:2204.06033. DOI: 10.1145/3530019.3530022

Habibzadeh, F., & Yadollahie, M. (2010). Are shorter article titles more attractive for citations? Cross-sectional study of 22 scientific journals. *Croatian Medical Journal, 51*(2), 165–170. DOI: 10.3325/cmj.2010.51.165 PMID: 20401960

Jacques, T. S., & Sebire, N. J. (2010). The impact of article titles on citation hits: An analysis of general and specialist medical journals. *JRSM Short Reports, 1*(1), 2. DOI: 10.1258/shorts.2009.100020 PMID: 21103094

Lee, P.-S., West, J. D., & Howe, B. (2016). Viziometrics: Analyzing visual information in the scientific literature. *arXiv preprint arXiv:1605.04951*.ar5iv+2arXiv+2SpringerLink+2

Lei, S., Yang, R., & Huang, C.-R. (2021). *Automatic Analysis of Linguistic Features in Journal Articles of Different Academic Impacts with Feature Engineering Techniques*. arXiv preprint arXiv:2111.07525.

Letchford, A., Moat, H. S., & Preis, T. (2015). The advantage of short paper titles. *Royal Society Open Science, 2*(8), 150266. DOI: 10.1098/rsos.150266 PMID: 26361556

Liu, J., Xia, F., Feng, X., Ren, J., & Liu, H. (2022). Deep graph learning for anomalous citation detection. *IEEE Transactions on Neural Networks and Learning Systems, 1–14*. https://arxiv.org/abs/2202.11360

Lu, C., Bu, Y., Dong, X., Wang, J., Ding, Y., Larivière, V., Sugimoto, C. R., Paul, L., & Zhang, C. (2019). Analyzing linguistic complexity and scientific impact. *Journal of Informetrics, 13*(3), 817–829. DOI: 10.1016/j.joi.2019.07.004

Marshall, G. C., Jay, C., & Freitas, A. (2021). Number and quality of diagrams in scholarly publications is associated with number of citations. In *Diagrammatic Representation and Inference* (pp. 512–519). Springer., DOI: 10.1007/978-3-030-86062-2_52

McCannon, B. C. (2019). Readability and research impact. *Economics Letters, 180*, 76–79. DOI: 10.1016/j.econlet.2019.02.017

Mercier, D., Rizvi, S. T. R., Rajashekar, V., Dengel, A., & Ahmed, S. (2020). *ImpactCite: An XLNet-based method for Citation Impact Analysis*. arXiv preprint arXiv:2005.06611.

Nazir, S., Asif, M., Ahmad, S., Aljuaid, H., Iftikhar, R., Nawaz, Z., & Ghadi, Y. Y. (2022). Important Citation Identification by Exploding the Sentiment Analysis and Section-Wise In-Text Citation Weights. *IEEE Access : Practical Innovations, Open Solutions, 10*, 87990–88000. DOI: 10.1109/ACCESS.2022.3199420

Nieminen, P., Carpenter, J., Rücker, G., & Schumacher, M. (2006). The relationship between quality of research and citation frequency. *BMC Medical Research Methodology*, *6*(1), 42. DOI: 10.1186/1471-2288-6-42 PMID: 16948835

Paiva, C. E., Lima, J. P. S. N., & Paiva, B. S. R. (2012). Articles with short titles describing the results are cited more often. *Clinics (São Paulo)*, *67*(5), 509–513. DOI: 10.6061/clinics/2012(05)17 PMID: 22666797

Porwal, R., & Devare, M. (2024). Scientific impact analysis: Unraveling the link between linguistic properties and citations. *Journal of Informetrics*, *18*(1), 101252. DOI: 10.1016/j.joi.2024.101526

Purba, C. R., Anggraini, Y., Sari, P., Pangaribuan, W., & Pane, I. I. I. (2023). Article sentence analysis: Use of clauses and phrases in scientific sentences. *Lingüística*, *12*(1), 19–25. DOI: 10.24114/jalu.v11i4.43164

Saragih, E. (2023). Sentence complexity analysis in selected students' scientific papers: A closer look on abstract section. *E-Structural (English Studies on Translation, Culture, Literature, and Linguistics)*, 6(1), 70–83.

Stokes, C., Setlur, V., Cogley, B., Satyanarayan, A., & Hearst, M. (2022). Striking a balance: Reader takeaways and preferences when integrating text and charts. *arXiv preprint arXiv:2208.01780.*arXiv

Teplitskiy, M., Duede, E., Menietti, M., & Lakhani, K. R. (2020). *Citations Systematically Misrepresent the Quality and Impact of Research Articles: Survey and Experimental Evidence from Thousands of Citers*. arXiv preprint arXiv:2002.10033.

Tschalzev, A., Purucker, L., Lüdtke, S., Hutter, F., Bartelt, C., & Stuckenschmidt, H. (2025). Unreflected use of tabular data repositories can undermine research quality. *arXiv preprint arXiv:2503.09159*.

Vyas, V., Ravi, K., Ravi, V., Uma, V., Setlur, S., & Govindaraju, V. (2020). *Article citation study: Context enhanced citation sentiment detection*. arXiv preprint arXiv:2005.04534.

Wang, J., Liu, Y., Li, P., Lin, Z., Sindakis, S., & Aggarwal, S. (2023). Overview of data quality: Examining the dimensions, antecedents, and impacts of data quality. *Journal of the Knowledge Economy*. Advance online publication. DOI: 10.1007/s13132-022-01096-6 PMID: 40479478

Wright, D., & Augenstein, I. (2021). CiteWorth: Cite-Worthiness Detection for Improved Scientific Document Understanding. arXiv preprint arXiv:2105.10912. DOI: 10.18653/v1/2021.findings-acl.157

Yitzhaki, M. (2014). The effect of characteristics of title on citation rates of articles. *Scientometrics*, *101*(2), 1195–1205. DOI: 10.1007/s11192-013-1118-1

KEY TERMS AND DEFINITIONS

Bag of Words (BoW): Collection of individual words, ignoring grammar and word order, but keeping track of the word frequency. It represents the words in the vector format and numerical representation.

Continuous Bag of Words (CBOW): A Neural Network-based model tries to predict a target word based on its context words (surrounding words) within a fixed window.

Graph Neural Network (GNN): A neural network that learns to make predictions or extract patterns from graph-structured data by aggregating and transforming information from a node's neighbors' nodes.

H-Index: Hirsch index of a researcher with value h if they have at least h papers that have each been cited h times or more.

I10 Index: The i10-index is the number of academic publications by a researcher that have received at least 10 citations each.

Skip-Gram: It is a neural network-based model that predicts surrounding context words given a target word.

Type Token Ratio (TTR): It is the ratio of the number of unique words (types) to the total number of words (tokens) in a text.

Word Sense Disambiguation (WSD): It is the process of automatically determining the correct sense dictionary meaning of a word with multiple meanings based on its context in a sentence or document.

Chapter 9
Artificial Intelligence in Scholarly Investigation: Transforming Research and Ethics

Muhammad Irfan
http://orcid.org/0009-0007-2462-2129
Marmara University, Turkey

ABSTRACT

The chapter investigates how Artificial Intelligence (AI) affects academic research by boosting efficiency and analysis automation while providing predictive insights. The fast pace of knowledge production by AI systems brings new challenges involving data integrity and authorship alongside potential bias issues. The chapter examines how Artificial Intelligence affects peer review and interdisciplinary work while improving research transparency and advocates for ethical oversight and responsible application. The balance between opportunities and risks demonstrates why transparency and accountability must be central to AI-based academic research.

INTRODUCTION: THE PROMISE AND PARADOX OF AI IN SCHOLARSHIP

The integration of Artificial Intelligence (AI) into academic research methodologies marks a notable change in thinking, revolutionizing how scholarly investigations are conducted and knowledge is produced (Zahra & Rautela, 2024). With its unparalleled prowess in processing vast and intricate datasets, AI empowers researchers to uncover hidden patterns and insights that were previously beyond the reach of conventional methods. This transformative capability extends across various research activities, from automating literature reviews and predictive mod-

DOI: 10.4018/979-8-2600-2373-0.ch009

eling to accelerating peer review procedures. However, this technological frontier presents a profound paradox. While AI's potential to accelerate discovery and expand the boundaries of knowledge is undeniable, its rapid adoption introduces a host of complex ethical, epistemological, and practical challenges that demand urgent and rigorous examination. The very tools that promise to enhance intellectual rigor also risk introducing opaque biases, eroding traditional notions of authorship, and creating new forms of academic inequality. This chapter critically navigates the inherent tension at the heart of AI-driven research. It delves into the multifaceted impact of AI on academic scholarship, focusing specifically on the epistemological shifts, technological advancements, and ethical dilemmas that define this evolving landscape. By balancing an appreciation for AI's transformative power with a critical eye toward its inherent risks, this analysis seeks to chart a course for its responsible and equitable integration into the future of research.

METHODOLOGICAL APPROACH AND GROUNDING

To comprehensively explore AI's multifaceted impact on scholarly research, a mixed-methods approach emerges as a particularly robust and appropriate framework. Combining qualitative and quantitative data allows for a richer and more nuanced understanding of AI's effects across various dimensions of academic inquiry, including methodological advancements, data processing, and ethical issues. This approach, integrating numerical data with narrative insights, offered a more holistic perspective on AI's transformative effects on academic research methodologies and outcomes. Qualitative interviews provided detailed, nuanced insights into individual researcher experiences with AI tools, capturing the richness of human perspectives and ethical considerations. Simultaneously, quantitative measures can uncover broader usage patterns and statistically demonstrate how AI affects productivity levels (Muskat et al., 2012). This balanced approach allowed for both a deep understanding of the complexities of human experience and the application of statistical rigor for broader generalization, ensuring a comprehensive and robust investigation.

To illustrate how this methodology provided a holistic understanding, consider the issue of AI in peer review. A quantitative survey might reveal that 75% of journals in a field are experimenting with AI tools to find reviewers. While this number indicates a trend, it doesn't explain the 'why.' Qualitative interviews with editors and reviewers can then uncover the nuanced experiences behind this statistic: the pressures to speed up publication, the ethical anxieties about algorithmic bias in manuscript evaluation, and the lived reality of trusting a 'black box' system. By triangulating the 'what' (quantitative data) with the 'why' and 'how' (qualitative insights), a much richer and more valid picture emerges. The mixed-methods design offers significant advantages in data analysis. By combining qualitative and quantitative data analysis techniques, researchers can uncover hidden patterns and themes that might remain elusive when using a single-method approach. The synergistic combination of qualitative and quantitative data proves essential for documenting the intricate interactions between AI methods and human researchers, allowing for a more thorough exploration of the complexities inherent in digital knowledge generation (Muskat et al., 2012). Furthermore, a mixed-methods methodology enhances study validity and reliability by mitigating potential biases. The convergent corroboration provided by both qualitative and quantitative analyses strengthens the study's empirical basis and bolsters confidence in the findings.

The ability of mixed methods to effectively examine ethical and social consequences represents another key advantage, directly addressing the ethical imperatives researchers have highlighted throughout this chapter. The increasing adoption of AI in academic research raises multifaceted ethical concerns regarding bias, transparency, and equity. A mixed-methods approach allowed researchers to examine these issues more comprehensively, integrating empirical data analysis with critical evaluation. Qualitative research methods effectively surface participants' ethical concerns, capturing the nuanced lived experiences of researchers engaging with AI. Quantitative analysis, in turn, can determine the prevalence and intensity of these concerns across diverse academic environments, providing a broader statistical context for the qualitative findings.

The mixed-methods framework also facilitated the nuanced examination of methodological advancements brought about by AI technologies. By combining qualitative and quantitative research approaches, the authors gained a deeper understanding of how AI tools are transforming research paradigms. Qualitative data revealed the specific ways researchers are adapting their methods and workflows in response to AI, while quantitative data measured the impact of these changes on research efficiency and outcomes. Examples include AI tool applications for data transcription, thematic coding, and predictive analytics, all of which contribute to enhanced data-driven decision-making capabilities (Roe & Perkins, 2024). However, effectively managing the intricate nature of handling diverse data types and mastering multiple research methodologies requires meticulous strategic planning and rigorous oversight, particularly in addressing ethical concerns related to authorship and data protection in AI-driven research activities. Therefore, the continued collaboration between researchers, policymakers, and technologists remains essential to fully unlock AI's transformative potential while safeguarding academic integrity and ethical research practices.

To further contextualize research investigation, researchers conducted a systematic literature review of current research on AI adoption within academic environments. This review reveals an evolving field characterized by both significant potential benefits and considerable challenges. The systematic literature review highlights AI's profound impact on higher education, transforming teaching and administrative methods, while simultaneously prompting urgent discussions about ethical applications, data protection concerns, and potential over-reliance on automated systems. Literature underscores the necessity for a balanced approach to AI integration, one that maximizes its advantages while effectively mitigating its drawbacks.

Literature consistently points to significant learning enhancements facilitated by AI, particularly through personalized teaching approaches, leading to improved educational outcomes and increased student engagement (Allam, 2025). AI-driven tools like ChatGPT and similar platforms are shown to expedite various academic tasks through automated feedback systems and efficient evaluation processes, freeing up educators to focus more on pedagogical strategies and student mentorship (Castillo-Martínez et al., 2024). Moreover, AI demonstrably accelerates systematic literature reviews themselves, through automation of data collection and analysis stages, enhancing methodological accuracy while still requiring human oversight and critical interpretation of results.

However, alongside these benefits, literature acknowledges a range of challenges and concerns. Ethical and privacy concerns emerge as particularly pressing, stemming from the large-scale data collection capabilities of AI systems and the potential for misuse of sensitive student and research data (Allam, 2025; Mabona et al., 2024). Furthermore, excessive dependence on AI technology raises concerns about the potential erosion of students' critical thinking and problem-solving abilities, underscoring the need for thoughtful and proportionate integration of AI in educational settings. Significantly, the scholarly discourse reveals a notable gap in robust empirical studies examining the long-term impacts of AI advancements and academic institutions' preparedness for effectively and ethically implementing these technologies. Research reviews consistently suggest future research directions emphasizing interdisciplinary efforts to refine AI integration within educational frameworks, alongside the development of robust policies that prioritize human-centric principles and stringent data protection measures (Allam, 2025). These recommended approaches align closely with the principles of Sociotechnical Systems Theory, advocating for technological advancements to be carefully integrated with social and ethical considerations, ensuring that AI serves as a supportive tool rather than a replacement for essential human roles in education and research (Mabona et al., 2024).

While systematic reviews provide a broad overview of AI's academic impact, qualitative research methods, specifically case studies, phenomenological analysis, and expert interviews, offer essential in-depth insights into lived experiences and ethical nuances often missed by purely quantitative approaches. These qualitative methodologies, with their focus on firsthand experiences, cultural factors, and organizational norms, provided richer and more contextualized understandings of AI deployment and usage patterns within academic research settings. Case studies, for instance, effectively illuminate societal and ethical challenges arising from AI implementation. Analysis of case studies focusing on facial recognition technologies, for example, reveals industry practices such as deflection and strategic reform employed to address ethical concerns (Wen & Holweg, 2024). Other case-based studies demonstrate the collaborative frameworks necessary for ethical AI development, establishing design principles that prioritize user values and ethical considerations (Lase & Nkosi, 2023).

Phenomenological analysis offers a different, but equally valuable, perspective by investigating subjective experiences with AI systems. This approach effectively revealed the fundamental changes AI technologies are bringing to learning processes and social work interactions. Phenomenological research examining university students' interactions with generative AI uncovers core themes related to students' adaptation to new educational contexts and the co-evolution of human cognitive processes and AI capabilities. Furthermore, phenomenological viewpoints contribute to the ongoing philosophical debate about AI's capacity to mimic human consciousness, revealing the inherent limitations that distinguish even advanced machine learning outcomes from essential human cognitive features (Lumbreras & Garrido-Merchán, 2024).

Expert interviews serve as a vital medium for understanding professional and public opinions regarding AI's role in academia. Research interviews facilitated the exploration of common beliefs, ethical concerns, and the institutional power structures shaping AI adoption. Ethnographic framing within expert interviews further illuminated the forces shaping AI research and governance, providing nuanced insights into the negotiation and legitimation processes undertaken by societal actors in relation to emerging technologies. These qualitative methodologies provided rich, contextualized insights that were then integrated with broader quantitative data patterns to construct a more comprehensive and holistic understanding of AI's impact. Critically, incorporating perspectives from artistic and humanistic domain enhances authors' understanding of AI's broader socio-technical consequences, promoting the development of AI systems that are not only effective but also inclusive and ethically sound.

THE RESHAPING OF THE RESEARCH WORKFLOW

Artificial Intelligence is not merely a new tool; it is an advanced collaborator that is fundamentally redefining the entire research workflow. Research institutions require robust AI typologies to manage diverse AI applications, utilizing conceptual models encompassing technical, functional, and contextual dimensions. Public sector frameworks like Ballester (2021) highlight AI's governmental impact, emphasizing policy analysis. The OECD Framework bridges AI technology and policy, promoting trustworthy AI. Classification systems like "Switch," "Ladder," and "Matrix" (Mökander et al., 2022) aid AI governance by aligning AI features with organizational goals. Controlled vocabularies and AI-powered systems using BERT (Sachini et al., 2022) enhance AI research organization. Business classifications map AI across sectors, revealing industry connections. Non-deterministic AI necessitates scrutiny, especially in critical sectors like aviation (Tejasen et al., 2022). Ongoing typology refinement is essential to incorporate technical advancements and evolving ethical and societal implications, ensuring continued relevance.

By automating routine tasks and enabling a level of computational analysis previously unattainable, AI is augmenting human cognitive abilities and reshaping how knowledge is discovered, synthesized, and validated. This automation of routine yet time-consuming tasks is evident across the entire research lifecycle. For instance, AI is becoming crucial in academic librarianship, where it aids in hypothesis generation and overall workflow enhancement. Publishing platforms with integrated AI tools like Manubot now streamline manuscript preparation and citation management, freeing researchers to dedicate more of their time to core scholarly activities like conceptualization and interpretation. This is further evidenced in specific disciplines, such as the use of machine learning for the efficient screening of abstracts in psychology, which automates a traditionally labor-intensive task. A pivotal development in AI's application to research is the emergence of generative AI models, notably Generative Adversarial Networks (GANs) and Generative Pre-trained Transformers (GPT) (Baradziej, 2023; Edam, 2025). A pivotal development in AI's application to research has been the rise of models that don't just analyze information but actually create it. Think of it this way: for a long time, AI was like a super-fast file clerk, brilliant at sorting existing data. But 'generative' AI turned it into a creative partner. These models are not merely analytical tools; they represent a new class of methodologies capable of advanced predictive analytics and the identification of gaps within existing literature. By enabling researchers to explore uncharted territories in their fields, generative AI fosters innovative approaches to research inquiry. Complementing these advancements, Natural Language Processing (NLP) capabilities are significantly enhancing the efficiency and depth of literature reviews. NLP tools can rapidly analyze extensive bodies of academic text, identifying contemporary trends, subtle thematic connections, and critical insights with unprecedented speed and accuracy (Agrawal et al., 2024). This automation extends to routine yet time-consuming tasks like compiling bibliographies and generating reference lists, which allows researchers to dedicate more of their time to core scholarly activities like conceptualization and interpretation.

Beyond literature analysis, AI has revolutionized data analysis and pattern recognition at a foundational level. The foundation of this AI-driven transformation lies in its capacity for autonomous data processing and its ability to reveal hidden patterns through sophisticated machine learning techniques, including deep learning and natural language processing. These technological advancements significantly enhance data analysis operations, enabling the identification of valuable insights that conventional methods often miss. AI-driven systems demonstrate a remarkable ability to transform non-linearly separable data into linearly separable structures, simplifying subsequent analysis and creating novel pathways for discovering complex patterns. Self-Adaptive Neural Networks (SANNs), for example, exhibit superior capabilities in identifying subtle patterns within intricate datasets, particularly in biological data analysis, utilizing innovative similarity matching methods and error accumulation tactics to achieve enhanced accuracy.

This enhanced capability for analyzing vast datasets is not merely an endpoint; it serves as a powerful new engine for the very beginning of the research process: hypothesis generation. Sophisticated algorithms are playing an increasingly vital role in this process, working in tandem with human cognition, and in some instances, challenging traditional approaches. Through the analysis of extensive interdisciplinary databases and scholarly resources, generative AI and machine learning systems can detect novel patterns, correlations, and anomalies that can serve as the bedrock for developing groundbreaking hypotheses. This synergistic approach, combining data-driven analysis techniques with established literature-based methods, demonstrably enhances research accuracy. For example, research by Lin et al., (2024) indicates a 7.44% improvement in deception detection accuracy and a 14.19% improvement in AI-generated content detection when utilizing such combined methodologies. This evidence underscores AI's dual potential: both to refine existing analytical frameworks and to expand the horizons of scientific research.

The emergence of Large Language Models (LLMs) such as ChatGPT, capable of analyzing vast scientific literature collections, has further catalyzed this redefinition of hypothesis generation. While acknowledging their inherent error rates, these AI models provide a valuable tool for "algorithmic creativity," fostering the development of innovative research pathways. In fields like psychology, researchers are increasingly integrating causal knowledge graphs with LLMs to generate hypotheses that not only rival expert-level understanding but, in some cases, surpass those produced by standalone LLMs (Lin et al., 2024). Looking ahead, AI-powered automated discovery processes are poised to drive rapid advancements in academic research, significantly expanding the reach and scope of investigative inquiry.

This evolving human-AI symbiosis transforms the entire research workflow by distributing cognitive labor between researchers and machines. This constructive interaction simplifies routine tasks, such as literature review and data extraction, while simultaneously enabling levels of computational complexity and exploratory depth that were previously unattainable. Researchers from fields as varied as biology, computer science, mathematics, and social sciences are increasingly collaborating to address shared methodological challenges, particularly in the development of effective machine learning algorithms and interpretability frameworks. The "human-in-the-loop" approach is a crucial element of this collaborative research paradigm, emphasizing the ongoing need for human oversight and interaction to refine and validate AI system outputs (Hutson & Plate, 2024). In this model, AI and human creativity become mutually amplifying forces: AI systems accelerate knowledge acquisition, while human researchers ensure ethical considerations and nuanced interpretation.

AI functions as a "cognitive extender," significantly enhancing human cognitive capacities by improving memory function, boosting creative output, and sharpening critical thinking skills (Najem et al., 2024). Cognitive Artificial Intelligence (CAI) demonstrates AI's capacity to mimic human reasoning, enabling systems to act rationally within the parameters of their training data and pre-set objectives, as highlighted by Sumari & Ahmad (2018). This collaborative relationship fundamentally transforms task execution by distributing cognitive workloads between humans and machines.

This collaborative dynamic even extends to the final stages of research, such as peer review. AI-driven systems are showing promise in accelerating the peer review process. By assisting reviewers in evaluating the relevance and originality of submitted manuscripts, AI tools can potentially reduce review delays and enhance the overall quality of peer evaluation (Baradziej, 2023; Edam, 2025). It is crucial to emphasize that while AI tools can provide valuable support, human experts remain central to the peer review process, retaining the ultimate authority in judging the quality and significance of scholarly work.

A UNIFIED FRAMEWORK FOR ETHICAL AND SOCIETAL CHALLENGES

The integration of AI into the research workflow, while powerful, is fraught with profound ethical and societal challenges that strike at the core of academic values. These issues are not peripheral but are deeply embedded in the design, deployment, and use of AI systems. Addressing them requires a unified framework that considers bias and fairness, transparency and accountability, integrity and authorship, and equity and access.

BIAS AND FAIRNESS: PERPETUATING AND AMPLIFYING INEQUALITY

Expanding on the ethical challenges, researchers now focus specifically on algorithmic bias, a pervasive issue that arises from the use of algorithmic decision-making systems across various sectors, including academia. The risk of embedded biases, which can perpetuate and even amplify discriminatory practices, is a significant concern. The emergence of biases can occur at various stages – during data collection, model training, and system deployment – reflecting and often reinforcing societal prejudices already present within the training datasets. For example, AI-based recruitment tools trained on historical data that is skewed against specific demographic groups are prone to generating biased hiring recommendations (Pulivarthy & Whig, 2025). The combination of model design choices and training objectives can further intensify these existing biases. Prioritizing performance metrics over equitable outcomes, for instance, often results in marginalized groups experiencing disproportionate harm. Moreover, feedback loops can inadvertently exacerbate these inequalities. The practice of repeatedly targeting specific neighborhoods based on predictions from biased predictive policing algorithms, for example, can lead to skewed crime data, further undermining the fairness and objectivity of these algorithmic systems.

The manifestation of these biases typically results in discriminatory practices, often disproportionately impacting specific gender or racial groups, particularly in areas such as loan approvals and hiring procedures, as documented by (Y. Kim et al., 2024). When these discriminatory outcomes intersect with pre-existing perceptions of social inequality, public trust in AI systems erodes, particularly within communities already facing marginalization. Researchers are actively developing fairness-aware algorithms, incorporating constraints designed to achieve a more equitable balance between system performance and fair treatment (Pulivarthy & Whig, 2025). Bias-detection techniques, employing methods such as re-sampling, adjustments to model parameters, and post-processing output modifications, offer potential pathways to mitigate these issues and promote greater fairness. Furthermore, the development of robust ethical and regulatory frameworks is essential to promote transparency and accountability in AI systems, enabling diverse stakeholders to meaningfully influence AI development and deployment. However, the intricate and constantly evolving nature of biases means that complete removal is unattainable. This ongoing challenge underscores the crucial need for continuous research, stronger theoretical foundations in fairness and ethics, and vigilant monitoring of AI systems to mitigate algorithmic bias and its potentially harmful consequences. To move beyond simply acknowledging bias, institutions must develop and enforce mandatory bias-auditing frameworks. Similar to how institutional review boards (IRBs) oversee human subject research, these frameworks would require researchers to document their datasets, test their models for discriminatory outcomes against protected categories, and report on mitigation strategies before the research can be published.

TRANSPARENCY AND ACCOUNTABILITY: NAVIGATING THE "BLACK BOX"

The intricate nature of AI algorithms raises critical questions about transparency and accountability. The lack of clear explanations for AI-driven decisions and outcomes makes it challenging for researchers and stakeholders to ensure the trustworthiness of AI-assisted methodologies. This "black box" problem is exemplified in healthcare AI systems used for patient risk assessment. While these systems can effectively predict patient risk, their complex neural network architectures often preclude a clear understanding of their decision-making processes. For instance, a hospital employing an AI algorithm to assess emergency room patients may find that the system effectively predicts complications but cannot readily explain *why* a patient with chest pain receives a high-risk score. This opacity presents challenges for medical staff in verifying the relevance of identified risk factors, ensuring algorithm reliability across diverse patient populations, and establishing accountability for adverse outcomes. While techniques like LIME and SHAP offer post-hoc explanations, they provide only approximations, underscoring a fundamental tension in AI development: increased power and complexity often come at the cost of transparency and interpretability. This tension raises significant questions about organizational decision management when full system comprehension is unattainable.

In response, the growing demand for explainable AI (XAI) systems is therefore essential to maintain trustworthiness and ensure dependability in AI-driven knowledge creation, directly addressing the transparency and accountability concerns discussed in previous sections.

INTEGRITY AND AUTHORSHIP: REDEFINING SCHOLARLY NORMS

Data accuracy issues, alongside the inherent opacity of AI systems, raise broader ethical questions concerning authorship responsibilities and intellectual property rights in AI-mediated research. As AI tools become more deeply integrated into academic activities, defining the boundaries between human and machine contributions becomes increasingly complex. This complexity leads to significant concerns about work attribution and the ethical utilization of AI-generated content in scholarly publications. The potential for misuse extends beyond plagiarism to the deliberate fabrication of research data. For instance, AI-generated deepfakes could be used to create fraudulent medical images or falsify visual evidence in social science research, posing a profound threat to empirical integrity. Furthermore, an over-reliance on AI risks eroding students' and researchers' critical thinking and analytical skills, creating a dependency that undermines core educational goals. Alongside these concerns are significant issues of data privacy and security. The management of large datasets by AI systems demands a delicate equilibrium between leveraging data for insights and protecting sensitive personal information. These challenges underscore the urgent need for the development of ethical standards that prioritize transparency, accountability, and clear guidelines for the responsible implementation of AI in research (Baradziej, 2023; Edam, 2025). The scholarly community must proactively address the potential for AI tools to facilitate new forms of plagiarism and data misuse (Agrawal et al., 2024), ensuring the preservation of research integrity in this evolving technological landscape.

EQUITY AND ACCESS: CONFRONTING THE DIGITAL DIVIDE

The benefits of AI in research are not being distributed evenly, creating new forms of inequality and reinforcing existing ones. The differential access to and utilization of these technologies across academic communities can create "algorithmic knowledge hierarchies." Higher-ranked and better-funded universities with advanced AI infrastructure gain a significant advantage in knowledge production and dissemination, potentially widening the gap with less-resourced institutions and exacerbating global academic inequalities. Systematic guidelines are crucial to ensure equitable AI access, considering diverse user needs. Universal Design for Learning (UDL) frameworks promote accessible AI instruction for diverse learners (Lin et al., 2024). AI certifications integrating ethics and societal impact can broaden participation across disciplines. Technologists should prioritize diversity in AI design, serving varied user groups including marginalized communities. Generative AI offers opportunities for accessible instructional content. Inclusive online platforms should leverage AI for personalized learning and community building, as emphasized by the AIISE framework for inclusive STEM education (Roski et al., 2024). AI can foster a more inclusive economy by expanding resource access, requiring collaboration to address digital skill gaps. Purposefully, representative data collection is needed to train inclusive AI. Developing universally accessible, anti-ableist AI remains a challenge, demanding ongoing updates to design and evaluation standards amidst rapid AI advancements.

EPISTEMOLOGICAL AND PHILOSOPHICAL TRANSFORMATIONS

The integration of artificial intelligence into academic research is catalyzing profound epistemological and philosophical transformations, fundamentally altering how knowledge is produced, validated, and conceptualized. This shift moves beyond mere efficiency gains to challenge the very nature of inquiry itself. It requires a deep examination of how we know what we know in an age where knowledge is increasingly co-created with intelligent machines.

THE SHIFT TO ALGORITHMIC AND NETWORKED KNOWLEDGE

The integration of AI into academic research necessitates a critical examination of epistemological shifts in knowledge production. Algorithm-generated material, while potentially insightful and efficient, does not inherently carry the same epistemological weight as knowledge produced through traditional scholarly methods. As researchers aim to establish credibility in academic work, the authors traditionally rely on traceable processes: authors dedicate time to research, develop arguments from synthesized information, and explicitly connect their work to prior studies through citations. This process creates an "accountability chain," providing a transparent lineage from source material to the final scholarly product. AI disrupts this established chain. AI systems learn from vast and often opaque datasets, making it challenging to pinpoint the specific sources that influenced their outputs. The information genealogy in AI-generated content becomes a complex, interwoven network, complicating traditional notions of verification and validation.

This shift from linear, mechanistic perspectives to more interconnected systems of understanding can be understood through various epistemological lenses. Quantum Epistemology, for example, offers a compelling framework for interpreting this transformation. The shift toward Quantum Epistemology can be understood through a simple analogy. Traditional knowledge production often resembled an assembly line—linear, sequential, and deterministic. In contrast, the new model, which resonates with algorithmic structures, is more like a collaborative interdisciplinary research team. Knowledge emerges not from a straight line but from the complex, non-linear, and interconnected interactions between diverse experts and data sources, where the final insight is greater than the sum of its parts. This understanding of knowledge arising from interactive networks mirrors a broader epistemological movement away from simple, linear causality towards acknowledging the complex and relational nature of understanding.

Consider, for instance, a researcher using AI to assist in drafting a climate change research paper. While the AI may generate accurate summaries, validating these summaries independently becomes challenging. Unlike human researchers who provide explicit citations, the AI synthesizes information based on complex, often untraceable patterns within its training data. This difference raises fundamental questions about the nature of evidence and justification in AI-mediated scholarship.

The evolving epistemological landscape leads us to consider "Algorithmic Epistemologies," which redefine algorithms not merely as computational tools, but as active co-creators of knowledge (Maalsen, 2023). Contemporary research practices provide tangible examples of this emerging framework. Recommendation algorithms within academic research databases exemplify this active role. These algorithms transcend simple search functionalities, actively shaping scholarly research trajectories by suggesting related studies and revealing novel connections and research avenues. The function of algorithms has thus evolved beyond mere computational support to become an integral part of knowledge creation, influencing researchers' conceptual frameworks and investigative directions.

From this perspective, algorithms actively participate in knowledge acquisition by transforming data through decomposition, recompositing, and partitioning, establishing a modular framework for epistemic analysis (Aradau & Blanke, 2022). Modern genomic research vividly demonstrates this modular approach. Biological systems are broken down into components for algorithmic analysis and then reassembled to uncover previously hidden patterns. For instance, algorithms used in cancer genetics research dissect large genetic mutation datasets to identify subtle connections and therapeutic targets. This algorithmic decomposition and reintegration methodology has facilitated breakthroughs in personalized medicine, achievements often unattainable through conventional linear analysis methods.

Algorithmic Bayesian Epistemology offers a further nuanced perspective by integrating insights from algorithms with Bayesian frameworks (Neyman, 2024). This approach emphasizes the pragmatic constraints researchers face in real-world scenarios, such as limited data and computational power. Contemporary climate modeling exemplifies this balance. These models combine historical climate datasets with current observations, while acknowledging computational limitations, to produce probabilistic future climate forecasts. This methodology operates under the premise that perfect knowledge is often unattainable, focusing instead on achieving optimal solutions within existing resource and data quality constraints.

The rise of big data analytics in social sciences further underscores this epistemological transition. Digital Methods, integrating with existing theoretical frameworks, represent a move toward an abductive and intersubjective pluralistic knowledge framework (Amaturo & Aragona, 2021). Social network analysis, transformed by digital methods, exemplifies this shift. Researchers now employ algorithmic techniques, instead of traditional surveys or interviews, to analyze vast volumes of social media data, revealing intricate patterns of human social behavior and influence. This methodology embodies abductive reasoning, using algorithmic analysis to discover patterns and generate hypotheses, rather than solely relying on pre-established theoretical structures. Urban studies, similarly, has embraced algorithmic analysis of diverse data streams – mobile phone movement patterns, social media interactions – to gain deeper understandings of city dynamics. By algorithmically integrating multiple data sources and theoretical perspectives, new knowledge emerges that transcends traditional disciplinary boundaries. Educational research, once again, provides a clear manifestation of this epistemological transformation. Modern learning analytics platforms apply advanced algorithms to analyze student behavior, performance, and engagement. These systems often reveal unexpected patterns and relationships, expanding authors' understanding of learning processes beyond the limitations of predefined metrics.

TECHNOLOGICAL MEDIATION AND THE CO-CREATION OF KNOWLEDGE

Building upon the understanding of epistemological shifts, technological mediation models provide a crucial lens through which to examine AI's active participation in transforming knowledge production and validation. AI empowers human researchers not simply by increasing efficiency in managing large datasets and generating rapid insights, but by fundamentally reshaping and augmenting the very process of knowledge creation.

Cognitive Mediation Networks Theory (CMNT) further illuminates this perspective, arguing that the development of "Sophotechnic Mediation" creates a novel form of cognitive interaction with AI, profoundly altering individual information processing methods (de Souza et al., 2024). Consider researchers utilizing AI-powered literature review tools. Scholars who adopt these systems experience a fundamental change in their engagement with academic literature. Instead of traditional sequential reading of papers, they often begin with AI-generated summaries, fostering a collaborative understanding between human and machine intelligence. AI technology also plays a transformative role in collective memory and historical consciousness. Machine-led data management allows individuals and communities to engage in dialogic interactions, shifting the very historical knowledge that is produced (Matei, 2024). For example, historians utilizing AI systems to analyze historical documents are transforming the practice of historiography. Traditional historical research involved scholars meticulously reading archives and establishing connections through human memory and critical thinking. AI systems now enable rapid analysis of vast collections of historical texts, detecting patterns and relationships that would require years of human research alone. This integration of AI with historian expertise creates an “augmented historiography,” enriching and accelerating historical scholarship.

These AI-driven advancements in academic practices extend beyond mere efficiency gains. Consider the transformation of academic writing practices. AI writing tools now assist researchers by suggesting relevant citations, identifying argumentative gaps, and even generating alternative sentence structures. The writing process itself evolves into a collaborative endeavor, a dynamic intellectual dialogue between human creativity and machine analysis.

To fully appreciate the magnitude of these changes, compare modern doctoral research methods to those prevalent just two decades ago. Today’s doctoral students can leverage AI systems to process extensive literature, identify emerging research trends, and connect with international scholars, unconstrained by the limitations of physical library access or manual note-taking. Researchers experience not only enhanced efficiency but also a fundamental transformation in how knowledge is discovered, verified, and disseminated.

This deep entanglement of AI in the research process is captured by the term “Epistemolog-IA”. The concept of “Epistemolog-IA” succinctly captures the profound interconnection between artificial intelligence and epistemology (Palencia, 2024). It underscores AI's transformative effects on both knowledge itself and researchers’ perceptions of reality. AI systems in medical diagnosis, for example, transcend mere clinical data processing; they revolutionize the very construction and validation of medical knowledge. AI's ability to detect subtle patterns in radiological images, often imperceptible to human experts, challenges established medical expertise, prompting fundamental inquiries into the nature of diagnostic knowledge. This epistemological shift extends into computational linguistics, where large language models (LLMs) exhibit capabilities that challenge traditional assumptions about language learning and understanding. Furthermore, AI's ability to generate new scientific hypotheses by analyzing vast collections of research papers transforms researchers into understanding of scientific knowledge development and progression. This capability, however, also highlights both the strengths and limitations of machine-based knowledge creation.

CRITICAL THEORIES AND PHILOSOPHICAL TENSIONS

This epistemological revolution is accompanied by significant philosophical tensions and ethical risks. AI's integration into research raises philosophical tensions regarding human interpretative authority and the nature of knowledge. While AI algorithms advance, human creativity remains characterized by open-ended exploration, unlike AI's algorithmic constraints, even with advancements like GANs (Dwivedi et al., 2023). AI's increasing autonomy challenges human preeminence in knowledge creation, sparking ethical debates about AI consciousness and moral responsibility. This challenge to human preeminence in knowledge creation is not entirely new; it is a modern-day manifestation of questions Alan Turing posed in the 1950s about machine intelligence. However, generative AI's capacity for creating seemingly novel text forces us to move beyond Turing's imitation game to directly confront the nature of creativity and authorship in a mediated world. Human oversight remains crucial for ethical AI operation. Digital humanism advocates for AI prioritizing human values, preventing workforce replacement (Nowotny, 2022). The line between human and machine knowledge blurs as algorithms influence collective understanding. Integrating AI innovation while preserving human insight and ethical principles is crucial. The task is to harness AI's potential while protecting human creativity and ethical knowledge production.

Critics rightly argue that over-reliance on machine-generated insights can disregard essential subjective perspectives and reflective thought, potentially leading to a simplistic understanding of knowledge (Fisher, 2022). Critics like Fisher (2022) warn that over-reliance on AI-generated insights could lead to a 'subversion of critical knowledge'. The danger is not just that AI might be wrong, but that its efficiency may cause researchers to devalue the slower, more reflective, and often ambiguous process of human intuition, which is essential for true breakthroughs and deep understanding. This concern is amplified when considering the potential for “algorithmic harm” and the exacerbation of bias and discrimination (Maalsen, 2023). Consider AI systems used in predictive policing or recidivism risk assessment. While these systems analyze extensive case law and demographic data to forecast recidivism rates, they risk diminishing the importance of judicial discretion and human empathy. Algorithmic predictions, in such scenarios, can overshadow a judge's nuanced understanding of human nature and contextual factors, illustrating the tension between machine efficiency and essential human judgment.

Educational environments are particularly vulnerable to the challenges of algorithmic harm. An AI-driven student assessment system, while efficient in processing large volumes of written work, may misjudge unique creative expressions due to its reliance on fixed patterns. This can inadvertently reinforce cultural biases and stifle diverse modes of knowledge creation by enforcing uniform thinking. Such scenarios highlight how biases embedded within algorithms can perpetuate existing social inequalities and generate new forms of epistemic injustice. Environmental science research provides another compelling example. AI systems evaluating climate data for environmental predictions often prioritize measurable data, potentially overlooking the crucial context provided by Indigenous knowledge systems and traditional environmental wisdom. The reduction of intricate ecological relationships to computational models risks losing essential contextual understanding derived from generational observations and culturally embedded knowledge. This tension is evident across multiple disciplines. In art history and criticism, for example, while AI analysis of artistic styles can reveal unknown patterns, it also risks reducing aesthetic appreciation to a formalistic study of characteristics, potentially missing the deeper cultural and emotional dimensions that human critics discern. Similarly, while systems like Transkribus and ChatGPT can improve quantitative analysis within the humanities, their contributions are often offset by a lack of nuanced human understanding, highlighting the persistent gap between computational processing and qualitative interpretation.

These examples collectively underscore the intricate interplay between computational effectiveness and human discernment in contemporary knowledge creation. AI systems offer unprecedented analytical capabilities, yet human subjectivity and ethical considerations must remain integral to ensure a balanced and nuanced approach to knowledge generation in the digital age. The successful co-existence of algorithmic insights and human wisdom requires a deliberate and thoughtful integration, ensuring that technological progress enhances, rather than diminishes, human understanding.

Having explored the epistemological and ethical dimensions of AI in academic research, researchers now employ critical theories and Science and Technology Studies (STS) frameworks to further analyze AI's role in knowledge production. STS provides a crucial lens for understanding how social and technological interactions shape the creation and validation of knowledge. This perspective reveals that AI-driven processes are not operating in a vacuum, but are deeply embedded within ethical, organizational, and cultural contexts. STS frameworks allow us to move beyond a purely technical assessment of AI's capabilities to a more nuanced understanding of its socio-technical implications.

Drawing on STS frameworks, the authors recognize that technological deployments invariably occur within established power structures and institutional hierarchies. The impact of AI tools introduced into academic settings is thus mediated by departmental budgets, institutional priorities, and pre-existing professional relationships. Departments with greater financial resources are more likely to adopt advanced AI technologies, potentially exacerbating existing disparities in research capabilities and academic outcomes. This observation aligns with researchers' earlier discussion of algorithmic knowledge hierarchies and the uneven distribution of AI's benefits across academic institutions.

ETHICAL RAMIFICATIONS AND THE IMPERATIVE FOR GLOBAL GUIDELINES

The rapid proliferation of generative AI systems also presents immediate ethical ramifications, particularly concerning plagiarism. AI-generated text can closely mimic human writing, raising concerns about the potential for misuse and the need for robust mechanisms to maintain scholarly publication integrity. Furthermore, the use of AI systems to manage large datasets raises significant privacy and data protection concerns, demanding heightened attention to the secure storage and sharing of sensitive research data. Let's say a team of medical researchers using a powerful AI system to analyze a dataset containing thousands of patient records to identify new patterns in disease progression. This dataset is filled with highly sensitive and personal information, including names, genetic markers, and confidential health histories. The AI system, possibly running on a third-party cloud server, processes this information. If that system has security vulnerabilities or if the data wasn't perfectly anonymized, a breach could expose the private medical details of every person in the study. This represents a catastrophic failure of data protection, with severe consequences for patient privacy. Therefore, the global research community urgently requires standardized ethical guidelines that transcend national borders to establish uniform norms for responsible AI use in academia (Baradziej, 2023; Edam, 2025).

BALANCING INNOVATION AND ETHICAL RESPONSIBILITY

The introduction of AI into academic research represents an unparalleled opportunity to accelerate discovery and expand knowledge production. However, realizing this potential requires a firm commitment to ethical standards, methodological transparency, and robust governance frameworks. The academic community must strategically navigate the balance between AI's transformative benefits and its potential to disrupt traditional notions of authorship and research ethics. Fostering steadfast partnerships between researchers, academic institutions, and policymakers is essential to ensure the responsible utilization of AI's transformative power, advancing scholarly research while upholding the rigorous and innovative nature of scientific discourse. Moving forward, initiative-taking engagement with the ethical, epistemological, and technological dimensions of AI in research will be crucial for harnessing its benefits while mitigating its risks, ensuring a future where AI serves to enhance, rather than undermine, the integrity and value of academic scholarship.

HUMAN-MACHINE COLLABORATION AND ETHICAL CONSIDERATIONS

STS research emphasizes the crucial role of human-machine collaboration in ensuring ethical standards and maximizing AI's effectiveness in serving academic goals (Dinçer, 2024; Tomczyk et al., 2024). AI's power lies in augmenting human expertise, not replacing it. AI excels at identifying patterns within large datasets and facilitating interdisciplinary partnerships to address complex problems in fields such as healthcare, environmental science, and social policymaking. In medical research, AI systems can analyze massive datasets encompassing patient records, genetic information, and clinical trial data, detecting complex patterns indicative of potential drug interactions or disease relationships. However, human researchers provide the essential medical context to these findings, designing validation studies and evaluating ethical implications for patient care. AI, in this context, functions as a powerful tool to enhance human medical expertise, requiring professional human supervision to maintain clinical relevance and uphold ethical standards.

Environmental sciences offer another compelling illustration of this partnership. AI systems analyze vast datasets from satellites, oceanic sensors, and weather stations to uncover complex patterns in climate change studies, patterns that might elude human observers. For example, an AI system is tasked with analyzing vast datasets of high-resolution satellite imagery of the Amazon rainforest, which it receives daily. A team of human observers could never manually review this data. The AI is trained to detect subtle changes in forest cover, looking for complex patterns that might signal illegal activity—patterns that might otherwise elude human observers. It doesn't just look for large clear-cut areas; it identifies the faint, new lines of makeshift logging roads, gradual thinning of the canopy over time, and specific geometric shapes inconsistent with natural forest loss. Environmental scientists then interpret these patterns through the lens of established climate models, considering the influence of local ecosystems and human activities. Suppose the AI flags remote, supposedly protected region where it has detected a new, branching network of these faint roads. An environmental scientist receives this alert. They then interpret this data through the lens of established climate and ecological models. The scientist can determine if the pattern matches slash-and-burn agriculture or if it indicates more organized, industrial logging. By cross-referencing the AI's findings with data on local ecosystems, indigenous territories, and rainfall patterns, they can assess the potential impact of this specific activity. This synergistic combination of AI analysis and human expertise allows researchers to tackle environmental challenges in ways that surpass the capabilities of either humans or machines working in isolation.

Social policy research introduces even more nuanced dynamics to human-machine collaboration. For instance, an AI system is tasked with processing a city's vast and varied datasets. It analyzes demographic data from the census, economic indicators like local business closures, public transportation routes, and anonymized social media trends related to job-seeking and community sentiment. The AI detects a strong correlation: several specific neighborhoods consistently show the highest rates of unemployment among 18–24-year-olds. It further correlates this with limited public transport access to the city's main commercial hubs and a recent wave of retail job losses within those neighborhoods. The AI has effectively identified *what* the problem is and *where* it is most concentrated. Now, a team of sociologists and social policy researchers receives the AI's report. They know the correlation is just a starting point. Their work is to uncover the "why." They investigate the history of these neighborhoods, discovering that past industrial decline and discriminatory housing policies ("redlining") led to generational poverty and isolation. Moreover, through community focus groups and interviews, they learn that a simple lack of jobs isn't the only issue. There's a deep-seated distrust of city-run employment programs and a cultural stigma against the low-wage service jobs available in other parts of the city. Also, the researchers evaluate the ethics of potential solutions. For example, a purely data-driven solution might be to simply offer subsidized bus passes, but this could force young people into long commutes for precarious work, which is not an ethically sound or sustainable solution.

So, AI systems can process demographic data, economic indicators, and social media trends to identify emerging social issues. However, human researchers remain indispensable for interpreting cultural contexts, historical factors, and evaluating the ethical implications of these identified patterns. While AI tools might detect correlations between socioeconomic factors and urban inequality, human insight is crucial to understanding underlying historical patterns and crafting culturally appropriate and ethically sound policy solutions.

Despite the considerable benefits AI offers, its integration into research methodologies introduces significant ethical challenges. The use of AI-generated content, for instance, presents risks to academic integrity, including the potential for manipulated data and fabricated references (Dinçer, 2024). This necessitates robust oversight mechanisms to protect research honesty and rigor, echoing researchers' earlier concerns about maintaining research integrity in the age of AI. These ethical considerations underscore the critical role of human supervision and institutional guidelines in mitigating the potential misuse of AI-generated outputs and ensuring responsible AI implementation in academic research, reinforcing the imperative for ethical frameworks discussed in the initial sections of this chapter.

THE IMPERATIVE OF HUMAN OVERSIGHT AND ETHICAL REFLECTION

The transformative role of AI in research methodologies is undeniable, driving innovation across fields from genomics to climate science by automating routine tasks and revealing new research possibilities. However, the rapid advancement and widespread adoption of AI systems necessitate the development of comprehensive strategies that proactively recognize and mitigate inherent biases, address misinformation, and safeguard human decision-making authority. STS scholars, through their analysis of AI integration within social, cultural, and institutional contexts, effectively highlight both the potential benefits and inherent challenges. Maintaining human oversight, fostering ethical reflection, and promoting critical engagement with AI are crucial for safeguarding the integrity of academic knowledge production (Dinçer, 2024; Tomczyk et al., 2024). As AI becomes increasingly integrated into all facets of scholarly activity, researchers must actively address its broader societal and ethical consequences. Adhering to STS principles, grounded in socio-technical awareness, will help ensure that AI remains a valuable *tool* in knowledge creation, rather than an unconstrained force reshaping academic norms and values. By embracing collaborative methodologies, promoting transparent practices, and establishing robust ethical guidelines, the academic community can harness AI's transformative potential while simultaneously safeguarding the thoroughness, rigor, and ethical integrity of scholarly research.

DISCIPLINARY IMPACT: AI'S ROLE ACROSS HUMANITIES, SOCIAL SCIENCES, AND STEM FIELDS

Artificial Intelligence is transforming research across STEM, Humanities, and Social Sciences. In STEM, AI revolutionizes data analysis and pattern recognition, accelerating research and enabling interdisciplinary innovation (Kondaveeti et al., 2024). Automation tools enhance efficiency, though ethical concerns regarding data privacy and bias are paramount, necessitating robust guidelines. In parallel, humanities are also being transformed by AI. This transformative effect is not confined to STEM. In the humanities, AI tools are used to analyze vast textual archives, identifying stylistic patterns to attribute authorship or tracing the evolution of ideas across centuries of literature, thereby bridging quantitative analysis with qualitative interpretation. Thus, it is enabling in-depth analyses of cultural patterns (Gefen et al., 2021) and fostering new interdisciplinary fields like digital humanities. This bridges the sciences and humanities, with the latter providing crucial ethical frameworks for AI development, emphasizing human-centered values. In conclusion, AI offers unprecedented efficiency and interdisciplinary opportunities across academia but demands a balanced approach that harmonizes technological progress with humanistic values to safeguard ethical depth and rigor across all disciplines.

INTERDISCIPLINARY COLLABORATION: AI FOSTERING NEW RESEARCH MODALITIES

AI's rapid progress is driving interdisciplinary collaborations and innovation across sectors. Environmental science uses AI for climate change and biodiversity loss, merging algorithmic insights with ecological knowledge. Agriculture leverages AI to enhance food security, integrating ethics, economics, and environmental stewardship (Ryan et al., 2023). LLMs are revolutionizing negotiation, though ethical vigilance is crucial. Generative AI tools like ChatGPT benefit manufacturing, finance, retail, and transportation, fostering cross-functional teams (Rane, 2023). Finance combats fraud and personalizes services with AI. Transportation optimizes routes and coordination. Healthcare addresses aging-related diseases like Alzheimer's through interdisciplinary AI collaborations (Abadir et al., 2024). These partnerships highlight AI's pervasive influence and the necessity for ethical, stakeholder-oriented methodologies, emphasizing ethical AI design and agile research management.

CONCLUSION: CHARTING A COURSE FOR RESPONSIBLE AI IN SCHOLARSHIP

The integration of Artificial Intelligence into academic research marks a fundamental paradigm shift, an unparalleled opportunity to accelerate discovery and expand the frontiers of knowledge. From automating literature reviews to revealing previously hidden patterns in vast datasets, AI's transformative potential is undeniable. However, this power is inextricably linked with profound ethical, epistemological, and societal challenges that strike at the very heart of scholarly integrity. The central thesis of this work is that navigating this new landscape requires more than just technological adoption; it demands a steadfast, proactive commitment to balancing innovation with ethical responsibility through robust governance and methodological transparency.

The analysis has shown that AI is not a neutral tool; it actively reshapes the nature of academic inquiry. It disrupts the traditional "accountability chain" of knowledge production by operating on vast, often opaque datasets, making the validation of its outputs a critical challenge. This "black box" problem, coupled with the risk of AI-generated fabrications or "hallucinations," renders the foundations of scholarship vulnerable and necessitates a move toward Explainable AI (XAI). Furthermore, the manuscript has underscored how algorithmic bias can perpetuate and amplify societal inequities if left unchecked, while the rise of "algorithmic knowledge hierarchies" threatens to widen the digital divide between institutions. These challenges, alongside the complexities of redefining authorship and intellectual property in an era of "mediated creativity," demand urgent attention from the entire academic community.

Despite these hurdles, the opportunities are immense. AI is revolutionizing the entire research workflow, functioning as a "cognitive extender" that augments human intellect rather than replacing it. By automating laborious tasks, it frees researchers to focus on higher-order conceptualization, analysis, and interpretation. AI's capacity for data analysis and pattern recognition is fostering new methodological innovations and driving unprecedented interdisciplinary collaboration across STEM, the social sciences, and the humanities. When deployed thoughtfully within a "human-in-the-loop" framework, AI and human creativity become mutually amplifying forces, enabling researchers to tackle complex problems that were previously intractable.

Moving forward, charting a course for responsible AI in scholarship requires a coordinated, multi-stakeholder effort. The following recommendations provide a framework for action:

- **For Academic Institutions:** It is imperative to develop and implement clear, comprehensive institutional policies and ethical guidelines for AI use. These frameworks must prioritize transparency, accountability, and the mitigation of bias. Furthermore, institutions must invest in robust AI literacy programs to equip both faculty and students with the critical skills needed to engage with these tools responsibly.
- **For Researchers and Educators:** A culture of critical engagement is paramount. Researchers must insist on methodological transparency, meticulously documenting AI tools and models to ensure reproducibility. Adopting a "human-in-the-loop" model ensures that human expertise and ethical judgment remain central to the research process, particularly in peer review and the final interpretation of results.
- **For Policymakers and the Global Community:** The rapid, borderless nature of AI necessitates the development of standardized, global ethical guidelines to establish uniform norms for responsible AI use in academia. Efforts must support the development of fairness-aware algorithms and promote inclusive design principles to ensure equitable access and prevent the exacerbation of existing inequalities.

Ultimately, the successful integration of AI into scholarship hinges on our ability to embed our core academic values into the technologies we create and use.

The future is not a binary choice between humanistic tradition and technological progress, but a collaborative synthesis of both. By fostering steadfast partnerships, promoting transparent practices, and adhering to rigorous ethical standards, the academic community can harness AI's transformative power to advance scholarly research while safeguarding the integrity, rigor, and equity that define scientific and intellectual discourse.

REFERENCES

Abadir, P., Oh, E., Chellappa, R., Choudhry, N., Demiris, G., Ganesan, D., Karlawish, J., Marlin, B., Li, R. M., Dehak, N., Arbaje, A., Unberath, M., Cudjoe, T., Chute, C., Moore, J. H., Phan, P., Samus, Q., Schoenborn, N. L., Battle, A., & Walston, J. D. (2024). Artificial Intelligence and Technology Collaboratories: Innovating aging research and Alzheimer's care. *Alzheimer's & Dementia*, *20*(4), 3074–3079. DOI: 10.1002/alz.13710

Agrawal, A., McHale, J., & Oettl, A. (2024). Artificial intelligence and scientific discovery: A model of prioritized search. *Research Policy*, *53*(5), 104989. DOI: 10.1016/j.respol.2024.104989

Allam, H. (2025). *The Role of AI and Living Intelligence in Higher Education: Potential Applications and Challenges.*

Amaturo, E., & Aragona, B. (2021). Digital methods and the evolution of the epistemology of social sciences. *Data Science and Social Research II: Methods, Technologies and Applications*, 1–8.

Aradau, C., & Blanke, T. (2022). *Algorithmic reason: The new government of self and other*. Oxford University Press. DOI: 10.1093/oso/9780192859624.001.0001

Ballester, O. (2021). An artificial intelligence definition and classification framework for public sector applications. *DG. O2021: The 22nd Annual International Conference on Digital Government Research*, 67–75.

Baradziej, S. (2023). The influence of Large Language Models on systematic review and research dissemination. *Septentrio Conference Series, 1.*

Castillo-Martínez, I. M., Flores-Bueno, D., Gómez-Puente, S. M., & Vite-León, V. O. (2024). AI in higher education: A systematic literature review. *Frontiers in Education*, *9*, 1391485. DOI: 10.3389/feduc.2024.1391485

de Souza, B. C., de Andrade Neto, A. S., & Roazzi, A. (2024). The generative AI revolution, cognitive mediation networks theory and the emergence of a new mode of mental functioning: Introducing the Sophotechnic Mediation scale. *Computers in Human Behavior: Artificial Humans*, *2*(1), 100042. DOI: 10.1016/j.chbah.2024.100042

Dinçer, S. (2024). The use and ethical implications of artificial intelligence in scientific research and academic writing. *Educational Research & Implementation*, *1*(2), 139–144. DOI: 10.14527/edure.2024.10

Dwivedi, Y. K., Kshetri, N., Hughes, L., Slade, E. L., Jeyaraj, A., Kar, A. K., Baabdullah, A. M., Koohang, A., Raghavan, V., Ahuja, M., Albanna, H., Albashrawi, M. A., Al-Busaidi, A. S., Balakrishnan, J., Barlette, Y., Basu, S., Bose, I., Brooks, L., Buhalis, D., & Wright, R. (2023). Opinion Paper:"So what if ChatGPT wrote it?" Multidisciplinary perspectives on opportunities, challenges, and implications of generative conversational AI for research, practice, and policy. *International Journal of Information Management*, *71*, 102642. DOI: 10.1016/j.ijinfomgt.2023.102642

Edam, S. M. I. (2025). Restructuring the Landscape of Generative AI Research. In *Impacts of Generative AI on the Future of Research and Education* (pp. 287–334). IGI Global.

Fisher, E. (2022). *Algorithms and subjectivity: The subversion of critical knowledge*. Routledge. DOI: 10.4324/9781003196563

Gefen, A., Saint-Raymond, L., & Venturini, T. (2021). AI for digital humanities and computational social sciences. *Reflections on Artificial Intelligence for Humanity*, 191–202.

Hutson, J., & Plate, D. (2024). Disrupting Algorithmic Culture: Redefining the Human (ities). In *Generative AI in Teaching and Learning* (pp. 1–30). IGI Global.

Kim, Y., Kim, D., Choi, J., Park, J., Oh, N., & Park, D. (2024). A survey on integration of large language models with intelligent robots. *Intelligent Service Robotics*, *17*(5), 1091–1107. DOI: 10.1007/s11370-024-00550-5

Kondaveeti, H. K., Kumar, S. V. S., Manusree, A. V. N., Vatsavayi, V. K., & Ananthachari, P. (2024). Role of AI in Academic Research. In *Utilizing AI Tools in Academic Research Writing* (pp. 1–17). IGI Global. DOI: 10.4018/979-8-3693-1798-3.ch001

Lase, E. M., & Nkosi, F. (2023). Human-Centric AI: Understanding and Enhancing Collaboration between Humans and Intelligent Systems. *Algorithm Asynchronous*, *1*(1), 33–40. DOI: 10.61963/jaa.v1i1.49

Lin, T., Song, K., Jiang, Z., Kang, Y., Yuan, W., Li, X., Sun, C., Huang, C., & Liu, X. (2024). Towards human-like perception: Learning structural causal model in heterogeneous graph. *Information Processing & Management*, *61*(2), 103600. DOI: 10.1016/j.ipm.2023.103600

Lumbreras, S., & Garrido-Merchán, E. (2024). Insights from Saint Teresa and Saint Augustine on Artificial Intelligence: Discussing Human Interiority. *Scientia et Fides*, *12*(2), 265–295. DOI: 10.12775/SetF.2024.025

Maalsen, S. (2023). Algorithmic epistemologies and methodologies: Algorithmic harm, algorithmic care and situated algorithmic knowledges. *Progress in Human Geography*, *47*(2), 197–214. DOI: 10.1177/03091325221149439

Mabona, A., Van Greunen, D., & Kevin, K. (2024). Integration of Artificial Intelligence (AI) in Academic Libraries: A Systematic Literature Review. *2024 IST-Africa Conference (IST-Africa)*, 1–9.

Matei, S. (2024). Generative artificial intelligence and collective remembering. The technological mediation of mnemotechnic values. *Journal of Human-Technology Relations, 2*.

Mökander, J., Juneja, P., Watson, D. S., & Floridi, L. (2022). The US Algorithmic Accountability Act of 2022 vs. The EU Artificial Intelligence Act: What can they learn from each other? *Minds and Machines*, *32*(4), 751–758. DOI: 10.1007/s11023-022-09612-y

Muskat, M., Blackman, D. A., & Muskat, B. (2012). Mixed methods: Combining expert interviews, cross-impact analysis, and scenario development. *Electronic Journal of Business Research Methods*, *10*(1), 9–21.

Najem, N. R., Salman, A. S., Nas, Y. F., Abu-AlShaeer, M. J., Basheer, B. M., Khaddad, A., & Monadhel, H. (2024). Human-AI Symbiosis: Investigating Real-Time Neural Link Integrations for Enhanced Cognitive Abilities. *2024 36th Conference of Open Innovations Association (FRUCT)*, 664–674.

Neyman, E. (2024). Algorithmic Bayesian Epistemology. *ArXiv Preprint ArXiv:2403.07949*.

Nowotny, H. (2022). *Digital Humanism: Navigating the Tensions Ahead.*

Palencia, M. G. P. (2024). Epistemolog-IA: La confluencia de la Inteligencia Artificial y la epistemología en el desarrollo científico contemporáneo. *Ciencia Latina Revista Científica Multidisciplinar*, *8*(4), 11236–11257. DOI: 10.37811/cl_rcm.v8i4.13264

Pulivarthy, P., & Whig, P. (2025). Bias and Fairness Addressing Discrimination in AI Systems. In *Ethical Dimensions of AI Development* (pp. 103–126). IGI Global.

Rane, N. (2023). ChatGPT and Similar Generative Artificial Intelligence (AI) for Smart Industry: role, challenges, and opportunities for industry 4.0, industry 5.0 and society 5.0. *Challenges and Opportunities for Industry, 4*.

Roe, J., & Perkins, M. (2024). Generative AI and Agency in Education: A Critical Scoping Review and Thematic Analysis. *ArXiv Preprint ArXiv:2411.00631*.

Roski, M., Sebastian, R., Ewerth, R., Hoppe, A., & Nehring, A. (2024). Learning analytics and the Universal Design for Learning (UDL): A clustering approach. *Computers & Education, 214*, 105028. DOI: 10.1016/j.compedu.2024.105028

Ryan, M., Isakhanyan, G., & Tekinerdogan, B. (2023). An interdisciplinary approach to artificial intelligence in agriculture. *NJAS: Impact in Agricultural and Life Sciences, 95*(1), 2168568. DOI: 10.1080/27685241.2023.2168568

Sachini, E., Sioumalas-Christodoulou, K., Christopoulos, S., & Karampekios, N. (2022). AI for AI: Using AI methods for classifying AI science documents. *Quantitative Science Studies, 3*(4), 1119–1132. DOI: 10.1162/qss_a_00223

Sumari, A. D. W., & Ahmad, A. S. (2018). Cognitive artificial intelligence: Concept and applications for humankind. *Intelligent System, 23*, 55. DOI: 10.5772/intechopen.72764

Tejasen, K. T. J., Raju, P., Ryan, W., Jordan, A., & Yang, R. (2022). Defining an Initial Classification Scheme for Non-Deterministic AI Technologies. *2022 Integrated Communication, Navigation and Surveillance Conference (ICNS)*, 1–10.

Tomczyk, P., Brüggemann, P., & Doligalski, T. (2024). The automation of science? Possibilities and boundaries of AI applications for conducting systematic literature reviews. *International Journal of Artificial Intelligence Tools, 33*(06), 2450023. DOI: 10.1142/S0218213024500234

Wen, Y., & Holweg, M. (2024). A phenomenological perspective on AI ethical failures: The case of facial recognition technology. *AI & Society, 39*(4), 1929–1946. DOI: 10.1007/s00146-023-01648-7

Zahra, W., & Rautela, G. (2024). Revolutionizing Learning Landscapes: Unleashing the Potential of AI in the Realm of Academic Research. In *Artificial Intelligence: A Multidisciplinary Approach towards Teaching and Learning* (pp. 242–264). Bentham Science Publishers.

KEY TERMS AND DEFINITIONS

Epistemological Shift: The advancement of AI research methods leads to a fundamental change in knowledge production, validation, and understanding because they challenge conventional human-focused academic study approaches.

Explainable AI (XAI): This represents a research domain focused on creating AI models with transparent decision processes that humans can interpret to maintain accountability in AI research.

Generative Adversarial Networks (GANs): These represent an AI technique based on dual neural networks which include a generator and a discriminator that collaborate to produce and critique synthetic data for research development and predictive modeling.

Mediated Creativity: It represents a partnership between human researchers and AI systems to produce new knowledge by utilizing AI capabilities for large dataset analysis, argument refinement, and research gap identification.

Mode 4 Knowledge Production: It operates as a transdisciplinary research framework which combines information from various fields to demonstrate how AI synthesizes different data sources and perspectives for complex problem-solving.

Natural Language Processing (NLP): This represents an AI division that teaches computers to comprehend human language and produce text-based content which supports academic research through literature reviews and text analysis as well as summarization.

The Black Box Problem: This problem in AI emerges from deep learning models whose decision-making processes lack transparency and interpretability which prevents researchers from understanding the source of AI-generated outputs.

The Cognitive Mediation Networks Theory (CMNT): This explains how artificial intelligence systems modify human cognitive methods and information consumption which results in a novel knowledge interaction termed "sophotechnic mediation."

Compilation of References

Abadin, A. F. M., Sulaiman, R., & Hasan, M. K. (2024). Randomization strategies in image steganography techniques: A review. *Computers, Materials & Continua*, *80*(2), 1861–1896. DOI: 10.32604/cmc.2024.050834

Abadir, P., Oh, E., Chellappa, R., Choudhry, N., Demiris, G., Ganesan, D., Karlawish, J., Marlin, B., Li, R. M., Dehak, N., Arbaje, A., Unberath, M., Cudjoe, T., Chute, C., Moore, J. H., Phan, P., Samus, Q., Schoenborn, N. L., Battle, A., & Walston, J. D. (2024). Artificial Intelligence and Technology Collaboratories: Innovating aging research and Alzheimer's care. *Alzheimer's & Dementia*, *20*(4), 3074–3079. DOI: 10.1002/alz.13710

Abdallah, M. (2025). Advancing decision-making in AI through Bayesian inference and probabilistic graphical models. *Symmetry*, *17*(5), 635. DOI: 10.3390/sym17050635

Abd-El-Atty, B., Abd El-Latif, A. A., & Amin, M. (2017). New quantum image steganography scheme with Hadamard transformation. Proceedings of the International Conference on Advanced Intelligent Systems and Informatics 2016 2, Abd EL-Latif, A. A., Abd-El-Atty, B., & Venegas-Andraca, S. E. (2019). A novel image steganography technique based on quantum substitution boxes. *Optics & Laser Technology*, *116*, 92–102.

Abdeljaber, A., Al Smadi, S., Talib, M. A., & Abdallah, M. (2025). Comparative Analysis of Machine Learning and Conventional Methods for Waste Generation Forecasting. *Cleaner Engineering and Technology*, *27*, 100992. Advance online publication. DOI: 10.1016/j.clet.2025.100992

Abduljabbar, R., Dia, H., Liyanage, S., & Asadi Bagloee, S. (2019). Applications of Artificial Intelligence in Transport: An Overview. *Sustainability (Basel)*, *11*(1), 189. DOI: 10.3390/su11010189

Abdulla, A. A. (2024). Digital image steganography: Challenges, investigation, and recommendation for the future direction. *Soft Computing*, *28*(15), 8963–8976. DOI: 10.1007/s00500-023-09130-8

Acharya, K., Raza, W., Dourado, C., Velasquez, A., & Song, H. H. (2023). Neurosymbolic reinforcement learning and planning: A survey. *IEEE Transactions on Artificial Intelligence*, *5*(5), 1939–1953. DOI: 10.1109/TAI.2023.3311428

Agar, N., Whatley, S., & Weijers, D. (2024). How to Think about Progress.

Aghdam, M. A., Bozdag, S., & Saeed, F. (2025). Machine-learning models for Alzheimer's disease diagnosis using neuroimaging data: Survey, reproducibility, and generalizability evaluation. *Brain Informatics*, *12*(8), 8. Advance online publication. DOI: 10.1186/s40708-025-00252-3

Agrawal, A., McHale, J., & Oettl, A. (2024). Artificial intelligence and scientific discovery: A model of prioritized search. *Research Policy*, *53*(5), 104989. DOI: 10.1016/j.respol.2024.104989

Ahaggach, H., Abrouk, L., & Lebon, É. (2024). Systematic mapping study of sales forecasting: Methods, trends, and future directions. *Forecasting*, *6*(3), 28. DOI: 10.3390/forecast6030028

Ahmad, S., Ogala, J. O., Ikpotokin, F., Arif, M., Ahmad, J., & Mehfuz, S. (2024). Enhanced CNN-DCT steganography: Deep learning-based image steganography over cloud. *SN Computer Science*, *5*(4), 408. DOI: 10.1007/s42979-024-02756-x

Ahn, S., Chertkov, M., Weller, A., & Shin, J. (2018). Bucket renormalization for approximate inference. Proceedings of Machine Learning Research, 80, 1–10. http://proceedings.mlr.press/v80/ahn18a/ahn18a.pdf

ALabaichi, A., Al-Dabbas, M. a. A. A. K., & Salih, A. (2020). Image steganography using least significant bit and secret map techniques. *International journal of electrical & computer engineering (2088-8708), 10*(1).

AlAli, A., & Anifowose, F. (2022). Seismic velocity modeling in the digital transformation era: A review of the role of machine learning. *Journal of Petroleum Exploration and Production Technology*, *12*(1), 1–14. DOI: 10.1007/s13202-021-01304-0

Alexan, W., Mamdouh, E., Aboshousha, A., Alsahafi, Y. S., Gabr, M., & Hosny, K. M. (2024). Stegocrypt: A robust tri-stage spatial steganography algorithm using TLM encryption and DNA coding for securing digital images. *IET Image Processing*, *18*(13), 4189–4206. DOI: 10.1049/ipr2.13242

Al-Garadi, M. A., Yang, Y. C., & Sarker, A. (2022). The Role of Natural Language Processing during the COVID-19 Pandemic: Health Applications, Opportunities, and Challenges. *Healthcare (Basel), 10*(2270), 2270. Advance online publication. DOI: 10.3390/healthcare10112270

Ali, H. (2023). Artificial intelligence in multi-omics data integration : Advancing precision medicine, biomarker discovery and genomic-driven disease interventions. *International Journal of Science and Research Archive, 08*(01), 1012–1030. DOI: 10.30574/ijsra.2023.8.1.0189

Aljuhani, M., Ashraf, A., & Edison, P. (2024). Use of Artificial Intelligence in Imaging Dementia. *Cells, 13*(1965). DOI: 10.62486/latia202492

Allam, H. (2025). *The Role of AI and Living Intelligence in Higher Education: Potential Applications and Challenges.*

Alotaibi, J. (2025). Enhancing Traffic Accident Severity Prediction: Feature Identification Using Explainable AI. *Vehicles (Basel), 7*(2), 38. DOI: 10.3390/vehicles7020038

Alowais, S. A., Alghamdi, S. S., Alsuhebany, N., Alqahtani, T., Alshaya, A. I., Almohareb, S. N., Aldairem, A., Alrashed, M., & Saleh, K. (2023). Revolutionizing healthcare: The role of artificial intelligence in clinical practice. *BMC Medical Education, 23*(1), 689. DOI: 10.1186/s12909-023-04698-z

Alsadi, B., Musleh, S., Al-Absi, H. R. H., Refaee, M., Qureshi, R., El Hajj, N., & Alam, T. (2024). An ensemble-based machine learning model for predicting type 2 diabetes and its effect on bone health. *BMC Medical Informatics and Decision Making, 24*(144), 144. Advance online publication. DOI: 10.1186/s12911-024-02540-0

ALSAFFAWI, Z. S. Y. (2016). Image steganography by using exploiting modification direction and knight tour algorithm. *Journal of Al-Qadisiyah for computer science and mathematics, 8*(1), 1-11.

Al-Salhi, Y. E., & Lu, S. (2016). Quantum image steganography and steganalysis based on LSQu-blocks image information concealing algorithm. *International Journal of Theoretical Physics, 55*, 3722–3736. DOI: 10.1007/s10773-016-3001-3

Altememy, H. A., Mohammed, B. A., Hsony, M. K., Hassan, A. Y., Mazhair, R., Dawood, I. I., & Sharif, H. R. (2023). The influence of the artificial intelligence capabilities of higher education institutions in Iraq on students' academic performance: The role of AI-based technology application as a mediator. *Eurasian Journal of Educational Research, 104*(104), 267–282.

Alvi, J., Arif, I., & Nizam, K. (2024). Advancing financial resilience: A systematic review of default prediction models and future directions in credit risk management. *Heliyon, 10*(21), e39770. DOI: 10.1016/j.heliyon.2024.e39770 PMID: 39553697

Alwadee, E. J., Sun, X., Qin, Y., & Langbein, F. C. (2024). LATUP-Net: A Lightweight 3D Attention U-Net with Parallel Convolutions for Brain Tumor Segmentation. *Computers in Biology and Medicine, 184*(109353), 109353. Advance online publication. DOI: 10.1016/j.compbiomed.2024.109353

Amaturo, E., & Aragona, B. (2021). Digital methods and the evolution of the epistemology of social sciences. *Data Science and Social Research II: Methods, Technologies and Applications*, 1–8.

Ang, K. L. M., Seng, J. K. P., Ngharamike, E., & Ijemaru, G. K. (2022). Emerging Technologies for Smart Cities' Transportation: Geo-Information, Data Analytics and Machine Learning Approaches. *ISPRS International Journal of Geo-Information, 11*(2), 85. DOI: 10.3390/ijgi11020085

Ansari, Y., Mourad, O., Qaraqe, K., & Serpedin, E. (2023). Deep learning for ECG Arrhythmia detection and classification: An overview of progress for period 2017–2023. *Frontiers in Physiology, 14*(1246746), 1246746. Advance online publication. DOI: 10.3389/fphys.2023.1246746

Aradau, C., & Blanke, T. (2022). *Algorithmic reason: The new government of self and other*. Oxford University Press. DOI: 10.1093/oso/9780192859624.001.0001

Arsenault, P.-D., Wang, S., & Patenaude, J.-M. (2025). A survey of explainable artificial intelligence (XAI) in financial time series forecasting. *ACM Computing Surveys, 3*(1), 1–25. DOI: 10.1145/3729531

Artiemjew, P., & Kislak-Malinowska, A. (2020). Indiscernibility mask key for image steganography. *Computers, 9*(2), 38. DOI: 10.3390/computers9020038

Askin, S., Burkhalter, D., Calado, G., & El Dakrouni, S. (2023). Artificial Intelligence Applied to clinical trials: Opportunities and challenges. *Health and Technology, 13*(2), 203–213. DOI: 10.1007/s12553-023-00738-2

Attia, Z. I., Friedman, P. A., Noseworthy, P. A., Lopez-Jimenez, F., Ladewig, D. J., Satam, G., Pellikka, P. A., Munger, T. M., Asirvatham, S. J., Scott, C. G., Carter, R. E., & Kapa, S. (2019). Age and Sex Estimation Using Artificial Intelligence from Standard 12-Lead ECGs. *Circulation: Arrhythmia and Electrophysiology, 12*(9), e007284. Advance online publication. DOI: 10.1161/CIRCEP.119.007284

Attia, Z. I., Noseworthy, P. A., Lopez-Jimenez, F., Asirvatham, S. J., Deshmukh, A. J., Gersh, B. J., Carter, R. E., Yao, X., Rabinstein, A. A., Erickson, B. J., Kapa, S., & Friedman, P. A. (2019). An artificial intelligence-enabled ECG algorithm for the identification of patients with atrial fibrillation during sinus rhythm: A retrospective analysis of outcome prediction. *Lancet*, *394*(10201), 861–867. DOI: 10.1016/S0140-6736(19)31721-0

Avazov, K., Mirzakhalilov, S., Umirzakova, S., Abdusalomov, A., & Cho, Y. I. (2024). Dynamic Focus on Tumor Boundaries: A Lightweight U-Net for MRI Brain Tumor Segmentation. *Bioengineering (Basel, Switzerland)*, *11*(1302), 1302. Advance online publication. DOI: 10.3390/bioengineering11121302

Avula, R., & Tummala, S. (2021). Assessing the impact of data quality on predictive analytics in healthcare: Strategies, tools, and techniques for ensuring accuracy, completeness, and timeliness in electronic health records. *Sage Science Review of Applied Machine Learning*, *4*(2), 31–47.

Badalotti, D., Agrawal, A., Pensato, U., Angelotti, G., & Marcheselli, S. (2024). Development of a Natural Language Processing (NLP) model to automatically extract clinical data from electronic health records: Results from an Italian comprehensive stroke center. *International Journal of Medical Informatics*, *192*(105626), 105626. Advance online publication. DOI: 10.1016/j.ijmedinf.2024.105626

Badings, T., Simão, T. D., Suilen, M., & Jansen, N. (2023). Decision-making under uncertainty: Beyond probabilities. *SN Computer Science*, *4*(4), 353. DOI: 10.1007/s42979-023-01770-9 PMID: 37128512

Baldini, G., Botterman, M., Neisse, R., & Tallacchini, M. (2018). Ethical design in the internet of things. *Science and Engineering Ethics*, *24*(3), 905–925. DOI: 10.1007/s11948-016-9754-5 PMID: 26797878

Ballester, O. (2021). An artificial intelligence definition and classification framework for public sector applications. *DG. O2021: The 22nd Annual International Conference on Digital Government Research*, 67–75.

Baradziej, S. (2023). The influence of Large Language Models on systematic review and research dissemination. *Septentrio Conference Series, 1*.

Barbieri, L., Savazzi, S., & Nicoli, M. (2021). Decentralized Federated Learning for Road User Classification in Enhanced V2X Networks. *2021 IEEE International Conference on Communications Workshops (ICC Workshops)*, 1-6. https://www.semanticscholar.org/paper/Decentralized-Federated-Learning-for-Road-User-in-Barbieri-Savazzi/3ecf7fa75f06b14a37756fa1d9fe42920efa3a91

Barman, A., Roy, S. K., Das, S., & Dutta, P. (2024). Exploring the Horizons of Meta-Learning in Neural Networks: A Survey of the State-of-the-Art. *IEEE Transactions on Emerging Topics in Computational Intelligence*.

Baron, P. R. (2018). Ethical inclusive curricula design: Conversational teaching and learning. *South African Journal of Higher Education*, *32*(6), 326–350. DOI: 10.20853/32-6-2987

Beckers, T. (2023). Data-driven Bayesian control of port-Hamiltonian systems. *IEEE Control Systems Letters*, *7*, 3046–3051. DOI: 10.1109/LCSYS.2023.3294239

Bengesi, S., El-Sayed, H., Sarker, M. K., Houkpati, Y., Irungu, J., & Oladunni, T. (2024). Advancements in Generative AI: A Comprehensive Review of GANs, GPT, Autoencoders, Diffusion Model, and Transformers. *IEEE Access : Practical Innovations, Open Solutions*, *12*, 69812–69837. DOI: 10.1109/ACCESS.2024.3397775

Bernacki, M. L., Greene, M. J., & Lobczowski, N. G. (2021). A systematic review of research on personalized learning: Personalized by whom, to what, how, and for what purpose (s)? *Educational Psychology Review*, *33*(4), 1675–1715. DOI: 10.1007/s10648-021-09615-8

Besold, T. R., Bader, S., Bowman, H., Domingos, P., Hitzler, P., Kühnberger, K. U., . . . Zaverucha, G. (2021). Neural-symbolic learning and reasoning: A survey and interpretation 1. In Neuro-Symbolic Artificial Intelligence: The State of the Art (pp. 1-51). IOS press.

Bess, J. L., Johnstone, D. B., & Dee, J. R. (2023). Understanding college and university organization: Theories for effective policy and practice: Volume II—Dynamics of the system. Routledge.

Bessant, J. (2018). *The great transformation: History for a techno-human future*. Routledge. DOI: 10.4324/9781315643533

Bilal, A., Imran, A., Baig, T. I., Liu, X., Abouel Nasr, E., & Long, H. (2024). Breast cancer diagnosis using support vector machine optimized by improved quantum inspired grey wolf optimization. *Scientific Reports*, *14*(10714), 10714. Advance online publication. DOI: 10.1038/s41598-024-61322-w

Bohra, N., Kumari, A., Mishra, V. K., Soni, P. K., & Balyan, V. (2025). Intelligence-Based Strategies with Vehicle-to-Everything Network: A Review. *Future Internet*, *17*(2), 79. DOI: 10.3390/fi17020079

Bousetouane, F. (2025). Physical AI agents: Integrating cognitive intelligence with real-world action. *Journal of Artificial Intelligence Research*, *74*, 1–30. DOI: 10.32388/HA0F5Z

Bown, O. (2021). *Beyond the creative species: Making machines that make art and music*. Mit Press. DOI: 10.7551/mitpress/10913.001.0001

Braiek, H. B., & Khomh, F. (2025). Machine learning robustness: A primer. In Elsevier eBooks (pp. 37–71). DOI: 10.1016/B978-0-44-323761-4.00012-2

Brass, J., & Lynch, T. L. (2020). Personalized learning: A history of the present. *Journal of Curriculum Theorizing*, *35*(2). Advance online publication. DOI: 10.63997/jct.v35i2.807

Brendel, M., Su, C., Bai, Z., Zhang, H., Elemento, O., & Wang, F. (2022). Application of Deep Learning on Single-cell RNA Sequencing Data Analysis: A Review. *Genomics, Proteomics & Bioinformatics*, *20*(5), 814–835. DOI: 10.1016/j.gpb.2022.11.011

Buehler, H., Horvath, B., Limmer, Y., & Schmidt, T. (2025). Uncertainty-aware strategies: A model-agnostic framework for robust financial optimization through subsampling. SSRN Electronic Journal. DOI: 10.2139/ssrn.5286592

Cai, Z., Liu, L., Chen, B., & Wang, Y. (2021). Artificial intelligence: From beginning to date.

Calin, O. (2020). *Deep learning architectures*. Springer International Publishing. DOI: 10.1007/978-3-030-36721-3

Callaham, M., Wears, R. L., & Weber, E. (2006). The relationship between quality of research and citation frequency. *BMC Medical Research Methodology*, *6*(1), 42. DOI: 10.1186/1471-2288-6-42 PMID: 16948835

Castelnovo, A., Crupi, R., Greco, G., Regoli, D., Penco, I. G., & Cosentini, A. C. (2022). A clarification of the nuances in the fairness metrics landscape. *Scientific Reports*, *12*(4209), 4209. Advance online publication. DOI: 10.1038/s41598-022-07939-1

Castillo-Martínez, I. M., Flores-Bueno, D., Gómez-Puente, S. M., & Vite-León, V. O. (2024). AI in higher education: A systematic literature review. *Frontiers in Education*, *9*, 1391485. DOI: 10.3389/feduc.2024.1391485

Chakraborti, T., Banerji, C. R. S., Marandon, A., Hellon, V., Mitra, R., Lehmann, B., Bräuninger, L., McGough, S. F., Tuğbay, T., Frangi, A. F., Bianconi, G., Li, W., Rackham, O., Parasher, D., & Harbron, C. (2025). Personalized uncertainty quantification in artificial intelligence. *Nature Machine Intelligence*, *7*(4), 312–325. DOI: 10.1038/s42256-025-01024-8

Changder, S., & Debnath, N. C. (2009). A new approach for steganography in Bengali text. *Journal of Computational Methods in Sciences and Engineering*, *9*(s1), S111–S122. DOI: 10.3233/JCM-2009-0240

Chen, M. K. (2025). A comparative study of neurosymbolic AI approaches to interpretable logical reasoning. arXiv. https://doi.org/DOI: 10.48550/ARXIV.2508.03366

Chen, C., Liu, B., Wan, S. H., Qiao, P., & Pei, Q. Q. (2021). An edge traffic flow detection scheme based on deep learning in an intelligent transportation system. *IEEE Transactions on Intelligent Transportation Systems*, *22*(3), 1840–1852. DOI: 10.1109/TITS.2020.3025687

Chen, M., Copley, S. J., Viola, P., Lu, H., & Aboagye, E. O. (2023). Radiomics and artificial intelligence for precision medicine in lung cancer treatment. *Seminars in Cancer Biology*, *93*, 97–113. DOI: 10.1016/j.semcancer.2023.05.004

Chithaluru, P., Reddy, V. K., Narsimhulu, P., & Kumar, M. (2025). DNA computing for the smart wireless sensor networks. In *Blockchain and Digital Twin for Smart Healthcare* (pp. 395–417). Elsevier. DOI: 10.1016/B978-0-443-30300-5.00022-1

Churchill, R., Apps, T., Batt, J., Beckman, K., Grainger, P., Holloway, J., & Shaw, K. (2024). *Teaching: Making a difference*. John Wiley & Sons.

Clement, M. C. (2018). *What successful teachers do: a dozen things to ensure student learning*. Rowman & Littlefield.

Colavizza, G., Hrynaszkiewicz, I., Staden, I., Whitaker, K., & McGillivray, B. (2019). The citation advantage of linking publications to research data. *arXiv preprint arXiv:1907.02565*.

Collins, A., & Halverson, R. (2018). *Rethinking education in the age of technology: The digital revolution and schooling in America*. Teachers College Press.

Cong, S., & Zhou, Y. (2023). A review of convolutional neural network architectures and their optimizations. *Artificial Intelligence Review*, *56*(3), 1905–1969. DOI: 10.1007/s10462-022-10213-5

Corrêa, N. K., Galvão, C., Santos, J. W., Del Pino, C., Pinto, E. P., Barbosa, C., Massmann, D., Mambrini, R., Galvão, L., Terem, E., & Oliveira, N. (2023). Worldwide AI ethics: A review of 200 guidelines and recommendations for AI governance. *Patterns (New York, N.Y.)*, *4*(10), 100857. DOI: 10.1016/j.patter.2023.100857 PMID: 37876898

Costanzo, M. R., Stevenson, L. W., Adamson, P. B., Desai, A. S., Heywood, J. T., Bourge, R. C., Ms, J. B., & Abraham, W. T. (2016). Interventions Linked to Decreased Heart Failure Hospitalizations During Ambulatory Pulmonary Artery Pressure Monitoring. *JACC. Heart Failure*, *4*(5), 333–344. DOI: 10.1016/j.jchf.2015.11.011

Cristescu, R., Mogg, R., Ayers, M., Albright, A., Murphy, E., Sher, X., Liu, X. Q., Lu, H., Nebozhyn, M., Lunceford, J. K., Joe, A., Cheng, J., Webber, A. L., Ibrahim, N., Plimack, E. R., Ott, P. A., Seiwert, T. Y., Mcclanahan, T. K., Tomassini, J. E., & Kaufman, D. (2018). Pan-tumor genomic biomarkers for PD-1 checkpoint blockade– based immunotherapy. *Science*, *362*(6411), eaar3593. Advance online publication. DOI: 10.1126/science.aar3593

Cross, J. L., Choma, M. A., & Onofrey, J. A. (2024). Bias in medical AI: Implications for clinical decision-making. *PLOS Digital Health*, *3*(11), e0000651. Advance online publication. DOI: 10.1371/journal.pdig.0000651

Damadam, S., Zourbakhsh, M., Javidan, R., & Faroughi, A. (2022). An Intelligent IoT Based Traffic Light Management System: Deep Reinforcement Learning. *Smart Cities*, *5*(4), 1293–1311. DOI: 10.3390/smartcities5040066

de Souza, B. C., de Andrade Neto, A. S., & Roazzi, A. (2024). The generative AI revolution, cognitive mediation networks theory and the emergence of a new mode of mental functioning: Introducing the Sophotechnic Mediation scale. *Computers in Human Behavior: Artificial Humans*, *2*(1), 100042. DOI: 10.1016/j.chbah.2024.100042

Devare, M. H. (2019a). Cloud computing and innovations. In Kecskemeti, G. (Ed.), *Applying integration techniques and methods in distributed systems and technologies* (pp. 1–33). IGI Global Scientific Publishing., DOI: 10.4018/978-1-5225-8295-3.ch001

Devare, M. H., & Devare, A. M. (2026). Predictive Maintenance Using Sensor Data Processing. In Habib, M. (Ed.), *AI-Driven Smart Industrial Technologies* (pp. 175–210). IGI Global Scientific Publishing., DOI: 10.4018/979-8-3693-7994-3.ch008

Dhar, S., & Sahu, A. K. (2024). Digital to quantum watermarking: A journey from past to present and into the future. *Computer Science Review*, *54*, 100679. DOI: 10.1016/j.cosrev.2024.100679

Díaz-Rodríguez, N., Del Ser, J., Coeckelbergh, M., de Prado, M. L., Herrera-Viedma, E., & Herrera, F. (2023). Connecting the dots in trustworthy Artificial Intelligence: From AI principles, ethics, and key requirements to responsible AI systems and regulation. *Information Fusion*, *99*, 101896. DOI: 10.1016/j.inffus.2023.101896

Dinçer, S. (2024). The use and ethical implications of artificial intelligence in scientific research and academic writing. *Educational Research & Implementation, 1*(2), 139–144. DOI: 10.14527/edure.2024.10

Ding, H., Du, Y., & Xia, Z. (2025). Urban Road Anomaly Monitoring Using Vision-Language Models for Enhanced Safety Management. *Applied Sciences (Basel, Switzerland), 15*(5), 2517. DOI: 10.3390/app15052517

Dong, Y., & Yan, R. (2024). A new integrated steganography scheme for quantum color images. *The Journal of Supercomputing, 80*(16), 24758–24780. DOI: 10.1007/s11227-024-06332-1

Duan, X., Guo, D., Liu, N., Li, B., Gou, M., & Qin, C. (2020). A new high capacity image steganography method combined with image elliptic curve cryptography and deep neural network. *IEEE Access : Practical Innovations, Open Solutions, 8*, 25777–25788. DOI: 10.1109/ACCESS.2020.2971528

Duan, X., Li, B., Guo, D., Zhang, Z., & Ma, Y. (2020). A coverless steganography method based on generative adversarial network. *EURASIP Journal on Image and Video Processing, 2020*(1), 1–10. DOI: 10.1186/s13640-020-00506-6

Duffield, S., Donatella, K., Chiu, J., Klett, P., & Simpson, D. (2024). Scalable Bayesian learning with posteriors. arXiv. DOI: 10.48550/ARXIV.2406.00104

Dwivedi, Y. K., Kshetri, N., Hughes, L., Slade, E. L., Jeyaraj, A., Kar, A. K., Baabdullah, A. M., Koohang, A., Raghavan, V., Ahuja, M., Albanna, H., Albashrawi, M. A., Al-Busaidi, A. S., Balakrishnan, J., Barlette, Y., Basu, S., Bose, I., Brooks, L., Buhalis, D., & Wright, R. (2023). Opinion Paper:"So what if ChatGPT wrote it?" Multidisciplinary perspectives on opportunities, challenges, and implications of generative conversational AI for research, practice, and policy. *International Journal of Information Management, 71*, 102642. DOI: 10.1016/j.ijinfomgt.2023.102642

Edam, S. M. I. (2025). Restructuring the Landscape of Generative AI Research. In *Impacts of Generative AI on the Future of Research and Education* (pp. 287–334). IGI Global.

Eggers, J. J., Baeuml, R., & Girod, B. (2002). Communications approach to image steganography. Security and watermarking of Multimedia Contents IV.

Elwarraki, O., Aammou, S., Jdidou, Y., & Lahiassi, J. (2023). Toward the future of personalized learning: Emerging trends and challenges in recommendation systems. ICERI2023 Proceedings, 7226-7235.

Estrada, M., Mension, J., & Salicrú, M. (2021). Operation of transit corridors served by two routes: Physical design, synchronization, and control strategies. *Transportation Research Part C, Emerging Technologies, 130*, 103283. DOI: 10.1016/j.trc.2021.103283

European Medicines Agency. (2024). *Reflection paper on the use of Artificial Intelligence (AI) in the medicinal product lifecycle.* https://www.ema.europa.eu/en/documents/scientific-guideline/draft-reflection-paper-use-artificial-intelligence-ai-medicinal-product-lifecycle_en.pdf

Faghani, S., Gamble, C. U., & Erickson, B. J. (2024). Uncover this tech term: Uncertainty quantification for deep learning. *Korean Journal of Radiology, 25*(4), 395. DOI: 10.3348/kjr.2024.0108 PMID: 38528697

Fang, J., Yu, Y., Zhao, C., & Zhou, J. (2021, February). Turbotransformers: an efficient gpu serving system for transformer models. In *Proceedings of the 26th ACM SIGPLAN Symposium on Principles and Practice of Parallel Programming* (pp. 389-402). DOI: 10.1145/3437801.3441578

Fantazzini, D. (2024). Adaptive conformal inference for computing market risk measures: An analysis with four thousand crypto-assets. *Journal of Risk and Financial Management, 17*(6), 248. DOI: 10.3390/jrfm17060248

Farhud, D. D., & Zokaei, S. (2021). Ethical issues of artificial intelligence in medicine and healthcare. *Iranian Journal of Public Health, 50*(11), i–v. DOI: 10.18502/ijph.v50i11.7600

Fazi, M. B. (2021). Beyond human: Deep learning, explainability and representation. *Theory, Culture & Society, 38*(7-8), 55–77. DOI: 10.1177/0263276420966386

Felix, C. V. (2020). The role of the teacher and AI in education. In *International perspectives on the role of technology in humanizing higher education* (pp. 33–48). Emerald Publishing Limited. DOI: 10.1108/S2055-364120200000033003

Fellows, M., Kaplowitz, B., de Witt, C., Schroeder, S., & Whiteson, S. (2024). Bayesian exploration networks. arXiv. DOI: 10.48550/ARXIV.2308.13049

Fieguth, P. (2022). *An introduction to pattern recognition and machine learning.* Springer. DOI: 10.1007/978-3-030-95995-1

Finn, E. (2017). What algorithms want: Imagination in the age of computing. mit Press.

Fisher, E. (2022). *Algorithms and subjectivity: The subversion of critical knowledge.* Routledge. DOI: 10.4324/9781003196563

Fitz, S., & Romero, P. (2021). Neural networks and deep learning: A paradigm shift in information processing, machine learning, and artificial intelligence. The Palgrave handbook of technological finance, 589-654.

Foster, I., Kesselman, C., Nick, J. M., & Tuecke, S. (2002). *The physiology of the grid: An open grid services architecture for distributed systems integration*. Global Grid Forum.

Foster, I., Kesselman, C., & Tuecke, S. (2001). The Anatomy of the Grid: Enabling Scalable Virtual Organizations. *International Journal of High Performance Computing Applications*, *15*(3), 200–222. DOI: 10.1177/109434200101500302

Fozap, F. M. P. (2025). Hybrid machine learning models for long-term stock market forecasting: Integrating technical indicators. *Journal of Risk and Financial Management*, *18*(4), 201. DOI: 10.3390/jrfm18040201

Freiesleben, T., König, G., Molnar, C., & Tejero-Cantero, Á. (2024). Scientific Inference with Interpretable Machine Learning: Analyzing Models to Learn About Real-World Phenomena. In *Minds and Machines* (Vol. 34, Issue 32). Springer Netherlands. DOI: 10.1007/s11023-024-09691-z

Fridgeirsson, E. A., Williams, R., Rijnbeek, P., Suchard, M. A., & Reps, J. M. (2024). Comparing penalization methods for linear models on large observational health data. *Journal of the American Medical Informatics Association : JAMIA*, *31*(7), 1514–1521. DOI: 10.1093/jamia/ocae109

Gade, K. R. (2021). Data-driven decision making in a complex world. *Journal of Computational Innovation*, *1*(1).

Gagliardi, G., Gallelli, V., Violi, A., Lupia, M., & Gario, G. (2024). Optimal Placement of Sensors in Traffic Networks Using Global Search Optimization Techniques Oriented towards Traffic Flow Estimation and Pollutant Emission Evaluation. *Sustainability (Basel)*, *16*(9), 3530. DOI: 10.3390/su16093530

Gawande, M. S., Zade, N., Kumar, P., Gundewar, S., Weerarathna, I. N., & Verma, P. (2025). The role of artificial intelligence in pandemic responses: From epidemiological modeling to vaccine development. *Molecular Biomedicine*, *6*(1), 1. Advance online publication. DOI: 10.1186/s43556-024-00238-3

Gefen, A., Saint-Raymond, L., & Venturini, T. (2021). AI for digital humanities and computational social sciences. *Reflections on Artificial Intelligence for Humanity*, 191–202.

Geirhos, R., Jacobsen, J. H., Michaelis, C., Zemel, R., Brendel, W., Bethge, M., & Wichmann, F. A. (2020). Shortcut learning in deep neural networks. *Nature Machine Intelligence*, *2*(11), 665–673. DOI: 10.1038/s42256-020-00257-z

George, A. S. (2024). Democratizing Compute Power: The Rise of Computation as a Commodity and its Impacts. *Partners Universal Innovative Research Publication*, *2*(3), 57–74.

George, R., Navanesan, L., & Thangathurai, K. (2024). Revisiting the steganography techniques with a novel region-based separation approach. *Multimedia Tools and Applications*, *83*(28), 71089–71114. DOI: 10.1007/s11042-023-17961-8

Ghasemieh, A., & Kashef, R. (2024). Advanced Monocular Outdoor Pose Estimation in Autonomous Systems: Leveraging Optical Flow, Depth Estimation, and Semantic Segmentation with Dynamic Object Removal. *Sensors (Basel)*, *24*(24), 8040. DOI: 10.3390/s24248040 PMID: 39771776

Ginghina, O., Hudita, A., Zamfir, M., Spanu, A., Mardare, M., Bondoc, I., Buburuzan, L., Georgescu, S. E., Costache, M., Negrei, C., Nitipir, C., & Galateanu, B. (2022). Liquid Biopsy and Artificial Intelligence as Tools to Detect Signatures of Colorectal Malignancies: A Modern Approach in Patient's Stratification. *Frontiers in Oncology*, *12*(856575), 856575. Advance online publication. DOI: 10.3389/fonc.2022.856575

Girdea, M., Dumitriu, S., Fiume, M., Bowdin, S., Boycott, K. M., Chénier, S., Chitayat, D., Faghfoury, H., Meyn, M. S., Ray, P. N., So, J., Stavropoulos, D. J., & Brudno, M. (2013). PhenoTips: Patient phenotyping software for clinical and research use. *Human Mutation*, *34*(8), 1057–1065. DOI: 10.1002/humu.22347

Golchha, R., Sahu, M., & Bhateja, V. (2025). Quantum-based deep learning method for recognition of facial expressions. *Neural Computing & Applications*, *37*(16), 1–11. DOI: 10.1007/s00521-024-10968-8

Goldstein, N. D., Levasseur, M., & Mcclure, L. A. (2020). On the Convergence of Epidemiology, Biostatistics, and Data Science. *Harvard Data Science Review*, *2*, 2. DOI: 10.1162/99608f92.9f0215e6

Goodman, J., & Salow, B. (2023). Belief revision from probability. *Epistemic Theory of Conditionals*, *379*, 25. DOI: 10.4204/epcts.379.25

Gosangi, R., Arora, R., Gheisarieha, M., Mahata, D., & Zhang, H. (2021). *On the Use of Context for Predicting Citation Worthiness of Sentences in Scholarly Articles*. arXiv preprint arXiv:2104.08962 DOI: 10.18653/v1/2021.naacl-main.359

Graf-Vlachy, L., Graziotin, D., & Wagner, S. (2022). *Text and Team: What Article Metadata Characteristics Drive Citations in Software Engineering?* arXiv preprint arXiv:2204.06033. DOI: 10.1145/3530019.3530022

Green, S. L., & Wright, C. F. (2017). Retaining first generation underrepresented minority students: A struggle for higher education. *The Journal of Educational Research, 11*(3).

Grunova, D., Bakratsi, V., Vrochidou, E., & Papakostas, G. A. (2024). Machine learning for anomaly detection in industrial environments. *Engineering Proceedings, 70*(1), 25. DOI: 10.3390/engproc2024070025

Guan, B., Xu, D., & Li, Q. (2020). An efficient commutative encryption and data hiding scheme for HEVC video. *IEEE Access : Practical Innovations, Open Solutions, 8*, 60232–60245. DOI: 10.1109/ACCESS.2020.2983330

Guo, A., & Yuan, C. (2021). Network Intelligent Control and Traffic Optimization Based on SDN and Artificial Intelligence. *Electronics (Basel), 10*(6), 700. DOI: 10.3390/electronics10060700

Gupta, S., Goyal, A., & Bhushan, B. (2012). Information hiding using least significant bit steganography and cryptography. *International Journal of Modern Education and Computer Science, 4*(6), 27. DOI: 10.5815/ijmecs.2012.06.04

Gupta, U., Paluru, N., Nankani, D., Kulkarni, K., & Awasthi, N. (2024). A comprehensive review on efficient artificial intelligence models for classification of abnormal cardiac rhythms using electrocardiograms. *Heliyon, 10*(5, e26787), e26787. Advance online publication. DOI: 10.1016/j.heliyon.2024.e26787

Gurovich, Y., Hanani, Y., Bar, O., Nadav, G., Fleischer, N., Gelbman, D., Basel-Salmon, L., Krawitz, P. M., Kamphausen, S. B., Zenker, M., Bird, L. M., & Gripp, K. W. (2019). Identifying facial phenotypes of genetic disorders using deep learning. *Nature Medicine, 25*(1), 60–64. DOI: 10.1038/s41591-018-0279-0

Habibzadeh, F., & Yadollahie, M. (2010). Are shorter article titles more attractive for citations? Cross-sectional study of 22 scientific journals. *Croatian Medical Journal, 51*(2), 165–170. DOI: 10.3325/cmj.2010.51.165 PMID: 20401960

Hameed, M. A., Abdel-Aleem, O. A., & Hassaballah, M. (2023). A secure data hiding approach based on least-significant-bit and nature-inspired optimization techniques. *Journal of Ambient Intelligence and Humanized Computing, 14*(5), 4639–4657. DOI: 10.1007/s12652-022-04366-y

Hannun, A. Y., Rajpurkar, P., Haghpanahi, M., Tison, G. H., Bourn, C., Turakhia, M. P., & Ng, A. Y. (2019). Cardiologist-Level Arrhythmia Detection and Classification in Ambulatory Electrocardiograms Using a Deep Neural Network. *Nature Medicine*, *25*(1), 65–69. DOI: 10.1038/s41591-018-0268-3

Han, Y. W., Du, X., Zhang, H. M., Ni, J. F., & Fan, F. Y. (2024). Does smart home adoption reduce household electricity-related CO2 emissions? Evidence from Hangzhou city, China. *Energy*, *289*, 129890. DOI: 10.1016/j.energy.2023.129890

Han, Y., Cai, J., Ma, E., Du, S., & Lin, J. (2023). Understanding smart city practice in urban china: A governance perspective. *Sustainability (Basel)*, *15*(9), 7034. DOI: 10.3390/su15097034

Hao, C., Yang, X., Ma, Q., Qu, D., Wang, R., & Zhang, T. (2024). Quantum audio LSB steganography with entanglement-assisted modulation. *Quantum Information Processing*, *23*(3), 106. DOI: 10.1007/s11128-024-04312-1

Harati, H., Sujo-Montes, L., Tu, C. H., Armfield, S. J., & Yen, C. J. (2021). Assessment and learning in knowledge spaces (ALEKS) adaptive system impact on students' perception and self-regulated learning skills. *Education Sciences*, *11*(10), 603. DOI: 10.3390/educsci11100603

Hassija, V., Chamola, V., Mahapatra, A., Singal, A., Goel, D., Huang, K., Scardapane, S., Spinelli, I., Mahmud, M., & Hussain, A. (2024). Interpreting black-box models: A review on explainable artificial intelligence. *Cognitive Computation*, *16*(1), 45–74. DOI: 10.1007/s12559-023-10179-8

Hastawan, A. F., & Septiana, R. (2020). Hiding multiple secret information using dynamic image bit manipulation. Journal of Physics: Conference Series, Heidari, S., Pourarian, M. R., Gheibi, R., Naseri, M., & Houshmand, M. (2017). Quantum red–green–blue image steganography. *International Journal of Quantum Information*, *15*(05), 1750039.

Haugeland, J., Craver, C. F., & Klein, C. (Eds.). (2023). *Mind Design III: Philosophy, Psychology, and Artificial Intelligence*. MIT press.

Haydari, A., & Yilmaz, Y. (2022). Deep reinforcement learning for intelligent transportation systems: A survey. *IEEE Transactions on Intelligent Transportation Systems*, *23*(1), 11–32. DOI: 10.1109/TITS.2020.3008612

Helmy, M. (2024). Audio transmission based on hybrid crypto-steganography framework for efficient cyber security in wireless communication system. *Multimedia Tools and Applications*, *84*(18), 18893–18917. DOI: 10.1007/s11042-023-17921-2

Hernandez-Olivan, C., & Beltran, J. R. (2022). Music composition with deep learning: A review. Advances in speech and music technology: computational aspects and applications, 25-50.

Hijazi, A., Bifulco, C., Baldin, P., & Galon, J. (2024). Digital Pathology for Better Clinical Practice. *Cancers, 16*(1686). DOI: 10.3390/cancers16091686

Hosmer, D. W., Jr., Lemeshow, S., & Sturdivant, R. X. (2013). Applied Logistic Regression. In *John Wiley & Sons, Hoboken, NJ.* DOI: 10.1002/9781118548387

Hospedales, T., Antoniou, A., Micaelli, P., & Storkey, A. (2021). Meta-learning in neural networks: A survey. *IEEE Transactions on Pattern Analysis and Machine Intelligence*, *44*(9), 5149–5169. PMID: 33974543

Hossain, E., Rana, R., Higgins, N., Soar, J., Barua, P. D., Pisani, A. R., & Turner, K. (2023). Natural Language Processing in Electronic Health Records in relation to healthcare decision-making: A systematic review. *Computers in Biology and Medicine*, *155*, 106649. Advance online publication. DOI: 10.1016/j.compbiomed.2023.106649

Huang, S., Nianguang, C. A. I., Penzuti Pacheco, P., Narandes, S., Wang, Y., & Wayne, X. U. (2018). Applications of support vector machine (SVM) learning in cancer genomics. *Cancer Genomics & Proteomics*, *15*(1), 41–51. DOI: 10.21873/cgp.20063

Hu, K., Wang, M., Ma, X., Chen, J., Wang, X., & Wang, X. (2024). Learning-based image steganography and watermarking: A survey. *Expert Systems with Applications*, *123715*, 123715. Advance online publication. DOI: 10.1016/j.eswa.2024.123715

Huo, L., Chen, R., Wei, J., & Huang, L. (2024). A high-capacity and high-security image steganography network based on chaotic mapping and generative adversarial networks. *Applied Sciences (Basel, Switzerland)*, *14*(3), 1225. Advance online publication. DOI: 10.3390/app14031225

Huo, Y., Qiao, Y., & Liu, Y. (2024). A deep learning-based steganography method for high dynamic range images. *The Visual Computer*, *40*(11), 7887–7903. DOI: 10.1007/s00371-023-03214-0

Hurtado-Gómez, J., Romo, J. D., Salazar-Cabrera, R., Pachón de la Cruz, Á., & Madrid Molina, J. M. (2021). Traffic Signal Control System Based on Intelligent Transportation System and Reinforcement Learning. *Electronics (Basel)*, *10*(19), 2363. DOI: 10.3390/electronics10192363

Hutson, J., & Plate, D. (2024). Disrupting Algorithmic Culture: Redefining the Human (ities). In *Generative AI in Teaching and Learning* (pp. 1–30). IGI Global.

Hu, X., Li, S., Ying, Q., Peng, W., Zhang, X., & Qian, Z. (2024). Establishing robust generative image steganography via popular stable diffusion. *IEEE Transactions on Information Forensics and Security*, *19*, 8094–8108. DOI: 10.1109/TIFS.2024.3444311

Hyun Lim, S., Hersi, M., Krishnan, R., Montroy, J., Rook, B., Farrah, K., Chung, Y. E., Stevens, A., Zafack, J., Wong, E., Forbes, N., Killikelly, A., Young, K., & Tunis, M. (2024). COVID-19 vaccine evidence monitoring assisted by artificial Intelligence: An emergency system implemented by the Public Health Agency of Canada to capture and describe the trajectory of evolving pandemic vaccine literature. *Vaccine: X*, *21*(100575), 100575. Advance online publication. DOI: 10.1016/j.jvacx.2024.100575

Imam, F., Musilek, P., & Reformat, M. Z. (2024). Parametric and Nonparametric Machine Learning Techniques for Increasing Power System Reliability: A Review. *Information (Basel)*, *15*(37), 37. Advance online publication. DOI: 10.3390/info15010037

Islam, K. R., Prithula, J., Kumar, J., Tan, T. L., Reaz, M. B. I., Sumon, M. S. I., & Chowdhury, M. E. H. (2023). Machine Learning-Based Early Prediction of Sepsis Using Electronic Health Records: A Systematic Review. *Journal of Clinical Medicine*, *12*(5658), 5658. Advance online publication. DOI: 10.3390/jcm12175658

Jacques, T. S., & Sebire, N. J. (2010). The impact of article titles on citation hits: An analysis of general and specialist medical journals. *JRSM Short Reports*, *1*(1), 2. DOI: 10.1258/shorts.2009.100020 PMID: 21103094

Janson, L., & Lempert, M. (2024). ARTISTS AND MACHINE INTELLIGENCE.

Javed, H., El-Sappagh, S., & Abuhmed, T. (2025). Robustness in deep learning models for medical diagnostics: Security and adversarial challenges towards robust AI applications. *Artificial Intelligence Review*, *58*(12), 12. Advance online publication. DOI: 10.1007/s10462-024-11005-9

Jayaraman, P., Desman, J., Sabounchi, M., Nadkarni, G. N., & Sakhuja, A. (2024). A Primer on Reinforcement Learning in Medicine for Clinicians. *NPJ Digital Medicine*, *7*(337), 337. Advance online publication. DOI: 10.1038/s41746-024-01316-0

Jiang, L., Zuo, H. J., & Chen, C. (2025). Artificial intelligence in echocardiography: Applications and future directions Luying. *Fundamental Research (Beijing)*. Advance online publication. DOI: 10.1016/j.fmre.2025.01.020

Jiang, N., Zhao, N., & Wang, L. (2016). LSB based quantum image steganography algorithm. *International Journal of Theoretical Physics*, *55*(1), 107–123. DOI: 10.1007/s10773-015-2640-0

Jiang, X., Hu, Z., Wang, S., & Zhang, Y. (2023). Deep Learning for Medical Image-Based Cancer Diagnosis. *Cancers (Basel)*, *15*(3608), 3608. Advance online publication. DOI: 10.3390/cancers15143608

Kadem, K. H., & Mohammed, M. F. (2024). OptiFusion steganography method based on masking OFDM signal in Gaussian beam intensity. *Journal of Optics*.

Kallick, B., & Zmuda, A. (2017). *Students at the center: Personalized learning with habits of mind*. Ascd.

Kallis, R., Di Sorbo, A., Canfora, G., & Panichella, S. (2019, September). Ticket tagger: Machine learning driven issue classification. In *2019 IEEE International Conference on Software Maintenance and Evolution (ICSME)* (pp. 406-409). IEEE. DOI: 10.1109/ICSME.2019.00070

Kanyongo, W., & Ezugwu, A. E. (2023). Machine learning approaches to medication adherence amongst NCD patients: A systematic literature review. *Informatics in Medicine Unlocked*, *38*(101210), 101210. Advance online publication. DOI: 10.1016/j.imu.2023.101210

Karalis, V. D. (2024). The Integration of Artificial Intelligence into Clinical Practice. *Applied Biosciences*, *3*(1), 14–44. DOI: 10.3390/applbiosci3010002

Kaur, S., Singh, S., Kaur, M., & Lee, H. N. (2022). A systematic review of computational image steganography approaches. *Archives of Computational Methods in Engineering*, *29*(7), 4775–4797. DOI: 10.1007/s11831-022-09749-0

Kawasaki, A., Brunel, H., Ide, R., Suzuki, T., Kashiwazaki, T., Inoue, A., & Takase, K. (2025). Real-time observation of picosecond-timescale optical quantum entanglement towards ultrafast quantum information processing. *Nature Photonics*, *19*(3), 1–6. DOI: 10.1038/s41566-024-01589-7

Kayyali, M. (2021). Positive impact of high technology on higher education.

Kayyali, M. (2024 A). Global Perspectives on Personalized Learning: Case Studies and Best Practices. In Transforming Education for Personalized Learning (pp. 66-84). IGI Global.

Kayyali, M. (2024 C). Immersive Technologies: Virtual and Augmented Reality in Higher Education. In Reshaping learning with next generation educational technologies (pp. 99-114). IGI Global.

Kayyali, M. (2025 a). Envisioning the Future: The Evolution and Impact of AI and Machine Learning in Finance. In Utilizing AI and Machine Learning in Financial Analysis (pp. 193-212). IGI Global Scientific Publishing.

Kayyali, M. (2025 b). Ethical Implications of Generative AI in Education: Privacy, Bias, and Integrity. In Transformative AI Practices for Personalized Learning Strategies (pp. 185-218). IGI Global Scientific Publishing.

Kayyali, M. (2025 B). The Future of AI in Education: Predictions and Emerging Trends. Next-Generation AI Methodologies in Education, 367-406.

Kayyali, M. (2025 c). Generative AI and Education: Transforming Teaching and Learning Through Collaborative Intelligence. In Humans and Generative AI Tools for Collaborative Intelligence (pp. 25-52). IGI Global Scientific Publishing.

Kayyali, M. (2026 a). Case Studies in Competitive Intelligence: Real-World Applications in Global Industries. In Competitive Intelligence in the Digital Age: Strategies for Business and Technology Leadership (pp. 37-64). IGI Global Scientific Publishing.

Kayyali, M. (2026 b). Ethical AI and Automation in the Workplace. In Leading Inclusive Workplaces Through Digital Transformation and Organizational Change (pp. 103-138). IGI Global Scientific Publishing.

Kayyali, M. (2026 c). Machine Learning and Bias: Creating Inclusive AI Systems for All. In AI and New Forms of Exclusion (pp. 143-166). IGI Global Scientific Publishing.

Kayyali, M. (2026 d). The Digital Transformation of Education: Opportunities and Challenges for Communication. Effects of Education Communication in Digital Learning Environments, 433-472.

Kayyali, M. (2026 e). The Evolution of Artificial Intelligence in Education: From Theory to Practice. In Responsible AI Integration in Education (pp. 119-150). IGI Global Scientific Publishing.

Kayyali, M. (Ed.). (2024 D). Building Resiliency in Higher Education: Globalization, Digital Skills, and Student Wellness: Globalization, Digital Skills, and Student Wellness. IGI Global.

Kayyali, M. (2020). Pros and Cons of University Rankings. *Online Submission*, *1*(1), 1–6.

Kayyali, M. (2024). B). Future possibilities and challenges of AI in education. In *Transforming education with generative AI: Prompt engineering and synthetic content creation* (pp. 118–137). IGI Global Scientific Publishing. DOI: 10.4018/979-8-3693-1351-0.ch006

Kayyali, M. (2025). A). The Impact of Personalized Learning on Student Engagement and Achievement in STEAM. In *Integrating Personalized Learning Methods Into STEAM Education* (pp. 51–78). IGI Global Scientific Publishing. DOI: 10.4018/979-8-3693-7718-5.ch003

Keil, D., & Olendzenski, M. (2023). Exaggerated claims of artificial general intelligence.

Khalifa, M., & Albadawy, M. (2024). Artificial Intelligence for Clinical Prediction: Exploring Key Domains and Essential Functions. *Computer Methods and Programs in Biomedicine Update*, *5*(100148), 100148. Advance online publication. DOI: 10.1016/j.cmpbup.2024.100148

Khan, A., Rauf, Z., Sohail, A., Khan, A. R., Asif, H., Asif, A., & Farooq, U. (2023). A survey of the vision transformers and their CNN-transformer based variants. *Artificial Intelligence Review*, *56*(S3, Suppl 3), 2917–2970. DOI: 10.1007/s10462-023-10595-0

Khan, A., Sohail, A., Zahoora, U., & Qureshi, A. S. (2020). A survey of the recent architectures of deep convolutional neural networks. *Artificial Intelligence Review*, *53*(8), 5455–5516. DOI: 10.1007/s10462-020-09825-6

Khan, M. A., & Park, H. (2024). Exploring Explainable Artificial Intelligence Techniques for Interpretable Neural Networks in Traffic Sign Recognition Systems. *Electronics (Basel)*, *13*(2), 306. DOI: 10.3390/electronics13020306

Khokhar, P. B., Gravino, C., & Palomba, F. (2025). Advances in artificial intelligence for diabetes prediction: Insights from a systematic literature review. *Artificial Intelligence in Medicine*, *164*(103132), 103132. Advance online publication. DOI: 10.1016/j.artmed.2025.103132

Kim, J., Greenberg, D. E., Pifer, R., Jiang, S., Xiao, G., Shelburne, S. A., Koh, A., Xie, Y., & Zhan, X. (2020). VaMPR: VAriant Mapping and Prediction of antibiotic resistance via explainable features and machine learning. *PLoS Computational Biology*, *16*(1), e1007511. Advance online publication. DOI: 10.1371/journal.pcbi.1007511

Kim, Y., Kim, D., Choi, J., Park, J., Oh, N., & Park, D. (2024). A survey on integration of large language models with intelligent robots. *Intelligent Service Robotics, 17*(5), 1091–1107. DOI: 10.1007/s11370-024-00550-5

Kingsley, K. A., & Barmawi, A. M. (2020). Improving Data Hiding Capacity in Code Based Steganography using Multiple Embedding. *J. Inf. Hiding Multim. Signal Process., 11*(1), 14–43.

Klusowski, J. M., & Tian, P. M. (2023). Large scale prediction with decision trees. *Journal of the American Statistical Association, 118*(543), 1835–1847. DOI: 10.1080/01621459.2022.2126782

Kneusel, R. T. (2023). *How AI works: from sorcery to science*. No Starch Press.

Kondaveeti, H. K., Kumar, S. V. S., Manusree, A. V. N., Vatsavayi, V. K., & Ananthachari, P. (2024). Role of AI in Academic Research. In *Utilizing AI Tools in Academic Research Writing* (pp. 1–17). IGI Global. DOI: 10.4018/979-8-3693-1798-3.ch001

Konduru, U. R., Nagarajan, A. P., & Sai, C. V. S. (2024). An improved performance of reversible data hiding in encrypted images using decision tree algorithm. *Engineering Applications of Artificial Intelligence, 137*, 109100. DOI: 10.1016/j.engappai.2024.109100

Krause, A., & Hübotter, J. (2025). Probabilistic artificial intelligence. *arXiv preprint arXiv:2502.05244*.

Kumar, R., & Jung, K.-H. (2020). Robust reversible data hiding scheme based on two-layer embedding strategy. *Information Sciences, 512*, 96–107. DOI: 10.1016/j.ins.2019.09.062

Kumar, S., Singh, A., & Kumar, M. (2019). Information hiding with adaptive steganography based on novel fuzzy edge identification. *Defence Technology, 15*(2), 162–169. DOI: 10.1016/j.dt.2018.08.003

Kunhoth, J., Subramanian, N., Al-Maadeed, S., & Bouridane, A. (2023). Video steganography: Recent advances and challenges. *Multimedia Tools and Applications, 82*(27), 41943–41985. DOI: 10.1007/s11042-023-14844-w

Kuppusamy, P., Ramya, K., Rani, S. S., Sivaram, M., & Dhasarathan, V. (2020). A novel approach based on modified cycle generative adversarial networks for image steganography. *Scalable Computing: Practice and Experience, 21*(1), 63–72. DOI: 10.12694/scpe.v21i1.1613

Kuznetsov, O., Frontoni, E., & Chernov, K. (2024). Beyond traditional steganography: Enhancing security and performance with spread spectrum image steganography. *Applied Intelligence*, *54*(7), 5253–5277. DOI: 10.1007/s10489-024-05415-z

Kwon, D., Kang, H., Lee, D., & Kim, Y. C. (2025). Deep learning-based prediction of atrial fibrillation from polar transformed time-frequency electrocardiogram. *PLoS One*, *20*(3), e0317630. Advance online publication. DOI: 10.1371/journal.pone.0317630

Lase, E. M., & Nkosi, F. (2023). Human-Centric AI: Understanding and Enhancing Collaboration between Humans and Intelligent Systems. *Algorithm Asynchronous*, *1*(1), 33–40. DOI: 10.61963/jaa.v1i1.49

Lee, P.-S., West, J. D., & Howe, B. (2016). Viziometrics: Analyzing visual information in the scientific literature. *arXiv preprint arXiv:1605.04951*.ar5iv+2arXiv+2SpringerLink+2

Lee, C. S., & Lee, A. Y. (2020). How artificial intelligence can transform randomized controlled trials. *Translational Vision Science & Technology*, *9*(2), 9. Advance online publication. DOI: 10.1167/tvst.9.2.9

Lee, C.-F., Shen, J.-J., Agrawal, S., Wang, Y.-X., & Lee, Y.-H. (2020). Data hiding method based on 3D magic cube. *IEEE Access : Practical Innovations, Open Solutions*, *8*, 39445–39453. DOI: 10.1109/ACCESS.2020.2975385

Lee, H., Chatterjee, I., & Cho, G. (2023). AI-Powered Intelligent Seaport Mobility: Enhancing Container Drayage Efficiency through Computer Vision and Deep Learning. *Applied Sciences (Basel, Switzerland)*, *13*(22), 12214. DOI: 10.3390/app132212214

Lee, J., Das, D., Choo, J., & Choi, S. (2023). Towards open-set test-time adaptation utilizing the wisdom of crowds in entropy minimization. *Proceedings of the IEEE/CVF International Conference on Computer Vision (ICCV)*, 14991–15000. DOI: 10.1109/ICCV51070.2023.01501

Lei, S., Yang, R., & Huang, C.-R. (2021). *Automatic Analysis of Linguistic Features in Journal Articles of Different Academic Impacts with Feature Engineering Techniques*. arXiv preprint arXiv:2111.07525.

Leonardi, S., Distefano, N., & Gruden, C. (2025). Advancing Sustainable Mobility: Artificial Intelligence Approaches for Autonomous Vehicle Trajectories in Roundabouts. *Sustainability (Basel)*, *17*(7), 2988. DOI: 10.3390/su17072988

Letchford, A., Moat, H. S., & Preis, T. (2015). The advantage of short paper titles. *Royal Society Open Science*, *2*(8), 150266. DOI: 10.1098/rsos.150266 PMID: 26361556

Levantis, N., & Sgora, A. (2024, May). Algorithmic Decision Making in Education: Challenges and Opportunities. In *2024 IEEE Global Engineering Education Conference (EDUCON)* (pp. 1-7). IEEE. DOI: 10.1109/EDUCON60312.2024.10578645

Liang, Y., You, J., Wang, R., Qin, B., & Han, S. (2024). Urban Transportation Data Research Overview: A Bibliometric Analysis Based on CiteSpace. *Sustainability (Basel)*, *16*(22), 9615. DOI: 10.3390/su16229615

Li, F., Li, L., Zeng, Y., Yu, J., & Qin, C. (2025). Adversarial multi-image steganography via texture evaluation and multi-scale image enhancement. *Multimedia Tools and Applications*, *84*(9), 5793–5823. DOI: 10.1007/s11042-024-18920-7

Li, K., Chen, L., Cai, X., Cai, X., Lu, Y., Luo, S., Wang, W., Jiang, L., Wu, G., & Jia, Z. (2025). A Bayesian network approach to predicting severity status in nuclear reactor accidents with resilience to missing data. *Entropy (Basel, Switzerland)*, *18*(11), 2684. DOI: 10.3390/e18112684

Lin, C. H., Yu, C. T., Chen, Y. L., Lin, Y. Y., & Chiao, H. T. (2025). Simulated Adversarial Attacks on Traffic Sign Recognition of Autonomous Vehicles. *Engineering Proceedings*, *92*(1), 15. DOI: 10.3390/engproc2025092015

Lindebaum, D., Vesa, M., & Den Hond, F. (2020). Insights from "the machine stops" to better understand rational assumptions in algorithmic decision making and its implications for organizations. *Academy of Management Review*, *45*(1), 247–263. DOI: 10.5465/amr.2018.0181

Lin, T., Song, K., Jiang, Z., Kang, Y., Yuan, W., Li, X., Sun, C., Huang, C., & Liu, X. (2024). Towards human-like perception: Learning structural causal model in heterogeneous graph. *Information Processing & Management*, *61*(2), 103600. DOI: 10.1016/j.ipm.2023.103600

Lin, Y., Tang, J., Guo, J., Wu, S., & Li, Z. (2025). Advancing AI-enabled techniques in energy system modeling: A review of data-driven, mechanism-driven, and hybrid modeling approaches. *Energies*, *18*(4), 845. DOI: 10.3390/en18040845

Liu, J. M., Li, J. Y., Chen, Y., Lian, S., Zeng, J. Q., Geng, M. S., Zheng, S. J., Dong, Y. A., He, Y., Huang, P., Zhao, Z., Yan, X., Hu, Q., Wang, L., Yang, D., Zhu, Z., Sun, Y., Shang, W., Wang, D., & Chen, X. M. (2023). Multi-scale urban passenger transportation CO_2 emission calculation platform for smart mobility management. *Applied Energy*, *331*, 120407. DOI: 10.1016/j.apenergy.2022.120407

Liu, J., Xia, F., Feng, X., Ren, J., & Liu, H. (2022). Deep graph learning for anomalous citation detection. *IEEE Transactions on Neural Networks and Learning Systems, 1–14*. https://arxiv.org/abs/2202.11360

Liu, L., Liu, X., Wang, D., & Yang, G. (2024). Enhancing image steganography security via universal adversarial perturbations. *Multimedia Tools and Applications, 84*(3), 1303–1315. Advance online publication. DOI: 10.1007/s11042-024-19122-x

Liu, S., Li, H., Kun, W., Zhang, Z., & Wu, H. (2022). How do transportation influencing factors affect air pollutants from vehicles in china? Evidence from threshold effect. *Sustainability (Basel), 14*(15), 9402. DOI: 10.3390/su14159402

Liu, T., & Qiu, Z. (2002). A DWT-based color image steganography scheme. 6th International Conference on Signal Processing, 2002., Liu, J., Ke, Y., Zhang, Z., Lei, Y., Li, J., Zhang, M., & Yang, X. (2020). Recent advances of image steganography with generative adversarial networks. *IEEE Access : Practical Innovations, Open Solutions, 8*, 60575–60597. DOI: 10.1109/ACCESS.2020.2983175

Liu, Z., Chen, H., & Sun, S. (2020). Research on covert communication security based on screen content coding. *IEEE Access : Practical Innovations, Open Solutions, 8*, 22275–22280. DOI: 10.1109/ACCESS.2020.2968740

Li, X., Chen, L., Fu, T., Fu, Z., & Gao, Y. (2025). Coverless image steganography based on semantic-controlled text-to-image generation. *IEEE Transactions on Circuits and Systems for Video Technology, 35*(8), 8391–8405. DOI: 10.1109/TCSVT.2025.3545067

Li, X., Chen, L., Lai, J., Fu, Z., & Liu, S. (2024). GAN-based image steganography by exploiting transform domain knowledge with deep networks. *Multimedia Systems, 30*(4), 224. DOI: 10.1007/s00530-024-01427-4

Li, X., & Wang, Z. (2024). Vaccine for digital images against steganography. *Scientific Reports, 14*(1), 21340. Advance online publication. DOI: 10.1038/s41598-024-72693-5

Li, X., & Wang, Z. (2025). Image vaccine against steganography in encrypted domain. *Scientific Reports, 15*(1), 4046. Advance online publication. DOI: 10.1038/s41598-025-88384-8

Li, Z., & Bors, A. G. (2020). Steganalysis of meshes based on 3D wavelet multiresolution analysis. *Information Sciences, 522*, 164–179. DOI: 10.1016/j.ins.2020.02.061

Lones, M. A. (2024). Avoiding common machine learning pitfalls. *Patterns (New York, N.Y.), 5*(10), 101046. DOI: 10.1016/j.patter.2024.101046 PMID: 39569205

Lopez, C., Tucker, S., Salameh, T., & Tuckera, C. (2018). An unsupervised machine learning method for discovering patient clusters based on genetic signatures. *Journal of Biomedical Informatics, 85*, 30–39. DOI: 10.1016/j.jbi.2018.07.004

Lu, C., Bu, Y., Dong, X., Wang, J., Ding, Y., Larivière, V., Sugimoto, C. R., Paul, L., & Zhang, C. (2019). Analyzing linguistic complexity and scientific impact. *Journal of Informetrics, 13*(3), 817–829. DOI: 10.1016/j.joi.2019.07.004

Lumbreras, S., & Garrido-Merchán, E. (2024). Insights from Saint Teresa and Saint Augustine on Artificial Intelligence: Discussing Human Interiority. *Scientia et Fides, 12*(2), 265–295. DOI: 10.12775/SetF.2024.025

Luo, J., Zhou, R.-G., Liu, X., Hu, W., & Liu, G. (2019). A novel quantum steganography scheme based on ASCII. *International Journal of Quantum Information, 17*(04), 1950033. DOI: 10.1142/S0219749919500333

Luque-Fernandez, M. A., Schomaker, M., Rachet, B., & Schnitzer, M. E. (2018). Targeted maximum likelihood estimation for a binary treatment: A tutorial. *Statistics in Medicine, 37*(16), 1–17. DOI: 10.1002/sim.7628

Lu, S.-P.. (2021). Large-capacity image steganography based on invertible neural networks. In *Proceedings of the IEEE/CVF Conference on Computer Vision and Pattern Recognition*. IEEE. DOI: 10.1109/CVPR46437.2021.01067

Maalsen, S. (2023). Algorithmic epistemologies and methodologies: Algorithmic harm, algorithmic care and situated algorithmic knowledges. *Progress in Human Geography, 47*(2), 197–214. DOI: 10.1177/03091325221149439

Mabona, A., Van Greunen, D., & Kevin, K. (2024). Integration of Artificial Intelligence (AI) in Academic Libraries: A Systematic Literature Review. *2024 IST-Africa Conference (IST-Africa)*, 1–9.

Madhu, D., Vasuhi, S., & Samydurai, A. (2024). Dynamic 8-bit XOR algorithm with AES crypto algorithm for image steganography. *Signal, Image and Video Processing, 18*(S1, Suppl 1), 429–445. DOI: 10.1007/s11760-024-03165-6

Mahayuddin, Z. R., & Saif, A. (2022). Moving object detection using semantic convolutional features. *Journal of Information Systems and Technology Management, 7*(29), 24–41. DOI: 10.35631/JISTM.729003

Maleki, F., Ovens, K., Najafian, K., Forghani, B., Reinhold, C., & Forghani, R. (2020). Overview of machine learning part 1: Fundamentals and classic approaches. *Neuroimaging Clinics of North America, 30*(4), e17–e32. DOI: 10.1016/j.nic.2020.08.007 PMID: 33039003

Malgaroli, M., Hull, T. D., Zech, J. M., & Althoff, T. (2023). Natural language processing for mental health interventions: A systematic review and research framework. *Translational Psychiatry, 13*(309), 309. Advance online publication. DOI: 10.1038/s41398-023-02592-2

Mallet, A., Cogranne, R., & Bas, P. (2024, June). Linking intrinsic difficulty and regret to properties of multivariate Gaussians in image steganalysis. In *Proceedings of the 2024 ACM Workshop on Information Hiding and Multimedia Security* (pp. 31–39). ACM. DOI: 10.1145/3658664.3659643

Mandal, A., Banerjee, S., & Panigrahi, P. K. (2023). Hybrid phase-based representation of quantum images. *International Journal of Theoretical Physics*, *62*(6), 115. DOI: 10.1007/s10773-023-05354-4

Mandal, P. C., Mukherjee, I., Paul, G., & Chatterji, B. N. (2022). Digital image steganography: A literature survey. *Information Sciences*, *609*, 1451–1488. DOI: 10.1016/j.ins.2022.07.120

Manduchi, L., Meister, C., Pandey, K., Bamler, R., Cotterell, R., Däubener, S., Fellenz, S., Fischer, A., Gärtner, T., Kirchler, M., Kloft, M., Li, Y., Lippert, C., de Melo, G., Nalisnick, E., Ommer, B., Ranganath, R., Rudolph, M., Ullrich, K., . . . Fortuin, V. (2024). On the challenges and opportunities in generative AI. arXiv. https://doi.org//arXiv.2403.00025DOI: 10.48550

Manheim, D. (2023). Building less-flawed metrics: Understanding and creating better measurement and incentive systems. *Patterns (New York, N.Y.)*, *4*(10), 100842. DOI: 10.1016/j.patter.2023.100842 PMID: 37876897

Maniriho, P., & Ahmad, T. (2019). Information hiding scheme for digital images using difference expansion and modulus function. *Journal of King Saud University. Computer and Information Sciences*, *31*(3), 335–347. DOI: 10.1016/j.jksuci.2018.01.011

Manuilova, N., Khairullina, L., Khabibullina, G., Minnegalieva, C. B., Makletsov, S., Bronskaya, V., & Kharitonova, O. (2020). Wavelet method of hiding text information in audio signals. *Journal of Physics: Conference Series*, *1515*(3), 032056. DOI: 10.1088/1742-6596/1515/3/032056

Mao, F. F., Wei, Y. F., & Ren, J. Y. (2024). Are Smart Cities Smarter? The Impact of Smart City Policy on Digital Autonomy of Cities in China. *Polish Journal of Environmental Studies*, *33*(3), 2209–2222. DOI: 10.15244/pjoes/174837

Markauskaite, L., Marrone, R., Poquet, O., Knight, S., Martinez-Maldonado, R., Howard, S., Tondeur, J., De Laat, M., Buckingham Shum, S., Gašević, D., & Siemens, G. (2022). Rethinking the entwinement between artificial intelligence and human learning: What capabilities do learners need for a world with AI? *Computers and Education: Artificial Intelligence*, *3*, 100056. DOI: 10.1016/j.caeai.2022.100056

Markolf, S. A., Chester, M. V., Eisenberg, D. A., Iwaniec, D. M., Davidson, C. I., Zimmerman, R., Miller, T. R., Ruddell, B. L., & Chang, H. (2018). Interdependent infrastructure as linked social, ecological, and technological systems (SETSs) to address lock-in and enhance resilience. *Earth's Future*, *6*(12), 1638–1659. DOI: 10.1029/2018EF000926

Marshall, G. C., Jay, C., & Freitas, A. (2021). Number and quality of diagrams in scholarly publications is associated with number of citations. In *Diagrammatic Representation and Inference* (pp. 512–519). Springer., DOI: 10.1007/978-3-030-86062-2_52

Martín, A., Hernández, A., Alazab, M., Jung, J., & Camacho, D. (2023). Evolving generative adversarial networks to improve image steganography. *Expert Systems with Applications*, *222*, 119841. Advance online publication. DOI: 10.1016/j.eswa.2023.119841

Martínez-García, M., & Hernández-Lemus, E. (2022). Data integration challenges for machine learning in precision medicine. *Frontiers in Medicine*, *9*, 784455. DOI: 10.3389/fmed.2021.784455 PMID: 35145977

Masters, K. (2023). Ethical use of artificial intelligence in health professions education: AMEE Guide No. 158. *Medical Teacher*, *45*(6), 574–584. DOI: 10.1080/0142159X.2023.2186203 PMID: 36912253

Matei, S. (2024). Generative artificial intelligence and collective remembering. The technological mediation of mnemotechnic values. *Journal of Human-Technology Relations, 2*.

McCannon, B. C. (2019). Readability and research impact. *Economics Letters*, *180*, 76–79. DOI: 10.1016/j.econlet.2019.02.017

Meder, B., Asselbergs, F. W., & Ashley, E. (2025). Artificial intelligence to improve cardiovascular population health. *European Heart Journal*, *00*(20), 1–10. DOI: 10.1093/eurheartj/ehaf125

Meng, R., Cui, Q., Zhoul, Z., Yuan, C., & Sun, X. (2020). A Novel Steganography Algorithm Based on Instance Segmentation. *Computers, Materials & Continua*, *63*(1), 183–196. DOI: 10.32604/cmc.2020.05317

Mercier, D., Rizvi, S. T. R., Rajashekar, V., Dengel, A., & Ahmed, S. (2020). *ImpactCite: An XLNet-based method for Citation Impact Analysis*. arXiv preprint arXiv:2005.06611.

Michailidis, P., Dimitriadou, A., Papadimitriou, T., & Gogas, P. (2022). Forecasting Hospital Readmissions with Machine Learning. *Healthcare (Basel), 10*(981), 981. Advance online publication. DOI: 10.3390/healthcare10060981

Mienye, I. D., Swart, T. G., & Obaido, G. (2024). Recurrent neural networks: A comprehensive review of architectures, variants, and applications. *Information (Basel), 15*(9), 517. DOI: 10.3390/info15090517

Mîndrilă, D. (2023). Bayesian latent class analysis: Sample size, model size, and classification precision. *Mathematics, 11*(12), 2753. DOI: 10.3390/math11122753

Mohamed, K. I. E. S., & Nadia, K. I. E. S. (2024). Adapting to the Transformation of Education: New Challenges for Teachers. *Journal of Languages and Translation, 4*(1), 80–88. DOI: 10.70204/jlt.v4i1.310

Mohammed, E. M., Fakhrudeen, A. M., & Alani, O. Y. (2024). Detection of Alzheimer's disease using deep learning models: A systematic literature review. *Informatics in Medicine Unlocked, 50*(101551), 101551. Advance online publication. DOI: 10.1016/j.imu.2024.101551

Mohsen, B. M. (2024). AI-Driven Optimization of Urban Logistics in Smart Cities: Integrating Autonomous Vehicles and IoT for Efficient Delivery Systems. *Sustainability (Basel), 16*(24), 11265. DOI: 10.3390/su162411265

Mökander, J., Juneja, P., Watson, D. S., & Floridi, L. (2022). The US Algorithmic Accountability Act of 2022 vs. The EU Artificial Intelligence Act: What can they learn from each other? *Minds and Machines, 32*(4), 751–758. DOI: 10.1007/s11023-022-09612-y

Mon, E. E., Ochiai, H., Komolkiti, P., & Aswakul, C. (2022). Real - world sensor dataset for city inbound-outbound critical intersection analysis. *Scientific Data, 9*(1), 357. Advance online publication. DOI: 10.1038/s41597-022-01448-6

Moreno-Vozmediano, R., Huedo, E., Montero, R. S., & Llorente, I. M. (2025). AI-Driven Resource Allocation and Auto-Scaling of VNFs in Edge-5G-IoT Ecosystems. *Electronics (Basel), 14*(9), 1808. DOI: 10.3390/electronics14091808

Mpanya, D., Celik, T., Klug, E., & Ntsinjana, H. (2021). Predicting mortality and hospitalization in heart failure using machine learning: A systematic literature review. *International Journal of Cardiology. Heart & Vasculature, 34*(100773), 100773. Advance online publication. DOI: 10.1016/j.ijcha.2021.100773

Muralidharan, T., Cohen, A., Cohen, A., & Nissim, N. (2022). The infinite race between steganography and steganalysis in images. *Signal Processing, 201*, 108711. Advance online publication. DOI: 10.1016/j.sigpro.2022.108711

Murgatroyd, S. (2024). *The future of higher education in an age of artificial intelligence*. Ethics International Press.

Muskat, M., Blackman, D. A., & Muskat, B. (2012). Mixed methods: Combining expert interviews, cross-impact analysis, and scenario development. *Electronic Journal of Business Research Methods*, *10*(1), 9–21.

Mustafa, N. A. A. (2020). Text hiding in text using invisible character. *International Journal of Electrical and Computer Engineering*, *10*(4), 3550. DOI: 10.11591/ijece.v10i4.pp3550-3557

Na, D. (2020). DNA steganography: Hiding undetectable secret messages within the single nucleotide polymorphisms of a genome and detecting mutation-induced errors. *Microbial Cell Factories*, *19*(1), 1–9. DOI: 10.1186/s12934-020-01387-0 PMID: 32527315

Naderalvojoud, B., & Hernandez-Boussard, T. (2024). Improving machine learning with ensemble learning on observational healthcare data. *AMIA ... Annual Symposium Proceedings - AMIA Symposium. AMIA Symposium*, **•••**, 521–529.

Nahar, M., & Kamal, A. (2024). Dna steganography: Embedding the secret messages using glass stack method and detecting errors made by different attacks. *International Journal of Computers and Applications*, *46*(7), 508–525. DOI: 10.1080/1206212X.2024.2347456

Naidu, D., Tirpude, S., Kalyani, K., Bongirwar, V., & Sharma, T. (2020). Data hiding using meaningful encryption algorithm to enhance data security. *International Journal (Toronto, Ont.)*, *9*(2).

Najem, N. R., Salman, A. S., Nas, Y. F., Abu-AlShaeer, M. J., Basheer, B. M., Khaddad, A., & Monadhel, H. (2024). Human-AI Symbiosis: Investigating Real-Time Neural Link Integrations for Enhanced Cognitive Abilities. *2024 36th Conference of Open Innovations Association (FRUCT)*, 664–674.

Nambiar, A., Harikrishnaa, S., & Sharanprasath, S. (2023). Model-agnostic explainable artificial intelligence tools for severity prediction and symptom analysis on Indian COVID-19 data. *Frontiers in Artificial Intelligence*, *6*(1272506), 1272506. Advance online publication. DOI: 10.3389/frai.2023.1272506

Narushynska, O., Doroshenko, A., Teslyuk, V., Antoniv, V., & Arzubov, M. (2025). Enhancing hierarchical classification in tree-based models using level-wise entropy adjustment. *Big Data and Cognitive Computing*, *9*(3), 65. DOI: 10.3390/bdcc9030065

Nasarudin, N. A., Al Jasmi, F., Sinnott, R. O., Zaki, N., Al Ashwal, H., Mohamed, E. A., & Mohamad, M. S. (2024). A review of deep learning models and online healthcare databases for electronic health records and their use for health prediction. *Artificial Intelligence Review*, *57*(9), 249. Advance online publication. DOI: 10.1007/s10462-024-10876-2

Nasir, F., Rahman, S., & Nasir, N. (2025). Breast Cancer Detection Using Convolutional Neural Networks : A Deep Learning-Based Approach. *Cureus*, *17*(5). Advance online publication. DOI: 10.7759/cureus.83421

Nasr, M. A., El-Shafai, W., El-Rabaie, E. S. M., El-Fishawy, A. S., El-Hoseny, H. M., Abd El-Samie, F. E., & Abdel-Salam, N. (2024). A robust audio steganography technique based on image encryption using different chaotic maps. *Scientific Reports*, *14*(1), 22054. DOI: 10.1038/s41598-024-70940-3

Nazir, S., Asif, M., Ahmad, S., Aljuaid, H., Iftikhar, R., Nawaz, Z., & Ghadi, Y. Y. (2022). Important Citation Identification by Exploding the Sentiment Analysis and Section-Wise In-Text Citation Weights. *IEEE Access : Practical Innovations, Open Solutions*, *10*, 87990–88000. DOI: 10.1109/ACCESS.2022.3199420

Neyman, E. (2024). Algorithmic Bayesian Epistemology. *ArXiv Preprint ArXiv:2403.07949.*

Nguyen, T., Raghu, M., & Kornblith, S. (2020). Do wide and deep networks learn the same things? uncovering how neural network representations vary with width and depth. arXiv preprint arXiv:2010.15327.

Nicholas, G., & Bhatia, A. (2023). Lost in translation: large language models in non-English content analysis. arXiv preprint arXiv:2306.07377.

Nieminen, M. (2023). The Transformer Model and Its Impact on the Field of Natural Language Processing.

Nigam, N., Singh, D. P., & Choudhary, J. (2023). A Review of Different Components of the Intelligent Traffic Management System (ITMS). *Symmetry*, *15*(3), 583. DOI: 10.3390/sym15030583

Noaeen, M., Naik, A., Goodman, L., Crebo, J., Abrar, T., Abad, Z. S. H., Bazzan, A. L. C., & Far, B. (2022). Reinforcement learning in urban network traffic signal control: A systematic literature review. *Expert Systems with Applications*, *199*, 116830. DOI: 10.1016/j.eswa.2022.116830

Nord-Bronzyk, A., Savulescu, J., Ballantyne, A., Braunack-Mayer, A., Krishnaswamy, P., Lysaght, T., Ong, M. E. H., Liu, N., Menikoff, J., Mertens, M., & Dunn, M. D. (2025). Assessing Risk in Implementing New Artificial Intelligence Triage Tools—How Much Risk is Reasonable in an Already Risky World? *Asian Bioethics Review, 17*(1), 187–205. DOI: 10.1007/s41649-024-00348-8

Norori, N., Hu, Q., Aellen, F. M., Faraci, F. D., & Tzovara, A. (2021). Addressing bias in big data and AI for health care: A call for open science. *Patterns (New York, N.Y.), 2*(10), 100347. Advance online publication. DOI: 10.1016/j.patter.2021.100347

Nowotny, H. (2022). *Digital Humanism: Navigating the Tensions Ahead.*

Oinas-Kukkonen, H., Pohjolainen, S., & Agyei, E. (2022). Mitigating issues with/of/for true personalization. *Frontiers in Artificial Intelligence, 5*, 844817. DOI: 10.3389/frai.2022.844817 PMID: 35558170

Oladele, O. K. (2024). Machine Learning Algorithms for Analyzing Medical Imaging and Improving Diagnostic Accuracy.

Olawade, D. B., Wada, O. J., David-Olawade, A. C., Kunonga, E., Abaire, O., & Ling, J. (2023). Using artificial intelligence to improve public health: A narrative review. *Frontiers in Public Health, 11*(1196397), 1196397. Advance online publication. DOI: 10.3389/fpubh.2023.1196397

Paiva, C. E., Lima, J. P. S. N., & Paiva, B. S. R. (2012). Articles with short titles describing the results are cited more often. *Clinics (São Paulo), 67*(5), 509–513. DOI: 10.6061/clinics/2012(05)17 PMID: 22666797

Paiva, S., Abdul Ahad, M., Tripathi, G., Feroz, N., & Casalino, G. (2021). Enabling Technologies for Urban Smart Mobility: Recent Trends, Opportunities and Challenges. *Sensors (Basel), 21*(6), 2143. DOI: 10.3390/s21062143 PMID: 33803903

Palencia, M. G. P. (2024). Epistemolog-IA: La confluencia de la Inteligencia Artificial y la epistemología en el desarrollo científico contemporáneo. *Ciencia Latina Revista Científica Multidisciplinar, 8*(4), 11236–11257. DOI: 10.37811/cl_rcm.v8i4.13264

Palla, U., & Iwunwa, M. G. C. (2025). Leveraging predictive models to enhance infection control and reduce cross-contamination in public health settings. *International Journal of Research Publication and Reviews, 6*(1), 407–422. DOI: 10.55248/gengpi.6.0125.0212

Pandey, S. C., & Kumari, P. V. (2025). Adaptive Al-Driven Toll Management: Enhancing Traffic Flow and Sustainability Through Real-Time Prediction, Allocation, and Task Optimization. *Future Transportation, 5*(1), 21. DOI: 10.3390/futuretransp5010021

Panigrahi, R., & Padhy, N. (2025). An effective steganographic technique for hiding the image data using the LSB technique. *Cyber Security and Applications, 3*, 100069. DOI: 10.1016/j.csa.2024.100069

Pan, N., Qin, J., Tan, Y., Xiang, X., & Hou, G. (2020). A video coverless information hiding algorithm based on semantic segmentation. *EURASIP Journal on Image and Video Processing, 2020*(1), 1–18. DOI: 10.1186/s13640-020-00512-8

Pantanowitz, L., Hanna, M., Pantanowitz, J., Lennerz, J., Henricks, W. H., Shen, P., Quinn, B., Bennet, S., & Rashidi, H. H. (2024). Regulatory Aspects of Artificial Intelligence and Machine Learning. *Modern Pathology, 37*(100609), 100609. Advance online publication. DOI: 10.1016/j.modpat.2024.100609

Papadimitroulas, P., Brocki, L., Christopher Chung, N., Marchadour, W., Vermet, F., Gaubert, L., Eleftheriadis, V., Plachouris, D., Visvikis, D., Kagadis, G. C., & Hatt, M. (2021). Artificial intelligence: Deep learning in oncological radiomics and challenges of interpretability and data harmonization. *Physica Medica, 83*, 108–121. DOI: 10.1016/j.ejmp.2021.03.009

Pedro, F., Subosa, M., Rivas, A., & Valverde, P. (2019). Artificial intelligence in education: Challenges and opportunities for sustainable development.

Perez, K., Wisniewski, D., Ari, A., Lee, K., Lieneck, C., & Ramamonjiarivelo, Z. (2025). Investigation into Application of AI and Telemedicine in Rural Communities: A Systematic Literature Review. *Healthcare (Basel), 13*(324), 324. Advance online publication. DOI: 10.3390/healthcare13030324

Pietikäinen, M. (2024). From the middle of nowhere to a world-class scientist in computer vision and artificial intelligence.

Porwal, R., & Devare, M. (2024). Scientific impact analysis: Unraveling the link between linguistic properties and citations. *Journal of Informetrics, 18*(1), 101252. DOI: 10.1016/j.joi.2024.101526

Pramanik, S. (2024). A new method for locating data hiding in image steganography. *Multimedia Tools and Applications, 83*(12), 34323–34349. DOI: 10.1007/s11042-023-16762-3

Pulicharla, M. R. (2025). Neurosymbolic AI: Bridging neural networks and symbolic reasoning.

Pulivarthy, P., & Whig, P. (2025). Bias and Fairness Addressing Discrimination in AI Systems. In *Ethical Dimensions of AI Development* (pp. 103–126). IGI Global.

Purba, C. R., Anggraini, Y., Sari, P., Pangaribuan, W., & Pane, I. I. I. (2023). Article sentence analysis: Use of clauses and phrases in scientific sentences. *Lingüística, 12*(1), 19–25. DOI: 10.24114/jalu.v11i4.43164

Qraitem, M., Kularatne, D., Forgoston, E., & Hsieh, M. A. (2020). Bridging the gap: Machine learning to resolve improperly modeled dynamics. *Physica D. Nonlinear Phenomena, 414*, 132736. DOI: 10.1016/j.physd.2020.132736

Quazi, S. (2022). Artificial intelligence and machine learning in precision and genomic medicine. *Medical Oncology (Northwood, London, England), 39*(120), 120. Advance online publication. DOI: 10.1007/s12032-022-01711-1

Rachael, O., Misra, S., Ahuja, R., Adewumi, A., Ayeni, F., & Mmaskeliunas, R. (2020). Image steganography and steganalysis based on least significant bit (LSB). *Proceedings of ICETIT 2019: Emerging trends in information technology* DOI: 10.1007/978-3-030-30577-2_97

Ragab, M., Abdushkour, H. A., Maghrabi, L., Alsalman, D., Fayoumi, A. G., & AL-Ghamdi, A. (2023). Improved Artificial Rabbits Optimization with Ensemble Learning-Based Traffic Flow Monitoring on Intelligent Transportation System. *Sustainability (Basel), 15*(16), 12601. DOI: 10.3390/su151612601

Rahman, A., Debnath, T., Kundu, D., Khan, M. S. I., Aishi, A. A., Sazzad, S., Sayduzzaman, M., & Band, S. S. (2024). Machine learning and deep learning-based approach in smart healthcare: Recent advances, applications, challenges and opportunities. *AIMS Public Health, 11*(1), 58–109. DOI: 10.3934/publichealth.2024004

Rahman, S., Uddin, J., Hussain, H., Shah, S., Salam, A., Amin, F., de la Torre Díez, I., Vargas, D. L. R., & Espinosa, J. C. M. (2025). A novel and efficient digital image steganography technique using least significant bit substitution. *Scientific Reports, 15*(1), 107. DOI: 10.1038/s41598-024-83147-3

Rajkomar, A., Dean, J., & Kohane, I. (2019). Machine Learning in Medicine. *The New England Journal of Medicine, 380*(14), 1347–1358. DOI: 10.1056/NEJMra1814259

Random, S. S. U. T. (2020). An effective and secure digital image steganography scheme using two random function and chaotic map. *Journal of Theoretical and Applied Information Technology, 98*(01).

Rane, N. (2023). ChatGPT and Similar Generative Artificial Intelligence (AI) for Smart Industry: role, challenges, and opportunities for industry 4.0, industry 5.0 and society 5.0. *Challenges and Opportunities for Industry, 4.*

Rane, N., Choudhary, S., & Rane, J. (2023). Education 4.0 and 5.0: Integrating artificial intelligence (AI) for personalized and adaptive learning.

Rane, N., Choudhary, S. P., & Rane, J. (2024). Ensemble deep learning and machine learning: Applications, opportunities, challenges, and future directions. *Studies in Medical and Health Sciences*, *1*(2), 18–41. DOI: 10.48185/smhs.v1i2.1225

Raptis, S., Ilioudis, C., & Theodorou, K. (2024). From pixels to prognosis: Unveiling radiomics models with SHAP and LIME for enhanced interpretability. *Biomedical Physics & Engineering Express*, *10*(3), 035016. DOI: 10.1088/2057-1976/ad34db PMID: 38498925

Rashid, A., & Kausik, M. D. A. K. (2024). AI revolutionizing industries worldwide: A comprehensive overview of its diverse applications. *Hybrid Advances*, *7*(100277), 100277. Advance online publication. DOI: 10.1016/j.hybadv.2024.100277

Regan, L., Hopson, L. R., Gisondi, M. A., & Branzetti, J. (2022). Creating a better learning environment: A qualitative study uncovering the experiences of Master Adaptive Learners in residency. *BMC Medical Education*, *22*(1), 141. DOI: 10.1186/s12909-022-03200-5 PMID: 35241060

Regan, P. M., & Jesse, J. (2019). Ethical challenges of edtech, big data and personalized learning: Twenty-first century student sorting and tracking. *Ethics and Information Technology*, *21*(3), 167–179. DOI: 10.1007/s10676-018-9492-2

Reidenberg, J. R., & Schaub, F. (2018). Achieving big data privacy in education. *Theory and Research in Education*, *16*(3), 263–279. DOI: 10.1177/1477878518805308

Reis, M. J. C. S. (2025). Internet of Things and Artificial Intelligence for Secure and Sustainable Green Mobility: A Multimodal Data Fusion Approach to Enhance Efficiency and Security. *Multimodal Technologies and Interaction*, *9*(5), 39. DOI: 10.3390/mti9050039

Ren, C., & Wu, B. (2024). A robust joint coverless image steganography scheme based on two independent modules. *Cybersecurity*, *7*(1), 73. Advance online publication. DOI: 10.1186/s42400-024-00299-5

Roe, J., & Perkins, M. (2024). Generative AI and Agency in Education: A Critical Scoping Review and Thematic Analysis. *ArXiv Preprint ArXiv:2411.00631.*

Roski, M., Sebastian, R., Ewerth, R., Hoppe, A., & Nehring, A. (2024). Learning analytics and the Universal Design for Learning (UDL): A clustering approach. *Computers & Education*, *214*, 105028. DOI: 10.1016/j.compedu.2024.105028

Rothman, D. (2021). *Transformers for Natural Language Processing: Build innovative deep neural network architectures for NLP with Python, PyTorch, TensorFlow, BERT, RoBERTa, and more*. Packt Publishing Ltd.

Rustad, S., Andono, P. N., & Shidik, G. F. (2023). Digital image steganography survey and investigation (goal, assessment, method, development, and dataset). *Signal Processing*, *206*, 108908. Advance online publication. DOI: 10.1016/j.sigpro.2022.108908

Ryan, M., Isakhanyan, G., & Tekinerdogan, B. (2023). An interdisciplinary approach to artificial intelligence in agriculture. *NJAS: Impact in Agricultural and Life Sciences*, *95*(1), 2168568. DOI: 10.1080/27685241.2023.2168568

Sachini, E., Sioumalas-Christodoulou, K., Christopoulos, S., & Karampekios, N. (2022). AI for AI: Using AI methods for classifying AI science documents. *Quantitative Science Studies*, *3*(4), 1119–1132. DOI: 10.1162/qss_a_00223

Sadaf, M., Iqbal, Z., Javed, A. R., Saba, I., Krichen, M., Majeed, S., & Raza, A. (2023). Connected and Automated Vehicles: Infrastructure, Applications, Security, Critical Challenges, and Future Aspects. *Technologies*, *11*(5), 117. DOI: 10.3390/technologies11050117

Saeidi, Z., Yazdi, A., Mashhadi, S., Hadian, M., & Gutub, A. (2024). High performance image steganography integrating IWT and Hamming code within secret sharing. *IET Image Processing*, *18*(1), 129–139. DOI: 10.1049/ipr2.12938

Sahu, A. K., & Swain, G. (2022). High fidelity based reversible data hiding using modified LSB matching and pixel difference. *Journal of King Saud University. Computer and Information Sciences*, *34*(4), 1395–1409. DOI: 10.1016/j.jksuci.2019.07.004

Saif, A. S., & Mahayuddin, Z. R. (2021). Crowd density estimation from autonomous drones using deep learning: Challenges and applications. *Journal of Engineering and Science Research*, *5*(6), 1–6. DOI: 10.26666/rmp.jesr.2021.6.1

Saif, A. S., Mahayuddin, Z. R., & Arshad, H. (2021). Vision-Based Efficient Collision Avoidance Model Using Distance Measurement. In *Soft Computing Approach for Mathematical Modeling of Engineering Problems* (p. 12). Taylor & Francis. DOI: 10.1201/9781003138341-12-12

Saif, F. S., & Mahayuddin, Z. R. (2022). Vision based 3D object detection using deep learning: Methods with challenges and applications towards future directions. *International Journal of Advanced Computer Science and Applications*, *13*(11), 203–214. DOI: 10.14569/IJACSA.2022.0131123

Saltz, J., Gupta, R., Hou, L., Kurc, T., Singh, P., Nguyen, V., Samaras, D., Shroyer, K. R., Zhao, T., Batiste, R., Van Arnam, J., Caesar-Johnson, S. J., Demchok, J. A., Felau, I., Kasapi, M., Ferguson, M. L., Hutter, C. M., Sofia, H. J., Tarnuzzer, R., & Thorsson, V. (2018). Spatial Organization and Molecular Correlation of Tumor-Infiltrating Lymphocytes Using Deep Learning on Pathology Images. *Cell Reports*, *23*(1), 181–200. DOI: 10.1016/j.celrep.2018.03.086

Saragih, E. (2023). Sentence complexity analysis in selected students' scientific papers: A closer look on abstract section. *E-Structural (English Studies on Translation, Culture, Literature, and Linguistics)*, 6(1), 70–83.

Sarker, I. H. (2021). Machine Learning: Algorithms, Real-World Applications and Research Directions. *SN Computer Science*, *2*(160), 160. Advance online publication. DOI: 10.1007/s42979-021-00592-x

Scharp, D., Hobensack, M., Davoudi, A., & Topaz, M. (2024). Natural Language Processing Applied to Clinical Documentation in Post-acute Care Settings: A Scoping Review. *Journal of the American Medical Directors Association*, *25*(1), 69–83. DOI: 10.1016/j.jamda.2023.09.006

Schildt, H. (2017). Big data and organizational design–the brave new world of algorithmic management and computer augmented transparency. *Innovation (North Sydney, N.S.W.)*, *19*(1), 23–30. DOI: 10.1080/14479338.2016.1252043

Schouten, G. (2017). On meeting students where they are: Teacher judgment and the use of data in higher education. *Theory and Research in Education*, *15*(3), 321–338. DOI: 10.1177/1477878517734452

Seele, P. (2023). Technology Ethics: Origins, Paradigms and Implications for Business and Society. In *Encyclopedia of Business and Professional Ethics* (pp. 1751–1755). Springer International Publishing. DOI: 10.1007/978-3-030-22767-8_1268

Sena, J., Mostafiz, M. T., Zhang, J., Davidson, A. E., Bandyopadhyay, S., Nerella, S., Ren, Y., Ozrazgat-Baslanti, T., Shickel, B., Loftus, T., Schwartz, W. R., Bihorac, A., & Rashidi, P. (2024). Wearable sensors in patient acuity assessment in critical care. *Frontiers in Neurology*, *15*(1386728), 1386728. Advance online publication. DOI: 10.3389/fneur.2024.1386728

Serrano, D. R., Luciano, F. C., Anaya, B. J., Ongoren, B., Kara, A., Molina, G., Ramirez, B. I., Sánchez-Guirales, S. A., Simon, J. A., Tomietto, G., Rapti, C., Ruiz, H. K., Rawat, S., Kumar, D., & Lalatsa, A. (2024). Artificial Intelligence (AI) Applications in Drug Discovery and Drug Delivery: Revolutionizing Personalized Medicine. *Pharmaceutics*, *16*(1328), 1328. Advance online publication. DOI: 10.3390/pharmaceutics16101328

Setiadi, D. R. I. M. (2021). PSNR vs SSIM: Imperceptibility quality assessment for image steganography. *Multimedia Tools and Applications*, *80*(6), 8423–8444. DOI: 10.1007/s11042-020-10035-z

Setiadi, D. R. I. M. (2022). Improved payload capacity in LSB image steganography uses dilated hybrid edge detection. *Journal of King Saud University. Computer and Information Sciences*, *34*(2), 104–114. DOI: 10.1016/j.jksuci.2019.12.007

Shah, M., & Sureja, N. (2025). A comprehensive review of bias in deep learning models: Methods, impacts, and future directions. *Archives of Computational Methods in Engineering*, *32*(1), 255–267. DOI: 10.1007/s11831-024-10134-2

Shariatmadar, K., Yorke-Smith, N., Osman, A., Cuzzolin, F., Hallez, H., & Moens, D. (2025). Generalized decision focused learning under imprecise uncertainty—Theoretical study. arXiv. https://doi.org/DOI: 10.48550/ARXIV.2502.17984

Shariatmadar, K. (2024). Generalization of total uncertainty in AI: A theoretical study. arXiv. DOI: 10.48550/ARXIV.2408.00946

Sharma, K., & Giannakos, M. (2020). Multimodal data capabilities for learning: What can multimodal data tell us about learning? *British Journal of Educational Technology*, *51*(5), 1450–1484. DOI: 10.1111/bjet.12993

Sheikhalishahi, S., Miotto, R., Dudley, J. T., Lavelli, A., Rinaldi, F., & Osmani, V. (2019). Natural language processing of clinical notes on chronic diseases: Systematic review. *JMIR Medical Informatics*, *7*(2), e12239. Advance online publication. DOI: 10.2196/12239

Sheller, M. J., Edwards, B., Reina, G. A., Martin, J., Pati, S., Kotrotsou, A., Milchenko, M., Xu, W., Marcus, D., Colen, R. R., & Bakas, S. (2020). Federated learning in medicine: Facilitating multi-institutional collaborations without sharing patient data. *Scientific Reports*, *10*(12598), 12598. Advance online publication. DOI: 10.1038/s41598-020-69250-1

Shulajkovska, M., Smerkol, M., Noveski, G., Bohanec, M., & Gams, M. (2024). Artificial Intelligence-Based Decision Support System for Sustainable Urban Mobility. *Electronics (Basel)*, *13*(18), 3655. DOI: 10.3390/electronics13183655

Shulajkovska, M., Smerkol, M., Noveski, G., & Gams, M. (2024). Enhancing Urban Sustainability: Developing an Open-Source Al Framework for Smart Cities. *Smart Cities*, *7*(5), 2670–2701. DOI: 10.3390/smartcities7050104

Shute, V., & Towle, B. (2018). Adaptive e-learning. In *Aptitude* (pp. 105–114). Routledge.

Sidqi, H. M. (2020). Efficient Multi-Secret Digital Images Steganography. *Egyptian Computer Science Journal, 44*(1).

Sieg, S. (2023). AI Art and Its Limitations: Narrow Intelligence and Visual Indulgence (Master's thesis).

Simkins, S., & Maier, M. (Eds.). (2023). *Just in Time Teaching: Across the Disciplines, and Across the Academy*. Taylor & Francis.

Singh, R. P., Hom, G. L., Abramoff, M. D., Campbell, J. P., & Chiang, M. F. (2020). Current challenges and barriers to real-world artificial intelligence adoption for the healthcare system, provider, and the patient. *Translational Vision Science & Technology, 9*(2), 45–45. DOI: 10.1167/tvst.9.2.45 PMID: 32879755

Singh, V., Sahana, S. K., & Bhattacharjee, V. (2022). Nature-inspired Cloud-Crowd computing for intelligent transportation system. *Sustainability (Basel), 14*(23), 16322. DOI: 10.3390/su142316322

Smail, D. (2018). *Illusion and reality: The meaning of anxiety*. Routledge. DOI: 10.4324/9780429475733

Smys, S., Chen, J. I. Z., & Shakya, S. (2020). Survey on neural network architectures with deep learning. [JSCP]. *Journal of Soft Computing Paradigm, 2*(03), 186–194. DOI: 10.36548/jscp.2020.3.006

Song, B., Wei, P., Wu, S., Lin, Y., & Zhou, W. (2024). A survey on deep-learning-based image steganography. *Expert Systems with Applications, 124390*, 124390. Advance online publication. DOI: 10.1016/j.eswa.2024.124390

Song, C., Shin, S. Y., & Shin, K. S. (2024). Implementing the dynamic feedback-driven learning optimization framework: A machine learning approach to personalize educational pathways. *Applied Sciences (Basel, Switzerland), 14*(2), 916. DOI: 10.3390/app14020916

Son, H., Jang, J., Park, J., Balog, A., Ballantyne, P., Kwon, H. R., Singleton, A., & Hwang, J. (2025). Leveraging Advanced Technologies for (Smart) Transportation Planning: A Systematic Review. *Sustainability (Basel), 17*(5), 2245. DOI: 10.3390/su17052245

Stech, E. P., Grierson, A. B., Chen, A. Z., Sharrock, M. J., Mahoney, A. E. J., & Newby, J. M. (2020). Intensive one-week internet-delivered cognitive behavioral therapy for panic disorder and agoraphobia: A pilot study. *Internet Interventions : the Application of Information Technology in Mental and Behavioural Health, 20*(100315), 100315. Advance online publication. DOI: 10.1016/j.invent.2020.100315

Stevens, D., Lane, D. A., Harrison, S. L., Lip, G. Y. H., & Kolamunnage-Dona, R. (2021). Modelling of longitudinal data to predict cardiovascular disease risk: A methodological review. *BMC Medical Research Methodology*, *21*(283), 283. Advance online publication. DOI: 10.1186/s12874-021-01472-x

Stoddard, H. A., Lee, A. C., & Gooding, H. C. (2024). Empowerment of learners through curriculum co-creation: Practical implications of a radical educational theory. *Teaching and Learning in Medicine*, , 1–7. PMID: 38332636

Stokes, C., Setlur, V., Cogley, B., Satyanarayan, A., & Hearst, M. (2022). Striking a balance: Reader takeaways and preferences when integrating text and charts. *arXiv preprint arXiv:2208.01780*.arXiv

Subramanian, N., Elharrouss, O., Al-Maadeed, S., & Bouridane, A. (2021). Image steganography: A review of the recent advances. *IEEE Access : Practical Innovations, Open Solutions*, *9*, 23409–23423. DOI: 10.1109/ACCESS.2021.3053998

Sumari, A. D. W., & Ahmad, A. S. (2018). Cognitive artificial intelligence: Concept and applications for humankind. *Intelligent System*, *23*, 55. DOI: 10.5772/intechopen.72764

Supriya, K. S., & Lovesum, S. P. J. (2024). Review on lightweight cryptography techniques and steganography techniques for IoT environment. *International Journal of System Assurance Engineering and Management*, *15*, 4210–4228. DOI: 10.1007/s13198-024-02476-8

Su, S., Liu, J., Wang, Y., & Dong, K. (2024). Research on topological characteristics of spatial network based on complex network theory and its applications. *Mathematics*, *12*(23), 3746. DOI: 10.3390/math12233746

Su, W., Ni, J., & Sun, Y. (2024). StegaStyleGAN: Towards generic and practical generative image steganography. [). AAAI Press.]. *Proceedings of the AAAI Conference on Artificial Intelligence*, *38*(1), 240–248. DOI: 10.1609/aaai.v38i1.27776

Tabirca, A. I., Dumitrescu, C., & Radu, V. (2025). Enhancing banking transaction security with fractal-based image steganography using Fibonacci sequences and discrete wavelet transform. *Fractal and Fractional*, *9*(2), 95. Advance online publication. DOI: 10.3390/fractalfract9020095

Tan, S., Taeihagh, A., & Baxter, K. (2022). The risks of machine learning systems. arXiv preprint arXiv:2204.09852.

Tang, W., Rao, Y., Yang, Z., Peng, F., Cui, X., Huang, J., & Zhu, P. (2025). Reversible generative steganography with distribution-preserving. *Cybersecurity*, *8*(1), 18. DOI: 10.1186/s42400-024-00317-6

Tang, Y., Kurths, J., Lin, W., Ott, E., & Kocarev, L. (2020). Introduction to focus issue: When machine learning meets complex systems: Networks, chaos, and nonlinear dynamics. *Chaos (Woodbury, N.Y.), 30*(6), 063151. DOI: 10.1063/5.0016505 PMID: 32611112

Tan, Y., Xiang, X., Qin, J., & Tan, Y. (2024). Robust coverless image steganography based on human pose estimation. *Knowledge-Based Systems, 296*, 111873. Advance online publication. DOI: 10.1016/j.knosys.2024.111873

Tao, X. Y., Cheng, L., Zhang, R. H., Chan, W. K., Chao, H., & Qin, J. (2024). Towards Green Innovation in Smart Cities: Leveraging Traffic Flow Prediction with Machine Learning Algorithms for Sustainable Transportation Systems. *Sustainability (Basel), 16*(1), 251. DOI: 10.3390/su16010251

Tejasen, K. T. J., Raju, P., Ryan, W., Jordan, A., & Yang, R. (2022). Defining an Initial Classification Scheme for Non-Deterministic AI Technologies. *2022 Integrated Communication, Navigation and Surveillance Conference (ICNS)*, 1–10.

Teney, D., Peyrard, M., & Abbasnejad, E. (2022). Predicting is not understanding: Recognizing and addressing underspecification in machine learning. *European Conference on Computer Vision (ECCV)*. https://arxiv.org/abs/2207.02598 DOI: 10.1007/978-3-031-20050-2_27

Teplitskiy, M., Duede, E., Menietti, M., & Lakhani, K. R. (2020). *Citations Systematically Misrepresent the Quality and Impact of Research Articles: Survey and Experimental Evidence from Thousands of Citers*. arXiv preprint arXiv:2002.10033.

Titarenko, L., & Little, C. B. (2017). International cross-cultural online learning and teaching: Effective tools and approaches. *American Journal of Distance Education, 31*(2), 112–127. DOI: 10.1080/08923647.2017.1306767

Tomczyk, P., Brüggemann, P., & Doligalski, T. (2024). The automation of science? Possibilities and boundaries of AI applications for conducting systematic literature reviews. *International Journal of Artificial Intelligence Tools, 33*(06), 2450023. DOI: 10.1142/S0218213024500234

Trezza, A., Visibelli, A., Roncaglia, B., Spiga, O., & Santucci, A. (2024). Unsupervised Learning in Precision Medicine: Unlocking Personalized Healthcare through AI. *Applied Sciences (Basel, Switzerland), 14*(9305), 9305. Advance online publication. DOI: 10.3390/app14209305

Trongtirakul, T., Panetta, K., Grigoryan, A. M., & Agaian, S. S. (2025). A novel entropy-based approach for thermal image segmentation using multilevel thresholding. *Electronics (Basel), 27*(5), 526. DOI: 10.3390/e27050526 PMID: 40422480

Tschalzev, A., Purucker, L., Lüdtke, S., Hutter, F., Bartelt, C., & Stuckenschmidt, H. (2025). Unreflected use of tabular data repositories can undermine research quality. *arXiv preprint arXiv:2503.09159.*

Tsvetanov, F. (2024). Integrating AI Technologies into Remote Monitoring Patient Systems. *Engineering Proceedings*, *70*(54), 54. Advance online publication. DOI: 10.3390/engproc2024070054

U.S. Food & Drug Administration. (2021). *Artificial Intelligence/Machine Learning (AI/ML)-Based Software as a Medical Device (SaMD) Action Plan.* DOI: 10.1145/3447548.3470823

Uppalaiah, B., Mallikarjuna Reddy, D., Rajalakshmi, K., Vignesh, P., Govindan, V., & Donganont, S. (2025). Hybrid modeling approaches for predicting COVID-19 mortality: A comparative study across USA, France, and India. *Results in Engineering*, *26*(105092), 105092. Advance online publication. DOI: 10.1016/j.rineng.2025.105092

Urbaite, G. (2025). When AI hesitates: Methods for identifying and managing model uncertainty. *LUMIN*, *2*(3), 36–45. Advance online publication. DOI: 10.69760/lumin.2025000203

Vaca-Recalde, M. E., Marcano, M., Matute, J., Hidalgo, C., Martinez-Rodriguez, B., Bilbao-Arechabala, S., Jorge-Hernandez, F., Murgoitio, J., Rastelli, J. P., & Santaella, J. (2024). Connected and Intelligent Framework for Vehicle Automation in Smart-Ports. *IEEE Access : Practical Innovations, Open Solutions*, *12*, 120347–120361. DOI: 10.1109/ACCESS.2024.3434628

Vaccaro, M., Almaatouq, A., & Malone, T. (2024). When Are Combinations of Humans and AI Useful: A systematic review and meta-analysis. *Nature Human Behaviour*, *8*(12), 2293–2303. https://arxiv.org/abs/2405.06087. DOI: 10.1038/s41562-024-02024-1

Valaboju, V. K. (2024). The Synergy of Just-in-Time Learning and Artificial Intelligence: Revolutionizing Personalized Education. [IJCET]. *International Journal of Computer Engineering and Technology*, *15*(5), 707–715.

Varghese, F., & Sasikala, P. (2023). A detailed review based on secure data transmission using cryptography and steganography. *Wireless Personal Communications*, *129*(4), 2291–2318. DOI: 10.1007/s11277-023-10183-z

Varnosfaderani, S. M., & Forouzanfar, M. (2024). The Role of AI in Hospitals and Clinics: Transforming Healthcare in the 21st Century. *Bioengineering (Basel, Switzerland), 11*(337), 337. Advance online publication. DOI: 10.3390/bioengineering11040337

Vaswani, A., Shazeer, N., Parmar, N., Uszkoreit, J., Jones, L., Gomez, A. N., & Polosukhin, I. (2017). Attention is all you need. *Advances in Neural Information Processing Systems*, , 30.

Verma, V., & Kumar, S. (2025). Quantum image encryption algorithm based on 3D-BNM chaotic map. *Nonlinear Dynamics, 113*(4), 3829–3855. DOI: 10.1007/s11071-024-10403-6

Vezhbovska, L., Boltenkov, A., Vaskialite, V., Lopukhova, N., & Dementovych, T. (2024). Global trends in educational environment design: From cultural dimensions to innovations. Research Journal in Advanced Humanities, 5(1).

Vieira, M., Galváo, G., Vieira, M. A., Véstias, M., Vieira, P., & Louro, P. (2024). Integration of Visible Light Communication, Artificial Intelligence, and Rerouting Strategies for Enhanced Urban Traffic Management. *Vehicles (Basel), 6*(4), 2106–2132. DOI: 10.3390/vehicles6040103

Visave, J. (2025). Transparency in AI for emergency management: Building trust and accountability. *AI and Ethics, 5*(4), 3967–3980. Advance online publication. DOI: 10.1007/s43681-025-00692-x

Vujović, Ž. (2021). Classification model evaluation metrics. *International Journal of Advanced Computer Science and Applications, 12*(6), 170–185. DOI: 10.14569/IJACSA.2021.0120670

Vyas, V., Ravi, K., Ravi, V., Uma, V., Setlur, S., & Govindaraju, V. (2020). *Article citation study: Context enhanced citation sentiment detection*. arXiv preprint arXiv:2005.04534.

Waldt, G. V. D. (2024). Constructing theoretical frameworks in social science research. *Discourse (Berkeley, Calif.), 20*(1), 1468. DOI: 10.4102/td.v20i1.1468

Wang, D., Liu, J., & Chen, L.. (2024). Implicit neural representation steganography by neuron pruning. *Multimedia Systems, 30*(5), 266. DOI: 10.1007/s00530-024-01476-9

Wang, J., & Li, J. (2024). Artificial intelligence empowering public health education: Prospects and challenges. *Frontiers in Public Health, 12*(1389026), 1389026. Advance online publication. DOI: 10.3389/fpubh.2024.1389026

Wang, J., Liu, Y., Li, P., Lin, Z., Sindakis, S., & Aggarwal, S. (2023). Overview of data quality: Examining the dimensions, antecedents, and impacts of data quality. *Journal of the Knowledge Economy*. Advance online publication. DOI: 10.1007/s13132-022-01096-6 PMID: 40479478

Wang, K., Zhao, Y., Gangadhari, R. K., & Li, Z. (2021). Analyzing the Adoption Challenges of the Internet of Things (loT) and Artificial Intelligence (Al) for Smart Cities in China. *Sustainability (Basel)*, *13*(19), 10983. DOI: 10.3390/su131910983

Wang, L., Zhang, X., Li, Q., Zhang, M.-T., Su, H., Zhu, J., & Zhong, Y. (2023). Incorporating neuro-inspired adaptability for continuous learning in artificial intelligence. *Nature Machine Intelligence*, *5*(12), 1356–1368. DOI: 10.1038/s42256-023-00747-w

Wang, S., Sang, J., Song, X., & Niu, X. (2015). Least significant qubit (LSQb) information hiding algorithm for quantum image. *Measurement*, *73*, 352–359. DOI: 10.1016/j.measurement.2015.05.038

Wang, Y., Wang, Y., Zhang, T., Yu, Y., Cheung, S. C., Yu, H., & Zhu, Z. (2023, November). Can machine learning pipelines be better configured? In *Proceedings of the 31st ACM Joint European Software Engineering Conference and Symposium on the Foundations of Software Engineering* (pp. 463-475). DOI: 10.1145/3611643.3616352

Wen, Y., & Holweg, M. (2024). A phenomenological perspective on AI ethical failures: The case of facial recognition technology. *AI & Society*, *39*(4), 1929–1946. DOI: 10.1007/s00146-023-01648-7

Wiegrebe, S., Kopper, P., Sonabend, R., Bischl, B., & Bender, A. (2024). Deep learning for survival analysis: a review. In *Artificial Intelligence Review* (Vol. 57, Issue 65). Springer Netherlands. DOI: 10.1007/s10462-023-10681-3

Williamson, B. (2017). Who owns educational theory? Big data, algorithms and the expert power of education data science. *E-Learning and Digital Media*, *14*(3), 105–122. DOI: 10.1177/2042753017731238

Woźniak, K., Ogiela, M. R., & Ogiela, L. (2025). A Two-Phase Embedding Approach for Secure Distributed Steganography. *Sensors (Basel)*, *25*(5), 1448. DOI: 10.3390/s25051448 PMID: 40096275

Wright, D., & Augenstein, I. (2021). CiteWorth: Cite-Worthiness Detection for Improved Scientific Document Understanding. arXiv preprint arXiv:2105.10912. DOI: 10.18653/v1/2021.findings-acl.157

Wu, M., Zhou, J., Peng, Y., Wang, S., & Zhang, Y. (2023, December). Deep learning for image classification: a review. In International Conference on Medical Imaging and Computer-Aided Diagnosis (pp. 352-362). Singapore: Springer Nature Singapore.

Wu, F., Shen, T., Bäck, T., Chen, J., Huang, G., Jin, Y., Kuang, K., Li, M., Lu, C., Miao, J., Wang, Y., Wei, Y., Wu, F., Yan, J., Yang, H., Yang, Y., Zhang, S., Zhao, Z., Zhuang, Y., & Pan, Y. (2024). Knowledge-empowered, collaborative, and co-evolving AI models: The post-LLM roadmap. *Engineering.* Advance online publication. DOI: 10.1016/j.eng.2024.12.008

Wu, N., Yang, Z., Yang, Y., Li, L., Shang, P., Ma, W., & Liu, Z. (2020). STBS-Stega: Coverless text steganography based on state transition-binary sequence. *International Journal of Distributed Sensor Networks*, *16*(3), 1550147720914257. DOI: 10.1177/1550147720914257

Xie, J., Luo, X., Deng, X., Tang, Y., Tian, W., Cheng, H., Zhang, J., Zou, Y., Guo, Z., & Xie, X. (2023). Advances in artificial intelligence to predict cancer immunotherapy efficacy. *Frontiers in Immunology*, *13*(1076883), 1076883. Advance online publication. DOI: 10.3389/fimmu.2022.1076883

Xie, Q. W., Shi, K., Wu, X., Huang, W. L., Zheng, X. L., & Li, Y. J. (2023). Transportation Efficiency Evaluation Under the Policies of Energy Savings and Emissions Reduction. *IEEE Intelligent Transportation Systems Magazine*, *15*(6), 192–211. DOI: 10.1109/MITS.2023.3301877

Yadav, G. S., & Ojha, A. (2018). Hamiltonian path based image steganography scheme with improved imperceptibility and undetectability. *Applied Soft Computing*, *73*, 497–507. DOI: 10.1016/j.asoc.2018.08.034

Yang, Z., Wei, N., Liu, Q., Huang, Y., & Zhang, Y. (2020). GAN-TStega: Text steganography based on generative adversarial networks. Digital Forensics and Watermarking: 18th International Workshop, IWDW 2019, Chengdu, China, November 2–4, 2019, Revised Selected Papers 18

Yang, H., Xu, Y., Liu, X., & Ma, X. (2024). PRIS: Practical robust invertible network for image steganography. *Engineering Applications of Artificial Intelligence*, *133*, 108419. Advance online publication. DOI: 10.1016/j.engappai.2024.108419

Yang, J., Dung, N. T., Thach, P. N., Phong, N. T., Phu, V. D., Phu, K. D., Yen, L. M., Thy, D. B. X., Soltan, A. A. S., Thwaites, L., & Clifton, D. A. (2024). Generalizability assessment of AI models across hospitals in a low-middle and high income country. *Nature Communications*, *15*(8270), 8270. Advance online publication. DOI: 10.1038/s41467-024-52618-6

Yang, Q., Feng, X., & Wei, L. (2025). Image Similarity Quantum Algorithm and Its Application in Image Retrieval Systems. *Entropy (Basel, Switzerland), 27*(2), 137. DOI: 10.3390/e27020137 PMID: 40003134

Yang, S., Tian, H., Sun, L., & Yu, X. (2019, June). From one-size-fits-all teaching to adaptive learning: The crisis and solution of education in the era of AI. [). IOP Publishing.]. *Journal of Physics: Conference Series, 1237*(4), 042039. DOI: 10.1088/1742-6596/1237/4/042039

Yang, Y.. (2024). Diffstega: Towards universal training-free coverless image steganography with diffusion models. arXiv. https://arxiv.org/abs/2407.10459

Yanuar, M. R., Apriono, C., & Syawaludin, M. F. (2024). Image-to-image steganography with Josephus permutation and least significant bit (LSB) 3-3-2 embedding. *Applied Sciences (Basel, Switzerland), 14*(16), 7119. Advance online publication. DOI: 10.3390/app14167119

Yao, Y., Wang, J., Chang, Q., Ren, Y., & Meng, W. (2024). High invisibility image steganography with wavelet transform and generative adversarial network. *Expert Systems with Applications, 249*, 123540. Advance online publication. DOI: 10.1016/j.eswa.2024.123540

Yeh, J.-Y., Chen, C.-C., Liu, P.-L., & Huang, Y.-H. (2020). High-payload data-hiding method for AMBTC decompressed images. *Entropy (Basel, Switzerland), 22*(2), 145. DOI: 10.3390/e22020145 PMID: 33285920

Yigitcanlar, T., & Cugurullo, F. (2020). The Sustainability of Artificial Intelligence: An Urbanistic Viewpoint from the Lens of Smart and Sustainable Cities. *Sustainability (Basel), 12*(20), 8548. DOI: 10.3390/su12208548

Yilmaz, L., & Liu, B. (2022). Model credibility revisited: Concepts and considerations for appropriate trust. *Journal of Simulation, 16*(3), 312–325. DOI: 10.1080/17477778.2020.1821587

Yin, J. H., & Song, H. Y. (2023). Does the perception of smart governance enhance commercial investments? Evidence from Beijing, Shanghai, Guangzhou, and Hangzhou. *Heliyon, 9*(8), e19024. DOI: 10.1016/j.heliyon.2023.e19024 PMID: 37609407

Yin, J. H., Song, H. Y., & Zeng, K. X. (2022). Does a smart business environment promote corporate investment? a case study of Hangzhou. *PLoS One, 17*(7), e0269089. DOI: 10.1371/journal.pone.0269089 PMID: 35793371

Yitzhaki, M. (2014). The effect of characteristics of title on citation rates of articles. *Scientometrics, 101*(2), 1195–1205. DOI: 10.1007/s11192-013-1118-1

Yonck, R. (2020). *Heart of the machine: Our future in a world of artificial emotional intelligence*. Arcade.

Yoon, M., Lee, J., & Jo, I. H. (2021). Video learning analytics: Investigating behavioral patterns and learner clusters in video-based online learning. *The Internet and Higher Education, 50*, 100806. DOI: 10.1016/j.iheduc.2021.100806

Younus, Z. S., & Hussain, M. K. (2022). Image steganography using exploiting modification direction for compressed encrypted data. *Journal of King Saud University. Computer and Information Sciences, 34*(6), 2951–2963. DOI: 10.1016/j.jksuci.2019.04.008

Yuan, S., Mao, X., Chen, L., & Xue, Y. (2013). Quantum digital image processing algorithms based on quantum measurement. *Optik (Stuttgart), 124*(23), 6386–6390. DOI: 10.1016/j.ijleo.2013.05.063

Zafar, I., Anwar, S., Kanwal, F., Yousaf, W., Un Nisa, F., Kausar, T., ul Ain, Q., Unar, A., Kamal, M. A., Rashid, S., Khan, K. A., & Sharma, R. (2023). Reviewing methods of deep learning for intelligent healthcare systems in genomics and biomedicine. *Biomedical Signal Processing and Control, 86*(105263), 105263. Advance online publication. DOI: 10.1016/j.bspc.2023.105263

Zahra, W., & Rautela, G. (2024). Revolutionizing Learning Landscapes: Unleashing the Potential of AI in the Realm of Academic Research. In *Artificial Intelligence: A Multidisciplinary Approach towards Teaching and Learning* (pp. 242–264). Bentham Science Publishers.

Zantvoort, K., Scharfenberger, J., Boß, L., Lehr, D., & Funk, B. (2023). Finding the Best Match — a Case Study on the (Text-)Feature and Model Choice in Digital Mental Health Interventions. In *Journal of Healthcare Informatics Research* (Vol. 7). DOI: 10.1007/s41666-023-00148-z

Zenati, A., Ouarda, W., & Alimi, A. M. (2020). SSDIS-BEM: A new signature steganography document image system based on beta elliptic modeling. *Engineering Science and Technology, an International Journal, 23*(3), 470–482. DOI: 10.1016/j.jestch.2019.09.002

Zhang, D., Feng, T., Xue, L., Wang, Y., Dong, Y., & Tang, J. (2025). Parameter-Efficient Fine-Tuning for Foundation Models. arXiv preprint arXiv:2501.13787.

Zhang, F., Kreuter, D., Chen, Y., Dittmer, S., Tull, S., Shadbahr, T., Schut, M., Asselbergs, F., Kar, S., Sivapalaratnam, S., Williams, S., Koh, M., Henskens, Y., de Wit, B., D'Alessandro, U., Bah, B., Secka, O., Nachev, P., Gupta, R., & Schönlieb, C. B. (2024). Recent methodological advances in federated learning for healthcare. *Patterns (New York, N.Y.)*, *5*(6), 101006. Advance online publication. DOI: 10.1016/j.patter.2024.101006

Zhang, H., Sun, S., Hu, L., & Meng, F. (2023). A novel data hiding scheme based on improved diamond encoding in IWT domain. *Multimedia Tools and Applications*, *82*(12), 18727–18745. DOI: 10.1007/s11042-022-14235-7 PMID: 36250182

Zhang, S., Xiao, Y., Tian, H., & Li, X. (2025). A multi-image steganography: ISS. *Cybersecurity*, *8*(1), 20. Advance online publication. DOI: 10.1186/s42400-024-00333-6

Zhang, T., Abd-El-Atty, B., Amin, M., & El-Latif, A. (2016). QISLSQb: A quantum image steganography scheme based on Least Significant Qubit. *International Conference on Mathematical, Computational and Statistical Sciences and Engineering*.

Zhang, X. F., & Fan, D. C. (2023). Collaborative emission reduction research on dual - pilot policies of the low-carbon city and smart city from the perspective of multiple innovations. *Urban Climate*, *47*, 101364. DOI: 10.1016/j.uclim.2022.101364

Zhang, X., Han, N., & Zhang, J. (2024). Comparative analysis of VGG, ResNet, and GoogLeNet architectures evaluating performance, computational efficiency, and convergence rates. *Applied and Computational Engineering*, *44*(1), 172–181. DOI: 10.54254/2755-2721/44/20230676

Zhang, Y.-P., Zhang, X.-Y., Cheng, Y.-T., Li, B., Teng, X.-Z., Zhang, J., Lam, S., Zhou, T., Ma, Z.-R., Sheng, J.-B., Tam, V. C. W., Lee, S. W. Y., Ge, H., & Cai, J. (2023). Artificial intelligence-driven radiomics study in cancer: The role of feature engineering and modeling. *Military Medical Research*, *10*(22), 22. Advance online publication. DOI: 10.1186/s40779-023-00458-8

Zhang, Y., Wang, S., Li, T., Liu, B., & Pan, D.-B. (2020). Modulus calculations on prime number algorithm for information hiding with high comprehensive performance. *IEEE Access : Practical Innovations, Open Solutions*, *8*, 85309–85320. DOI: 10.1109/ACCESS.2020.2992690

Zhang, Z., Fu, G., Ni, R., Liu, J., & Yang, X. (2020). A generative method for steganography by cover synthesis with auxiliary semantics. *Tsinghua Science and Technology*, *25*(4), 516–527. DOI: 10.26599/TST.2019.9010027

Zhan, Y., Hao, Y., Wang, X., & Guo, D. (2025). Advances of artificial intelligence in clinical application and scientific research of neuro-oncology: Current knowledge and future perspectives. *Critical Reviews in Oncology/Hematology*, *209*(104682), 104682. Advance online publication. DOI: 10.1016/j.critrevonc.2025.104682

Zhou, X. L., Jia, Y. W., Bai, C., Zhu, H. P., & Chan, S. X. (2022). Multi-object tracking based on attention networks for Smart City system. *Sustainable Energy Technologies and Assessments*, *52*(C), 102216. DOI: 10.1016/j.seta.2022.102216

Zhou, Z., Bao, Z., Jiang, W., Huang, Y., Peng, Y., Shankar, A., Maple, C., & Selvarajan, S. (2024). Latent vector optimization-based generative image steganography for consumer electronic applications. *IEEE Transactions on Consumer Electronics*, *70*(1), 4357–4366. DOI: 10.1109/TCE.2024.3354824

Zhu, H. Y., Shen, L. Y., & Ren, Y. T. (2022). How can smart city shape a happier life? The mechanism for developing a Happiness Driven Smart City. *Sustainable Cities and Society*, *80*, 103791. DOI: 10.1016/j.scs.2022.103791

Zhu, H., Sun, Y., & Yang, J. (2025). Towards responsible artificial intelligence in education: A systematic review on identifying and mitigating ethical risks. *Humanities & Social Sciences Communications*, *12*(1), 1111. Advance online publication. DOI: 10.1057/s41599-025-05252-6

Zuluaga-Gomez, J., Nigmatulina, I., Prasad, A., Motlicek, P., Khalil, D., Madikeri, S., Tart, A., Szoke, I., Lenders, V., Rigault, M., & Choukri, K. (2023). Lessons Learned in Transcribing 5000 h of Air Traffic Control Communications for Robust Automatic Speech Understanding. *Aerospace (Basel, Switzerland)*, *10*(10), 898. DOI: 10.3390/aerospace10100898

About the Contributors

Poshan (Sam) Yu is a Chinese-Australian professional with an astonishingly diverse background and an extensive collection of remarkable accomplishments. In the academic sphere, he currently teaches at the University of Victoria Program at Soochow University. Previously, he held the position of an external professor of financial technology and finance at SKEMA Business School. He also serves as a visiting researcher at the Australian Studies Centre of Shanghai University, a guest professor at emlyon business school China, and an adjunct faculty member at George Washington University's master (finance) program at Renmin University of China. As a visiting professor at Krirk University in Thailand and an EU-Asia research coordinator at the European Business Institute in Luxembourg, he brings a truly global perspective to his teaching and research activities. He is a member of the IP & Innovation Researchers of Asia (IPIRA) Network and the Global South Dialogue on Economic Crime (GSDEC), further enriching his academic engagement. His prior role as a casual academic at the University of South Australia Business School has significantly enhanced and diversified his academic portfolio. From September 2020 to February 2021, he held the position of visiting scholar at The Chinese University of Hong Kong on two occasions. His scholarly pursuits are extensive and multifaceted. As an editor for the European Academic Journal (Special Issue) - European Business Institute in Luxembourg, an editor for Humanities & Social Sciences Communications (an SSCI-indexed journal), and an associate editor for the International Journal of Interdisciplinary Research in Social Science, he plays a crucial role in the dissemination of knowledge. He is an ad hoc reviewer for a number of prestigious journals and academic presses, including Applied Economics, Applied Artificial Intelligence, Cogent Economics & Finance, Humanities and Social Sciences Communications, Journal of Chinese Economic and Business Studies, Journal of Digital Learning and Education, The Singapore Economic Review, ILMA Journal of Social Sciences & Economics, Journal of Environmental Issues and Climate Change, Advances in Global Economic and Business Journal, The

Interdisciplinary Social Sciences Journal Collection, Common Ground Research Networks, Imprint - Xi'an Jiaotong-Liverpool University, Innovative Teaching and Learning, IBT Journal of Business Studies, Journal of Infrastructure Policy and Development, and Innovative Informatics and Artificial Intelligence Research. Moreover, he is an international editorial advisory board member for several edited books such as Advancing STEM Education and Innovation in a Time of Distance Learning (Scopus-indexed), Multidisciplinary Perspectives Towards Building a Digitally Competent Society (Scopus-indexed), Handbook of Research on SDGs for Economic Development, Social Development, and Environmental Protection, and Implications for Entrepreneurship and Enterprise Development in the Blue Economy. He has released more than 12 journal articles, among which 6 are listed as ABDC: B/SSCI. He has also contributed over 70 peer-reviewed book chapters imprinted by renowned publishers like IGI Global, Routledge, and Springer. He has edited 22 books, with 14 English-edited books indexed by Scopus and 6 Chinese-edited books. Notably, the book about Innovation & Exploration: The Development of FinTech in Jiangsu China has received the 14th Outstanding Achievement Award of Philosophy and Social Sciences in Suzhou and the 3rd prize of the 2018 Jiangsu Provincial Education Science Research Achievement Award by Jiangsu Provincial Department of Education. His receipt of four Xi'an Jiaotong-Liverpool University (XJTLU) National University Teaching Innovation Awards from 2016 to 2020 and being recognized as a top contender in the same national competition in 2016 led to his appointment as the Institute of Leadership and Education Advanced Development (ILEAD) Research Fellow by XJTLU. In 2021, he received The Outstanding Contribution Award for Industrial Research Development in China, CIE100 issued by Wisdom China Magazine: Beijing. Beyond academia, he is actively involved in various industries. He is an entrepreneur and venture capitalist, collaborating with alumni and senior faculty members from Cambridge University. Additionally, he is a guest financial news commentator on over 30 media platforms in China. In the business world, he holds significant positions. He is a regional partner in China for FasterCapital based in Dubai, United Arab Emirates. He also serves as vice president at Tinbowah Investment in Beijing and as an honorary vice president of the Belt and Road Blockchain Association. Furthermore, he mentors businesses for AIC RAISE in Coimbatore, India, the Griffith Industry Mentoring Program in Australia, and University College London Innovation & Enterprise. In 2023, he was invited to act as a venture capital panel judge and mentor at 'Y&Archer A Stream 2023' conference in Jeju, South Korea. His research interests are broad and encompass financial technology, regulatory technology, blockchain, web 3.0 in financial services, generative AI, public-private partnerships, mergers and acquisitions, private equity, venture capital, startups, family offices, IoTs, supply chain finance, intellectual property, art finance, wine, back-door listing, intangible cultural heritage, and Chinese economy & policy. His extensive experience in international fintech, edtech, startup, social media, and cleantech companies across India, the UK, Australia, Hong Kong, and China is truly remarkable. His three-year tenure in significant leadership positions within the Chinese-Australian media marketing and public relations sector, along with his role as an OzAsia Festival Ambassador in Australia, has exerted a profound influence on his current modus operandi as an academic and business consultant. Additionally, it has considerably broadened his perspective within the international multicultural arts community and enlarged his business network. This multifaceted experience has furnished him with a more comprehensive and inclusive outlook on academia, industry, and research. He is fully dedicated to making substantial contributions in these areas and is keen on furthering his development in the future. Incidentally, Sam has an inclination towards wine, arts, and reading.

James Mulli is the Founder, Program Director and Academic Dean of the European Business Institute, Luxembourg. He lectures in Applied Blockchain Technologies and Artificial Intelligence integration, post-graduate Corporate Finance & Business Statistics, and Managerial Accounting. He has held lectureships at in Luxembourg, China, the USA, Kenya and Germany. Dr. Mulli is a former director of two successful New York based multinational conglomerates and has valuable experience in the field as an NASD Series 7 compliance officer for the broker dealer Heyka Capital Management. He worked as a Portfolio Manager for the Soros Fund Management's Quantum Industrial Partners and holds a Doctorate and Masters degree from Saint Johns University, New York, and an MBA from New Hampshire Plymouth State University with specialization in Investment and Finance. Dr. Mulli is an international educator, and educational technology consultant with a keen interest in looking over the horizon at how technology is shaping the world. His search for trends in emerging technologies allows him to be an educator who applies skills to help students thrive. He is the founder of Technology Enabled Learning - Africa, and European Business Institute, Luxembourg, both non-for-profit educational providers whose initiative is to support existing Institutions in developing e-learning . His belief is that education is the silver bullet for development and through existing expertise and support infrastructure, EBI can provide the needed "jump-start" to institutions in Europe, Africa, Asia and beyond. Dr. Mulli is a Rockefeller Foundation Grant Recipient, and a Prince Fellow Teaching Excellence recipient. He is a textbook author and has published numerous newspaper and magazine articles.

Zain Ali Shah Syed is currently affiliated with Soochow University.

Laila Umme holds a PhD in Computer Science and Information Technology from NED University of Engineering and Technology and a MS/BS in Computer Engineering from Sir Syed University of Engineering & Technology. Her PhD is in pure Software Engineering, focusing on "open source software". Her research interests include open-source software, IoT, computer programming, software engineering, Artificial Intelligence, and Machine Learning. Currently She is working as an Associate Professor in Computer Science Department at IoBM. She has 20 years of teaching experience and has published over 20 publications in international and national journals and conferences.

***

Anita Devare is passionate about the applied mathematics in engineering domain. She is interested in the mathematical modeling of the computational resources, and security techniques in the domain of Computer Science.

Manoj Devare received BSc & MSc degree from North Maharashtra University and PhD in Computer Science from Bharati Vidyapeeth University, India. He is working as Associate Professor at Amity Institute of Information Technology, Amity University Mumbai. He has 17 years of teaching and research experience in Computer Science. His PhD thesis was based on the Congestion Controlling in Homogeneous and Heterogeneous Computer Networks. Dr. Manoj won the "Best Paper Award", in ICSCI 2008. He has served as Post Doctorate Fellow at Centre of Excellence on HPC, Uni. of Calabria, Italy under young researcher scheme. He has been developed Desktop Cloud system. His research deals with IoT, Cloud, Machine Learning and innovative applications of those technologies to scientific problems. He has 02 Patents pending; he edited 05 book chapters, 09 Int. Journal papers, 15 conference Papers. He has delivered 08 national and international keynote speeches. He is connected with review process of reputed international journal papers, edited chapters from the reputed journals like Elsevier's FGCS, Springer's review system, Symbiosis International Journal.

Gao Yuan, an independent researcher, has research interests in economics, business finance, and fintech.

Emmanuel Ileberi received the B.Eng.degree in information technology and the M.Sc. degree in telecommunications systems and computer networks from the Belarusian State University of Informatics and radioelectronics Belarus, in 2017 and 2018 respectively, and obtained PhD degree in electrical and electronic engineering from the university of Johannesburg South Africa 2023

Muhammad Irfan received his bachelor's degree from Sukkur IBA University, where his final thesis explored the factors that hinder critical thinking skills of undergraduate students. He is currently a master's scholar in Educational Management and Supervision at Marmara University, Istanbul. In addition to his academic pursuits, he works as an English teacher, preparing students for IELTS and TOEFL exams, as well as conducting general English classes for managers and employees in corporate settings. His research interests include AI in education, AI and politics in education, critical thinking, and critical pedagogy.

Zainal Rasyid Mahayuddin is a Senior Lecturer in the Center for Artificial Intelligence Technology (CAIT), Faculty of Information Science and Technology, Universiti Kebangsaan Malaysia (UKM). He specializes in Simulation Modelling, Visual Computing, Mixed Reality (Virtual and Augmented Reality), Computer Vision, and Large Language Model (LLM).

Kunwar Pal has received his B.Tech degree in Computer Science and Engineering from KNIT, Sultanpur, M.E (CSE) from Punjab Engineering College, Chandigarh, and his Doctorate degree from Malaviya National Institute of Technology JaipurIndia in 2018. Presently he is working as an Assistant professor at National Institute of Technologyjalandhar, India. He is having more than 9 years of experience in education. His researchinterests include communication, network security, real time system, UAV path planning, Multimedia System, etc.

A F M Saifuddin Saif serves as a professor at Chicago State University. He served in various academic roles at many universities, including West Virginia University, Colorado State University, the University of Helsinki, and Aalto University. His research interests include Computer Vision, Image Processing, Deep Learning, Augmented Reality, and Virtual Reality.

Nwosu Obinnaya Chikezie Victor received his B. Tech degree in Geophysics from the Federal University of Technology Owerri, Nigeria, in 2007 and his M. Sc degree in Environmental Technology from Teesside University, England, in 2011. He has worked in companies ranging from Retail to Banking to Administration and Construction in Nigeria, England, and Canada. He was among a 14- person finalist for the "Falling Lab Johannesburg 2023 Competition", which he presented on "Breaking the Wall of Adopting AI to Maximize Construction Productivity". He has also done short certificate courses at the University of Alberta, Canada, Georgia Institute of Technology, USA, and Cape Peninsula University of Technology, South Africa. Nwosu Obinnaya Chikezie Victor is a Journal reviewer for Science Publishing Group and a guest contributing blogger for Smashoid.

Yannawar Pravin Laxmikant received his B.Sc Computer Science from Dr. Babasaheb Ambedkar Marathwada University, Aurangabad in June 1999, and M.Sc Computer Science from Department of Computer Science and Information Technology, Dr. Babasaheb Ambedkar Marathwada University, Aurangabad in June 2001 and the Ph.D(Computer Science), Department of Computer Science and Information Technology, Dr. Babasaheb Ambedkar Marathwada University Aurangabad in March 2011. He is a Member and Editorial of many journals.

Index

L

M

N

P

R

S

T

U

www.ingramcontent.com/pod-product-compliance
Lightning Source LLC
LaVergne TN
LVHW081533300926
849161LV00006B/1409
9798260023730